Aging in the Pas

This book is to be returned on
or before the date stamped below

STUDIES IN DEMOGRAPHY

General Editors

Eugene A. Hammel

Ronald D. Lee

Kenneth W. Wachter

Aging in the Past: Demography, Society, and Old Age

EDITED BY

David I. Kertzer
Peter Laslett

UNIVERSITY OF CALIFORNIA PRESS

Berkeley   Los Angeles   London

University of California Press
Berkeley and Los Angeles, California
University of California Press
London, England
Copyright © 1995 by The Regents of the University of California

Library of Congress Cataloging-in-Publication Data

Aging in the past : demography, society, and old age / edited by David
I. Kertzer and Peter Laslett.
    p.   cm. — (Studies in demography ; 7)
Includes bibliographical references and index.
ISBN 0-520-08465-9 (alk. paper). — ISBN 0-520-08466-7 (pbk.)
    1. Aged—History.   2. Old age—Social aspects.   3. Population—
History.   I. Kertzer, David I., 1948– .   II. Laslett, Peter.
III. Series: Studies in demography (Berkeley, Calif.) ; 7.
HQ1061.A463   1995
305.26′09—dc20   93-33288
                                                            CIP

Printed in the United States of America
1   2   3   4   5   6   7   8   9

The paper used in this publication meets the minimum requirements of American National
Standard for Information Sciences—Permanence of Paper for Printed Library Materials,
ANSI Z39.48-1984 ∞

To Matilda White Riley,
an inspiration to us all

CONTENTS

PREFACE

We present this volume to our readers in the confidence that they will acknowledge the importance of its subject and that they will accept the description of its content in the title of the first chapter, "Necessary Knowledge," necessary knowledge from the past. Old age and old people are now a commonplace theme in all Western and industrialized countries, which is understandable as people realize that their populations are exceedingly old and getting older. They are well aware of the implications for transfers between age groups and for generational justice, especially in the United States where the crises in welfare and health costs are persistent themes in the media and among politicians and administrators. Every such discussion begins with a rigmarole about aging, the facts being variously selected and interpreted, seldom with much accuracy or understanding and frequently in a way that misleads. Perpetually and inevitably, there is a lack of historical depth, with consequent obfuscation.

The attempt here is to fill out the historical horizon and to make use of it to clear away some of the misapprehensions. This is done in the recognition that we cannot expect to understand ourselves as we now are in the industrialized countries—and what we shall become—unless we also understand what we have been. It is not only true, as a case in point, that Western and Japanese populations are very, very old. It is also true that they are the oldest human populations that have ever existed and that they never will be young again. Indeed, all the other populations in the world will join them in their elderly condition and are beginning to do so already. Our hope is that this book may help those in the nonindustrial world take cognizance of what they are and of what they may become.

Although we shall claim that this is the first work of its kind to be published, it is far from the first book to be published on the history of aging.

In recent years such efforts have challenged many of the established assumptions about aging and enriched our understanding of how the nature of old age has changed through the centuries. In spite of these advances, our ignorance is still formidable. Meanwhile, the strictly demographic study of aging has been making progress, if not enough to satisfy us, and the historical side of that study has been going forward.

But historical demography, like demography itself, has been preoccupied for the most part with fertility and mortality. Lacking so far is a conjunction of the history of age and the old, that is to say, *how* we have become old, with its historical demography, *why* we have become old. Such is the need that is addressed in this volume, with the addition of some elements—rather few, because this is the most difficult and least cultivated part of the terrain—of comparative analysis. The significant contrast is between the condition of developed societies when they were younger and the condition of the developing nations of today.

In the discussions that have gone on between us as coeditors, we have been impressed with the intellectual vistas that open up once we adopt a viewpoint from the perspective of later life, rather than of youth, which is seemingly the natural and inevitable vantage point of our civilization. Like speleologists breaking for the first time into the ample space of a cave, we are overwhelmed by entirely unexplored avenues leading off in various directions in the crepuscular light.

But familiar territory also begins to look different. Such is the area of the history and the development, in relation to aging, of the co-resident domestic group. In his final chapter, David Kertzer is able to limn the contours of a new definition of arguably the most important, because the most widespread, form of that group, the nuclear family household. The informed reader may recognize that this new interpretation is scarcely consonant with the published views of Peter Laslett on the nuclear family household.

We hope that this difference of interpretation will add to the intellectual interest of our contributions to the volume. How long will it be before the study of aging loses that air of grayness and tedium that has always hung about everything to do with becoming old and is instead recognized as an arena of brilliant intellectual opportunity?

References are made in the introductory chapter to the collected volume published two decades ago, *Household and family in past time* (1972). There it was confessed that deliberate aim was being taken at the opening up of a new field of inquiry, and so it proved in the sequel. It has also transpired that the rigorous standards of data collection and analysis that were laid out at length in the introduction to that volume have been progressively neglected. So much has this been so that the controversies that have arisen about family and household at various times and at various places in the world seem to have become interchanges about approximations and impressions rather than about rigorously examined entities. The findings of family history are to that extent less significant or even trustworthy. It is fervently to be hoped that this will not come about in the field of the history and historical demography of aging.

This book is the product of our efforts to stimulate interest in these pursuits and to suggest the kinds of insights that can be obtained by paying more attention to demographic issues in conducting historical research on the lives of older people. Toward this end, a conference on the historical demography of aging was held at Bowdoin College Breckinridge Public Affairs Center in York, Maine, in spring 1990. Among the participants were historians, anthropologists, sociologists, economists, and demographers from several countries.

Our interest was in the interaction between demographic events and processes, on the one hand, and both societal age norms and individual-level behavior involving older people, on the other. While the emphasis was on demographic forces, these were examined in interaction with other relevant influences: economic, political, social, and cultural. The focus was on the West, both Europe and North America.

Of the thirteen chapters that follow, ten are revisions of papers first given at that conference. The focus is on a number of Western societies, including Britain, Italy, Hungary, and the Baltic states, though the United States receives the most attention. In his contribution, Gene Hammel provides a demonstration of the role to be played by microsimulation techniques in advancing the historical demography of aging, as he takes on the classic question of the prevalence of the stem family in the past.

In addition to those whose work is found in this volume, a number of other scholars participated in the Breckinridge conference. Their contributions have enriched these pages. We should particularly like to thank Matilda White Riley, Arthur Imhof, Tom Ericsson, Maris Vinovskis, Pier Paolo Viazzo, Richard Suzman, Timothy Guinnane, Jack Riley, Lee Craig, and Robert Whaples.

The conference was made possible by a grant (1R13 AG08429–01) from the National Institute on Aging (NIA). We would like to acknowledge the important role of Richard Suzman of the NIA in encouraging and nurturing this project. Further support for manuscript preparation was provided by the NIA supplement to Brown University's Population Studies and Training Center grant (NICHD P30 HD28251). We would also like to thank Bowdoin College and the staff of the Breckinridge Public Affairs Center for providing us with an idyllic setting for the conference. A final note of thanks is owed to Stanley Holwitz, of the University of California Press, for his continued encouragement and faith in this project.

CONTRIBUTORS

George Alter is Professor of History at the University of Indiana, Bloomington.

Rudolf Andorka is Rector of the University of Economic Sciences, Budapest.

Allen C. Goodman is Professor of Economics at Wayne State University.

Myron P. Gutmann is Professor of History at the University of Texas, Austin.

Michael R. Haines is Banfi Vintners Professor of Economics at Colgate University.

E. A. Hammel is Professor Emeritus of Anthropology and Demography at the University of California, Berkeley.

Tamara K. Hareven is Unidel Professor of Family Studies and History at the University of Delaware.

Nancy Karweit is Senior Research Associate, Center for the Study of the Social Organization of Schools, Johns Hopkins University.

David I. Kertzer is Paul Dupee University Professor of Social Science and Professor of Anthropology and History at Brown University.

Peter Laslett is a Fellow of Trinity College, Cambridge, and co-founder of the Cambridge Group for the History of Population and Social Structure.

Andrejs Plakans is Professor of History at Iowa State University.

Roger L. Ransom is Professor of History and Economics at the University of California, Riverside.

Daniel Scott Smith is Professor of History at the University of Illinois, Chicago.

Richard Sutch is Professor of Economics and History and Director of the Institute of Business and Economic Research at the University of California, Berkeley.

Peter Uhlenberg is Professor of Sociology at the University of North Carolina, Chapel Hill.

Richard Wall is the senior researcher at the Cambridge Group for the History of Population and Social Structure.

Charles Wetherell is Professor of History at the University of California, Riverside.

PART ONE

Introduction

ONE

Necessary Knowledge: Age and Aging in the Societies of the Past

Peter Laslett

For our purposes here, necessary knowledge, that is, necessary knowledge from the past, is a body of information that all persons must have to understand themselves as they are today. The historian, especially the historical sociologist, might claim that in theory at least the whole of history is relevant to present people and might demand a demonstration of how far age and aging should be accorded priority over other things that present people ought to be aware of. Such a demonstration is clearly required in the introduction to a book about aging in the past.

WHY DO PEOPLE HAVE TO KNOW ABOUT AGING IN THE PAST?

The populations of developed societies have grown old at an amazing pace. Within the last hundred years, and to a considerable degree within the last fifty years, the populations of Europe, North America, Australasia, and Japan have become far and away the oldest human populations of which we have knowledge. These populations are older—and still getting older—in two important senses: average individual lifetimes last for very much longer than they ever have before anywhere or at any time, and these populations have among them quite unprecedented numbers of elderly people. It is obvious that the situation could not always have been like this, and during the last century some European populations were getting younger. In England, for example, proportions of elderly people were decreasing slightly between 1800 and 1830. A knowledge of aging in the past, that is to say, the historical demography of aging, is evidently necessary in order to recognize how novel the situation now is in the advanced countries. There is no other way of grasping that fact.

I shall maintain that aging has been so sudden that there has not yet been time enough to take account of the transformation. Contemporary Europeans and citizens of societies of European origin must, along with the Japanese, be living in a state of cultural lag, even of false consciousness, at least to some degree. They are continuing to make assumptions about age and aging that, though they had always been true before the present century, have incontinently disappeared. They have to be brought up against the facts of aging as they always used to be and compare them with the very different facts as they now are.

The information produced by the historical demography of aging is therefore first and foremost knowledge with a view to ourselves. But the developed societies are not the only ones to be getting older in the last decade of the twentieth century. All contemporary populations are aging, including those classed as less developed or even "primitive." Young as they still are, sooner or later they will join the industrialized countries in their age-transformed condition. We shall illustrate this below for some Southeast Asian countries.

Nevertheless, the developed nations are much farther along the road. Except for Japan, they have spent a much longer time during the aging process than these other nations will, even though the change in the West has had to be described as so sudden and unexpected. It is the advanced countries that have to learn to adapt themselves, to modify their outlooks, to found the new institutions, to bring forth and develop the ideas and attitudes that are now for the first time required and that will be required into the indefinite future. At the present moment, they are in a situation not unlike that of Western Europe, especially of Britain, at the dawn of industrialization, the first to adventure into an entirely new world. The history of aging in the now developed countries has a significance for Brazil, shall we say, or India or China, analogous to that of the economic history of those developed countries, and the analogy is the more telling because of the fundamental similarity of demographic processes wherever and whenever they occur. The sooner the cultural lag or false consciousness, as I have called it, is made to disappear from the countries that already have age-transformed populations, the better for the world as a whole.[1] The first requirement is that the facts should be known, the historical facts in particular.

There is another reason why the historical demography of aging is highly significant. Together with gender, ethnicity, and class, aging is one of the four dimensions of individual and social experience, though it has hitherto been given much less attention than the other three. It has to be known how the age composition of societies has changed over time, along with the longevity and the life course of individuals, if a properly historical social analysis, a durational analysis, is to be undertaken. Until this is done, we shall not fully comprehend the societies in which our ancestors lived, nor shall we be able to grasp the contrast between their situation and our own. This means that we shall not be able to understand ourselves, to understand ourselves in time, to place ourselves in the procession, as I shall finally put it.

Remarkable as the aging of the populations of advanced societies has been, the phenomenon is rather more complex than it may seem and must be viewed in proper proportion. It is now frequently said that in a country like Britain, longevity has doubled and relative numbers of the old have trebled within the hundred years preceding our own day and that this has mostly happened within the lifetimes of its older citizens. As the figures in table 1.3 will demonstrate, however, this is somewhat of an overstatement as to changes in the two variables, though the historical period during which the change has occurred is correct.

In England the gain in expectation of life at birth over that period has been more like two-thirds for men and just slightly more for women, with a multiplication of some two and a half times for men and somewhat under three times for women in proportions over 60.[2] When the more revealing measures that are suggested below in the section "Experiential Measures in the Historical Demography of Aging" are applied, the change has been somewhat less than this in England with respect to longevity. Length of life after the fifteenth birthday, the suggested statistic for general comparison over periods of time, has not doubled but increased by more like a half, and at age 50, more appropriate for comparisons of this kind for those in later life, the rise is about one-half for men and two-thirds for women in Britain since the 1880s. If the share of those over age 60 of all those over age 25 is reckoned, the realistic experiential measure suggested for the weight in the population of senior people, there has been a twofold rather than a threefold gain, though rather less for men.

We need not exaggerate these historic changes, therefore, and we should be prepared to face the complications that arise when deciding on the most informative ways of describing them. In making out a case for the great importance of the history of aging, moreover, we must take due account of other drastic and unprecedented demographic changes that have recently taken place in Western countries and in Japan as well, though not to the same extent. The extraordinary increases in divorce, in births outside marriage, in numbers of persons living alone, and in consensual unions have gone forward over the last twenty or twenty-five years alongside the process of aging and have had their own individual and collective effects on social life. The combination of these developments with aging has made the position of the Western countries in the 1990s singular indeed. But these other alterations in behavior, though frequently dramatic, have been more recent and rather less general than aging, showing abrupt vicissitudes and varying from country to country.[3] Their occurrence, in my view, does nothing to modify the claim that the historical demography of aging represents necessary knowledge.

This is the first volume, as far as we know, ever to be devoted to the historical demography of aging. The introductory chapter accordingly begins with a discussion of it as a subject itself and an appreciation of the extent and reliability of its results. We go on to describe and discuss the course of aging in developed societies, under the heading "The Secular Shift in Aging," a shift from a lower plateau to a higher plateau that has taken place, as has been seen, for the most part during the present century. The two temporal areas will alternatively be referred to as the Before and the After.[4] We will insist that longevity, that is, expectation of life at birth and at later ages, is as important a constituent of the history of aging as proportions of elderly, though not generally recognized as such by demographers. New indicators will be suggested to supplement those in use at present, which are ineffective for historical purposes and removed from experience, experience in our own day as well as in the past.

No apology will be offered for giving so much space to these indicators and to the discussion of definitions, conventions, and measures for this newly emerging study. When in the early 1970s a book of this type was issued, opening up the then-novel field of the history of household and family (Laslett and Wall, *Household and family in past time,* with a comprehensive introduction by Laslett), much space had to be used in this way.

THE HISTORICAL DEMOGRAPHY OF AGING

Historical demography proper began its career fairly recently, in the 1960s. Statistics for age and aging have always been among its results, but it is only during the last year or two that much attention has been paid to them, and the information so far available is rather restricted. Scarcity of data imposes stringent limits on what can be accomplished by historical demography in any field. Fertility and mortality, both essential to the reconstruction of the history of aging, can only be worked out for societies that have recorded births, marriages, and deaths (or in Christian areas, baptisms, marriages, and burials), societies whose records of this kind are still extant and available for study. Migration, often critical in the study of age composition, generally requires information additional to the registration of vital events. The fact that these are preconditions of satisfactory analysis means that we shall never have anything like precise numerical knowledge of aging in wholly illiterate societies, past or present, or in literate communities that have failed to carry out the necessary recordings and to leave them to us for study.

Hence accurate estimates of life expectation and age composition even in highly civilized earlier populations like those of Greece or Rome, or in any European population before the end of the Middle Ages, will always elude us. Along with them go the peoples of the whole of the rest of the world in the premodern past, though here and there a tiny pool of uncertain light glimmers in the darkness, nearly always fitfully illuminating groups of elite individuals.

It has to be said that this enforced ignorance makes it difficult for us to observe at all closely any population that could be supposed to have the aging characteristics of a wholly traditional society of the preindustrial kind existing on the lower aging plateau in a wholly traditional world. It might be thought that the developing societies, especially the "primitive" ones, surviving in our own day would provide just what we would like to have, instances of something like "natural" aging. This is scarcely the case, however, because these contemporary societies, if they carry out the required registrations at all, do so at the behest of literate minorities whose very presence may alter their aging characteristics to some degree. Moreover, such "backward" communities exist in a world so dominated by the highly industrialized countries that their longevity and age structure are hardly likely to be at the traditional level.[5] We are in the same position as those who study birthrates, and our best chance of estimating a "natural" standard for aging lies in reconstructing the demographic history of the one or two countries that did maintain usable recordings for the whole of their populations during at least some stretches of time before the demographic transition and the secular shift. Since they have now become industrialized themselves, however, and since their material standards were probably already higher than those of the rest of humanity at the periods in the Before for which their situations with regard to aging can be recovered, the evidence of these countries is even less suited to show a "natural" aging condition than is the case with "natural" fertility.

Archaeodemography, the establishment of a general notion of vital rates through the examination of exhumed skeletal remains, has sometimes been used to prompt the record of the historical demography of aging (e.g., Laslett [1976] 1985: table 2a). Through this technique, indications of ages at death, of the life span, and of gender differentiation over the life course have been recovered; life tables have even been constructed. This evidence is all that is open to biologists of aging who have to interest themselves in the very distant past, distant enough to allow for natural selection. Historians concerned with much later periods have contrasted its outcomes with those derived from other sources with rather discouraging consequences. Although archaeodemography may serve for approximate aging estimates, the reckoning of limiting values for the most part, the sketchiness of its results, and questions as to their accuracy and representativeness prevent it from being a source of much importance for the historical demography of aging as it will be expounded in this volume.[6]

Studies of what could be termed the history of aging as distinct from the historical demography of aging are subject to somewhat the same judgment. Where particular written records have survived from the prestatistical era which can be manipulated for the purposes of demography, though not created to that end, they can yield some estimates of age. Conspicuous examples are Ulpian's life table (3d century A.D.) or the *inquisitiones post-mortem* in medieval England (inquiries at a landholder's death about his properties and claimants to them). The first appears in many works on mortality and life expectancy not concerned with history and the second, along with the evidence of poll taxes, in a comprehensive historical study such as J. C. Russell's *British medieval population* (1948) and in many more limited analyses.[7]

When proper allowance is made for their limitations, biases, and inaccuracies, materials of this kind are of considerable use to the historical demography of aging. They could not be said, however, themselves to constitute that study over tracts of time in which nothing more systematic, interconnected, and informative is, or can be, forthcoming. Every detail pertaining to aging in past time is important to this book. But if nothing of greater value to our purposes could be recovered for former generations, our present project could never have been undertaken.

There are yet other studies of particular subjects in the history of aging that are of relevance to our purposes, and they will be touched on when we come to the aging of particular groups and restricted areas and aging at particular times. But we must glance here at the general, outline histories of the topic that its salience at the present moment has given rise to. They seem to be of much more limited value than the writings we have gone over. Composed, like some of the special studies, with the use of traditional historical sources, mainly literary evidence, and sometimes with scant respect for demographic analysis or even demographic reality, they seem to be preoccupied with past ideas about the division of the life course. They are to be classed as histories of aging attitudes and attitudes to the old rather than as histories of aging and will perhaps impede the progress of the study rather than forward it.[8]

Nevertheless, no great stress will be laid on the contrast between the historical demography of aging and the history of aging. As we approach demographic analysis proper, however, it has to be pronounced that by and large the historical demography of aging is confined to the now developed countries and, with salient exceptions in the history of those developed countries themselves, to the period that is called the statistical era. The statistical era is the time during which states have carried out exact recording of vital events, analyzed and preserved those records, and made them accessible. For most of the developed countries, the statistical era begins some one hundred fifty years ago, in the middle of the nineteenth century, though a century earlier in Scandinavia, notably Sweden. For these Western nations a great deal of what the historical demographer wishes to know about age and aging can now be recovered. Census and local census-type materials, where and for what years they are open to examination,[9] make it possible also to investigate such things as the position in the household of persons of various ages, their kin relationships, and, by reference to their vital statistics, what has come to be called their life course transitions. Data of this kind have been extensively used in the chapters in this volume.

There are even some developed countries, notably those of Scandinavia, along with the Netherlands, Belgium, and Italy, where population registers were regularly maintained by local authorities in past periods and are now accessible. These are lists of all the inhabitants of a particular place distributed into households, giving ages and updated for every birth, marriage, death, entrance, or departure. In these very special cases, if the registers have survived, in principle virtually everything that the historical demographer wishes to know about aging is available.[10]

Since the 1950s and because of the activities of international statistical bodies such as the demographic division of the United Nations, data are plentiful for populations at all stages of development and multiply rapidly. Here the task of the historical demographer is to disentangle the figures that can be used to produce an intelligible account within that excessively narrow time period. As he or she works backward toward the beginnings of the statistical era, the evidence thins out rapidly, but in comparative terms the temporal depth remains woefully shallow. For by far the largest part of history in its conventional definition—past time during which written records were maintained and can be consulted—all there is to go on is demographic theory and analogy. This makes the historical demography of aging a very different pursuit from previously established forms of historical study. Not only is nearly all the available material confined to the last two or two and a half centuries, compressed so to speak in a dense layer on the surface of time, but almost all the notable action is in fact confined to that time space. The temptation that has to be resisted is to follow the unfortunate example of social scientists generally and to read history backward from the present moment. Our enterprise as to aging in the past is undeniably demanding and difficult, replete with somewhat hazardous inferential argument.

This comes out in the fact that the statements already made about necessary knowledge apply to all the world's populations over the whole of their history, while the relevant evidence is so recent and so concentrated. We have to do everything we can to make use of the records of a handful of national populations, as opposed to individual communities, for which reliable numerical knowledge of aging can be pushed back for a hundred years earlier than the statistical era, to the middle of the eighteenth century. France and the Scandinavian countries and parts of Italy are in this position. In one country, England, using the same means but in what might be called heroic form, the time horizon has been stretched backward another two hundred years to the mid-sixteenth century for the entire national population.[11] All these statistics from the time before the official statistical era have been derived from registrations made by the Christian church. We shall see, however, that even the four and a half centuries of the English historical record on aging, from the 1540s to the 1990s, are rather short for our purposes.

We now turn to the actual process of aging in populations of some size, nearly always national populations, and begin with the demographic transition itself.

THE AGING OF NATIONAL POPULATIONS

Since the demographic transition consists in a monotonic and irreversible fall in fertility and in mortality, from generally stable high levels to less stable low levels, it must always lengthen life and inevitably give rise, in due course, to an increase in the proportion of elderly people in a population. However, like fluctuations in total numbers, aging in this latter sense, that of our second aging variable, is a second-order demographic effect. The increase in proportions of elderly persons does not come about as a direct result of change in first-order variables such as fertility, mortality, and migration. It is an outcome of the interplay between those variables as they change over time, on the one hand, with the initial age composition of the population, on the other hand. It is the case, however, that in most situations, certainly those that characterize populations on the lower aging plateau, a fall in fertility that is as large and continuous as it has to be during the demographic transition always initiates and maintains a proportionate increase in the numbers of older persons. The part played by falling mortality, which goes forward at the same time, is negligible at these earlier stages of the change in age composition, though it is of course wholly responsible for increase in longevity.

The process is not easy to explain in terms accessible to those unfamiliar with demographic analysis. It is important to recognize that because the rise in the numbers and proportions of the old is a delayed rather than an immediate outcome of the demographic transition, the momentum which causes that rise continues after the transition is over. Different countries therefore show different patterns over time in changes in their age composition, in accordance with the differing calendar years over which they experience the transition and with the varying course that the transition may take. They also age at different speeds. We shall only be able to refer here to the historically more important of these differences between the records of the countries we are considering.[12]

Countries have also varied in the timing and pace of aging in our first sense, in longevity, though we shall not be able to linger on this matter either. But the recognition of longevity as of equal significance to change in age composition in the aging process and its analysis is an extremely important matter.

Life expectation has been regarded by demographers hitherto as a function of the mortality prevalent in any given population and as nothing more. Accordingly, it is classified by social scientists and by administrators as a measure of general health and well-being, not in itself as a manifestation of aging, individual or social. Since their interest stretches over the whole of the life course, it is expectation of life at birth that is the commanding statistic, worked out and cited almost to the exclusion of longevity at later ages, except of course when life expectation at subsequent birthdays is the particular interest in mind. From our point of view, that of historical sociology, this is wholly too narrow a view of longevity and has to be expanded. Expectation of life at every age and rises or falls in its duration, the probability at one birthday of reaching a particular later birthday, are all crucial aging phenomena on their own account, both for the individual and for society at large, in our own day and assuredly in the past. What people have always wanted and needed to know is how long persons like themselves are likely to live, their friends and their relatives included, and social scientists need to know this too, if they are to grasp the durational reality.

The historical aging process in national societies will therefore be discussed here in terms of two variables, not one, two variables treated as if they were discrete. The first is change in longevity, or life expectation, that is to say, not only average expectation at birth in a population but increasingly as we proceed expectations at later ages. The second is change in the proportions of the population of those in the higher age groups, generally those over 60 but increasingly the share that these older persons made up of all those in mid- and later life, that is, all those over age 25. Tables 1.1 and 1.2 set out the statistics of these two variables in their initial form, expectation of life at birth and proportions over 60, for the populations of a number of now-developed countries between the 1880s and the 1980s. Numbers in the final columns in both tables will give some idea of the extent of the rise in values between the last quarter of the nineteenth century and the present day.

It is evident from the figures that in the 1880s there were considerable differences between the selected countries with respect to the two chosen aging variables. It is also evident that low mortality (high expectation of life) was not always associated with large proportions of elderly people. This comes out clearly in the contrast in the tables between France, on the one hand, and England and Wales, on the other. Longevity was lower in France in the 1880s, yet France had a two-thirds larger proportion of persons over 60. This contrast is even more marked when it is recalled that in Britain there was in progress during the 1880s a considerable out-migration that had continued for a long time. This made the British population older than it would otherwise have been. What made Britain older in this sense, of course, made countries of immigration like the United States, Canada, and Australia younger, because many of the migrants were younger Britons. The

TABLE 1.1 Change in Life Expectancy (at Birth) during the Secular Shift, 1880s to 1980s

	1 1880s		2 1920s		3 1950s		4 1980s		5 Rise[a]	
	Male	Female	Male	Female	Male	Female	Male	Female	Male	Female
Australia	47.2	50.8	59.0	61.4	66.8	70.5	73.0	79.4	156	156
Belgium	43.8	46.9	56.2	59.8	62.9	68.3	70.4	76.9	161	164
Bulgaria	—	—	45.9	46.6	58.0	62.0	68.4	73.6	149	158
Canada	43.5	46.0	55.6	58.4	66.4	70.8	73.0	79.8	168	169
England and Wales	44.2	47.5	55.9	59.9	69.8	68.2	71.0	77.6	161	163
France	40.8	43.4	52.3	56.7	63.6	69.4	72.0	80.3	176	185
Germany	35.6	38.5	56.0	58.8	64.6	68.5	71.8	76.4	202	198
Greece	36.0[b]	37.5[b]	48.4	50.0	63.4	66.7	72.2	76.4	200[b]	204[b]
Italy	33.3	33.9	48.8	50.4	63.9	67.9	72.0	78.6	216	232
Japan	42.4	43.7	44.8	49.6	59.4	62.7	75.5	81.3	178	186
Spain	33.8	35.7	40.3	51.6	59.8	64.3	72.5	78.6	214	220
Sweden	48.5	54.1	57.5	60.2	69.1	72.3	74.2	77.0	153	142
Switzerland	43.3	45.7	54.5	57.5	66.3	70.5	73.9	80.7	171	176
U.S.A.	42.5[c]	44.5[c]	55.0[d]	57.1[d]	66.3	72.0	71.3	78.2	168[c]	173[c]

SOURCES: Dublin, Lotka, and Spiegelman 1949; National Statistical Yearbooks; Preston, Keyfitz, and Schoen 1971; and various.

[a]For Bulgaria, values from column 2 = 100; for all other countries, values from column 1 = 100.

[b]1879.

[c]1890s, Massachusetts whites only.

[d]Registration states (17% of U.S. population 1880s, 82% 1920s, whites only); see U.S. Bureau of the Census 1937.

TABLE 1.2 Change in Proportions over Age 60 during the Secular Shift, 1880s to 1990s

	1			2			3			4	5
	1880s			1920s			1950s			1980s–1990s	Change[a]
	Male	Female	Both	Male	Female	Both	Male	Female	Both	Both	
Australia	—	—	—	7.7	7.3	7.5	11.5	13.4	12.4	11.9	—
Belgium	9.4	10.2	9.8	9.4	10.9	10.1	14.4	16.6	15.5	15.8	161
Bulgaria	7.0	6.4	6.7	8.6	8.3	8.5	9.1	10.1	9.6	—	—
Canada	5.2	6.0	5.4	6.8	7.8	7.5	11.5	11.1	11.2	11.3	209
England and Wales	6.9	7.8	7.4	8.8	10.9	9.4	13.9	17.8	15.9	17.0	230
France	12.0	12.6	12.3	13.0	14.7	13.9	13.4	19.0	16.3	16.6	135
Germany	7.5	8.2	7.9	8.6	9.6	9.1	13.0	14.4	13.8	16.7	211
Greece	5.0	4.1	4.6	8.5	8.9	8.7	9.1	10.4	9.8	15.2	330
Italy	9.0	8.9	9.0	10.8	10.9	10.8	11.3	13.1	12.2	15.5	172
Japan	—	—	—	—	—	—	7.0	8.4	7.7	12.9	—
Spain	7.8	7.9	7.8	10.0	10.0	10.0	—	15.8	15.0	14.1	180
Sweden	8.4	10.2	9.4	11.1	13.3	12.2	14.2	15.8	15.0	17.7	188
Switzerland	8.6	9.1	8.8	8.3	10.1	9.2	12.7	15.4	14.1	16.3	185
U.S.A.	—	—	[5.4]b	6.7b	6.8b	6.7b	11.8	12.5	12.2	15.9	[294]

SOURCES: National Statistical Yearbooks; and various.

[a]Values from column 1 = 100.

bRegistration states (17% of U.S. population 1880s, 82% 1920s, whites only); see U.S. Bureau of the Census 1937.

variation between these populations and other similarly placed populations as they were in the 1880s and the rates of fall in fertility and mortality that ensued during the transition ensured that they would age at different paces. But the effect to which we have already referred, monotonic fall in fertility initiating and sustaining change in age composition, was a constant, and it could be shown that the accompanying fall in mortality had very little to do with it until the last decades of the secular shift.

We have now reached the point that has to be called the pons asinorum of demographic aging, a bridge that has to have been crossed by everyone undertaking historical analysis of the subject. It is universally assumed by those who have never had occasion to examine the issue that populations grow old invariably because deaths go down and life expectation goes up. This mistake is the more understandable in that the demographic transition itself starts in most cases with a fall in mortality. But it is a serious mistake, nevertheless, particularly often made by historians without demographic knowledge. They think it natural to expect that if there is evidence of rising longevity at a particular period, proportions of older persons must have been growing, and vice versa. It usually does not occur to them that a fall in births will work to expand the proportion of the elderly in the population, that this effect could be reinforced by the very young living longer, least of all that a fall in deaths might contract that proportion because, especially in the Before, such a high proportion of deaths happened to babies.

THE SECULAR SHIFT IN AGING

The secular shift in aging in England is set out schematically in figure 1.1 in ideal terms and on a scale that goes back for some eight centuries into the pretransitional past, in the Before, and is projected forward in the After some six centuries from the 1990s.

The general shape of the curves conveys the idea of the secular shift as an upward thrust from a lower aging plateau stretching backward in time from the last decade of the nineteenth century up to a much higher aging plateau sloping upwards and stretching forward from the first decades of the twenty-first century. But in this hypothetical model, the higher plateau is a particularly speculative construct, and its course over time after the first few decades of the twenty-first century is very uncertain. Projections made by demographers specify a range of alternative futures, some of which are quite extreme. These uncertainties make it necessary to represent the future courses of both longevity and proportions in later life as areas of possibility rather than as determinate lines. The earlier plateau and the rise from the lower level after the 1890s are, however, quite well documented for a number of populations, as will be shown. In England, its steepest climb in both graphs evidently took place between the 1920s and the 1950s. These

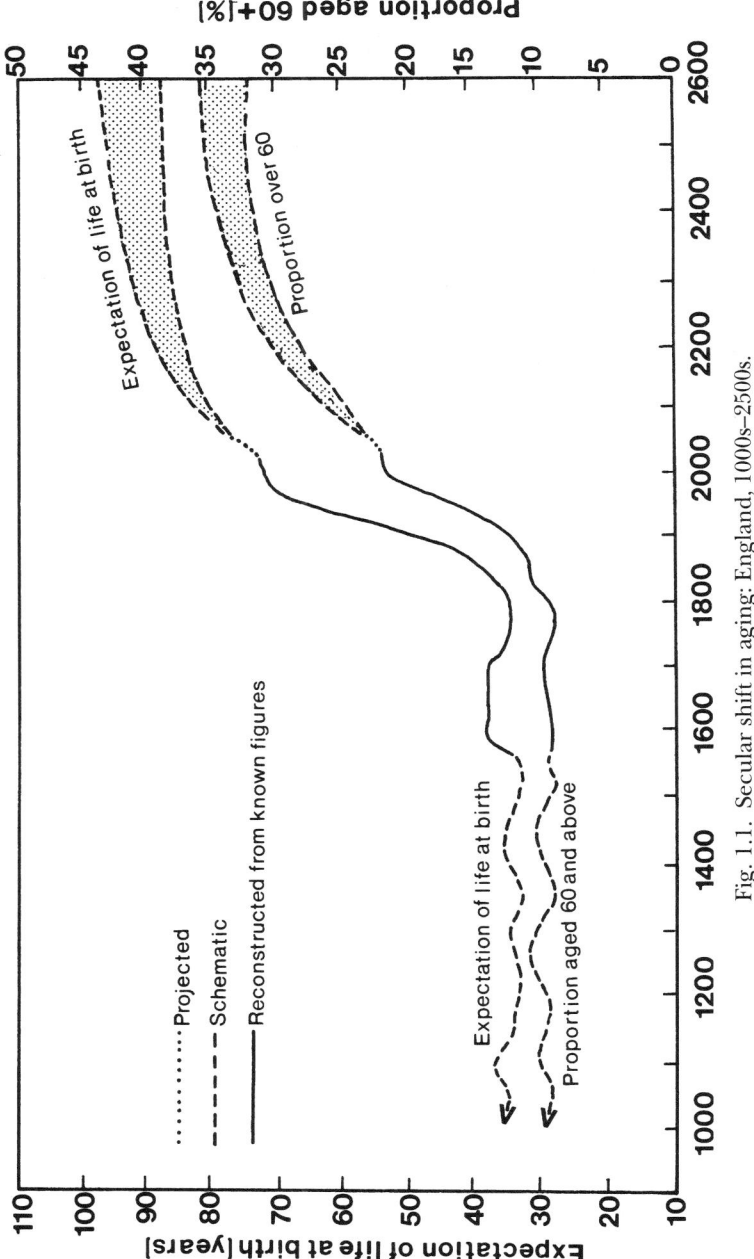

Fig. 1.1. Secular shift in aging: England, 1000s–2500s.

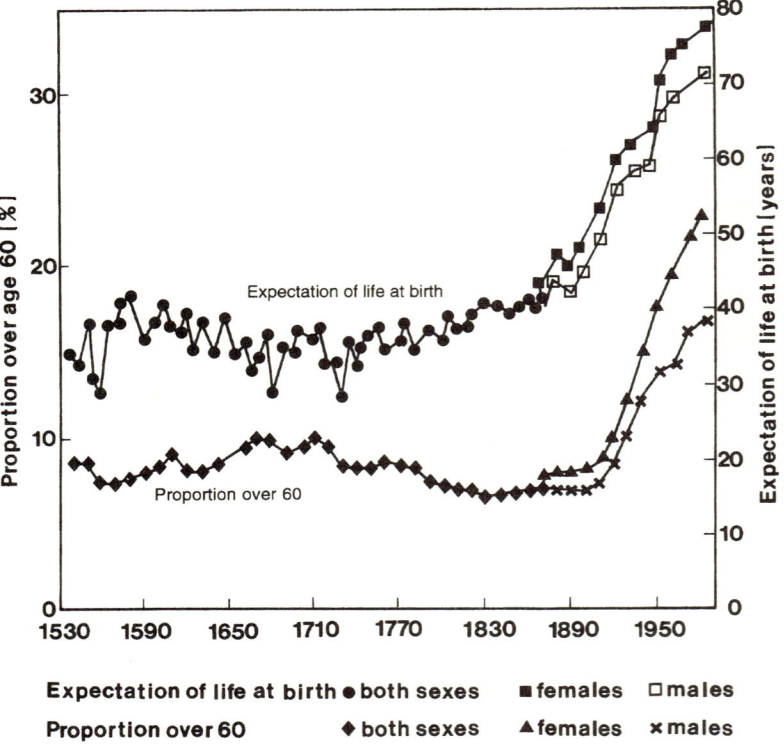

Fig. 1.2. Expectation of life at birth and proportion of population over age 60: England, 1540s–1990s.

effects are very clear in the detailed representation of data for England set out in figure 1.2 covering the four hundred fifty years over which the requisite data are available. It is not possible to divide the genders until the 1870s, but the widening gap between male and female as we approach the 1990s is unmistakable.[13] In figure 1.3, the English curves are set out again, along with directly comparable curves from France and Sweden, two other countries that also have evidence for both longevity and age composition stretching some way back from the beginnings of the statistical era, distinguishing male from female at the outset. Figure 1.4 compares Tuscany, that area of Italy in which Florence is situated, with England in expectation of life at birth for three hundred years after the early seventeenth century. The stretch of years between the 1640s and the 1890s in this figure represents the longest period during the Before over which life expectation at birth can at present be compared for two substantial European areas.

Apart from these pieces of relevant evidence, the English record is all we have to go on before about the year 1740 to assess the experience of aging

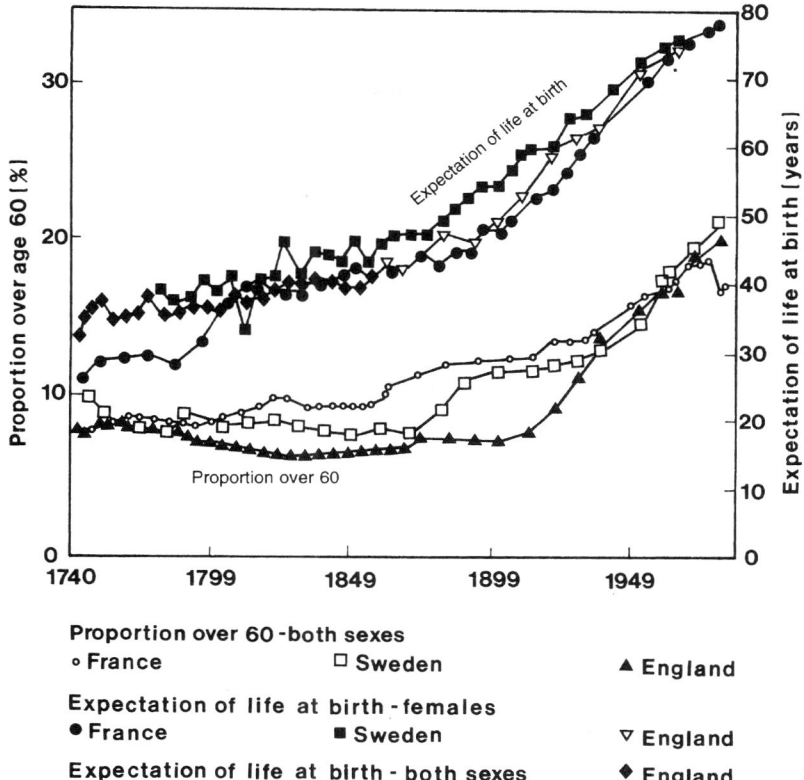

Fig. 1.3. Expectation of life at birth and proportion of population over age 60: England, France, and Sweden, 1740s–1990s.

in Western countries—and in large part, the experience of the world as a whole—in properly numerical terms. This makes the statistics from England (and in more recent years, from England and Wales) strategically so important that all the relevant numbers for that country have been set out as table 1.3.

With this spread of information about England before, during, and after the secular shift in aging before us, there are two issues that have to be confronted if we are to appreciate critically its significance for the course of aging over the centuries and for the general subject of the historical demography of aging. These two issues are whether the English curves exaggerate the steepness of the rise in the two chosen variables and so cannot be called typical of the movement in all the countries concerned and whether the Before and the After are in fact to be thought of as plateaus. The upper plateau can scarcely be our present concern. Only the analogy of the level trajectory of the lower plateau, which we are about to discuss, justifies the suggested

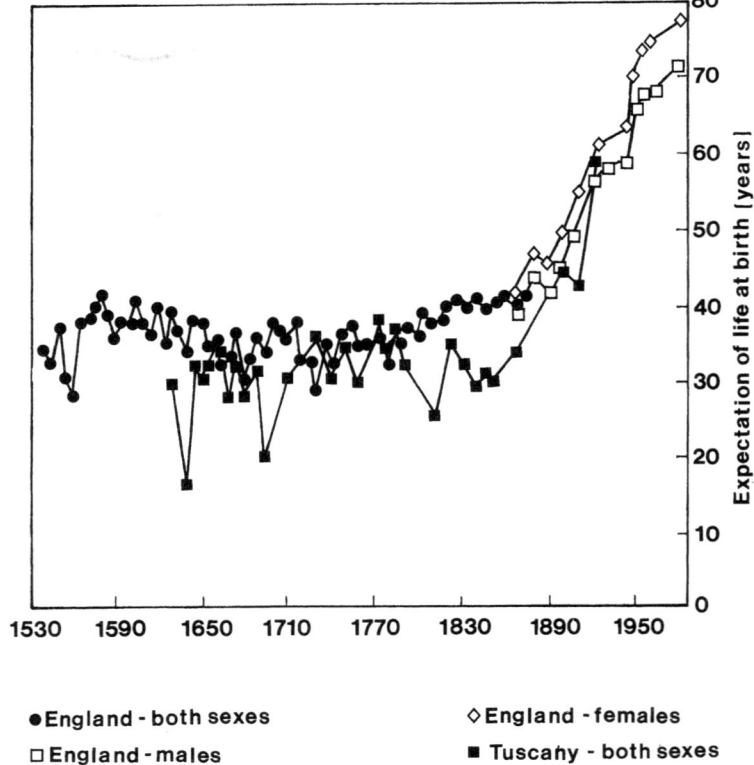

Fig. 1.4. Expectation of life at birth: England, 1540s–1990s, and Tuscany, 1630s–1930s. Data for Tuscany from Breschi 1990.

stretching forward of the higher plateau into the indefinite future, though the narrowing of gaps between survival curves in figure 1.5 hints at such a future development.[14] Its possible or probable existence, however, gives a striking appearance to the secular shift in relation to what came before. It is to the lower aging plateau that we have to direct our attention.

RELATIVE HISTORICAL CONSTANCY IN AGING BEFORE THE SECULAR SHIFT

Since England is unique in the way we have discussed above and since it was from the English evidence[15] that the model of the secular shift in aging was originally constructed (see Laslett 1984), the question of whether England has been typical is not without its importance. There would seem to be little doubt that this was so with respect to the increase in expectation of life at birth, the first of our aging variables. France and Sweden, whose curves

TABLE 1.3   Expectation of Life at Birth and Proportion over Age 60,
England, 1541–1991

Year	Expectation of Life at Birth[a]	Proportion over Age 60[b]	Year	Expectation of Life at Birth	Proportion over Age 60
1541	33.75	8.67	1746	35.34	7.99
1546	32.50	8.47	1751	35.57	8.22
1551	37.99	8.35	1756	37.29	8.37
1556	30.73	8.16	1761	34.23	8.60
1561	27.77	7.29	1766	35.04	8.76
1566	37.97	7.21	1771	35.60	8.50
1571	38.22	7.32	1776	38.17	8.36
1576	40.26	7.49	1781	34.72	8.24
1581	41.68	7.59	1786	35.93	7.97
1586	38.31	7.80	1791	37.33	7.41
1591	35.51	7.93	1796	36.76	7.37
1596	37.65	8.08	1801	35.89	7.26
1601	38.12	8.27	1806	38.70	6.99
1606	40.82	8.62	1811	37.59	6.89
1611	37.27	9.08	1816	37.86	6.86
1616	36.79	8.90	1821	39.24	6.68
1621	39.95	8.02	1826	39.92	6.54
1626	33.96	7.90	1831	40.80	6.56
1631	38.71	8.03	1836	40.15	6.58
1636	36.14	8.12	1841	40.28	6.58
1641	33.70	8.27	1846	39.56	6.57
1646	38.47	8.59	1851	39.56	6.56
1651	37.82	8.92	1856	40.39	6.80
1656	34.11	9.28	1861	41.19	6.87
1661	35.71	9.40	1866	40.32	6.93
1666	31.79	9.73	1871	41.31	7.05
1671	33.18	9.89			

Year	Expectation of Life at Birth[a]	Proportion over Age 60[b]	Year	Male	Female	Male	Female
1676	36.37	9.95					
1681	28.47	9.71					
1686	31.77	9.10	1881	44.2	47.5	6.9	7.8
1691	34.87	9.06	1891	41.9	45.7	6.8	7.9
1696	34.13	9.18	1901	48.0	51.6	6.8	8.0
1701	37.11	9.38	1911	49.4	53.4	7.3	8.6
1706	36.44	9.81	1921	55.9	59.9	8.7	10.0
1711	35.93	9.97	1931	58.4	62.4	10.7	12.3
1716	37.10	10.08	1941	59.4	63.9	—	—
1721	32.51	9.46	1951	66.2	71.2	14.6	17.7
1726	32.41	9.11	1961	67.9	73.8	15.3	17.9
1731	27.88	8.41	1971	68.8	75.0	15.9	21.9
1736	35.64	8.35	1981	69.8	76.2	16.2	22.7
1741	3170	8.11	1991	70.1	78.3	16.5	23.1

SOURCES: British official statistics; Wrigley and Schofield [1981] 1989.
[a]1541–1545 to 1871–1875: Mean, 36.45; standard deviation, 3.25; minimum, 27.77; maximum, 41.68.
[b]1541–1545 to 1871–1875: Mean, 8.31; standard deviation, 1.48; minimum, 6.54; maximum, 10.08.

for the course of this statistic over time are also depicted in figure 1.3, show a steep or very steep rise similar to that for England, a rise that began at some point in the last decade of the nineteenth century or the first decade of the twentieth. In the case of Tuscany in figure 1.4, the resemblance to the curve for England is quite striking, rather surprising in view of very different conditions of health and welfare. There seems to have been a slow upward incline of expectation of life at birth in all Western countries during the nineteenth century before the secular shift, and the Scandinavian countries were well above England by the time the really steep ascent began. Such a circumstance might be taken as putting England into the median position. Longevity has been excellently assessed in all now-developed countries for this period, and it is possible to be confident that England can stand for the rest. And if this was so in the run-up to the secular shift and for the shift itself, why should it not have been so in earlier decades and centuries?

The same cannot be so easily pronounced for our second aging variable, traced by the lower graph in figure 1.3, increase in proportions over the age of 60. Here the English figures show a tendency to fall in the earlier nineteenth century, as is evident in table 1.3, putting the English graph for proportions of elderly well below those for France and Sweden, and this can be confirmed in other countries. The subsequent precipitate ascent in England may well exaggerate the abruptness of the aging transformation at the secular shift. Even in other English-speaking populations, the share of the old rose more slowly than in the "mother country," though their character as immigrant receivers may have something to do with this.

The contrast between English experience of growth in the weight of older people in the population at large is particularly marked in relation to France. But it is well known that the demographic transition itself was more diffuse in France than elsewhere, and it has to be expected that in this respect the secular shift would also be more diffuse in that country. The general *allure*, as the French would themselves say, of the French curves is quite similar to that of the English and the Scandinavian. With such a small sample and in so novel and uncertain an area of investigation, the correspondence between these graphs seems acceptable. I am prepared to regard the shape of the secular shift in England as an ideal type of that development, ideal type in the sense used by Max Weber. We shall return to this point when we come to discuss more revealing aging measures than those we have used so far.

As for the levelness of the lower plateau, which is a way of expressing the long-term constancy of these two aging variables in historic populations, the course taken by the graphs in figure 1.3 certainly suggests that in the long term relative stability can be assumed as well. It is here that the length of the record over time becomes highly significant, so that even the near half-millennium covered by the English data may appear somewhat inadequate.

But the line representing the English statistics of proportions over 60 is conspicuously flat for the complete run, and those for the other countries being compared are very much the same for their interludes of record. A survey of the quinquennial figures for England contained in table 1.3 shows that proportions varied between extremes of 10.08 percent (maximum) in the years 1716 to 1720 and 6.54 percent (minimum) in the 1820s and 1830s but that three-fourths of the values fell between 6.80 percent and 8.50 percent. In spite of differences in the later eighteenth century and earlier nineteenth century, the impression of constancy remains with respect to the weight of older persons in the population at large. But we shall find ourselves wondering whether this was quite so evident for the proportion of elderly persons in the adult as opposed to the whole population and whether the rise was as considerable at the secular shift in that respect.

The course of expectation of life at birth before the secular shift has a much less even appearance than the course of proportions of elderly: ups and downs succeed each other in the English figures in a way that recalls the heraldic description *dancetty*. Nevertheless, the claim for an underlying constancy seems strong in this matter too. Variation between extremes of 41.68 years (maximum) in the 1580s and 27.77 years (minimum) in the 1560s— the propinquity in date of the maximal peak and minimal trough should be noted—is accompanied by a concentration of two-thirds of the values between 35 and 40 years. When the graphs for expectation of life at birth are smoothed by the use of moving averages,[16] they also have a decidedly even appearance. Work in progress at the Cambridge length of life project suggests a surprising stability over time in the longevity figures for elite groups, back to the later Middle Ages for British peers and members of Parliament, back to the beginning of the Christian era for Chinese mandarins. It seems safe to assume that the secular shift is properly represented by a sudden, precipitous rise from a lower plateau to a higher level in both dimensions.

The implications of these considerations for the historical demography of aging must be quite evident. Although they were subject to quite sharp fluctuations in life expectation at birth–and here the effects of epidemics, wars, and food shortages spring to mind—our ancestors never seem to have been subject to aging changes on anything like the scale that has been experienced by the populations going through the secular shift. Recovery in duration of life was rapid after episodes of disaster, though it must be remembered that this recovery consisted largely of better prospects for newly arrived infants and children. Proportions of elderly persons in the population at large remained fairly constant, showing the same tendency to revert to the average after rises and falls, for centuries on end as far as we can tell.

This conclusion is reinforced by demographic knowledge and demographic theory. Although we have had to recognize that no example of a population in what might be called a "natural" condition with respect to ag-

ing is or is likely to be available, demographers have had extremely wide experience of populations that had not yet entered the demographic transition, or are in its early stages and hence so far not much affected by the secular shift. Their aging characteristics are indeed plateaulike. Episodes of low
fertility along with relatively low mortality cannot have lasted long enough
among these populations for them to grow old in the dual fashion that has
been described for the secular shift. This has to be the case, since pretran-
sition populations had and still have high birth- and death rates by definition.

DURATION OF LIFE AT EVERY AGE AND
AGE COMPOSITION HISTORICALLY CONSIDERED:
THE RECTANGULAR SURVIVAL CURVE

The theme of the historical demography of aging has been treated so far as
if it were concerned only with those who reach, who have reached, or who
are likely to reach late life. This may seem appropriate because gerontology,
the scientific study of aging, is itself pursued in this way and because the
chapters that follow here deal with such topics, many of them belonging interestingly enough to the period of the secular shift when it occurred to the
population of the United States.

But the elderly have only ever been the topmost of the age levels of any
society, and aging at all the other, lower levels are alike of importance to the
social scientist, the historical sociologist especially. The system of distribut-
ing individuals into age groups—childhood, youth, middle age, and so on—
found, but in differing forms, in every society and at all times together with
the interrelationships between those groups and their members are all of
significance. Generational relationships are rightly recognized as a subject
for anthropological and sociological as well as for historical and gerontological research. Taken as a whole these studies go by the name of age structuring, until recently pursued mainly by anthropologists, though with some
reference to historical instances.[17] Analyses of how age structuring differs
from society to society and how far it has changed historically certainly belong with the historical demography of aging, since the relative size of age
groups will change with demographic change. What is more, all members
of all age groups above infancy bear the marks of their experiences as members of younger age groups. This highly significant fact is of greatest importance for those who have gone through the largest number of age divisions, or life course stages, that is to say, those who are old at any one time.[18]

Both expectation of life and the relative sizes of the membership of age
groups are relevant here once again. For it must never be forgotten that
everyone is always getting older at all points in the life course and that
prospective length of life to spend in each life course division, or in divisions

to come, makes a considerable difference to individual attitudes and other features of age structuring. The question that presents itself is how far expectation of life at all ages, not simply at birth, is likely to change over time (or to differ between countries and cultures) and how far relative age group sizes do the same.

An interesting conspectus of capacity to go on living and its fluctuations over time is provided in figure 1.5, which traces not so much values of years still to live as they have changed over the centuries but survival itself. Survival curves plot for successive dates the numbers of an original 1,000 newborn babies still alive after 1 year, 5 years, 10 years, 20 years, and so on, up to 85, or to 100 for the most recent case. The record is again the English one, the first country for which such estimates have become available so far into the past. Up to that for 1691–1695, each curve is based on evidence from one five-year period; after that the curves relate to briefer periods or a single year.

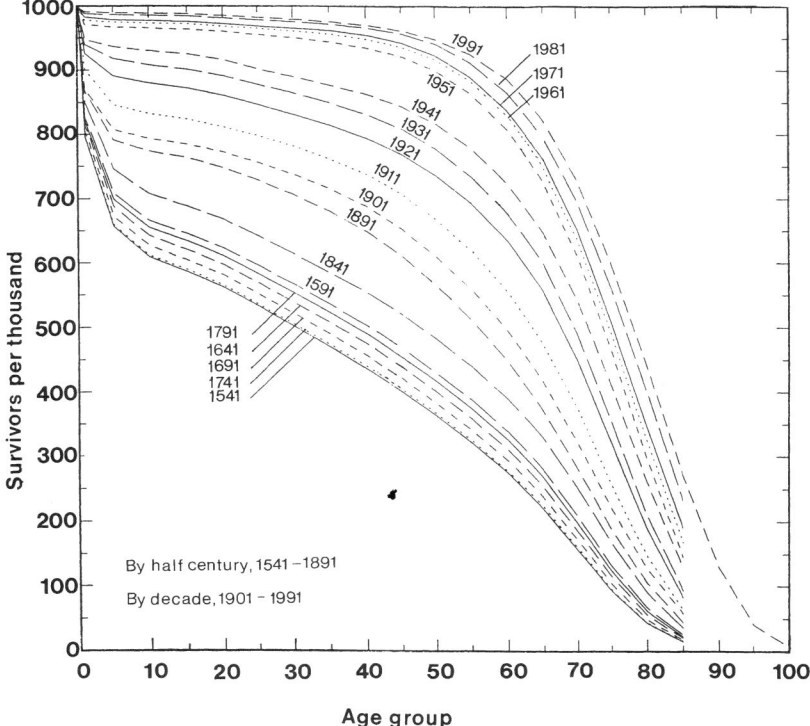

Fig. 1.5. Survival curves for cohorts of one thousand newborns, by age group: England, 1541–1991. Data from Cambridge Group back projection files and English Life tables up to no. 15. Work of James Oeppen.

The lower aging plateau is evident in the curves up to that for 1841–1845; here lines are separated by intervals of half a century each. These lines are not only very close together but they change positions with each other in an order that is certainly not chronological. The one for the five-year period 1691–1695, for example, traces a course only just above that for 1541–1545 and well below that for 1591–1595, which in its turn is closest to that for 1841–1845, nearly two hundred fifty years later. The run-up to the secular shift is visible in the wide gap between 1841–1845 and 1891, when mortality was evidently falling but at some ages may still not have been below the levels previously reached for an individual year or so on the lower aging plateau. The subsequent course of the secular shift itself shows up vividly in the more and more conspicuous spaces between successive curves, this time temporally successive curves and separated by ten-year and not by fifty-year intervals as is the case for the earlier lines. The approach to the higher aging plateau in our own day is strongly suggested by the marked narrowing of the spaces after 1951.

Students of aging will notice that the figure as a whole is reminiscent of the theory of what is called "The rectangularization of the survival curve," which is discussed in chapter 6 of *A fresh map of life* (Laslett 1989; see especially the revised version in press). This predictive theory, propounded by the American researcher James Fries and based on the very much more accurate survival curves now available, might provide a seductive concluding act to the historical drama we are commenting upon here. The finale would be a dramatic compression of mortality, showing itself in the survival curve pattern as a conspicuous narrowing of the gaps between the lines in figure 1.5, tending toward their elimination, particularly at the extreme right-hand side. Simultaneously these overlapping curves would change their shape even further in the direction shown forth in all their predecessors, tending more and more closely toward the rectangular. These shifts would indicate that survival will get better and better until finally virtually all persons born would be alive in their later 80s or their 90s. At some point during those years, it is further claimed, the end will come for a larger and larger number as time goes by, and after briefer and briefer final illness a "natural" death will supervene, a "natural" death at the completion of the "natural" span of human life.[19]

In Fries's model, then, morbidity, the tendency to fall ill, is to be compressed along with mortality. In favor of this dual hypothesis is that at all periods before the secular shift, on the lower aging plateau, that is to say, sickness and death were distributed over the whole life course: during and since the secular shift there has been an increasing tendency toward postponement to the later years. When the higher plateau succeeds after the secular shift is over, Fries's theory predicts that both sickness and death will be almost entirely concentrated within a very short period, most likely during the middle or late 80s of the life course. If the model were to be validated, its effect would indeed be that the survival curve will eventually become rectangular, fulfilling the tendency so conspicuous in our diagram of English development over half a millennium.

It is becoming evident, however, that survival curves in our own day are resistant to such an interpretation. Some of the number of competing theories of aging at the present time imply that they will finally approximate the rectangular shape. Otherwise the life span, known to be lengthening, will do so indefinitely. But the attractive thesis of a prospective compression of the incidence of final illness and death has to be regarded as not proven, a fact with evident implications for the uncertainties over the higher aging plateau. The issues it raises, however, decidedly intensify the interest of this topic in the historical demography of aging. For our present purposes, the significance of four and a half centuries of English survival curves, which as we have seen do not necessarily represent in detail what has gone on in other comparable populations, lies elsewhere. It is in the fact that their shape was indeed remarkably constant over time until the secular shift. Habits, attitudes, and institutional arrangements that were based on the assumption that most people would be alive in the same proportion of numbers at the same age as time went by and have roughly the same numbers of years to expect to live were apparently well founded.

It can be quite simply asserted, then, that over the three and a half centuries of English history before the secular shift for which the required knowledge has been established, age structuring was subject to very little change with respect to longevity. As has been hinted, the most interesting of the effects that finally supervened at the height of the shift itself is the emergence of the Third Age, which will be initially defined demographically in terms of survival by the establishment of a novel relationship between the number of those alive at age 25 and the number alive at age 70.

Exactly the same conclusion as to relative constancy during the Before can be drawn from figure 1.6, which traces the fluctuating boundaries between age groups composing the entire English population over the same long period. (Note that estimates before 1870 cover England and Wales; after 1870, the two entities can be distinguished in official figures.) All the age groups show continuity over time in their relative sizes until the secular shift sets in. It is true that the line bounding the elderly (those over 60, the lowest proportion of course until the end of the nineteenth century) is noticeably smoother than the lines bounding other age groups (0–4, 5–14, 15–24, 25–59). But all five boundaries are quite regular before the shift, regular, that is, within short-term fluctuation up and down. The only comparable reconstruction, that for Tuscany from 1810 to 1940, has a very similar pattern (Breschi 1990: 165). It seems to have been exceptional fertility falls in England during the 1550s and the 1640s to 1670s that led to the frontiers between shares of children (5–14) and adolescents (15–24) crossing each other for a little while. But otherwise age composition displays overall con-

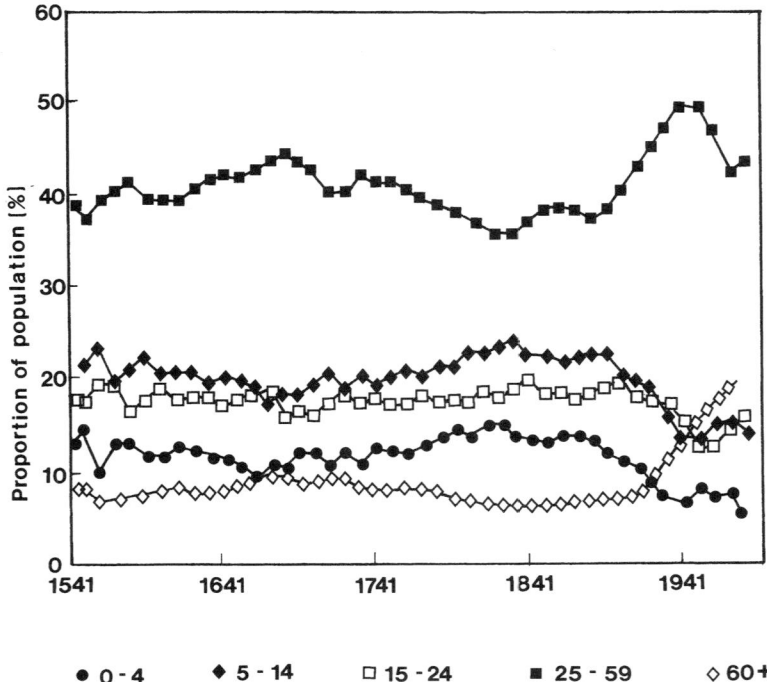

Fig. 1.6. Age composition of the population: England, 1540s–1990s.

stancy, and the statements made above about survival and life expectation apply here as well.

Stability in age composition did not survive the onset of the secular shift, and the area near the right margin of figure 1.6 demonstrates as much. Proportions over 60 rose abruptly until by the 1950s they became the second-largest age group and went on growing without interruption until the end. It is well known that this relative expansion was, is, and decidedly will be accompanied by a parallel change in composition within the open-ended group of those over 60. The very old—the 80s to 84s, 85s to 89s, the over 90s—will increase rapidly, along with their longevousness. This is a radical change from traditional age structure and one that creates an entirely novel and very formidable prospect for the present generation. Although we do not have the information to confirm the generalization in detail, it is very probable that at all earlier times the composition of the group of those very late in life tended to be constant in all larger populations.

Our ancestors, that is to say, those who were citizens of our countries before the secular shift in aging, could rely on a relatively stable age structure as well as a relatively static life expectation at every point in the age range.

All over their populations and at every period, the proportions of infants (0–4), children (5–14), adolescents (15–24), and those at working age stayed about the same, as did proportions of the elderly. The same statements could probably be made with some modification about the populations still on the lower aging plateau at the present time. The secular shift upsets this perennial pattern quite radically, and all age boundaries and traditional assumptions as to length of future life tend to lose their stability as the shift proceeds. The whole of the evidence we have so far surveyed suggests that this represents a unique occurrence in human history.

AGING BY LOCALITY AND BY SOCIAL GROUP

Up to this point, we have talked about duration of life and about age composition over long historical periods and always in terms of averages over whole populations. If we are to reconstruct the aging landscape and habits, attitudes, and institutional arrangements of the past, and if we are to get some insight into the results of the secular shift in aging, this procedure is satisfactory enough. Societywide beliefs and norms were based on perduring and very general experience, nationwide experience for the most part, and still are in whole tribes or whole societies, whatever is the proper unit to take. But it is of great importance to recognize that there could be very different situations with regard to aging in different localities and in different social groups before the shift, in spite of the continuities and the constraints on extreme variations that we have examined. Relative constancy did not necessarily obtain at the local level or among select samples of people during the Before.

Individual towns or villages, even fairly large areas with particular ecologies, could show noticeably irregular aging characteristics. At a place like Hartland in the English county of Devon, quite a sizable but isolated settlement at the end of a road leading up to higher land, expectation of life at birth could be maintained at something like fifty years for the three centuries from the mid-1500s to the mid-1800s. This was about ten years above the estimated peak level reached for the whole population of the country over that period and one not generally attained in England until after 1910. The operative cause was undoubtedly markedly lower infant and child mortality than elsewhere, though we shall see that this did not necessarily imply better survival in later life. Similar circumstances can be found in Oxfordshire villages at the same time.[20]

As for differences by social class and social group, it is natural to expect that there would have existed during the Before some form of hierarchy in longevity, descending from top to bottom of the society, a hierarchy that would be concealed by the averages we have cited. The landowning nobility and gentry could be supposed to have lived longer than the substantial farmers, the wealthy traders, the small landholders, and so on down through the modest tradesmen, the handicraft people, the laborers, and finally to the cottagers and paupers. Although this may have been the general tendency, and it can be confirmed for infants and children, there were surprising irregularities. In England during some of the earlier part of the period we can examine, the aristocracy actually died somewhat earlier on average than the rest of the population. Since their longevity was not higher at later ages, this may not have been due, as might be expected, so much to their having put their babies out to wet nurses rather than breast-feeding them themselves, like their social inferiors, and to the use of nourishment other than human milk (see Fildes 1986, 1988). There were evidently other causes such as a predilection of the nobility to lose their lives in warfare.[21] Of one thing we can be confident, however. Everywhere in the traditional world death came sooner among the inhabitants, even the richer inhabitants, of cities and towns than among the rural majority. The explanation is the life-endangering conditions of urban existence, of which putting children out to nurse was one.

A study of a particularly interesting example of a privileged group, the advocates of Edinburgh, has recently been published showing that these prosperous lawyers could expect to live after age 25 to 30—the start of their professional lives—for longer than the peers of the realm, and by the later eighteenth century, for as long as any of the select European groups that have been investigated.[22] Such bands of well-placed individuals could anticipate a considerably larger number of additional years after midlife than those in lowlier positions. But difference by locality was not confined to length of life: it existed in age composition. Wide variation is found from place to place in our second variable, proportions of elderly. In Arezzo, Italy, in 1427, 15.9 percent of the citizens were recorded as over 60 years old, half as many again as the maximum on the lower aging plateau for England and a figure well up to late-twentieth-century proportions in developed countries. The national census of Iceland in 1729 gives a figure of 16.7 percent.

Arezzo and Iceland were evidently exceptional cases, and we should be very cautious in trusting their accuracy. The other communities in the list of thirty or so from which these figures for proportions of elderly have been recovered for earlier times fall well within the limits given above for England before the shift, and some are as low as those for contemporary developing societies.[23] These exceptional figures, nearly all of them for relatively small bands of persons, may perhaps require us to modify a little the account that has been given of the contrast between the Before and the After. Their greatest significance for the historical sociology of aging, however, lies in two other circumstances of prime importance.

One is the caution that has always to be exercised in generalizing from the statistics of a group or a locality, either as to length of life or proportions elderly, to larger populations and to general conditions. Apart from the variability always encountered when numbers are restricted, there is the question of migration, migration that was never absent from preindustrial European society and the extent of which consistently surprises those who first encounter it. The immigration of poor elderly widows to places where public and charitable support might be forthcoming or the opposite, the emigration of younger people in search of employment opportunities, could easily make the share of the elderly in the population of a small community much larger, and the contrary effect might reduce that share accordingly. The chapter by Andrejs Plakans and Charles Wetherell in this volume discusses some of these issues in an eastern European context in the eighteenth century. Likewise in the matter of life expectation. It is transparently clear that one should not argue from the characteristics of a select group of the better off, or of a particularly favorably situated community, to a whole region or country. Great ingenuity is necessary if any guidance as to general conditions as to the life duration is to be gained from such evidence.[24]

The further point about arguing from figures from localities and from exceptional groups of people needs particular emphasis. In spite of the low or very low general expectation of life in the Before, particular individuals could live very long lives, even in places where mortality was high. Our early research into maximal length of life makes this evident. A survey at Cambridge of the information generously supplied by genealogists and local researchers, mostly studying their own forebears using parish registers and the official registration system, yielded the following results. Some 3,500 individuals were fairly reliably reported to have survived to age 80 or beyond, and a fair proportion of these died in their 90s. There were 89 (2.5 percent), 52 females and 37 males, who attained 100 years or more, 2 dying in the seventeenth century, 19 in the eighteenth century, 21 in the nineteenth century, and 47 in the twentieth century.[25] This may seem an unimpressive outcome, especially in view of the very numerous references to the extremely old, particularly to centenarians, in the literature of former times and up to our own day. But it could be said to indicate that survival to the tenth decade of life or, very, very occasionally, even to the eleventh decade (centenarians) was just a possibility on the lower plateau.

This exercise also demonstrates a salient fact about the very old, which no one interested in such matters can fail to observe. Both in the past and the present, in the developed countries, and those yet to undergo the secular shift, exaggeration of the later ages of individuals was and is lamentably widespread, especially when it comes to reaching 100. It is so for the alleged centenarians themselves, for their relatives and even for officials, local and national. It is blatantly evident on tombstone inscriptions and other family records. The worldwide interest in this topic continues, and even grows, not unexpectedly in view of the known tendency for the survival of ancients to increase. It may be intensified by the distinguished recognition given to cen-

tenarians, as for example by the telegrams sent out by the Queen of England
and by professional gerontologists who regularly include sessions on centenarians in their conferences, national and international, and who show little initial insight into the registration data. This encourages exaggeration
and the disposition to point to numbers of centenarians as a mark of pres-
tige, national and local. The historians of aging cannot be too heavily
warned against these distortive influences.

A particularly exasperating and highly misleading fable about survival to
a great age is the claim so often made for very special areas such as the Cau-
casus. Usually remote and mountainous, these are alleged not only to have
exceptionally high levels of survival but to produce centenarians at an un-
wonted rate. Such localities were extremely unlikely to have maintained the
highly reliable registration practices which alone would make such claims
acceptable, and the stories about them have been described as being "as
mythical as Methusaleh" (Laslett 1989: 109). It may be a long time before
the wheat is sorted from the chaff in these matters.

EXPERIENTIAL MEASURES IN THE HISTORICAL
DEMOGRAPHY OF AGING

We have yet to consider the actual impact of the secular shift in aging on the
societies in which it has so far occurred. Before we go on to a preliminary
assessment of these effects, however, we have to acquaint ourselves with the
experiential measures that have been alluded to already. These are numerical measures that it is hoped come closer to the personal and social realities of aging change over time and of aging differences between societies.
We shall then find it useful in relation to the secular shift to discuss an illustrative example of the application of the principles of the historical demography of aging and of the measures that will be suggested.

We begin with longevity and meet at the outset an obstacle to understanding that recalls the pons asinorum described earlier. It is natural for
someone unacquainted with what the demographers call the life table to
suppose that expectation of life—or average expectation of years still to
come, to give it its full title—is always highest at the very beginning, at age
0. But this is not so, except under the very special demographic circumstances of the advanced countries at the moment and over the last few
decades. Even in their case longevity is at its peak not at birth itself but a few
weeks later. In all other populations average expectation of years still to
come is higher at exact age 1 than at birth, higher again at age 2, and usually higher still at age 5, the expected peak value in all but contemporary developed countries. It can often be higher at age 15 or 20, or even sometimes
25 or 30. Let us take an example.

In the life table calculated for England and Wales as it was during the years 1989 to 1991, expectation of life for women was 78.67 years at age 0, 78.21 at 1, 75.29 at 5, and 64.41 at 15, all the later values being lower than the value at the beginning. For Canada in 1831, in contrast, it has been reckoned that expectation of life for women was 39.84 years at birth, 46.49 at age 1, 49.48 at 5, and 42.61 at 15, still over three years longer than at birth. The outstanding difference between the two populations, and such is always the case when comparing longevity between the Before and the After, was the very much higher infant and child mortality in Canada during the 1830s. The death rate of females in the first year of life in Canada in 1831 was 162.36 per thousand, whereas in England and Wales in 1989 to 1991, the corresponding figure was 6.78. In the second year in Canada, it was 135.76 and in England and Wales, 5.59.

If the rise in expectation of life in the Canadian figures at successive birthdays after the first seems paradoxical, because it appears to indicate that an individual person had longer to live at 2, 5, or 15 or later than at 0, this is due to the fact that the character of life expectation has not been recognized as an average, an average of the years still to be lived by a specific group of persons of a given age. Since such an average is the result of dividing the pooled total of years of life remaining to all members of the group by the number of members of that group, it must be possible for that average to go up rather than down after an interval during which an appreciable proportion have died.[26] This follows from the fact that such a loss could well reduce the numbers of persons surviving by relatively more, even very much more than it reduced pooled years still to live. Such would be the case in spite of the fact that the comparatively very large number of pooled years still to come would have been lessened by the years lived by those surviving through the interval, or through any part of it. A suitable metaphor might be that those still present at the end of the interval say to each other with some satisfaction, "Now that those unfortunates who were due to die during the interval are out of the way, we can all go on to live longer." Here the word "all" must be taken to indicate the new average of years remaining to each of them, that is, their expectation of life.

There are several implications of this explanation for the comparative study of longevity over time and between populations and for the selection of more realistic longevity measures. It demonstrates that expectation of life at birth has serious disadvantages as a measure, only appropriate for comparison of length of life between the populations of advanced societies in very recent times indeed. In the 1950s in the United Kingdom, longevity at age 1 was still nearly a year greater for females than it was at age 0 and over a year greater for males. The efficiency of expectation of life at age 0 as an indicator of the experience of longevity in other populations is obviously woefully impaired because it is so heavily affected by high death rates in the earliest years.

If we were to contrast the life expectation of Canadian women in 1831 at its maximum, that is, at age 5, with that of English women in 1989–1991 at its maximum, that is, at birth (49.48 years vs. 78.67 years), this would seem to be a more realistic comparison than that produced by contrasting expectation of life at birth on both sides. The outcome would be that there was a difference of 29.19 years in favor of the contemporary English women rather than 38.83, a substantial reduction of well over a quarter in the superiority of the present day. If both the populations had been on the lower aging plateau, of course, comparisons of maximum longevity would have to be for values at age 5 on both sides. Comparisons of this kind would have to be made, however, in the knowledge that babies and young children who would die before the age of 5 had been left out of account.

Nevertheless, the aging experiences of such young and very young persons might not necessarily be supposed to be of much significance to the subject we are pursuing, though reflecting on their position brings home the important fact that aging is different at different parts of the life course. The experience of proceeding from the fifth to the tenth birthday is certainly not the same as proceeding from the tenth to the fifteenth, let alone from the sixtieth to the sixty-fifth, and these obvious differences are even greater when the historical periods and social circumstances of the populations being compared are allowed for. It has to be reckoned that there is a degree of indeterminacy in comparing the experience of longevity over time and between societies and that there seems to be no easy way of overcoming it. This may be one of the reasons why demographers have not included longevity in their analysis of aging.

The compromise solution recommended here is that life expectation at age 15, not life expectation at age 0, should be taken as the value for comparing longevity between societies at all historical epochs and at all stages of development. This simple expedient has the following advantages over using expectation of life at birth. Taking life expectation at age 15 as the measure of longevity makes unnecessary the reckoning of life expectation at different ages on the different sides of the comparison. Moreover, it is a much better guide to changes in longevity in later life.

Taking up the contrast between Canadian women in 1831 and English women in 1989–1991 once again, the percentage difference in life expectation at birth was 97 percent, that is, English women had 97 percent longer to live than Canadian women as reckoned in this way. But at age 15 the difference was 51 percent in favor of modern English women, while at ages 50, 60, and 70, it was 50 percent, 57 percent, and 63 percent respectively, each value quite evidently considerably closer to the differential figure for expectation of life at 15 than the differential figure for expectation of life at birth. The value at age 5 would have similar advantages over expectation of life at birth as an indicator for this purpose, and it has the attraction that it is the highest longevity value for a very large proportion of all populations on the lower plateau. But expectation of life at 15 marks the point in the age range at which in many of them the average of years still to come ceases to be higher than expectation of life at birth. It could be said, moreover, that expectation of life at age 15 represents a closer approach to the median experience of longevity in the middle range of the population. But once again it has to be borne in mind that the aging experience of all immature persons is being omitted, and in populations on the lower aging plateau this means a quarter or even a third of the total.

If expectation of life at 15 is adopted as that measure of longevity that is least likely to misrepresent the aging experience of populations that are being compared, the question arises, what change might this imply for the secular shift in aging? Values for expectation of life at age 15 (e_{15}) are accordingly graphed in figure 1.7 for England, France, and Sweden, the countries shown in figure 1.3. Values for Canada, the United States, and Japan are also represented for as far back as records go.

Comparison of the curves in figure 1.7 for e_{15} with those in figure 1.3 for expectation of life at birth (e_0) makes it immediately apparent that the suddenness and steepness of the secular shift is much more pronounced with respect to longevity when expectation of life is reckoned for age 15. It is also evident that the experience of all the Western countries that appear in the figure has been very close, that England could indeed be taken for each of them without misrepresentation. Interesting, too, is the fact that the two North American, European-descended populations should follow the domestic European populations so faithfully but that their statistics are somewhat higher during the nineteenth century. The graph for Japan, however, though it follows a parallel course from a markedly inferior initial level, climbs from the lower to the higher plateau with an amazing steepness after the 1950s, almost vertically in fact, and rises above all the others. The aging trajectory for that country could be said to be something of a caricature of the secular shift as it has been experienced by Western countries, the extraordinary drop in the 1940s being an outcome of the Second World War. We shall return to these differences later on.

The generalizations that have been made about the secular shift, then, are emphatically confirmed for longevity by the use of the more realistic measure of life expectation at age 15. It might perhaps be asked why this indicator was not adopted at the outset. The answer has to be that it has a grave disadvantage in practice. Because the only statistic for longevity usually published for any population is expectation of life at birth, any other measure but this is very seldom likely to be available. For further discussion of this and other circumstances in the measurement of longevity in experiential

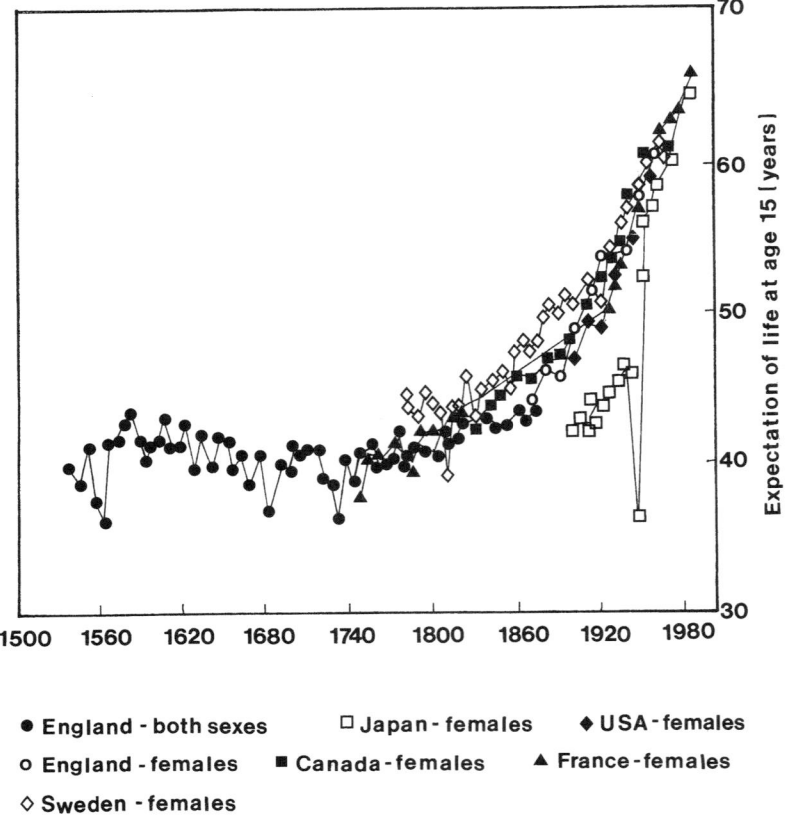

- ● England - both sexes   □ Japan - females   ◆ USA - females
- ○ England - females   ■ Canada - females   ▲ France - females
- ◇ Sweden - females

Fig. 1.7. Expectation of life at age 15: Canada, England, France, Japan, Sweden, and the United States.

terms, see the appendix to this chapter together with table 1.A1 and figure 1.A1. The outcome of our consideration of longevity to this point might have to be that we must continue to accept expectation of life at 0 as the standard measure but that this measure must be used bearing in mind all the drawbacks and obliquities that have been set out.

We are not quite at the end of the complications about the reckoning of longevity for comparative historical purposes. There is an important difference between what is called *period* or *generation* life expectation, which has been used so far, and *cohort* life expectation, which has not been mentioned.

Period life expectation is nearly always the one that is used. But it is a synthetic construct. In reckoning the total years still to live, which have to be averaged out among every member of the population in question, it assumes that the death rates being experienced at all ages during the year at issue remain the same over the whole time during which the people concerned will go on living. It is almost as if everyone had his or her whole life experience in the current year. In reality, of course, these mortality rates will undoubtedly change as the years go by, perhaps not by very much but by enough to make this synthetic calculation a hypothetical estimate. The enormous advantage of the period calculation, however, is that it can be done for any chosen year or, more usually, for any two or three years, provided only that mortality by age is completely known for the year or years concerned.

Cohort life expectation makes use of the actual number of deaths experienced by a cohort (persons born in the same year) from the time of its appearance until the last member of that cohort has died, that is, something like one hundred years later, or even more. Cohort life expectation, then, is about as realistic as such a statistic could be. But it has the enormous disadvantage that it can only be calculated after every member of the collection of people in which we are interested has ceased to exist. It is for this reason entirely impractical to recommend cohort life expectation as being more realistic and true to experience than period life expectation. Only for historians studying populations existing at least a century ago would cohort life expectation be of use. Though such a statistic could in theory be used for comparisons between past populations, all of which existed a century or more ago, it cannot be used for comparisons involving any more recently existing population. What is more, the necessary data for such calculations so far into the past only survive for a small number of historic populations. Nevertheless, cohort life expectation can usefully be calculated for some purposes on occasion, such as reckoning of the Third Age Indicator, which will concern us later on. It is available for English cohorts born between 1541 and 1781 and again for those born between 1841 and 1876.[27]

This brings us almost to the end of the considerations necessary in measuring expectation of life for historical purposes, though in the appendix to this chapter we shall look at yet a further possible indicator. This is the age at which there are a given number of years still to live (say, two years more or five years more), an age that differs in a most interesting way between the Before and the After. It goes down rather than up during and after the secular shift (compare especially Bourdelais 1993). As with all measures, that which is the most satisfactory, or perhaps in this case the least unsatisfactory, for general purposes may not be of much use for particular purposes. In describing the emergence of the Third Age as an outcome of the secular shift, a somewhat different statistic from that of e_{15} or of expected years still to live will be suggested in relation to longevity. This will be the chances of reaching age 70 from age 25, the Third Age Indicator, or 3AI. It would be possible to argue that from the point of view of the interests of most students of aging—and certainly of most of the contributors to this volume—the 3AI, reckoned either in the period or the cohort mode, might be even more realistic as a general measure than expectation of life at age 15, and closer to the experience of past people. I shall suggest later on that a low level of the 3AI might have disposed those people to write off the possibility of ever becoming old. These points are illustrated and enlarged in the appendix to this chapter.

Interesting as this possibility might be thought to be, the major concern of those who now study aging is in the numbers, experience, condition, and prospects of those already in late life and their relations with their juniors and their juniors with them. It is this concern that informs the suggestion of a revised measure of proportions in late life, our second aging variable, a measure more realistic than a simple fraction of older persons in the whole population. The realistic, experiential measure suggested here is the share of those over 60 of all adults, of all those over 25, in symbols $\frac{60+}{25+}$. A more detailed impression of the significance of older persons with respect to their numerical size in relation to that of other age bands, together with changes over time in such relationships, can be gained of course from figure 1.6.

This realistic age-proportional measure, relative weight of the elderly and old among all adults, passes over an even greater number of the nonadult, the immature, than the realistic longevity measure just discussed, life expectation at age 15. The justification for doing so is just as strong in my view, or perhaps even stronger. When attempting to sense the presence of those in late life in a society, it is not easy to see why every individual member of that society should weigh as much as every other. The young and very young are undeniably of significance in the social structure. We in our own day are not the first body of people to be conscious of the immature and maturing members of our society and of the crucial character of our relationships with them and theirs with us.[28] The young and the very young are also of evident importance because they are largely dependent and their numbers and proportions must be known to study support relationships and transfers between age groups. In this respect, the young are in a position very similar to that of the dependent old. These are highly significant examples of generational interchanges and of age structuring. Where changes in the proportions of age over time are accompanied by changes in the flow of support, with the result that some cohorts are privileged over other cohorts, a fascinating set of issues to do with intergenerational justice comes into view.[29]

These issues can certainly be classed as consequentially related to the historical demography of aging, but relationships as to aging experience between the various age groups are scarcely affected. Figure 1.8 traces the course of the ratio recommended, proportion of all adults who are over 60, for the four hundred fifty years of known English aging experience and the two hundred fifty years of French and Swedish experience, along with the briefer periods observable in Canada, the United States, and Japan. In my

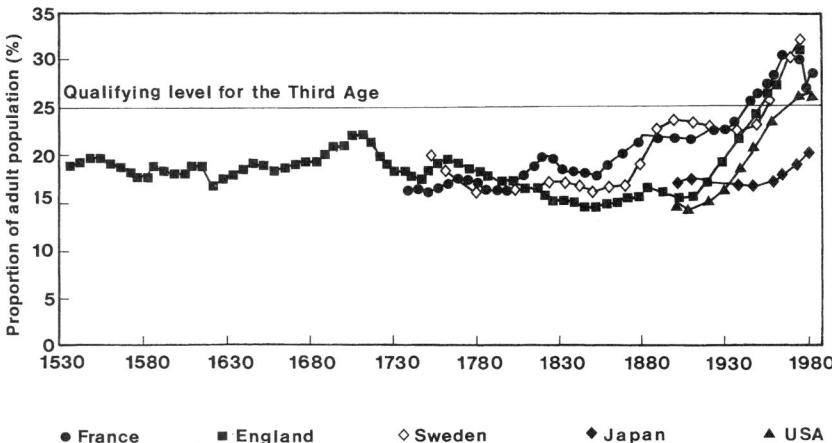

Fig. 1.8. Proportion of adult population (i.e., all those over age 25) over age 60: England, France, Japan, Sweden, and the United States.

view, it presents the clearest and most revealing comparative numerical account of the weight and importance of the elderly over the stretches of time which it is possible to observe and complements for aging experience of this kind the results we have just surveyed for the experience of longevity. The figure includes, it will be noticed, a line for the threshold of the Third Age, which, along with the 3AI itself, will be discussed below.

The features that stand out in figure 1.8 are once more the similarity with regard to the abruptness and the shape of the secular shift to what is to be seen for all the populations included in figure 1.3 and the somewhat greater unevenness of the lines, none of which shows quite the same smooth progression that marks the long English graph for proportions over 60 in the whole population portrayed in figure 1.2. The pronounced peak in the English profile in figure 1.8 during the early eighteenth century is somewhat disconcerting, since it reaches a height not seen again until the secular shift was well under way in the 1930s. At 22.4 percent, the proportion that those over 60 made of all English adults in the five-year period 1706 to 1710 was over two-thirds of its level now (1991 = 31.2 percent). It might be thought that the share of the elderly in the population was not as constant as has been made out, or that the experience of the English was less than representative.

Closer examination shows, however, that more modest peaks of this kind are present in the graphs for the other populations represented and that the general resemblance to the lines in figure 1.2 is quite pronounced. Once again the relative shortness of the lines in the figures, the woeful lack of temporal depth in our data, makes judgment difficult. Inspection of figure 1.6 and of the quinquennial figures in table 1.3 reveals that, during the

early decades of the eighteenth century, proportions over 60 were at their
highest in the whole English series before the 1930s and that the age band
25–69 fell into a trough at the same time. Though neither movement was
particularly sharp, their coincidence seems to have produced the effect we
are examining.

The adoption of a more realistic, experiential measure for proportions of
elderly scarcely confirms the arguments that have been presented using the
whole population as a divisor in quite the decisive way in which the substi-
tution of expectation of life at 15 does for longevity. The rise during the secular shift in the proportion of adults who were over 60 was only 57 percent
in England. But the dissonance cannot be said to affect in any great degree
the theory of relative constancy on the lower plateau, the abruptness of the
secular shift, or of the general typicality of the English data. The reexamination of the aging processes and particularly of the secular shift by the use
of experiential measures is highly illuminating, nevertheless. We shall find
this point confirmed as we take up an illustrative example in the aging history of two neighboring European countries whose comparative development has preoccupied us so much.

AGING IN FRANCE AND ENGLAND IN THE EIGHTEENTH AND
NINETEENTH CENTURIES: AN ILLUSTRATIVE EXAMPLE

The idiosyncratic demographic behavior of France has come up several
times, just as it tends to do in the discussion of the demographic transition
itself. It is of significance for understanding the secular shift in aging and
the emergence of the Third Age for the following reasons. If it could be
shown that French longevity, during the period when it is accurately known
for the later eighteenth century and nineteenth century, along with proportions of elderly rose to levels that have been claimed never to have been
reached before the secular shift was well under way in the twentieth century,
then the assertion that there was a sudden upthrust from plateau to plateau
would be less persuasive. So also would be the case for assuming an overall
constancy in aging in the Before and, by analogy, in the After.

Perhaps more important would be the effect on the claims made here
about the uniqueness of our own contemporary, developed societies. Experience of aging in a very important European nation during the eighteenth
century might have anticipated to a significant extent the experience that
has been described as confined to the developed countries at the present
day, though eventually to be shared by all societies. Since what happened in
France might well have happened elsewhere in the illimitable time space of
the Before, then it would be likely that all social structures along with their
constituted mentalities would have a resilience in the face of the effects of
pronounced aging built into them. The secular shift, though the very ex-

treme of change, could perhaps have been accommodated by the traditional social structure and so not have led to that incoherence which, as has
been claimed, marks the very old, developed societies of today.

Alternatively, if it could be assumed that France in the eighteenth century was the first country ever to have a foretaste of what was to come two
hundred years later, then the French attitudes and practices at that time
would have a peculiar significance in the history of aging. They would have
taken into account the aging experience not simply of a restricted locality,
or that of a select group, but of a whole national society, at that period a national society preeminent in the life of the Western world. During its Grand
Siècle, France was intellectually dominant in Europe, the center of the Enlightenment yet the seed bed of that revolutionism that was to shatter the political, cultural, and religious framework of the traditional European world.

Though no commentator on age and aging in France in the eighteenth
century has made statements as positive as these, a recent authoritative work
by a historian of aging, David Troyansky, *Old age in the Old Régime: Image and
experience in 18th-century France* (1989), certainly hints at them. He insists, quoting Pierre Chaunu, that the lengthening of human life was "the only great
event of the 18th century" (14) and sees this demonstrated in the literary and
cultural life of France at the time. They reveal in themselves, he seems to be
maintaining, that France was then already exceptionally old. The scene
changes for the nineteenth century, when French supremacy in these directions had disappeared and British industrialism had supplanted the Enlightenment as a hallmark of national success. Then it was the French statesmen
and wiseacres of the time rather than subsequent historians who interpreted
what they saw in a very different sense. They tended to blame French decline
after the revolutionary and Napoleonic interlude, the military reverses and
economic sluggishness, on the drag of excessive numbers of the old in the
population.[30] The object of this discussion is to show how easily interpretations
of this kind could have arisen when the historical demography of aging was
of an entirely unsystematic and impressionistic character and the comparative
historical evidence for the secular shift in aging had still to be worked out.

Now that we have something like principled, if often inferential, knowledge of aging in Western countries over the two centuries with which we are
here concerned, it is not difficult to see how ill-founded such judgments
must be for France during the century of the Enlightenment. The simple
juxtaposition in figure 1.3 of the French trajectories with those of England
and Sweden shows such judgments to be improbable, and the graphs in figures 1.7 and 1.8 should dispose of them altogether. When the records of
that country began in the 1740s, France was catching up to England and
Sweden in longevity (expectation of life at age 15) but never clearly sur-
passed them, and the rise was not exceptional but of the same order as the
fluctuations to be seen in longevity over the whole length of English record-

ings. Meanwhile, our more realistic indicator for the proportion of elderly among French adults behaved in rather the same way, except that it did go above the English level between 1800 and 1850 and was no doubt very high by European standards throughout the nineteenth century. But Swedish proportions were rising even faster and were well above the French by 1900, as were those of other Scandinavian countries. These circumstances for the French add particular significance to the possibility, suggested by recent work at Cambridge, that it was in the early eighteenth century that the longevity of adults amongst the elite began to differ from that of the masses in the Western populations.

If we were looking for an exceptional situation to justify an exceptional attitude arising from longevity and the relative weight of the elderly, it would not be in France over this period that we should be seeking it but rather in England. The population of that country was near or at the top of the scale of longevity in Europe from the 1740s to the 1940s and after the 1800s had an exceptionally low proportion of adults who were elderly. But this situation was certainly not to be classed as an anticipation of the present day, since while it continued the two aging indicators had opposite tendencies, high longevity and low proportions of elderly.

The imperfections of this illustrative example for the history of aging and its historical demography have to do with the methods and sources of historical sociology as well as the objective reality of the secular shift. Important and illuminating as may be the literature current in the past on the subject of aging and the elderly in the history of society and of culture, to seek in such sources indications of longevity in earlier times or of the numerical weight of the elderly in the adult population is a misdirected enterprise. It is particularly unfortunate, even potentially disastrous, when evidence of this kind alone survives to provide any indication of longevity or of proportions of elderly persons. The facts are, as we have seen, that such was the position as to knowledge of aging at almost all locations and points in time before the last two or three centuries of Western history.

With the rather uncertain exceptions cited earlier, such writings as the Old Testament, the poems of Homer, or the philosophical essays of medieval canonists and Renaissance philosophers contain practically all the evidence available. Under such circumstances, the proper policy for the historian is surely to make no attempt to use literary allusion as positive evidence for age and aging. The assumption has to be that the society in question must have been located at some level on the lower aging plateau, with the characteristics set out here for the Before and derived to a considerable extent from the theory and practice of demography in relation to primitive and developing societies. Textual allusions in such sources to growing old and to old people have to be taken as illustrative or complementary: their relationship to the demographic situation as it actually occurs can never be a reflection of reality.[31]

The title with which this discussion began, Troyansky's *Old age in the Old Régime,* is an attempt not so much to recover from cultural sources the facts about aging as to confirm from all the indications the author can lay his hands on that old people actually existed in some numbers in eighteenth-century France, so as to drive home his claim for the importance of aging under the Enlightenment and the Ancien Régime generally. It might be supposed this is something that any knowledge of the historical demography of aging would make unnecessary. Troyansky goes to considerable lengths in this enterprise, citing a rise in the proportion dying after the age of 60 or 70 in nine villages whose families have been reconstituted by French demographers; an increase in the age at death of French bishops; an inaccuracy in the low figures worked out for adults at Caen in 1988; a growth in the economy and its general capacity for supporting the dependent elderly; and many other circumstances. He even cites figures for proportions of adults who were over 60, a ratio similar to that used here, but using age 20 rather than age 25 in the denominator. It has not been possible to cover all the bewildering array of arguments he presents, arguments that sometimes suggest he has not yet got across the pons asinorum of aging. It should be clear from figures 1.7 and 1.8 that France only became exceptional with respect to the relative weight of elderly persons during the nineteenth century and that it was never exceptional in longevity before the mid-twentieth century. The disposition of historians to advance a confusing medley of numerical and seminumerical arguments of this kind has to be described as an obstacle in the way of the understanding of age and aging in the past.[32]

THE SECULAR SHIFT IN AGING: ITS GENERAL HISTORICAL POSITION AND ITS OUTCOMES

Industrialization and Modernization

The chapters in this volume can be read as a commentary on the results of the secular shift in aging, results that are shown to have been brought about during its historical course at particular places and for particular areas of activity. This is evident in Richard Wall's essay on the elderly in England and those with whom they resided, comparing the preindustrial past with the industrial present, the lower with the higher aging plateau in the language we have been using. Wall makes repeated references to the aging process, nearly all of them to rises in longevity, as does George Alter in analyzing railway pensions, though he refers to declining longevity as well. The other contributors make similar allusions, and it is evident that the secular shift is seldom far away from the changing situations that are being described, even when the subject is American home ownership or the elderly on the Texas frontier. The descriptions of facets of life as it was experienced by older persons at sites in traditional Europe—Hungarian experience in the case of Andorka, Latvian in the case of Plakans and Wetherell—seem deliberately aimed at conveying an impression of the position as it was in the Before. Some notion of what changed and what remained the same, a critical part of the task of historical sociology, can be gathered in this way.

Understandably, perhaps, considering the shortcomings of the available data that have had to concern us so much and the difficulties of the analysis, almost nothing is said in these chapters about the pace or extent of population aging change and their consequences. This introduction was not in the hands of the writers, and no compendium of the relevant demographic facts was available. None of our authors goes any way toward an estimation of the overall results of aging in Western societies, or of the historical situation and significance of the secular shift. Insofar as that estimation is yet feasible, it is very briefly attempted here, particular reference being made to such general outcomes as the transformation of the life course, the redirection of social transfers, and the swaying of the balance between the sexes leading to the feminization of the elderly population. Finally comes what in my view has to be called the most important of the outcomes for the present and future of developed societies and the future of societies yet to develop, that is, the emergence of the Third Age.

It cannot be expected that so profound a change in social relations and in the life of individuals should be adequately comprehended so soon after its crystallization as the present day, if indeed this change can yet be regarded as complete. This is particularly the case if, as has been claimed, the transformation itself has yet to be recognized and accepted and if even those who run the political and administrative systems of the advanced societies and determine their attitudes persist in a state of lagged awareness about the aging transformation. In the late 1980s, British Parliamentary candidates actually supposed that the way to get in touch with older voters was to go to the institutions where the infirm and dependent elderly lived "in spite of the fact that 96 percent of older people reside in ordinary housing."[33] No better case could be made for the historical demography of aging being necessary knowledge.

Singling out the effects of the secular shift is made peculiarly difficult because of the other major movements taking place during the century or so when the shift occurred. In most but certainly not all the countries, this was also the time of industrialization, of social and political mobilization, and finally of procreative transformation, the time in fact of all those movements that usually go under the unsatisfactory rubric "modernization." The particular results of radical aging have furthermore to be distinguished from those of other demographic changes to which it is causally connected, continuing shrinking fertility, perpetually lowering mortality, and radical change in marriage, all supposedly embraced within the overall "modernization" model. This is not the occasion for dwelling on the difficulties and the distortions, especially the historical distortions, that any such overarching concept as the modernization model is bound to bring about.[34] But certain distinctions can be made here.

The secular shift in aging was by no means necessarily associated with the other changes being mentioned and is not so today. In some important countries, in Germany and Italy, for example, or the Scandinavian countries and Spain, the phase of intense industrialization did coincide with the early part of the secular shift. But these instances can be misleading, especially when they are seen as historically parallel with what is happening in the now-developing countries.

Industrialization in Britain occurred wholly on the lower aging plateau and in that country, modernization, insofar as the concept is applicable at all, was complete before industrialization began. In France, as we have seen, the secular shift was considerably more diffuse over time than elsewhere. In China as well as in other East Asian countries, as we shall see, the shift is already in progress. The risk in China and especially in the really laggardly countries is that the shift will proceed so quickly that economic development will be behindhand in providing means of support for the hugely expanding elderly population.

It may turn out indeed to be a fortunate historical chance for the Western countries that they have not experienced the secular shift under the conditions and at the pace that seem likely to characterize its trajectories in other areas of the world. In short, an analysis of the historical position of the secular shift leads to the conclusion that it has been independent of these other changes, though causally connected with some of those that are clearly demographic. The interconnections supposed by the modernization model and its theory of convergence seem not to be evident, in spite of the difficulty of disentangling aging from those other threads in the skein.

Age Structuring and the Life Course

Some of the outcomes are fairly straightforward nevertheless and have been hinted at as the shift has been described. The transition from a position of perduring constancy in life expectation and in age structuring to one in which family members live in company with each other for longer and longer and age groupings undergo radical disturbance has upset the relationships between age groups. It has changed the life course of individuals along with the developmental cycle of the family and of the domestic group as a whole. The immemorial association in family time between the exit of the parental generation and the beginnings of the independent family life of the child generation has gone forever. The consequent proliferation and prolongation of the situation known as the empty nest stage, in which the parental couple stays together in the home after the departure of their children, a situation so familiar in the contemporary West, are almost exclu-

sively the result of aging. The accompanying phenomenon, the rapid rise of
the primary individual, that is, single persons living alone, has causes other
than aging, though this must be mainly responsible. Both existed in the Before, but it is probably the secular shift that has made them major characteristics of late-twentieth-century Western social structures.

As part of this development, age at inheritance has risen inordinately.

> Long-expected one-and-twenty
> Ling'ring year, at length is flown:
> Pride and pleasure, pomp and plenty,
> Great *** ****, are now your own.

Samuel Johnson's overfortunate youth, deliberately unnamed, be it noted,
whose father had evidently died long before the great day, would be more
like 58 or 60 years old at inheritance in contemporary Britain or America.

The accompanying elongation of vertical kin links, great-grandfather,
grandfather, father, son, grandson, great-grandson, or even great-great-
grandson, is entirely due to the secular shift. It reminds us that the populations of contemporary advanced societies, unlike any of their predecessors,
cannot be envisaged in pyramidal form with respect to the distribution of
age groups. They are more like rectangles posed on their shorter sides. The
shift in flows of support between generations, particularly the appearance
and spread of multiple dependency, in which a woman has at the same time
to attend to the needs of her children or grandchildren and to those of her
parents or even grandparents, is due to the same cause. This whole galaxy
of consequences of aging has been brilliantly described by Michael Anderson but in a strictly preliminary fashion, nevertheless, for it is scarcely possible yet to know how many changes of this character have been, are being,
or will be brought about.[35]

The least specific but still extremely important possible outcome of the
secular shift has still to be touched on. This is the possibility that the growth
in the relative weight of the elderly in the population—the ever-increasing
number of people with halting gaits, bent shoulders, lined faces, and shape-
less figures—brought into being a hostility and even a hatred that was absent or less prominent in the Before, became strident during the shift itself, and persists in the After. This is a topic of considerable controversy,
even of contradiction, and the interplay between demographic causes and
cultural influence is especially hard to unravel. For it has to be insisted, as
Daniel Scott Smith has repeatedly pointed out, that there was cultural
change with respect to the elderly during the secular shift which went on
separately from aging itself: mere demographic determinism is quite unacceptable in trying to understand what happened. There is a good case for
supposing that there was a change for the worse for elderly British people
in the later nineteenth and twentieth century, and historians of aging in the

United States are at odds as to when a similar but earlier change occurred in that country, although they seem convinced that it was an objective fact.[36]

Uncertainties such as these can only be registered here and remain for historians of aging to investigate further. We glance now at two sets of changes much more securely attached to lengthening longevity and population aging: feminization and retirement.

Effects on the Sex Ratio and on Retirement.   As is evident from figure 1.9, comparing the growth of proportions of elderly in England and France during the secular shift in aging, the process altered numerical relationships between the sexes in later life in a conspicuous way. The widening of the gap between female and male proportions of elderly persons is evident in France from the 1820s but came rather later in England. This effect intensified as the secular shift proceeded and has continued until the present day. There is some indication in table 1.2 that in the southern and eastern European countries, the sex ratio of the elderly had been more equal on the lower aging plateau just as it often is in developing societies in the contemporary world. In 1880, there were more old men than old women in Italy,

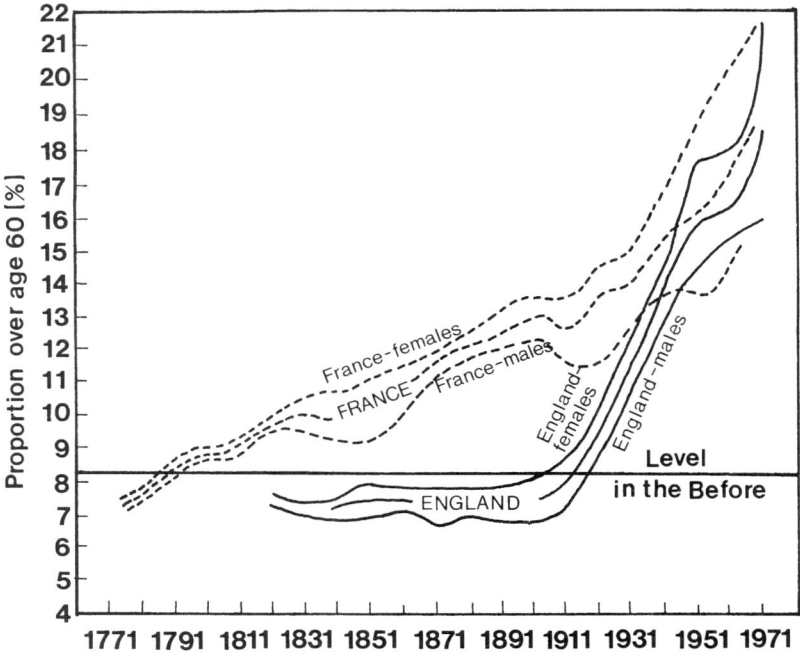

Fig. 1.9. Proportion of population over age 60: England and France, 1770s–1970s. Adapted from Laslett 1977.

Greece, and Bulgaria, as was the case in the eighteenth-century Hungarian village reported on by Rudolf Andorka in his contribution to this volume. The discrepancy in proportions lasted in Bulgaria into the 1920s, but at none of the dates in table 1.1 was expectation of life at birth higher for men than for women, close as the figures sometimes get. By the 1950s, the whole of Europe seems to have been fairly uniform as to the excess of women in the higher and highest age groups and as to their superior longevity.

We should not infer that this growing imbalance was caused by aging in a billiard ball sense; rather, the two accompanied each other, and living longer or being allowed to live longer gave women an opportunity, so to speak, to demonstrate more and more their superior capacity to persist in the face of natural hazards. However this may be, we have to recognize that in coming to terms with our age-transformed condition, we shall have to provide for a more and more feminine society of those in late life, with no tradition in our culture or in any culture to give us precedents or inspiration. We know little about the sex balance among senior people in the West before the secular shift, though in the small and unreliable samples analyzed for England (see Laslett 1977: 201–208), women already predominated in the seventeenth and eighteenth centuries, if not to the same degree that they do today. It would seem that neither in the Before nor in the After have social arrangements in this respect taken the facts of demography properly into account, though we are obviously less realistic than our forebears. The same indifference to, even defiance of, demographic "reality" is to be seen in the equally important matter of retirement.

Nothing whatever in the changes in age structure over the secular shift as portrayed in the figures could be said to justify the rapid and continuous withdrawal from the workforce at earlier and earlier ages that has marked recent Western social history. We have seen that the proportion in the working ages (15–59) was quite stable over the secular shift in England, though the mean age of the workforce has risen and will rise. As that change nears its end in the West, there is no surplus of older workers in the demographic sense in the way that there is a surplus of elderly women. Although account has to be taken of actions of government and employers in getting senior persons off the rolls of the employed, it is tempting to interpret retirement as a move by individual people in spite of demography, the assertion of a wish and a right to take advantage of lengthened life by changing the use of time. Above all this, of course, is the immense growth of wealth that was proceeding in all Western countries contemporaneously with the secular shift and that is doing so on an even greater scale in present-day Japan.[37]

The growth of retirement in spite of the lengthening of later life, like the growth we shall observe in solitary living in spite of greater opportunities for elder people to reside with their married children, illustrates the fact that demography does not always have the expected effect on life-course transitions, that fascinating topic handled in several of the chapters in this volume, particularly by Tamara Hareven and Peter Uhlenberg. We can go no farther in this direction here, but we must consider for a little while the familial effects of the shift, since the familial position of the elderly and old has been such a preoccupation of those who have pioneered the history of aging and who are well represented in our collection.

Familial Effects.   It might perhaps be expected that larger proportions of older people and the better survival of parents and grandparents would have led to an increase in multigenerational households all over Europe despite "modernization" as the secular shift proceeded, certainly in its early stages. It would seem, however, that this expectation is in general unjustifiable and that the effects were complex and multidirectional. Research has established (Wall 1989) that European countries vary very widely with respect to the living arrangements of their elderly citizens at the present day. There is no reason to suppose that this variation was less in the 1880s. It has been shown for England that while that society was on the lower aging plateau, independent living was quite a normal thing, though not very widespread for elderly people, even if they had married children with whom it was possible to co-reside. The tendency to live on their own is scarcely surprising in the European areas known to historical sociologists as maintaining neolocal household formation rules, that is, mostly the countries in the north and the west of Europe. In a nuclear family formed on such rules elderly persons have no right to join the families of their married children, any more than those married children have the right to rejoin the families of their parents. But it was always open to children to invite their parents into their households out of affection or because of failing health, or simply from a sense of duty. This evidently frequently happened. In southern and eastern Europe, where household formation rules were not the same, the secular shift may have progressively increased the proportion of multigenerational households, at least initially, but of this we have as yet little knowledge.[38]

In all developed Western countries, however, there has been the movement we have mentioned several times, one which is distinct from the secular shift and opposite in its impact on family forms, a tidal drift toward solitary living at every adult age, especially at late ages. In Asia, where about three-fourths of elderly persons in the 1990s live with their married offspring, the position has been very different.[39] It can be seen how intricate are the questions that have to be faced if the Western countries are to meet the challenge of providing precedents of use to those who will follow them on to the higher aging plateau.

There can be no doubt that the increase in the numbers of elderly, potentially dependent parents in European societies which came about as a result of the shift has led to an intensification of kin interchanges, particularly between mature children and their still-surviving parents. It is fascinating to see in a recent study of an industrializing town in the United Provinces where the population registers were kept how these interrelations grew more frequent and important in the later nineteenth and early twentieth century and how the domestic group itself frequently changed its structure in reaction to these developments (Janssens 1993). It can in general be said, however, that the final stage, the era of the older married couple living alone after the departure of their children and of the elderly solitary widow, widower, divorcée, divorcé, spinster, or bachelor had already begun by 1950.

Yet it is notorious that the image of the family group in the eyes of Western journalists, politicians, advertisers, and citizens themselves obstinately remains that of the married couple with two or more young children living with them. The great and growing numbers of elderly people living alone and the virtual absence of three-generational households have still to penetrate the consciousness of Western populations and to be recognized as a reality by Western politicians and intellectuals.

Effects on Social Transfers.   The secular shift, wherever and whenever it occurred, must have moved to some extent the burden of support for those at the working ages from maintaining large numbers of children to maintaining increasing numbers of the elderly. It seems unlikely that these changes would perforce have increased the total burden of dependency appreciably, since in most societies at most times dependent elderly persons are no more costly than dependent infants and children. We have just seen that support to the elderly in need was not necessarily given in the way of maintenance in the home, and it has now to be added that an appreciable proportion of that support, in England and perhaps other countries, took the form of transfers through the collectivity.

By collectivity is meant not simply the state but all agencies of social transfers that cannot be described as familial. The introduction of pensions in Bismarck's Germany and in Britain in 1908 marked an entirely new era in the extent and regularity of central state support for persons quitting the workforce. But the collectivity in European countries, evidently to varying degrees between country and country, had always taken rather more of a responsibility for demographic casualties such as failing elderly people than was realized until results of research on the point began to become available.[40]

The traditional English Poor Law has been shown to have been comparatively generous to the elderly, providing something like pensions to widows as early as the seventeenth century, even continuing that support under the much more parsimonious New Poor Law of early Victorian times. In addition to these sources, transfers to the dependent elderly from towns and charitable institutions of all kinds, together with a system of elderly privileges, such as licenses to beg, to glean after the harvest, to ransack the hedgerows for firewood, or even to pilfer, had been present in the traditional European social structure from time immemorial. There were multifarious arrangements for dealing with the incapacitated elderly, often agreed between the family and the collectivity, circulating them between households—of children, of kin, and of neighbors—and putting them into institutions where such existed. Nevertheless, transfers of this kind were unstable over time, plentiful at one period and scarce at others. There was evidently much ambivalence. But the truly decrepit, those entirely unable to care for themselves, could count more reliably on collective assistance. In England and probably elsewhere, it is an interesting fact that about the same proportions of old persons lived in institutions before the secular shift as do so today.

It seems clear, however, that the effect of the introduction of state pensions was to reduce the proportion of transfers reaching the elderly from these miscellaneous sources. After the middle of the twentieth century, very high proportions of the support of working-class elderly people began to come from the sole source of a state pension, a situation that seems to have become widespread elsewhere in Europe. It can certainly be observed among the workers of London in the 1930s.[41] The point of importance is that the increase in the longevity and numbers of older people at the secular shift elicited collective support on a larger scale but certainly did not bring it into being.

Although usually assigned to the invention and expansion of the welfare state, more recent scholarly opinion is that universal pensioning at a steadily increasing level of those past work in twentieth-century Europe is perhaps better regarded as a continuation of traditional policies into a time when the enormous increase in disposable wealth made it possible to contemplate transfers on such an unprecedented scale, even to a rapidly expanding and increasingly older population. It would seem that given in this way the means to live independently, older people readily did so. There were other effects as well. The state pension has been shown to have led, for example, to the decline of the responsibility felt by factory and other employers for members of their workforce who had grown old in their employment, providing not simply occasional pensions but also a scale of diminishing demands in the way of effort, by assigning workers near the end of their time to such tasks as being night watchmen.[42]

By the middle of the twentieth century, therefore, the secular shift had brought those retired from the workforce into direct contact with the nation state, in societies whose ever-increasing riches made it possible to support persons in later life at something like the level of workers in their active earning years. Except among the proletariat, savings over the life course, however, were surprisingly common even before the secular shift began, particularly in the United States, and were much enhanced in the decades of economic growth in the earlier twentieth century. Along with state support these resources gave to those in late life a prospect of personal independence on a mass scale quite unprecedented in the history of the old. Such were the financial prerequisites for the emergence of the Third Age in the fullest sense of that term, and they stand in exquisite contrast to the position as it was in all countries when they were on the lower aging plateau.

Nevertheless, dependent persons are always relatively poor, and dependent elderly proletarians in traditional societies like those of the preindustrial era in Europe are the poorest of all. The impression must not be given that the modestly placed 70-, 80-, and 90-year-olds of the past were ever anything but badly off in comparison to their juniors, and the historian is often puzzled that they managed to survive in the numbers that they did. In rich industrialized societies, as everyone should know, the working-class elderly are still wretchedly poor in comparison to the rest of the population. They are relatively poorer probably than the old persons of preindustrial times and getting relatively even poorer, at least in Britain. The outcome of this composite situation has been to create for contemporary citizens of developed nations a conviction that the now enormously expanded and expanding society of retired persons is an economic problem for themselves and a burden for posterity. They find it difficult to recognize that in the emergence of the Third Age their own personal future is being provided for in an entirely novel society.

THE EMERGENCE OF THE THIRD AGE

The definition of the stage of life which in European countries has come to be called the Third Age is still uncertain. The term belongs to a division of the life course into four ages, put forward in Britain during the 1980s, which is in increasing use there and in Australia but not so much in the United States and Canada. Many circumstances have to be taken into account in determining the character of the Third Age and in maintaining its independence of birthday age. The time of retirement from a job marks its beginning for most people, and for them the Third Age will last until death, or the onset of the Fourth Age.[43] Unless that interlude is substantial, the Third Age cannot come into being. The existence and development of retirement and the extent to which transfers and savings are adequate to make a life of self-realization possible for the retired are crucial circumstances. These, in turn, depend on the wealth of the society to which individuals of later life belong and on such things as the level of instruction, the numbers in education, and the availability of education over the whole life course. In this way, therefore, the emergence of the Third Age is inseparably bound up with national development and with political and social policy.

More fundamental perhaps than retirement from a job, especially for women, is the change in personal life that comes with the final departure of children from the parental family and the arrival of what has already been termed the empty nest stage of the development cycle of the family. There has to be a sense of release from the responsibilities and trammels of the Second Age and a recognition of the opportunity to live a life of self-fulfillment thereafter. It goes without saying that the physical condition of the retired person has to be good enough for her or him to seize that opportunity. Judging this circumstance depends on the reconstruction of the history of health over the life course. The assertions on this topic made by several of our contributors, especially by George Alter, hint at one of the most important of the tasks of the historical sociologist of aging. Though more usually justified by the intimidating growth in the cost of invalidism in late life, a theme not pursued here but evident in practically all of the discussions of the subject, its relevance to the emergence of the Third Age of independence and creativity is clear.[44]

The general theory of the emergence of the Third Age and of its relations with the Second and Fourth ages goes as follows. Though elements of such a life stage can be described during the Before, it could not properly exist then because its essential preconditions were absent, especially the demographic. The mass of individuals went without much in the way of an interlude between active life and old age, and old age was defined in terms corresponding largely to those we have used for the Fourth Age.[45] In the absence of widespread and compulsory state-guaranteed retirement, the transition was not dictated by calendar age and would vary with family and generational position, with social class and occupation, with the economic situation, but above all with physical and mental condition. There is ample evidence of this in the essays published here in Part IV, Retirement and Mortality.

Prior to all these necessary features of the Third Age, therefore, are the demographic conditions that permit a large enough proportion of the population to live for long enough after the Second Age is over. It is the theory of the early discussions of the Third Age and its emergence (Laslett 1984, 1987*a*, 1989) that all the circumstances named, along with others that have to be passed over for lack of space, began to exist for the first time in most of the countries of Europe and in countries with populations of European origin by the middle decades (1940–1960) of the twentieth century, though the countries of eastern Europe may have to be excepted. The demographic qualifications have had to be decided in an entirely arbitrary fashion, and the suggestion is that the Third Age can only be present when at least half of a country's male population can expect to survive from age 25 to age 70 and when at least a quarter of adults, those over 25, are beyond the age of 60 years.

As for the survival condition, in life table terms, numbers alive at age 70 divided by numbers alive at age 25 has to be equal to one-half or more ($l_{70}/l_{25} \geq .5$ for males). This is called the Third Age indicator, or 3AI.[46] In table 1.4, values of the 3AI are given for England at fifty-year intervals from

TABLE 1.4   Demographic Qualifications for the Third Age,
England and Britain, 1540s–1990s

Year	$3AI\ \dfrac{l_{70}{}^{a}}{l_{25}}$	$\dfrac{Number\ over\ Age\ 60^{b}}{Number\ over\ Age\ 25}$
1541–1545	.292	19.19
1591–1595	.348	18.43
1641–1645	.325	18.67
1691–1695	.310	20.53
1741–1745	.297	17.87
1791–1795	.338	16.90
1841–1845	.391	15.25
1881–1885	.374	16.47
1891	.301	16.21
1901	.375	15.42
1911	.416	15.66
1921	.492	17.23
1931	.497	19.66
1941	.471	21.82
1951	.532	24.50
1961	.581	26.77
1971	.625	30.08
1981	.634	31.73
1991	.690	31.21

SOURCE: Calculated from data in the files of the Cambridge Group for the
History of Population and Social Structure.
[a]Males only.
[b]Females and males.

the 1540s to the 1880s, along with proportions of adults over the age of 60, and at ten-year intervals thereafter until 1991. The fundamental differences between aging on the lower and higher plateaus are visible once again in the table, as is the complex relationship between the demographic transition and the secular shift. It will be noticed that the 3AI varied narrowly above and below .33 until 1901, a one-third chance for a male at age 25 ever attaining age 70. By 1951, however, the 3AI for men exceeded .5 for the first time, and proportions of all adults above the age of 60 exceeded a quarter for the first time by 1960. England (and Britain) had qualified demographically for the Third Age, on the criteria we are using, almost exactly at the midpoint of the twentieth century.

CLIMACTERIC IN THE MIDDLE OF THE TWENTIETH CENTURY

It would not be expected that all the developed countries should comport themselves in the same orderly fashion. It can be stated, nevertheless, that all the populations of the countries appearing in tables 1.1 and 1.2 had a

3AI for males of at least .5 by 1960 and some of them several decades earlier, but that none of them had a quarter of all adults over the age of 60 before the 1940s. Reference to figure 1.8, however, shows that within that
decade or its successor, every population represented except Japan had
risen decisively above the line denoted there as the qualifying level. In contrast, figure 1.10, with the further detail given in figure 1.11, shows that the
dates by which countries qualified with respect to survival were spread over
a much longer period. Sweden and New Zealand had a 3AI of .5 just after
1900; Denmark, by the 1920s; and the Netherlands and Italy (not in the figure), by the 1930s, still twenty years before the accession of the United Kingdom and thirty years before Japan.

It is only, therefore, when the course over time of our realistic, experiential indicator of the weight of older persons in a society is taken alongside
the course over time of the 3AI that England, or the United Kingdom, can

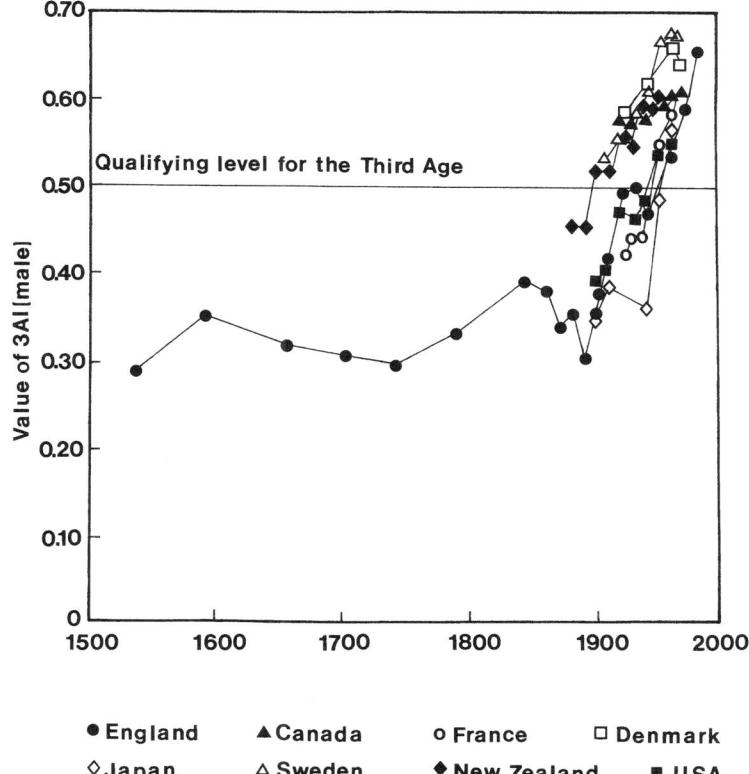

Fig. 1.10. 3AIs (males only): Canada, Denmark, England, France,
Japan, New Zealand, Sweden, and the United States. Data from National
Life Tables. $3AI = l_{70}/l_{25}$.

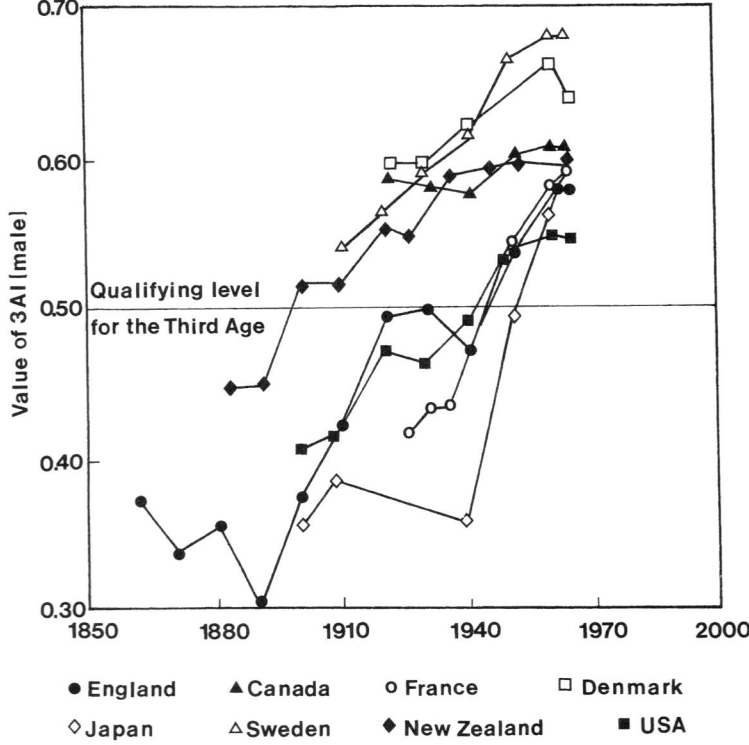

- England   ▲Canada   o France   □ Denmark
- ◇Japan   △Sweden   ◆ New Zealand   ■ USA

Fig. 1.11. Detail of figure 1.10.

still be said to have had the standard, the paradigmatic, experience of the secular shift in aging. The accession of that country to the Third Age in the 1950s can, under these highly specific conditions, be said to have marked the movement of the whole body of the rich, highly developed countries of western and northwestern Europe, with their companions overseas, into the new demographic era where the Third Age can exist. The most significant of all the outcomes of the secular shift in aging had unmistakably manifested itself in the West.

Yet another tilt of circumstance occurred in England in the 1950s. It must have been in this decade that the almost vertical upthrust of the secular shift began to bend over toward the higher aging plateau, problematic as that plateau may turn out to be in the next century. The demographic history of the other Western countries appearing in the figures we have been at such pains to compare with the English would most probably show this same slight change of direction detectable in the drawing together of the decadal survival curves in figure 1.5 at corresponding points in their aging trajectories. Inconspicuous as this reorientation may appear to be, this presaging of the disappearance of the secular shift and the succession of the higher plateau were pregnant with the future of aging in the Western societies we have lingered over. It is surely correct to think of the 1950s as the time of the "Great Climacteric" for the West in the history of age and aging. It remains to be seen what will correspond to it in the history of populations that have yet to be caught up in the secular shift.

AGE TRAJECTORIES OVER THE SECULAR SHIFT IN THE WEST AND IN SOME COUNTRIES OF EAST*

We have made use of the demographic statistics of Japan in the course of the argument, as a supplement and a contrast to those of the Western developed countries. We have also repeatedly asserted that the historical demography of aging in every country, and this means, of course, a collection consisting as to a vast majority of less-developed countries, will sooner or later follow the same course. The higher will succeed to the lower plateau in all of them, and the secular shift in aging will do much to transform their social landscapes.

Here we will make use of the Japanese data as well as data from one or two other East Asian countries to give substance to these propositions and to justify the statement made at the outset that the Western aging experience has a transcendent importance because it has happened first. With these additional facts in front of us, we shall proceed to a conclusion.

Because our sources for this section are published demographic statements, it will not be possible in this very brief exposition of such facts as have become known to us to keep to the experiential aging measures that have here been declared necessary for the comparative pursuit of the historical demography of aging. We shall have to content ourselves with the cruder measures we began with and which have been subjected to criticism. We shall proceed, moreover, in a summary fashion, by way of commentary on the six figures that follow.

In figure 1.12, two features have to be noticed. The first is that the trajectories of the growth in proportions of elderly (here those over 65 rather than those over 60) are measured on a scale of years from starting points placed thirty years apart, that of Japan from 1950 and that of China from 1980. This circumstance makes the second feature even more remarkable, that the two trajectories should follow each other so closely. This is in spite of the gap between their starting points, which implies that the shifts were initiated in very different world situations and very different local, North-

---

*Written with Zhongwei Zhao using the data and figures that he prepared. For an extended version, see Zhao in press.

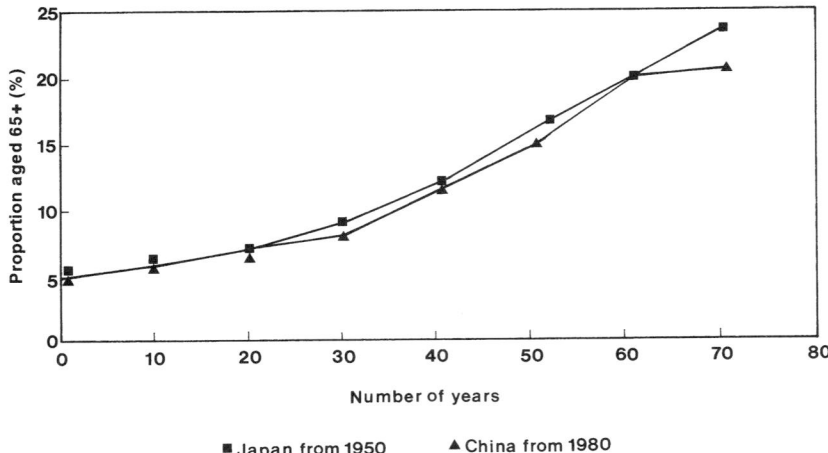

Fig. 1.12. Change in proportion of population age 65 and older: China, from 1950, and Japan, from 1980. Data from Keyfitz and Flieger 1986; Wu and Du 1992.

east Asian, North Pacific situations. The enormous dissimilarities between the two countries—in size, in culture, in social structure, in history (especially recent history), in wealth, in degree of development—seem not to have mattered.

This parallel effect is certainly surprising and suggests a definiteness and autonomy in the secular shift that could scarcely have been inferred from the evidence of the other countries we have surveyed. It is true that the comparison is largely based on projected trends of population aging (from the fourth decade in the case of Japan and the second in the case of China). It is also true that such projected results are essentially determined by the demographic parameters that have been used, and they could vary considerably according to the assumptions being made. But many other projected results indicate that in China, the aging trajectory is likely to be very similar to that which has been and will continue to be observed in Japan unless unexpected changes in fertility or mortality occur to alter them.[47] Short of an entirely improbable set of circumstances, or of borrowings from one set of projections to form the other, the trajectories and their close rapprochement must represent a genuine phenomenon.

In figure 1.13, four trajectories have been added to those represented in figure 1.12. The South Korean case is based mainly on forecasts, while the European cases rely to a far smaller extent on such projections. It is difficult to decide precisely the time when each population embarks on the secular shift, but for the purpose of comparing its speed in various countries, a starting point is arbitrarily chosen from the trajectory of the growth in propor-

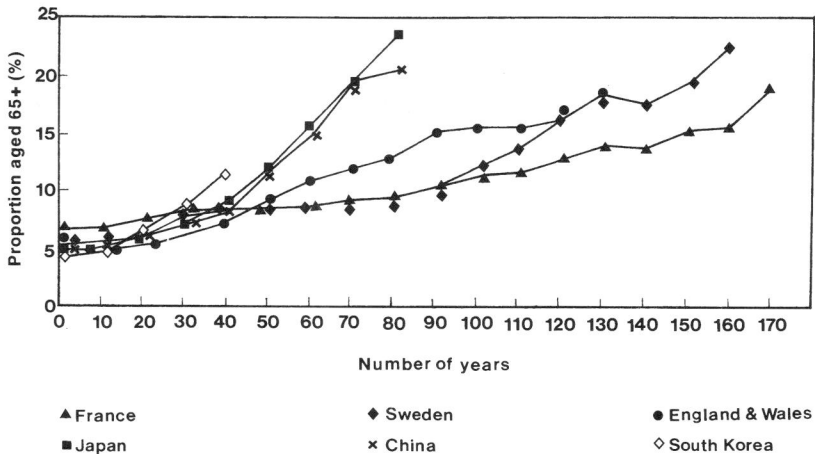

Fig. 1.13. Change in proportion of population age 65 and older: China, England and Wales, France, Japan, South Korea, and Sweden.

tions elderly. Here the point selected is that at which the proportion age 65 and over is close to 5 percent of the total population and thereafter rises rapidly and monotonically. Figure 1.13 shows that a rise in the proportions of those over 65 from a level of 5 percent to a level of 15 percent occupied about 150 years in France, about 115 years in Sweden, and about 90 years in England and Wales but about 60 years in China and Japan. In South Korea, if the projected trend continues after the year 2020, the increase in the proportion of the elderly may be even more rapid.

This conspicuous foreshortening of the time taken for drastic aging to occur has been noted before. In 1988, Naohiro Ogawa published figures showing that the years required for the proportion of the population over 65 to rise from 10 to 20 percent were 24 in Japan, 48 in Finland, the fastest European case, and ranged from 54 to 85 (Sweden) in the eight other European countries he selected (Ogawa 1988: table 8). All this implies that the secular shift has been very much briefer in Japan—about half of that in most northwestern European countries—and will no doubt be somewhat the same in China. The speeding up of the secular shift and the indication that it may intensify as country succeeds to country undergoing the shift in East Asia must be classed as singular phenomena.

We have dwelt a great deal upon the suddenness of the aging process in the West, on the extent to which it has been overlooked, and on consequent "false consciousness" about it. It seems that East Asia and perhaps other countries embarking or about to embark on the secular shift will undergo it with even greater rapidity. The Western precedent seems to be less helpful here. No one can yet tell what may happen in the way of social discontinuity and disorientation with regard to aging and age relationships after a shift of such rapidity.

A very similar reflection is suggested when figure 1.14 is added to the series, delineating comparisons in longevity. Here the time scale is a real one and the statistics observational. Once more the Southeast Asian populations have increased and are increasing their longevity far more quickly than ever the Europeans did, and they will outstrip them in short order if Japan is to be taken as precedent.

Figure 1.14 suggests something further (it suggests only, because the temporal depth is so shallow for the Asian populations). It may be—and the little historical work that has been done and that is known to us does nothing to contradict this—that expectation of life on the lower plateau in Asia, or in parts of Asia, was below what it was in Europe. There is a hint of this in the trajectory for Japan in figure 1.7. Early and near universal marriage for women, which we suppose to have been a widespread characteristic of

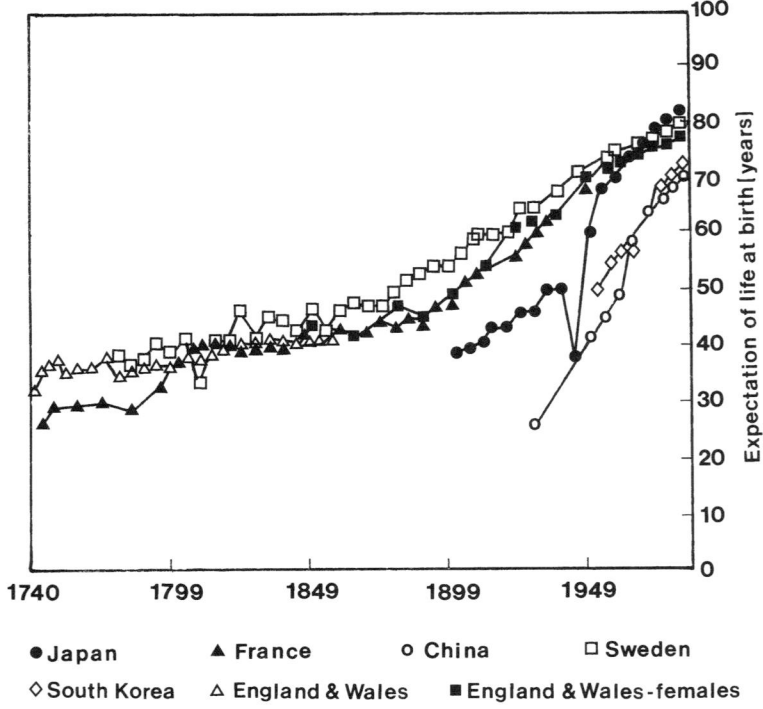

Fig. 1.14. Expectation of life at birth (females only): China, England and Wales, France, Japan, South Korea, and Sweden.

these countries, would certainly have made it possible for their populations to survive in the long term with lower expectation of life than has been found in the West in the past. We must be a little wary in comparison here, of course, because expectation of life at birth, which is all we have, may interfere a little with an objective contrast. But our knowledge of the plateau-like character of longevity over long periods certainly seems to imply that the rises in Japan, China, and South Korea are very unlikely to be a short-term variation in an otherwise generally even trajectory.

If this conjecture is correct, the lower longevity plateau in these countries may have been somewhat beneath that for Western populations but probably within its range of variation. We have as yet nothing to indicate the extent to which it was horizontal and flat. A further inference, therefore, that can be made from the figures is that the secular shift may start from a more modest level than that which obtained on the lower plateau in the West and so may have a longer slope upward. It could therefore take less time, travel farther, and be markedly steeper in these East Asian countries than it has been in Europe, America, and Australia. This would apply to both of our aging parameters, expectation of life and proportion in later life, and it has to be said that the first East Asian country to proceed through the shift, Japan, has displayed all these characteristics. The still more remote possibility that Western countries were perpetually somewhat longer lived than others on the lower plateau has no support known to us other than the indications of these figures. It is an intriguing possibility nevertheless.

Figures 1.15, 1.16, and 1.17 modulate the inferences we have made but certainly do not overset them. They are all in real time, over the period spec-

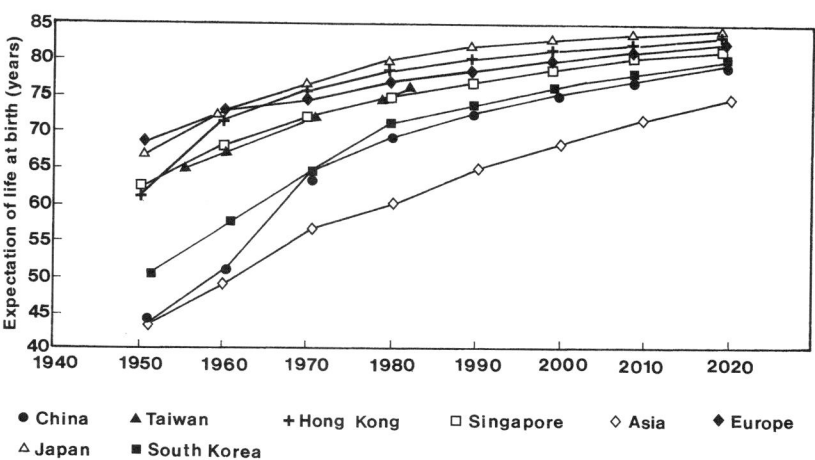

Fig. 1.15. Expectation of life at birth (females only): Asia, China, Europe, Hong Kong, Japan, Singapore, South Korea, and Taiwan, 1950–2020.

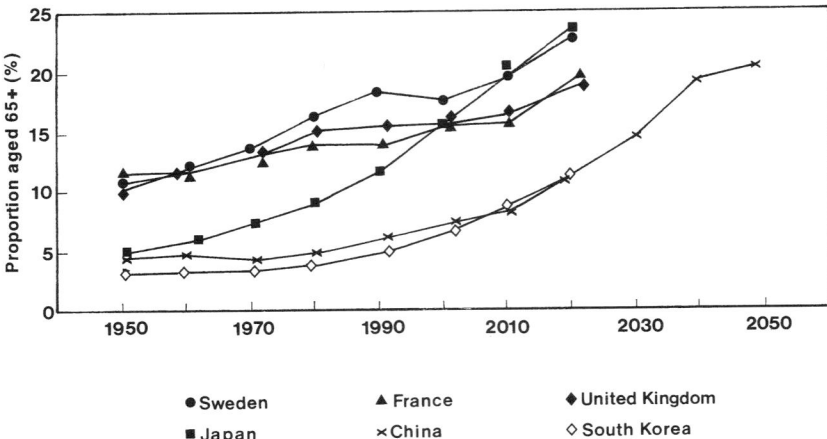

Fig. 1.16. Proportion of population age 65 and older: China, France, Japan, South Korea, Sweden, and the United Kingdom, 1950–2050. Data from Keyfitz and Flieger 1986; Wu and Du 1992.

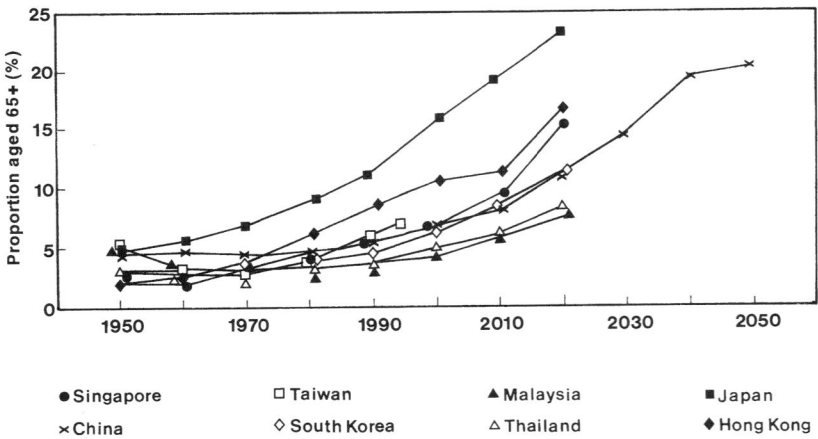

Fig. 1.17. Proportion of population age 65 and older: China, Hong Kong, Japan, Malaysia, Singapore, South Korea, Taiwan, and Thailand, 1950–2050.

ified. The trajectory shown in figure 1.15 for expectation of life in Asia as a whole during this interlude (taken from Keyfitz and Flieger 1990) does not suggest that the entire continent will have a longer-lived population than the West. The pattern of the lines in that figure points to East Asian exceptions, however, and hints once again that longevity could have been less before the secular shift began than in England (see, e.g., the figures in table 1.3, above). It is important to note that all the individual countries and areas shown in the figure have by now stepped over the threshold of the 3AI.

Figure 1.16 shows Japan overtaking European countries in proportions of elderly persons and rapidly acquiring the oldest age composition yet contemplated. The conceivable long-term difference between the Asian countries and the West with respect to both parameters on the lower plateau—Asia being the younger—is difficult to appreciate in view of the difference in the measures in figures 1.16 and 1.17 for proportions elderly from those used earlier, where proportions over 60 were used rather than proportions over 65.

But if it is remembered that proportions over 60 are likely to be about a third as high again as proportions over 65, a small margin in favor of the hypothesis is apparent. Finally, figure 1.17 makes it clear that in spite of the probability that all the Southeast Asian populations represented will show a similar pattern of change during the secular shift, the present temporal relationship between their trajectories is somewhat complex. The closeness of the observed and projected trajectories for Thailand and Malaysia, South Korea and China, Taiwan, Hong Kong, and Singapore brings us back to what was said about figure 1.12 as to the near-identity in the course of aging in Japan and China.

This exercise illustrates many of the issues about the Before and the After in aging, the two aging plateaus, and the secular shift in rather unexpected ways. It puts the historical aging processes that the Western developed countries have experienced into a comparative context. And it adds emphasis to the contention that the historical demography of aging has to be seen in the widest possible context over time—past, present, and future—and over all the world's political and cultural areas.

CONCLUSION: PROCESSIONAL KNOWLEDGE

A lengthy exposition has been required to demonstrate that the historical demography of aging is indeed necessary knowledge from the past. Some of this knowledge has had to be technical, even more of it numerical, not a little of it to consist in invoking visual judgment as to whether one line of a figure does or does not resemble other lines. These are not the usual qualities of historical discourse. And in the end, the knowledge and the inferences expounded turned out not to be from the past alone but from the past and the projected future, with the historically insubstantial present taking up a great deal of space.

For the title of a recent analysis of the grave issues of justice over time, the phrase "processional justice" had to be adopted.[48] It was found, and this will not surprise a demographer, that the realities to be understood escaped the analyst if they were confined to a time point. A cross-sectional view was only useful so far as it could indicate not only what is or was at a point in time but also what had been and would be. There is a similar logic in the use made of projections in the section above. We do not understand ourselves in time, and this understanding is the peculiar duty of the historical sociologist, unless we see ourselves as placed in a procession. Hence the description of necessary knowledge from the past as processional.

There are two further examples from the historical demography of aging that help us to grasp what we should be after. One was touched on in the discussion of the Third Age Indicator, the 3AI. If at the beginning of your productive life the expectation of ever growing old is so low that the prospect can be sensibly disregarded, then your attitude toward your late and very late life is likely to be quite different from that of a person who can confidently expect to be old. We do not know how far this did and does mark the attitude of people placed on the lower aging plateau. There, as table 1.4 and figure 1.10 show, the value of the 3AI was often below .33 and was likely to have been lower for a fair proportion of those "decreasing the wealth of the kingdom." We do know one relevant thing about their behavior as to age and aging, however. As late as the 1930s in England, working-class people failed to save for late life, but they did save penny by penny for their funerals (Johnson 1985), which could of course come at any age for them as it could for all their predecessors.

On the lower plateau, between 15 and 25 percent of an original male cohort were alive at the age of 70, whereas 65 to 75 percent are alive at that age today. If the proletarians did write off their old age in the Before, they were acting rationally, especially if public money was there to support them in old age as it certainly was in London during the 1930s. But they were behaving as if prompted by processional knowledge, knowledge of a kind that must inform the writing of the history of aging and especially its demography.

Our further example is the same set of circumstances looked at from another point of view. In discussing transfers of resources, social as well as familial, to those in late life in the West, it is properly supposed that the recipients receive these resources as of right, as a part of the normative structure of the society they live in. These rights have been of particular importance in the West because Western rules of household formation could be said to impose hardship on older people, especially widowed and decrepit older people. It does so by removing their children from their families at the marriage of those children, "nuclear family hardship" as it has come to be called.[49] On the lower aging plateau, these rights, although they can be supposed to have attached to every individual, were only ever exercised by very few. This is a point on which the strongest stress has to be placed. The others died too soon. However important their right to support at the end of their lives may have been to them when living, seen processionally, those rights were a nullity.

One way of looking at the much discussed crisis of support for the old in Western countries today is that the secular shift in aging makes it more and more difficult, perhaps in some estimates finally impossible, to sustain the inherited, perduring Western social structure in this regard. To recognize this possibility is also to practice processional thinking. Such thinking will be even more urgent in developing countries, as we have seen. It should be evident that responding to the acquisition of necessary knowledge from the past about aging, even in the preliminary fashion in which it has been done here, is to widen the intellectual horizon of historians, sociologists, and social scientists at large, as well as to explore a hitherto almost unknown area of the human reality. It does much to consolidate the concept of historical sociology and to demonstrate its overarching importance.

APPENDIX: INDICATORS FOR COMPARISON OF LONGEVITY

Measures of longevity are extensively discussed in the text above. The section, Experiential Measures in the Historical Demography of Aging, proposes that values for expectation of life at age 15 (e_{15}) be substituted for expectation of life at birth (e_0) as the most useful and revealing measure for comparing longevity between populations, particularly between those on the lower and the higher aging plateaus. It was pointed out, however, that this measure would only very seldom be available because expectation of life at birth alone is usually published in the relevant documents.

One of the objects of this appendix is to make it possible to proceed in a rough and ready fashion from e_0 to e_{15}. In columns 1 and 2 of table 1.A1, values for twenty-five "levels" of life expectation are set out for e_0 and e_{15}, and the trajectories of both are depicted in figure 1.A1, along with four other sets of statistics having to do with longevity. The source of all the information is the regional model life tables and stable populations published by Ansley Coale and Paul Demeny (2d ed., 1983, with the collaboration of Barbara Vaughan). All the statistics, except those for the 3AI (column 3), are for females.

The sets of tables ranged under the title "North" in that volume have been chosen for citation because the figures there seemed to correspond more closely than those in "East," "West," or "South" to the experience of England, at least up to the early nineteenth century, that is, on the lower aging plateau (see Wrigley and Schofield 1989: 110, 198, and passim). If, as is claimed in the text, English experience was in general typical of other Western countries, then the values in table 1.A1 can be regarded as indicative of Western demographic development as a whole. After the early nineteenth century, however, the English figures (and so perhaps those of contiguous European societies and their descendant societies overseas) resemble Coale and Demeny's "West" rather than "North," and this tendency must be allowed for when using the table.[50]

What follows is a discussion of the columns of the table and the corresponding lines in the figure, together with the character and values of the longevity indicators that the numbers in the columns represent.

TABLE 1.A1 Indicators Facilitating Comparisons in Longevity over Time and between Cultures

	1	*2*	*3*	*4*	*5*	*6*	*7*	*8*
	e_0	e_{15}	3AI (Males)	Mean Age at Death	5 Years to Come	10 Years to Come	12.5 Years to Come	Half of Cohort Dead
Level 1	20.0	32.8	.111	28.9	c.73	c.58	c.52	4
Level 2	22.5	34.3	.135	28.9	c.74	c.59	c.54	5
Level 3	25.0	35.8	.160	28.9	c.74	c.59	c.53	9
Level 4	27.5	37.2	.185	29.0	c.75	c.59	c.54	15
Level 5	30.0	38.6	.211	29.1	c.76	c.58	c.57	19
Level 6	32.5	40.0	.238	29.3	c.77	c.64	c.59	27
Level 7	35.0	41.3	.265	29.6	c.78	c.65	c.60	34
Level 8	37.5	42.6	.293	30.0	c.78	c.66	c.62	40
Level 9	40.0	44.0	.321	30.5	c.78	c.63	c.57	44
Level 10	42.5	45.3	.349	31.1	c.79	c.67	c.63	50
Level 11	45.0	46.6	.377	31.7	c.79	c.69	c.63	54
Level 12	47.5	47.9	.406	32.5	c.80	c.69	c.64	57
Level 13	50.0	49.0	.431	33.4	c.81	c.69	c.65	61
Level 14	52.5	50.2	.454	34.4	c.82	c.70	c.65	63
Level 15	55.0	51.4	.479	35.7	c.83	c.70	c.64	66
Level 16	57.5	52.6	.505	37.2	c.83	c.70	c.64	68
Level 17	60.0	53.8	.531	38.9	c.83	c.71	c.64	70
Level 18	62.5	55.1	.559	40.9	c.84	c.72	c.66	73
Level 19	65.0	56.4	.588	43.3	c.84	c.73	c.67	74
Level 20	67.5	57.7	.618	46.2	c.84	c.73	c.68	76
Level 21	70.0	59.0	.648	49.8	c.84	c.74	c.67	76
Level 22	72.5	60.3	.675	54.3	c.84	c.74	c.70	77
Level 23	75.0	62.0	.713	59.0	c.85	c.75	c.71	78
Level 24	77.5	63.8	.756	64.2	c.85	c.76	c.71	79
Level 25	80.0	65.8	.803	69.7	c.86	c.77	c.73	81

NOTE: Females only, except for column 3.

The numbers in column 1 (e_0) necessarily draw a straight line in the figure, since Coale and Demeny's tables were set up so as to make an e_0 of 20 for females the basis of level 1 and an e_0 of 22.5 as the basis for level 2, and so on, increasing by increments of 2.25 years up to an e_0 of 80. The relationship between columns 1 and 2 (e_0 and e_{15}) illustrates the points made in the text. Expectation of life at age 15 is as much as 12.8 years higher than that at e_0 when e_0 is 20 (level 1) years ($e_0/e_{15} = 1.64$), and this superiority diminishes gradually to 8.6 years when $e_0 = 30$ (level 5, multiplier 1.28) and to 2.8 (level 10, 1.06) when $e_0 = 42.5$. Longevity at age 15 does not fall below that at age 0 until a point between level 13 and level 14. Extrapolation will have to be made by users of the table: the figure for e_0 in question here is presumably about 51.5 years. Thereafter the value of e_{15} steadily falls below that for e_0, until at the highest level the difference is 14.2 years, proportionally about as much above e_0 as it is below it at the age of 20. This interesting relationship comes out clearly in figure 1.A1.

The course of the 3AI, column 3, the only set of figures for males in the table, was surveyed in the section, "The Emergence of the Third Age," above. This indicator shows a very considerable range of values and must be regarded as a highly sensitive and realistic measure of longevity experience. It can be seen that its course is parallel over most of its range to that of e_0 itself. It might be permissible to infer from these circumstances that when at level 16 female expectation of life at birth reaches 57.5 (male 53.8), the 3AI (male) reaches 0.5, the qualifying level in respect to longevity, it will be remembered, for the emergence of the Third Age.[51] It is interesting that at the highest levels, 22–25, the trajectory of the male 3AI ceases to be roughly linear and curves upward.

Mean age at death, column 4 in the table,[52] is sometimes used as an approximate indicator of longevity, which is the more understandable since details of the age of death of individuals on the lower plateau is the relevant evidence most likely to be available. Inspection of the table and the figure shows, however, that such a practice is almost entirely misleading, since the course of mean age at death is curvilinear and cannot be used as a guide to e_0 or e_{15} unless complicated calculations are made. It so happens that mean age at death is within a year or two of e_0 between levels 4 and 6 (e_0 27.5 to e_0 32.5), but the two curves diverge rapidly both above and below that narrow band. The distance is greatest at levels 17 to 19 (e_0 60 to e_0 65), when mean age at death is 20 years less than e_0 and 13 to 15 years less than e_{15}. The differences certainly narrow toward the highest levels. But it should be borne in mind that age at death is a function of population growth as well as of longevity, which makes matters even more intricate.

The full description of columns 5, 6, and 7 is mean age at which there are 5, 10, or 12.5 years still to live. Statistics of this kind have sometimes been recommended as measures of longevity and have an obvious usefulness from the point of view of individual experience.[53] It is instructive for an individual to know when she (or he) is on average within 5, 10, or 12.5 years of the end of life and particularly instructive when Third Age living has become possible from the point of view of longevity, that is (as we have seen), at levels above number 16 in our table.

What may seem astonishing is that the graphs representing values in columns 6 and 7, particularly even in their courses or consistently parallel to each other, rise so very gradually throughout the twenty-five levels of e_0. These two sets of values increase by only 35 percent and 40 percent while

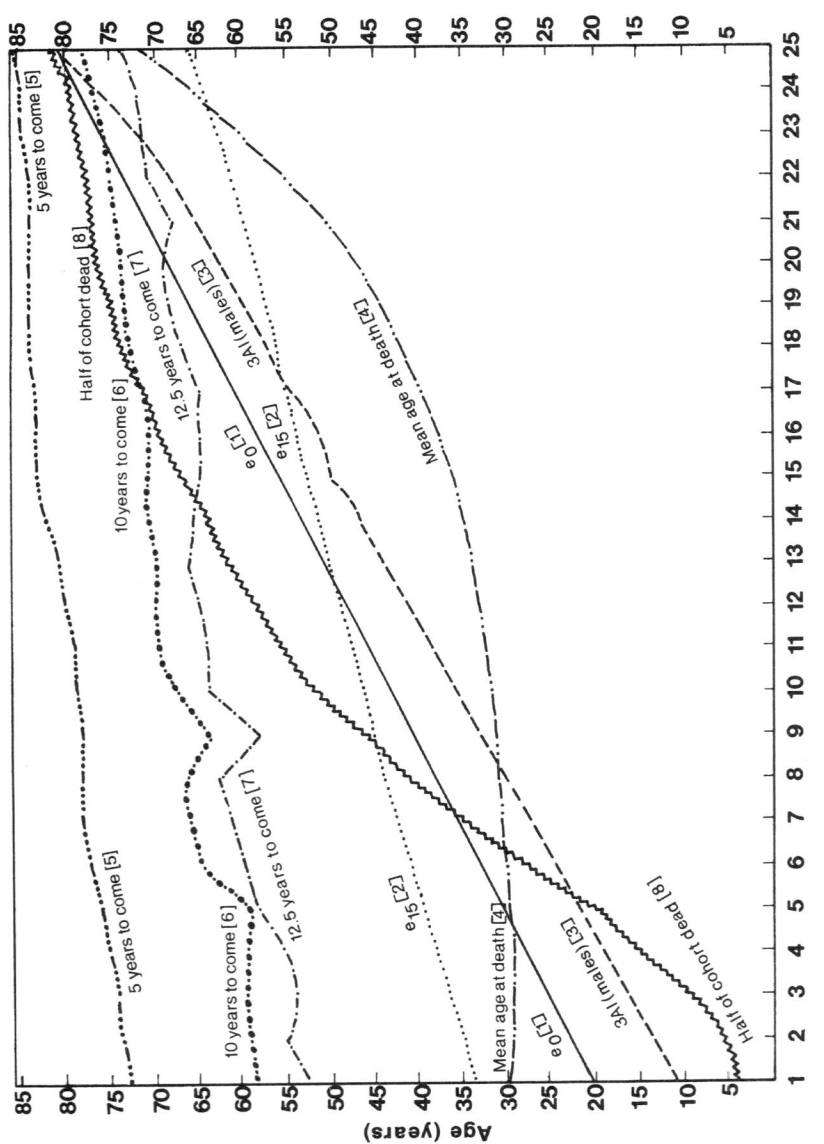

Fig. 1.A1. Longevity indicators. Females only, except males only for 3AI. Scale for 3AI is .01 that for age in years. Numbers in square brackets after the titles of the variables on the lines correspond to the columns of table 1.A1.

the 3AI rises by 800 percent, and in columns 4 and 8 the values are 266 percent and 2,025 percent. These circumstances make transparently clear once again a point already heavily stressed in the text: in spite of the fact that very few could expect to live to the later decades on the lower plateau, those women who did might continue for an appreciable number of additional years. If the general expectation of life was as low as the early 20s (and a dozen years higher at 15), a woman could expect to go on for another 12.5 years if she was one of those lucky enough to reach age 60. As for column 5, it makes very clear how much later in life that limit to expectation comes, even in situations where longevity is low.

The remaining column, 8, headed "half of cohort dead," should explain itself as the age by which one-half of a set of persons born in the same year have disappeared. It is even more sensitive as an indicator than the 3AI and so of considerable potential usefulness in longevity studies. This seems to be recognized, however, more by demographers studying animals than those studying people. Unfortunately, this final indicator, like those in all the columns except 5 (whose disadvantages have been set out), requires life tables if it is to be calculated. For the really detailed historical study of longevity, therefore, a series of time-separated life tables is necessary.

It can be tentatively suggested from this discussion and from an examination of the table and the figure that during the Before in the West, that is, on the lower aging plateau, for women in the West expectation of life at birth was on average at a value corresponding to a point between level 7 and level 8, that is, in the middle and late 30s, and expectation of life at age 15, in the early 40s. Something over a quarter of their male counterparts could expect to live until age 70 if they reached age 25, only about one-half of the proportion required to satisfy the longevity criterion for the Third Age. Average age at death for women was late 20s or early 30s, but women who reached the early 60s could expect to go on for 12.5 years more, for 10 years more if they attained the mid-60s, and for 5 years more in their early 80s. One-half of those born in the same year would, on average, be dead by their early 40s.

During the After, on the higher aging plateau as it is beginning to unfold, expectation of life for women at birth is likely to be in the 80s, probably inching upward: at age 15, in the mid-60s. Mean age at death is likely to be in the late 60s or early 70s, and the prospect of men surviving from 25 to 70—from the beginning of the Second Age to the middle of the Third Age—is over 80 percent. From the point of view of length of life, therefore, the Third Age will be absolutely securely established. In her early 70s on this higher plateau, a woman could probably expect to live for 12.5 years more, for 10 years more in her later 70s, and for 5 years more once over age 85. At an average age of over 80, probably slowly rising, one-half of all women born at the same date will still be alive.

It can be concluded with confidence that we inhabit an entirely different world with respect to length of life and experience of living it than our ancestors did, both as individuals and as a collective society. Necessary knowledge, indeed.

NOTES

1. See Laslett 1989 and the writings of Matilda White Riley (e.g., Riley 1987). On Europe, see particularly Laslett, "The aging of European populations and its social effects" (in press).

2. Tables 1.1 and 1.2 indicate that the original claim is nearer the truth for eastern Europe (including Germany) and also in some respects for southern Europe but is likewise too high for Britain's neighbors in western and northern Europe. If the whole depth of time before the 1880s is taken into account for England, however, longevity at birth has indeed doubled, and proportions of elderly have in fact trebled.

3. Nevertheless, they have been assembled under one heading and described as "The Second Demographic Transition," continuing falls in fertility and mortality being the leitmotiv. See van de Kaa 1987 and Lesthaeghe 1991–1992. It is interesting that demographers seem to have hesitated to include aging in the second demographic transition, though it is surely more clearly demographic than some of the other developments.

4. The terms "secular shift in aging," "lower and higher aging plateau," and "the Before" and "the After" were introduced in an attempt to distinguish aging from the other constituents of "modernization" and the aging process from the demographic transition or transitions. It was hoped to refer aging to the appropriate dates, periods, and stages of national development. See Laslett [1976] 1985 and 1984.

5. It is this which makes it inadvisable to use for properly historical purposes the demographic statistics ingeniously worked out by students of contemporary tribal communities. The remarkable results published in 1979 by Nancy Howell, *Demography of the Dobe !Kung,* for example, include aging estimates (see her chaps. 2 and 5) for an extant hunter-gathering society. But they do not necessarily indicate the situation during that era of universal hunter-gathering supposed to have preceded the agricultural era in which our own peasant ancestors lived.

6. For archaeodemography, see Acsádi and Nemeskéri 1970. Its inaccuracies and limitations are discussed in Petersen 1975.

7. For a specifically demographic work citing Ulpian's life table (considered by other demographers as lacking all basis in observation) and other historical fragments, see Dublin, Lotka, and Spiegelman [1936] 1948. It could be claimed that the parish registrations that yield the data for the demography of aging before the statistical era (see below) were likewise innocent of any demographic intent (see Laslett 1966) as were such sources as the censuses of China. It is the much more systematic character of the parish registers of the Christian church in European and European-decended societies and their persistence over long periods of early recordings that make them susceptible to satisfactory numerical analysis.

8. See my review of Georges Minois's *History of old age* (1989), ending "the hell with the Seven Ages of Man" (Laslett 1990).

9. Countries vary in this respect: the official U.S. census is closed for 50 years after being carried out, the British for 100 years. The Scandinavian countries are the most generous of access and their state-collected records go back as far as any of those elsewhere. Unfortunately, the original documentation for the censuses, even in countries like these, is very unevenly preserved. As for census-type documents drawn up before the statistical era, the situation is extremely uneven. In England, for example, whereas parochial registration of births, marriages, and deaths goes back to the 1530s and has made it possible to estimate age composition and life expectation, only about a dozen reliable census-type documents specifying ages are available before the official census began to record ages at the decennial census of 1831.

10. For examples, see Kertzer and Hogan 1989, Janssens 1993, and Bulder 1993.

11. These results are contained in Wrigley and Schofield [1981] 1989.

12. For an explication of demographic aging, particularly in relation to the demographic transition, see Chesnais [1986] 1992, esp. 274–289, and 1990. In accepting for the purposes of explanation the well-established model of the demographic transition, I have no wish to underwrite the functionalist theoretical framework or the assumption of inevitability as part of the modernization process which so often attaches to it. See the perceptive study by Simon Szreter (1993).

13. The recordings of baptisms, marriages, and burials from which the data used by Wrigley and Schofield [1981] (1989) for their monumental reconstruction were collected by several hundred volunteers (see their preface). Because gender is unspecified in the English parish registers that these volunteers used, they would have had to rely on given names and other clues to decide it. This was too laborious and uncertain a procedure to be worthwhile.

14. See the discussion in Laslett 1989, rev. ed., chap. 4, where possible projections for the twenty-first century in western Europe are considered. If substantiated, the more extreme of these forecasts would put life expectation at a maximum of 100 years at the end of that century rather than 85 years as indicated in figure 1.1. Under these extraordinary conditions, nothing like a plateau of the kind shown before the secular shift could be supposed.

15. Jacques Vallin (see Schofield, Reher, and Bideau 1991) suggests that the English evidence is not as reliable as the French because it depends to such an extent on model life tables, whereas the French is based on family reconstitutions. The English figures are, however, at present being checked against similar reconstitutions for English parishes. They are in general well confirmed. But it has to be accepted that English reconstitution evidence is never as reliable for this purpose as the French because English parish registers are less detailed in their descriptions of baptisms, marriages, and burials.

16. As has apparently been done by Vallin (1991: 48, fig. 3.3). The impression given by this figure is of a considerably less impressive climb at the end of the nineteenth century, and the appearance is more of a steady slope upward toward a substantial rise in the earlier 1900s. If the archaeodemographic evidence had been included in the analysis of longevity and a very much longer lapse of time thus taken into account, the impression of unceasing constancy would be very strong indeed.

17. See, for example, Kertzer and Schaie 1989, which includes historical studies of retirement both in Europe and America (Plakans 1989 [Europe], Vinovskis 1989 [America]).

18. Studies of these effects are particularly associated with Glen Elder and Tamara Hareven. See Hareven's chapter (with P. Uhlenberg) in this volume, with its references, and Elder 1974 and Hareven 1978.

19. See Fries 1980 and Fries and Crapo 1981. The critique in Laslett 1989, rev. ed., cites other discussions of their position, mostly dissenting from the claims made for the progressive compression of mortality and of morbidity in the final years. For the distribution of episodes of illness over the life course in the past as in the present and the drift toward their clustering in the later years, see the recent work of James C. Riley and others (e.g., Riley 1989). A research project on the statistical, demographic, and especially the historical aspects of life and death at the latest ages, concentrating on maximal length of life, is in progress at the Cambridge Group for the History of Population and Social Structure. It is working in conjunction with the Oldest Old Data Archive in Odense, Denmark, using the data so far assembled there. It has been incontrovertibly established that survival is decidedly improving at the latest ages at the present time, a circumstance not easy to reconcile with current compression of mortality in the oldest age group. See Kannisto 1994.

20. Estimates based on family reconstitutions at the Cambridge Group, subject to considerable uncertainty because of the difficulties of being confident of making reliable matches between personal names over periods of time greater than 50 years. The Oxfordshire villages were studied by Bridget Taylor.

21. On low life expectancy among British peers, see Hollingsworth 1964 and 1977. His estimates are now under further development at the Cambridge Group, where he has been kind enough to deposit the data.

22. Houston 1992, a very useful comparative analysis.

23. See Laslett 1977: 186. Iceland in 1729 did not have a population of what was even then thought of as on a national scale; there were only about 40,000 people. The aging peak of 1729 came in a year of disaster from smallpox, which seems to have affected younger people far more than the elderly. The Icelandic census gives 9.2 percent over 60 in 1703 and 8.7 percent in 1787.

24. See Houston 1992, where the issue is handled with considerable skill.

25. See the appendix for the surprisingly high survival of those who reached later life in the Before. Since this part of the chapter was written, evidence has been accumulating at Cambridge suggesting that the general expectation of elite groups having had longer lives than the rest of the population in the past may have to be revised, at least in respect to persons past infancy and childhood. An estimate by Roger Thatcher puts the total of centenarians in England and Wales at about 40 in 1861, and present evidence can be said to demonstrate what is claimed in the text: that it was possible to continue until very late life on the lower aging plateau and even to attain age 100.

26. The values for numbers alive at successive ages and the pooled total of years of life still left for them to live are standard features of the life table. Even in the clearest exposition of the life table, the major instrument of demographic analysis and particularly of mortality (Dublin, Lotka, and Spiegelman [1936] 1949) fails to explain to the uninitiated reader why expectation of life behaves in this way. The figures for England and Wales in 1989–1991 come from a provisional life table of the Government Actuary and those for Canada from Bourbeau and Legaré 1982. An even more elementary error about expectation of life is occasionally found in his-

torical discussions, that supposing longevity at birth of 70, then a person of 50 has twenty years to live. That this is a gross misconception should be obvious from the discussion in the text.

27. See Wrigley and Schofield 1989: 530, table A-3-2, and the Chester Beatty life tables. Japanese period life tables for dates over the century since 1891 have been used to work out generational (i.e., cohort) life tables. See Kobayashi and Nanjo 1988.

28. See Mitterauer 1992.

29. See Laslett, "Is there a generational contract?" in Laslett and Fishkin 1992, particularly the chapter in that volume by David Thomson.

30. On this topic, the supposition that an elderly population hinders national performance, see Laslett 1989, chap. 3; in relation to France, see Dyer 1977 and especially Bourdelais 1993, chap. 9.

31. For an attempt at a general theory of the proper use of evidence of this kind, especially literary evidence, when it cannot be supplemented and checked from other sources, see Laslett 1976.

32. It should be added that numbers of such specialist studies have avoided these tendencies, as, for example, those in this volume or in Pelling and Smith 1991 or Conrad and Kondratowicz 1993. Although the argument that France was already "modern" in terms of aging under the Enlightenment is not spelled out by Troyansky, it is not absent from all discussion of the topic.

33. See Laslett 1989: 105, quoting from Eric Midwinter.

34. See Szreter 1994 and Laslett 1987*a*, 1987*b*, and 1992 for the historical critique of modernization. Carmen Avalos del Pino is at present engaged at the Aging Unit of the Cambridge Group in the analysis of the results of attempting to apply the modernization model to aging in Catalonia during the secular shift. For the historical dissociation of constituents of modernization in the history of the West, see Laslett [1976] 1985, and for its relation with the so-called sexual revolution of the mid-twentieth century, see Laslett 1991.

35. See Anderson 1985. The accompaniment of the elongated vertical kin links, that is, the attenuation of lateral ones, is the result not of lengthened life but of declining fertility, an example of how intricate are the distinctions that have to be made. For the simulation of kin links over the life course, see Bongaarts, Burch, and Wachter 1987, especially the contributions of J. H. Reeves and J. E. Smith, and Laslett 1988*b*. Compare Ruggles 1994 and Zhao in press. The chapter by E. A. Hammel in this volume represents an advanced and sophisticated example of the use of simulation methods.

36. For England, see Laslett 1989, chap. 7, and for the United States, see, for example, Smith 1981 and the references in his contribution to this volume. On the two views of the change in the position of the elderly in America, see Fischer 1978 and Applebaum 1978.

37. On all these issues, see the considered discussion in Conrad 1991, with its references, and the facts set out in Laslett 1993.

38. On this paragraph, see Laslett 1989, chap. 8; 1977, chap. 5; and 1993; and compare the statements made by Hammel and the other authors in Part II, Living Arrangements, in this volume. Research is in progress at the Cambridge Group on the detailed social structure of thirteen English communities between 1891 and 1921 which may determine what effects the early path of the secular shift could have

had on the familial position of the elderly. Compare also Janssens 1992 and Bulder 1993 for the Netherlands with the work of Avalos del Pino (see note 34) for Catalonia, where she has shown that co-residence of parents with married children did indeed increase against the expectation raised by the modernization model.

39. See Laslett 1992; on the recent rapid rise in the primary individual, see Kobrin 1976. As for the United States, Steven Ruggles has laid it down that toward the end of the nineteenth century all parents who had a married child to reside with took up that familial position. It was only after that that the rise of the primary individual began. See Ruggles 1994 and compare Laslett 1989, rev. ed., chap. 9.

40. See Laslett 1988*a* and its references, especially to the work of David Thomson and Richard Smith. The amount provided for the dependent elderly seems to have varied extensively from country to country and locality to locality. It was almost never sufficient to support a penniless individual by itself. For the Dutch case, in which the support was particularly exiguous, see Bulder 1993. A somewhat skeptical view as to the collective support of the elderly is put by Thane 1993 and in her forthcoming book there cited.

41. See Gordon 1988.

42. See the chapter by Ransom and Sutch in this volume, and compare Riddle 1992. These developments are summarized in Laslett 1989, chap. 9.

43. The four-stage division of the life course is set out in Laslett 1989, where the Fourth Age is defined as one of final decrepitude and dependency, not a necessary stage of the life course of any individual and evidently subject to reduction and alleviation by medical progress and social policy. Along with the Third Age, it was intended to replace the blanket term "old age," which can now be considered obsolete. But the concept of a Fourth Age has been rejected by some authorities (see Young and Schuller 1991). In my own view the Fourth Age does represent a historical reality and its retention as a concept is required by the definition of the Third Age. See Laslett 1994, a review article on the Carnegie Enquiry into the Third Age in Britain, defending the Third Age against that Enquiry's decision to give it a chronological connotation covering a period of life between 50 and 74, a decision unacceptable to the originator of the concept and to those in the Third Age themselves.

44. The whole issue of life in the Third and Fourth ages has to be seen in relation to the analysis now proceeding of expectation of healthy active life as distinct from expectation of life as such. See discussion in Laslett 1989, rev. ed., chap. 5, and its references especially to the works of J.-M. Robine.

45. Nevertheless, there was a multiplicity of conventional ages of withdrawal, especially from public affairs ("Stepping Down," see Plakans 1989), affecting the better off for the most part, withdrawal into a retirement that might come in middle life and be ended by taking another office. This complicated situation is classically described by Keith Thomas (1976). The greater flexibility of transition into the final stage during the Before together with elements already present, which are characteristic of the Third Age, are discussed in Laslett 1989, rev. ed., and 1993. Bonfield (1989) considers the question of the Third Age during the Before in legal terms.

46. In Laslett 1987*a* and 1989, the proportional condition to be satisfied was different—at least 10 percent of the population over 65 years of age. Other demographic indicators associated with the longevity criterion for the appearance of the Third Age are found in the appendix.

47. For details of these projections and their results, see Ogawa 1988 and the following references for readers of Chinese: Yao Shuben 1989, Zeng Yi 1990, and Wu Cangping and Du Peng 1992.

48. Laslett and Fishkin 1992. The joint introduction bears this phrase as its title, and it is claimed that political theorists have a quite inadequate conception of justice over time and lack the concept of processional justice as well.

49. See Laslett 1988*a* and the introduction to Pelling and Smith 1991. Some scholars suppose that the Western familial system did specifically provide for old age dependency by requiring married children to take in aging parents (see the preface and Kertzer's concluding chapter to this volume). In my view the situation of such persons, many of whom had no surviving child, or none in a position to support them, was too miscellaneous for this to be so. Provision for support was ad hoc on the part of both family and collectivity, and the relationship may have been contractual, contractual between generations (see Laslett and Fishkin 1992).

50. It would not have been advisable to go over to "West" altogether for the later figures, because this would have sacrificed the continuity throughout the whole series which alone makes comparison possible over time.

51. Similar cross-comparisons can be made to estimate roughly other values of interest to the reader.

52. Values have been taken from the Stable Population Series for Model North, using the columns for a female gross reproduction rate of 2.25. This is only an approximate average for English historical experience and is badly out at higher levels. No correction has been made to remedy this for the reason given in note 50 above.

53. See especially Bourdelais 1993, chap. 7. His argument is that measures of this kind should be employed for preference in measuring longevity and that when converted into proportions over certain ages by an operation not easy to describe in the present context, should replace conventional aging indicators. The intriguing outcome is that countries like France, whose great age in proportional terms has been a major theme of this chapter, can actually be said to have grown younger in the twentieth century when his suggested indicators are applied.

REFERENCES

Acsádi, G., and J. Nemeskéri. 1970. *History of human life span and mortality.* Budapest: Akademiai Kaido.

Anderson, Michael. 1985. "The emergence of the modern life cycle in Britain." *Social History* 10(3): 69–87.

Applebaum, Andrew. 1978. *Old age in the new land.* Baltimore: Johns Hopkins University Press.

Bonfield, Lloyd. 1989. "Was there a 'third age' in the preindustrial English past?" In *An aging world,* ed. John M. Eekelar and D. Pearl, 37–53. Oxford: Oxford University Press.

Bongaarts, John, T. K. Burch, and Kenneth W. Wachter, eds. 1987. *Family demography: Methods and their application.* Oxford: Oxford University Press.

Bourbeau, R., and J. Legaré. 1982. *Evolution de la mortalité au Canada et au Québec, 1831–1931* [Evolution of mortality in Canada and Québec, 1831–1931]. Montréal: Presses de l'Université de Montréal.

Bourdelais, Patrice. 1993. *L'âge de la vieillesse* [The age of aging]. Paris: Odile Jacob.

Breschi, Marco. 1990. *La popolazione della Toscana dal 1640 al 1940* [The population of Tuscany from 1640 to 1940]. Florence, Italy: University of Florence, Department of Statistics.

Bulder, Elles. 1993. *The social economics of old age: Strategies to maintain income in the Netherlands 1880–1940.* Tinbergen Institute Research Series, no. 50 (P.O. Box 14791, 101LG, Amsterdam).

Chesnais, J.-C. 1990. "Demographic transition patterns and their impact on the age structure." *Population and Development Review* 16: 327–336.

———. [1986] 1992. *The demographic transition: Stages, patterns and economic implications.* Oxford: Oxford University Press. (Translation by E. and D. Kreager of *La transition démographique: Etapes, formes, implications économiques.* Paris: INED.)

Coale, Ansley J., Paul Demeny, and Barbara Vaughan. 1983. *Regional model life tables and stable populations.* 2d ed. New York and London: Academic Press.

Conrad, Christoph. 1991. "The emergence of modern retirement: Germany in international comparison." *Population* (Paris: INED), English selection no. 3.

Conrad, Christoph, and H.-J. Kondratowicz, eds. 1993. *Toward a cultural history of aging.* Berlin: Deutsche Centrum für Altersfrage.

Dublin, Louis I., A. J. Lotka, and M. Spiegelman. [1936] 1949. *Length of life: A study of the life table.* New York and London: Academic Press.

Dyer, Colin. 1977. *Population and society in twentieth-century France.* Sevenoaks: Hodder and Stoughton.

Elder, Glen. 1974. *Children of the Great Depression.* Chicago: University of Chicago Press.

Fildes, Valerie A. 1986. *Breasts, bottles and babies.* Edinburgh: Edinburgh University Press.

———. 1988. *Wet nursing: A history from antiquity to the present.* Oxford: Blackwell.

Fischer, David H. 1978. *Growing old in America.* New York: Oxford University Press.

Fries, James F. 1980. "Aging, natural death and the compression of morbidity." *New England Journal of Medicine* 303: 130–135.

Fries, James F., and L. M. Crapo. 1981. *Vitality and aging: Implications of the rectangular survival curve.* San Francisco: W. H. Freeman.

Gordon, Chris. 1988. "Familial support for the elderly in the past: The case of London's working class in the early 1930s." *Ageing and Society* 8(3): 287–320.

Hareven, Tamara. 1978. *Transitions: The family and the life course in historical perspective.* New York and London: Academic Press.

Hollingsworth, Thomas H. 1964. *The demography of the British peerage.* Supplement to *Population Studies* 18(2).

———. 1977. "Mortality in British peerage families since 1600." *Population* (Paris: INED), numéro spéciale.

Houston, Rab. 1992. "Mortality in early modern Scotland: The life expectancy of advocates." *Continuity and Change* 7(1): 47–69.

Howell, Nancy. 1979. *Demography of the Dobe !Kung.* New York and London: Academic Press.

Janssens, Angélique. 1993. *Family and social change: The household as a process in an industrializing community.* Cambridge: Cambridge University Press.

Johnson, Paul. 1985. *Saving and spending: The working class economy in Britain 1870–1939.* Oxford: Oxford University Press.

Kannisto, Väinö. 1994. *Development of oldest old mortality: Evidence from twenty-eight developed countries.* Monographs on Population Aging. Odense, Denmark: Odense University Press.

Kertzer, David I., and D. P. Hogan. 1989. *Family, political economy, and demographic change: The transformation of life in Casalecchio, Italy, 1861–1921.* Madison: University of Wisconsin Press.

Kertzer, David I., and K. W. Schaie, eds. 1989. *Age structuring in comparative perspective.* Hillsdale, N.J.: Lawrence Erlbaum.

Keyfitz, Nathan, and W. Flieger. 1990. *World population: An analysis of vital data.* Chicago: University of Chicago Press.

Kobayashi, Kazumasa, and Zenji Nanjo. 1988. *Generational life tables for Japan, based on period life tables covering the years 1891–1986.* Tokyo: Nihon University Press.

Kobrin, Frances E. 1976. "The primary individual and the family: Changes in living arrangements in the United States since 1940." *Journal of Marriage and the Family* 38(2).

Laslett, Peter, 1966. "The numerical study of English society." In *An introduction to English historical demography,* ed. E. A. Wrigley, 1–13. London: Weidenfeld.

———. 1972. "The history of the family." Introduction to *Household and family in past time,* ed. Peter Laslett, with Richard Wall, 1–89. Cambridge: Cambridge University Press.

———. 1976. "The wrong way through the telescope: A note on literary evidence in sociology and historical sociology." *British Journal of Sociology* 26: 319–342.

———. 1977. "The history of aging and the aged." In his *Family life and illicit love in earlier generations,* 174–213. Cambridge: Cambridge University Press.

———. [1965] 1983. *The world we have lost: English society before and after the coming of industry.* New York: Macmillan; London: Methuen.

———. 1984. "The significance of the past in the study of aging." Introduction to the special issue "History and Ageing." *Ageing and Society* 4(4): 379–389.

———. [1976] 1985. "Societal development and aging." In *Handbook of aging and the social sciences,* ed. R. H. Binstock and E. Shanas, 87–116. New York: Van Nostrand.

———. 1987*a*. "The emergence of the Third Age." *Ageing and Society* 7(2): 133–159.

———. 1987*b*. "The character of family history, its limitations and the conditions for its proper pursuit." *Journal of Family History* 12: 263–284.

———. 1988*a*. "Family, kinship and collectivity as systems of support in preindustrial Europe: A consideration of 'The nuclear hardship hypothesis.' " *Continuity and Change* 3(2): 153–175.

———. 1988*b*. "La parenté en chiffres" [Kinship in figures]. *Annales ESC: Economies, Societés, Civilizations* (Paris): 1–23.

———. 1989. *A fresh map of life: The emergence of the Third Age.* London: Weidenfeld; U.S. paperback ed., Cambridge: Harvard University Press, 1991; 2d rev. ed., London: Macmillan, 1995.

———. 1990. Review of G. Minois, *History of old age. Journal of the Social History of Medicine* 3(3): 461.

———. 1991. "Child, family and society." Address to the European Community, Luxembourg, May.

————. 1992. "The family in the industrializing East and the industrial West." Address to the International Conference on Family Formation and Dissolution, Perspectives from East and West, Taipei, Taiwan.

————. 1993. "What is old age?" Paper for the IUSSP Conference on Elderly Populations, Sendai, Japan.

————. 1994. Review article forthcoming in *Ageing and Society* on the final report and research papers of the Carnegie Enquiry into the Third Age.

————. In press. "The aging of European populations and its social effects." Part 1 of chap. 7 of vol. 3 of *L'histoire de la population Européenne*, Paris.

Laslett, Peter, and James S. Fishkin, eds. 1992. *Justice between age groups and generations.* New Haven: Yale University Press.

Lesthaeghe, Ronald. 1991–1992. "The second demographic transition in Western countries: An interpretation." IPD working paper, Free University, Brussels.

Minois, Georges. 1989. *History of old age.* Oxford: Polity Press, Blackwell.

Mitterauer, Michael. [1986] 1992. *A history of youth.* Trans. Graeme Dunphy. Oxford: Blackwell.

Ogawa, Naohiro. 1988. "Aging in China—Demographic alternatives." *Asia-Pacific Population Journal* 3(3): 21–64.

Pelling, Margaret, and Richard M. Smith, eds. 1991. *Life, death and the elderly: Historical perspectives.* London: Routledge.

Petersen, William. 1975. "A demographer's view of prehistoric demography." *Current Anthropology* 15(2): 134–156.

Plakans, Andrejs. 1989. "Stepping down in former times: A comparative assessment of 'retirement' in traditional Europe." In *Age structuring in comparative perspective,* ed. David I. Kertzer and D. W. Schaie, 175–195. Hillsdale, N.J.: Lawrence Erlbaum.

Riddle, S. M. 1992. Doctoral thesis on the elderly worker in England during the later 19th century and earlier 20th century, Cambridge Group.

Riley, James C. 1989. *Sickness, recovery and death.* London: Macmillan.

Riley, Matilda W. 1987. "On the significance of age in sociology." *American Sociological Review* 52: 1–14.

Ruggles, Steven. 1994. "The transformation of American family structure." *American Historical Review* 99(1): 103–128.

Russell, Josiah C. 1948. *British medieval population.* Albuquerque: University of New Mexico Press.

Schofield, Roger, David Reher, and Alain Bideau, eds. 1991. *The decline of mortality in Europe.* Oxford: Oxford University Press.

Smith, Daniel S. 1981. "Historical change in the household structure of the elderly in economically developed societies." In *Aging, stability and change in the family,* ed. R. W. Fogel, E. Hatfield, S. B. Kiesler, and E. Shanas, 91–114. New York and London: Academic Press.

Smith, James E. 1987. "The microsimulation of kin sets and kin counts." In *Family demography: Methods and their applications,* ed. John T. Bongaarts, T. K. Burch, and Kenneth W. Wachter, 249–260. Oxford: Oxford University Press.

————. 1991. "Aging together, aging alone." In *Life span extension: Consequences and open questions,* ed. Frederic C. Ludwig, 81–92. New York: Springer.

Szreter, Simon. 1993. "The idea of demographic transition and the study of fertility change." *Population and Development Review* 19(4): 659–701.

Thane, Pat. 1993. "Old age in English history." In *Toward a cultural history of aging,* ed. Christoph Conrad and H.-J. Kondratowicz, 17–37. Berlin: Deutsche Centrum für Altersfrage.

Thomas, Keith. 1976. "Age and authority in early modern England." *Proceedings of the British Academy* 62: 205–248.

Troyansky, David. 1989. *Old age in the Old Régime: Image and experience in 18th-century France.* Ithaca: Cornell University Press.

U.S. Bureau of the Census. 1937. *Vital statistics of the United States of America, Part 1.* Washington, D.C.: Government Printing Office.

Vallin, Jacques. 1991. "Mortality in Europe from 1720 to 1914: Long-term trends and changes in pattern by sex." In *The decline of mortality in Europe,* ed. Roger Schofield, D. Reher, and A. Bideau, 38–67. Oxford: Oxford University Press.

van de Kaa, D. J. 1987. "Europe's second demographic transition." *Population Bulletin* 42(1): 3–5.

Vinovskis, Maris A. 1989. "Stepping down in former times: The view from colonial and 19th-century America." In *Age structuring in comparative perspective,* ed. David I. Kertzer and K. W. Schaie, 215–225. Hillsdale, N.J.: Lawrence Erlbaum.

Wall, Richard. 1989. "The living arrangements of the elderly in Europe in the 1980s." In *Becoming and being old,* ed. Bill Bytheway, T. Keil, et al., 121–142. London: Sage.

Wrigley, E. A., and R. S. Schofield. [1981] 1989. *The population history of England 1541–1871: A reconstruction.* Cambridge: Cambridge University Press.

Wu, Cangping, and Peng Du. 1992. "Rethinking population aging in China." *Population Science of China* 3: 1–5. (In Chinese.)

Young, Michael, and Tom Schuller. 1991. *Life after work: The arrival of the ageless society.* London: Harper Collins.

Zhao, Zhongwei. In press. "Rapid demographic transition and its influence on kinship networks in East and South Asia, with particular reference to China." *Population Studies.*

PART TWO

Living Arrangements

Elderly Persons and Members of Their Households in England and Wales from Preindustrial Times to the Present

Richard Wall

There is, as Peter Laslett said, a deeply entrenched belief—or rather, misbelief—that in the past all older people in England (those over the age of 65) lived in families, either their own or those of their relatives, particularly those of their married children (Laslett 1989). A considerable amount of research has now been completed which shows that this is not the case, at least in preindustrial times, even though death rates were not so high as to prevent individuals from surviving long enough to see their children marry (Laslett 1977: 184; Laslett, Wachter, and Laslett 1978; Wall 1984, 1992). Disagreement continues, however, as to whether elderly parents were disinclined to co-reside with their married children because they wanted to remain independent as long as possible or whether co-residence was ruled out by the children because of the burden that would have been imposed on their own growing families immediately or in the future. Economic hardship (potential or current) is favored by Michael Anderson to account for the reluctance of the inhabitants of rural preindustrial England as well as of some nineteenth-century towns to welcome elderly persons into their households (Anderson 1972: 229). Laslett, however, appears to believe in the persistence over centuries in England of a family system that encouraged residential independence on the part of elderly parents (Laslett 1989: 119, 121).

This chapter presents a thorough reassessment of the living arrangements of the elderly in preindustrial England. In addition, the extent to which the family and household patterns of the elderly had changed by the end of the nineteenth century also receives consideration. Anderson has argued that the urban industrial revolution of the nineteenth century was associated with a considerable increase in the frequency of co-residence between parents and married children but with evidence of variation from place to place depending on the availability of employment for married women outside of the home, which encouraged co-residence as an elderly parent could provide child care (Anderson 1972: 223, 230). Also relevant, again according to Anderson, was the prosperity of the local community, with co-residence of parents and their married children only practical when the poverty was not too biting (Anderson 1972: 230). The expectation is, therefore, that the residence patterns of the elderly will have varied from one community to another. However, little hard evidence has yet been assembled on this point, either for nineteenth-century or preindustrial England. I hope to rectify this omission by noting the degree of local variation in the residence patterns of the elderly and relating this variation to particular features in the economy and social structure of the areas concerned, despite the fact that direct evidence on the living standards of specific populations in the past is particularly difficult to assemble.

Another factor that demands attention is the impact of the introduction of old age pensions in 1908 on the family and household patterns of the elderly. Prior to the Office of Population Censuses and Surveys making available to the ESRC Cambridge Group anonymized census data on thirteen communities from the period 1891–1921, it had been impossible to investigate this issue as public access to the records of the census (enumerators' books and householders' schedules) only becomes possible one hundred years after their compilation. Two competing hypotheses, however, already await examination (see Anderson 1972: 230–231). The first is that the award of a pension will have improved the ability of the elderly to maintain their residential independence; the second is that a co-resident elderly parent with a pension was a more attractive proposition to a married child as a potential co-resident as the income from the pension could help alleviate any temporary "life cycle" poverty in the child's family.

Finally, an attempt is made to chart the changes that have occurred in the residence patterns of the elderly since 1921, drawing on a number of local surveys and for recent times the Longitudinal Study of the Office of Population Censuses and Surveys. Explanations for such changes are then sought from a range of demographic, economic, and cultural factors. Demographic factors are important because of the potential impact on residence patterns of changes in the proportion of the population marrying, in fertility, and in the spacing of births, as well as an improvement in life expectancy, while economic factors may alter the ability and cultural factors the desire to maintain an independent household in old age.

THE "SAMPLE" POPULATIONS

It is somewhat ironic that households in preindustrial England have received more attention than have households in other parts of Europe, given that the census material that survives for preindustrial England is so much more fragmentary and poorer in quality than that which is available for other parts of Europe. For the period before 1800 in England and Wales, there are only about five hundred censuses, each listing the inhabitants of a particular parish or township at one point in time and no more than eight recording the ages of the inhabitants while also providing adequate detail on relationships of household members to the head of the household. It is impossible, therefore, to produce a random sample of preindustrial populations or to determine how representative the communities for which information does survive might be of English society in general. All that can be claimed is that surviving censuses come from many different parts of the country and from a variety of time periods.

For the purposes of analysis, the populations have been divided into two categories: a group of smaller communities and two larger communities, Lichfield and Stoke, both located in the county of Stafford and enumerated in 1692 and 1701, respectively. Ideally, each of the smaller communities should have been analyzed separately as well, given that the family and household patterns of the elderly may well have varied across both time and space just as did other features of the social structure (see Wall 1987, and for the dates of the censuses and the number of households in each community, see the note to table 2.1, below). In practice there are so few elderly recorded in some of these censuses that any such specific influences on residence patterns would be difficult to distinguish from the effects of random variation. Consequently, the only practical option is to analyze these communities as a group. On the plus side, it is possible to examine the nature of the economy of these smaller populations in some detail as in almost all cases the occupations of the male household heads were specified. This information is set out in table 2.1 and shows that despite the small size of these communities, agriculture was by no means the dominant employment. Farmers large and small (yeoman and husbandmen) represented less than a fifth of all heads of households and even together with the laborers, many of whom would not have been exclusively or perhaps even primarily involved in farm work, constituted slightly under half of all household heads. The remainder were employed in a wide range of manufacturing and service jobs. The majority of these were intended to meet the needs of the local community (as in the case of carpenters, blacksmiths, and wheelwrights, for example), but some were producing goods for more distant markets, as in the case of the nailers of Chilvers Coton. In view of the small size of these populations, however, it is appropriate to consider them as predominantly rural in character despite the presence of some protoindustrial employment.

The two larger populations fall into a quite different category. Lichfield was a city, and the cluster of settlements that would eventually become Stoke-on-Trent already had a reputation for the production of pottery. Both

TABLE 2.1 Occupations of Heads of Household in Preindustrial Rural England by Employment Sector

Employment Sector	*Occupation*	*Percentage of All Employed Heads*[a]
Primary	Yeoman or farmer	11
	Husbandman	7
	Fisherman	2
Laborer	Laborer (unspecified)	30
	Laborer (nonagricultural)	0
Manufacturing	Textiles	5
	Clothing	3
	Food	2
	Wood	4
	Leather	5
	Metal	2
	Tools and furniture	4
	Other products	2
Service	Building	4
	Mining and quarrying	5
	Transport	2
	Distribution and trade	4
	Service	4
	Clergy and professional	3
Other	Gentry	1
	Military	0
	Pauper	0
	Other	0
Total		100

SOURCES: Listings of the population of Ealing, Middlesex, in 1599 (86 households); Chilvers Coton, Warwickshire, in 1684 (176 households); Wetherby, Yorkshire, in 1776 (214 households); Corfe Castle, Dorset, in 1790 (256 households); Ardleigh, Essex, in 1796 (201 households).

[a]N = 823, employed household heads; N = 110, household heads with no occupation; total N = 933.

the censuses unfortunately lack information on the occupations of the inhabitants, but the character of each community is relatively clear from the remarks of travelers and later historians, while references about the relative wealth of the two populations can be derived from an analysis of the hearth tax. Daniel Defoe and Celia Fiennes both commented on Lichfield. Defoe, whether from personal inspection or not, found it "a fine, neat, well-built, and indifferent large city . . . a place of good conversation and good company, above all the towns in this county or the next, I mean Warwickshire or

Derbyshire" (Defoe [1928] 1974: 80). It was the presence in the close of clergy with positions in the cathedral and other wealthy residents, not included in the census, who earned Lichfield this reputation, but there was no doubt some benefit to the rest of the city, which was by far the larger and more populous part. Fiennes was far less impressed, wondering why the bishop and other officials together with the gentry did not remove to Coventry given that Lichfield "stands so low and watrish" (Fiennes 1947: 114).

Accounts of Stoke concentrate on its role as a center of manufacture rather than on what it looked like. Nineteenth-century historians of the pottery industry tended to refer rather disparagingly to the quality and scale of seventeenth-century production. Simeon Shaw and John Ward, for example, imply that no more than between five and eight men may have been employed at a single works and that the distribution of the coarse ware that they produced may seldom have extended farther than the neighboring towns and villages (Shaw [1829] 1970: 65, 96; Ward 1843: 46). There can be no doubt, however, that there was a considerable amount of industrial activity in the area even in the late seventeenth century. Robert Plot's near-contemporary account refers to peacock coal being dug at Handley Green, which is located within the area covered by the census of Stoke, and of iron ore being worked at Longdon (also part of Stoke), while Burslem and Keele contained, respectively, the greatest pottery in the country and one of the only two centers in the country for the manufacture of frying pans (Plot 1686: 122, 126, 158, 335–336). There is ample justification, therefore, for insisting on the independent analysis of the family and household patterns of the elderly in Stoke even though some areas that were included in the census, such as Seabridge, were still predominantly agricultural even in the early nineteenth century (Shaw [1829] 1970: 60).

It is to be expected that the population of Stoke would be considerably poorer than that of Lichfield. Analysis of the hearth tax from the second half of the seventeenth century tends to confirm this. Just over a quarter of chargeable households in Lichfield were assessed on just one hearth compared to two-thirds in Stoke. Twenty-six percent of households were certified as not chargeable in Lichfield against 42 percent of the households in Stoke, although over a third of all the households in Lichfield were themselves deemed too poor to pay either the poor or church rate (William Salt Archaeological Society 1921: 153f.; 1936: 145f.). Unfortunately, how many of this last type of household there may have been in Stoke is unknown, and if they have been included in the hearth tax returns rather than simply omitted, then the differences between Stoke and Lichfield in terms of relative wealth would be considerably less than has been suggested although not totally eliminated. There is some justification, therefore, for considering Stoke the poorer of the two populations, and it will be necessary to take note of this when examining the residence patterns of its elderly inhabitants.

For the period 1891–1921, it has been possible to select the populations it is intended to study in detail rather than rely on the chance survival of a few local censuses, as was the case with the preindustrial period. The choice was dictated by a number of factors. Most of the populations were of interest because aspects of their social structure in other time periods had already received attention, for example, Bethnal Green in the 1950s from Michael Young and Peter Willmott (1957), Swansea in 1960 from Colin Rosser and Chris Harris (1965), Stoke in the mid-nineteenth century through the work of Marguerite Duprée (1989), and working-class York at its end from the celebrated study by B. Seebohm Rowntree (1901). At the same time, care was also taken to ensure that the thirteen populations, all that could be obtained given both the limited research budget and the time that would be required to clean and organize the data, represented a range of geographic and economic environments. This process eventually led to the selection of two "rural" populations, one in the northwest of the country (Morland) and one in the southeast (close to Saffron Walden). Another largely rural population was located in the southwest in the rural district of Axminster but including also the small seaside resort of Seaton. Two additional rural areas surrounded the market towns of Abergavenny in Monmouthshire and Banbury in northeast Oxfordshire, although Abergavenny also embraced the coal and iron working district of Blaenavon. Other areas were primarily or even exclusively industrial: Earsdon, Northumberland, had coal mining; Bolton, Lancashire, specialized in cotton; and Stoke, Staffordshire, as already mentioned, was famous for its pottery and by the late nineteenth century had also developed mining and metal interests. Swansea, too, had an important metal industry, although it was chosen principally for its role as a major port. York was selected as a representative of a large provincial town. Its adult male population was employed in a wide variety of economic activities, with the food, transport, and construction sectors being the most important. Finally, three districts from within the London metropolitan area indicate the varied experiences of an inner-London population (Bethnal Green) and two suburban ones (Walthamstow and Pinner), the former very largely working class, the latter destined to be middle class but in 1891 only just beginning to experience the outward push of suburban London.

For the period after 1921, there are unfortunately only a few ad hoc surveys of a particular population at a particular date. These are also somewhat sparing in their details, indicating the numbers of elderly persons who lived alone, or alone but for the spouse, but rarely how many co-resided with their children (Wall 1992: 66–69). Such surveys suffice, however, to show the pace of change in both the household and the family patterns of the elderly before 1971 when the first of the random cross sections of the national population, taken every decade by the Office of Population Censuses and Surveys in connection with the Longitudinal Study, can be exploited to yield a fuller breakdown of relationships within households. Even this classification, however, is less complete than those obtained from the more flexible data sets that have been produced for the historical populations. It also has to be borne in mind that the Longitudinal Study data sets are too small to permit the study of residence patterns of geographic areas smaller than that of the region, while most historical data are derived from an analysis of residence patterns in particular localities. At present there is no viable alternative strategy. No detailed data set on household patterns at the level of the individual locality is available for the present-day population, while the production of random samples of the national populations in the past are so time consuming and expensive that only one (for 1851) has so far been attempted, with that yielding little more than an overview of family and household patterns (see Anderson 1988, 1990).

ELDERLY PERSONS AND THEIR CO-RESIDENTS IN PREINDUSTRIAL TIMES

There are any number of ways in which the household and family patterns of the elderly can be investigated. One of the more interesting approaches is to consider how many of the elderly were residentially isolated in that they lived either alone or with nonrelatives only. These two types of residence patterns are best considered in tandem as it is notoriously difficult to maintain a consistent definition of the household, and what one enumerator saw as a separate domestic group, another might subsume into a neighboring unit. The problem is serious enough in the nineteenth century when at least there was some attempt by a central authority, the Registrar General, to introduce and enforce a standard definition of the household (Wall 1982), but it is particularly acute with the earlier local censuses that were taken for a variety of purposes by different enumerators who, in compiling their lists of inhabitants, drew lines or left spaces between blocks of names but seldom recorded the procedures they had followed.

Another residence pattern that it is particularly important to distinguish involves those married couples who lived on their own, a very common pattern in contemporary Western societies and one that carries with it the threat of residential isolation should one of the partners die. Also of significance is the frequency of co-residence with a child, married or unmarried, with or without the presence of other people. There was, of course, no guarantee that child and parent would continue to co-reside until the latter's death, but at least there was a certain measure of security that care, economic support, and companionship would be provided if parents became dependent.

Data on these lines are set out in table 2.2 for preindustrial England, distinguishing the group of rural communities from the two urban areas of

Lichfield and Stoke. It is immediately apparent that five of the residence patterns that have been specified (living alone, with nonrelatives only, with a spouse alone, with a spouse and other persons, and with a child) capture the vast majority of the experience. For an elderly person to live with other relatives in the absence of a spouse or child was extremely uncommon in any of the communities. It is also apparent that relatively few elderly persons in preindustrial times lived totally alone: never more than 5 percent of elderly men and at most 16 percent of elderly women. As is argued above, however, those who lived only with nonrelatives should perhaps also be considered at risk of residential isolation. There were considerable numbers of such people, particularly women, in Lichfield and Stoke, reflecting perhaps the movement of women late in life into towns where there would be a broader range of cheaper accommodation. Taken together with the number of elderly who lived totally alone, it can be seen that about one in ten elderly men rising to a fifth in Stoke and around a third of elderly women rising to almost half in Lichfield were residentially isolated on the basis of the definitions set out above. These proportions are not substantially different from the proportions of persons who lived totally alone in England and Wales in 1971, as we shall see later. One important qualification has to be added. The censuses of both Lichfield and Stoke do not always specify the relationships of those persons who were not part of the nuclear family of the head of the

TABLE 2.2   Preindustrial England: Residence Patterns of Persons Aged 65+

	Residence Patterns[a]	Rural English Communities (1599–1796)	Lichfield (1692)	Stoke (1701)
Males	Alone	2%	3%	5%
	Nonrelatives only	11	8	15
	Spouse only	19	24	10
	Spouse and others (no child)	15	11	13
	Child with or without other persons	49	54	54
	Other relatives (no spouse or child)	4	0	3
	N	104	37	39
Females	Alone	16%	15%	8%
	Nonrelatives only	16	34	31
	Spouse only	17	8	3
	Spouse and others (no child)	9	7	7
	Child with or without other persons	37	34	46
	Other relatives (no spouse or child)	5	2	5
	N	101	67	39

[a]The residents of institutions are excluded from this and all subsequent tables.

household, and the number of occasions on which elderly women, in particular, lived only with nonrelatives may, in consequence, be overstated. In contrast, relationships in the censuses of the rural communities are well specified, and there seems no reason to doubt that overall a third of elderly women had no relative of any sort present in their households.

However, in all the preindustrial communities, urban as well as rural, more common than either living alone or with nonrelatives was for an elderly person to co-reside with a child. Around half of elderly men shared a household with a child, married or unmarried, as did more than a third of elderly women. That fewer elderly women than elderly men lived with a child may seem surprising, as it might have been expected that when elderly women were widowed they would be taken into the household of a married child. In fact, as table 2.3 makes clear, higher proportions of elderly women than of elderly men were living with a married child, but there were many more elderly men with a co-resident never-married child. Finally, it should be noted that it was relatively rare in preindustrial times for an elderly couple to live on their own. In Stoke, in particular, there were very few such households, but even in the rural communities fewer than a fifth of elderly men and women lived alone with their spouses. This is in marked contrast to the situation of the elderly in Britain today, when more than six in every ten elderly men and a third of elderly women are living just with their spouses (Arber and Ginn 1992: 99).

A different perspective on the residence patterns of elderly persons is suggested by measuring the frequency with which they lived with a range of related and unrelated persons regardless of the number and type of other persons who might (or might not) be present. Table 2.3 contains some data

TABLE 2.3   Preindustrial England: Percentage of Persons Aged 65+
with Co-residing Spouse, Child, or Nonrelatives

	Co-residents[a]	Rural English Communities (1599–1796)	Lichfield (1692)	Stoke (1701)
Males	Spouse	59	70	59
	Never-married child	38	46	51
	Ever-married child	12	8	3
	Nonrelatives	44	21	28
Females	Spouse	41	21	26
	Never-married child	21	25	31
	Ever-married child	17	9	15
	Nonrelatives	33	50	51

[a]Combinations of co-residents might be present in some cases, hence the percentages do not sum to 100.

along these lines for preindustrial England. For elderly men, the most likely co-resident was a spouse, followed in the case of Stoke and Lichfield by unmarried children. Co-residence with a married child was considerably rarer. Even in the rural communities, only just over 10 percent of elderly men lived with a married child. By contrast, the presence of a nonrelative, whether servant, boarder, or lodger, was somewhat more likely, and in the rural communities where 44 percent of elderly men had at least one nonrelative in their household, they were a more frequent co-resident than unmarried children.

The position of elderly women was somewhat different. In the first place, far fewer than was the case with elderly men lived with a spouse. This is only to be expected as in preindustrial times, like today, women generally outlived their spouses and were in any case on average a few years younger than their spouses on marriage or remarriage. Even so, approximately four in ten elderly women in the rural preindustrial communities were still married. That in Lichfield this proportion fell to about a fifth indicates there may well have been considerable variation from place to place in the pattern of living arrangements, probably reflecting on this occasion not only the higher mortality of urban areas but, as was suggested above, the movement of widows into localities offering a range of cheaper accommodation. Second, elderly women were less likely than were elderly men to live with an unmarried child. In this case it could be argued that the living arrangements of elderly men and women differ, because in a significant number of cases a radical reconstruction of the parental household occurred only after the death of the father. Such a reconstruction might involve both the departure and/or marriage of any children still resident and the movement of the newly widowed mother into the household of a married child. Only repetitive high-quality censuses or population registers, neither of which are available for preindustrial England, could enable the process to be traced in detail. The third point to make is that in both Lichfield and Stoke, half of all elderly women lived with a nonrelative, whereas fewer than a third of elderly men shared a household with a nonrelative. This reverses the situation in the rural communities, where elderly men were more likely to co-reside with nonrelatives than were elderly women. As noted above, the numbers of women in Lichfield and Stoke who co-resided with nonrelatives may be somewhat inflated because not all relationships between household members were identified in the censuses, but it is unlikely that so many relationships were unstated as to reduce the proportions of elderly women living with nonrelatives to the same level as those for elderly men.

ELDERLY PERSONS AND THEIR CO-RESIDENTS
BETWEEN 1891 AND 1921

The above account of the residence pattern of elderly people in preindustrial England can now be directly compared with the situation in the late nineteenth century and early twentieth century by drawing on the anonymized data that the Office of Population Censuses and Surveys has recently made available to the Cambridge Group. Table 2.4 parallels table 2.2 by indicating how many elderly men or women were residentially isolated, or lived with their spouses, either alone or with other people, or co-resided with a child at each of the censuses of 1891, 1901, 1911, and 1921. Few differences from preindustrial times are evident. For men the most dramatic change is the rise from a very low level in the proportions who lived with other relatives in the absence of their spouse or child. There may also have been a slight increase in the proportion of elderly men living entirely on their own. In the case of elderly women, it is clear that far fewer in the late nineteenth and early twentieth century than in preindustrial times lived with nonrelatives in the absence of relatives, while more co-resided either with a child or with other relatives in the absence of a spouse or child. Yet even after a century of great social and economic change it would be difficult to substantiate the claim that the households of either elderly men or elderly women in 1921 differed in fundamental respects from those formed by elderly people in preindustrial times. The other point worth making is how little alteration there was between 1891 and 1921 in the household and family patterns of the elderly. For elderly men there is evidence of a slight rise in the percentage living on their own, and there was also a steady increase in the proportions of both elderly men and elderly women resident with a child. These increases were balanced by a decrease in the proportions of elderly people who were still married but who did not co-reside with a

TABLE 2.4   Thirteen English and Welsh Communities, 1891–1921: Residence Patterns of Persons Aged 65+

	Residence Patterns	*1891*	*1901*	*1911*	*1921*
Males	Alone	5%	4%	6%	6%
	Nonrelatives only	13	11	12	11
	Spouse only	16	18	15	18
	Spouse and others (no child)	12	9	9	10
	Child with or without other persons	48	51	52	52
	Other relatives (no spouse or child)	6	6	5	6
	N	1,696	1,764	2,174	2,597
Females	Alone	11%	11%	10%	11%
	Nonrelatives only	13	10	12	10
	Spouse only	10	11	9	12
	Spouse and others (no child)	7	6	5	5
	Child with or without other persons	47	50	52	52
	Other relatives (no spouse or child)	12	12	12	10
	N	2,112	2,244	2,788	3,289

SOURCE: Anonymized data from the censuses of 1891–1921.

child. In all other respects it is impossible to detect any consistent trends affecting the residence patterns of the elderly in this period.

An absence of change between 1891 and 1921 does not, of course, pre-
clude significant developments between preindustrial times and the 1890s.
Detailed data on family and household patterns in almost any community
in the country can be abstracted from each of the decadal censuses beginning with 1851, but surprisingly few analyses have been completed given the
wealth of information available, and little enough has emerged even from
Anderson's 2 percent nationwide sample of enumerators' books from the
censuses of 1851. Anderson, however, has now calculated the proportions
of elderly men and women living alone, with nonrelatives only, with a child,
or with other relatives (Anderson 1988: 436).

Of the elderly men in 1851, 5 percent lived totally alone, 16 percent with
nonrelatives only, 5 percent with relatives other than a spouse and child,
and 45 percent with a child. Fewer elderly men co-resided with a child in
1851 than in preindustrial times or between 1891 and 1921. However, the
percentage who lived with nonrelatives in 1851 is considerably higher than
it was to be in the late nineteenth or early twentieth century and higher also
than what it had been in any of the preindustrial populations. The frequency with which elderly men lived with relatives other than a spouse or
child is also in excess of that occurring within the preindustrial communities, although generally below the levels recorded in the later years of the
nineteenth century and in the early part of the twentieth century. Finally,
the proportion of elderly men living alone in 1851 appears to differ little
from that between 1891 and 1921.

In a number of respects the situation with regard to the residence patterns of elderly women appears to be similar. For example, there is the same
rise between 1851 and the early twentieth century in the proportions who
shared a household with a child (46 percent in 1851 and between 47 percent
and 52 percent during the period 1891–1921), and the proportion who lived
with other relatives is, as is the case with elderly men, above that of preindustrial times but below that of the late nineteenth and early twentieth
century. Elderly women, like elderly men, were also more likely in 1851 to
be living only with nonrelatives than would elderly women in the late nineteenth and early twentieth century. The differences in their residence patterns as compared with those of elderly men lie in the fact that in 1851 they
appear to have been less likely to have lived alone than was the case either in
the late nineteenth century or in preindustrial times, while they were much
less likely compared to women in the preindustrial urban populations to have
lived with nonrelatives in the absence of any member of their own family.

The above account of family and household patterns of elderly people
between 1891 and 1921 can also be supplemented by measuring the frequency with which the elderly co-resided with a spouse, with never-married

or ever-married children, or with nonrelatives whether or not other persons were present. Data on these lines are set out in table 2.5 and point to a marked fall, particularly between 1911 and 1921, in the frequency with which both elderly men and elderly women lived with nonrelatives. The same decade also witnessed a substantial rise in the proportions living with a married child, perhaps as a result of the housing crisis that followed the end of the First World War (for a further account, see Wall 1989). Between 1891 and 1911, a steadily increasing proportion of elderly persons lived with an unmarried child. No definite trend, however, is visible as regards the proportion of elderly living with a spouse.

These proportions can now be compared with those that pertained in preindustrial England (see table 2.3). Focusing first on the situation of elderly men, it is apparent that by the end of the nineteenth century, fewer elderly men were living with a spouse than had been the case in preindustrial times. In addition, between 1891 and 1921, many fewer elderly men lived with a never-married child than had done so in Lichfield and Stoke. However, between 1891 and 1921, many more elderly men lived with their married children than had been the case in any of the preindustrial populations. Trends in the frequency with which elderly men co-resided with nonrelatives are, however, more difficult to interpret, as in 1891 it was somewhat more likely that elderly men would share a household with a nonrelative than would elderly men from Lichfield and Stoke but somewhat less likely than would men from the rural preindustrial populations.

In addition, a number of the contrasts between the living arrangements of elderly men in preindustrial times and at the end of the nineteenth century do not apply in the case of elderly women. First, the proportions of el-

TABLE 2.5   Thirteen English and Welsh Communities, 1891–1921: Percentage of Elderly Persons with Co-residing Spouse, Child, or Nonrelatives

	Co-residents[a]	1891	1901	1911	1921
Males	Spouse	57	56	55	57
	Never-married child	36	38	40	38
	Ever-married child	16	17	16	20
	Nonrelatives	35	31	31	25
Females	Spouse	30	31	29	32
	Never-married child	29	31	34	32
	Ever-married child	21	22	23	25
	Nonrelatives	34	29	29	24

SOURCE: Anonymized data from the censuses of 1891–1921.
[a]Combinations of co-residents might be present in some cases, hence the percentages do not sum to 100.

derly women still living with a spouse were some way below the proportion of elderly women in rural preindustrial England who co-resided with a spouse but were not as low as the proportions reported for the towns of Lichfield and Stoke. This contrasts with the situation of elderly men, who were less likely to be resident with a spouse than were men from any of the preindustrial populations. However, more elderly women were living with a never-married child in the nineteenth century than had lived with a never-married child in the rural communities in preindustrial times and by 1911 more even than had lived with a never-married child in Stoke in 1701. By contrast, the proportions of elderly men living with never-married children were much lower than they had been in preindustrial Stoke and Lichfield. The one major similarity in the trends over time in the residence patterns of elderly men and women was that co-residence with a married child had become much more probable by 1891.

A further perspective on the residence patterns of the elderly in the late nineteenth and early twentieth century requires that some account be taken of the degree of spatial variation. The data supplied by the Office of Population Censuses and Surveys are ideal for this purpose, because, as mentioned earlier, the thirteen populations were selected partly because of their geographic and economic diversity. To the extent, therefore, that household and family patterns are influenced by the nature of the local economy, the range of variation suggested is likely to embrace as much of the experience of the time as one could reasonably hope to cover, given that budgetary and time constraints precluded the taking of a proper national sample. Moreover, the focus on distinctive environments was enhanced due to the fact that from within each area a specific sample was drawn comprising a number of usually contiguous enumeration districts.

To illustrate the degree of variation from place to place in the residence patterns of the elderly, tables 2.6 and 2.7 set out the proportions of elderly in all thirteen communities in 1921 who were residentially isolated, or lived alone with their spouse or with their spouse and other persons but without a child, or lived with a child with or without other persons being present, or co-resided with more distant relatives. As measured by the coefficient of variation, there was least variation in the proportions of elderly men living with a child and most variation in the proportions living alone. Overall, about 6 percent of elderly men had no one else present in their household in 1921 (see table 2.4), whereas in Bethnal Green 14 percent lived alone and in Earsdon not one elderly man lived alone (table 2.6). By contrast, the percentage of elderly men co-residing with a child ranged from a high of 64 percent in Stoke to a low of 45 percent in Saffron Walden, Morland, and Bethnal Green. More variation is visible in the residence patterns of elderly women living with a child: the range extends from 63 percent in Stoke to 39 percent in Axminster.

TABLE 2.6 Thirteen English and Welsh Communities, 1921: Residence Patterns of Elderly Males

Residence Patterns	Abergavenny	Axminster	Banbury	Bethnal Green	Bolton	Earsdon
Alone	5%	4%	9%	14%	7%	0%
Nonrelatives only	18	8	8	10	12	11
Spouse only	12	24	22	21	15	17
Spouse and others (no child)	6	11	9	4	7	8
Child with or without other persons	51	49	49	45	56	58
Other relatives (no spouse or child)	7	4	2	6	4	6
N	249	226	249	125	104	146

Residence Patterns	Morland	Pinner	Saffron Walden	Stoke	Swansea	Walthamstow	York
Alone	9%	3%	12%	2%	6%	6%	5%
Nonrelatives only	6	13	3	12	8	12	11
Spouse only	18	14	23	8	16	18	19
Spouse and others (no child)	9	10	10	8	9	7	10
Child with or without other persons	45	54	45	64	54	53	50
Other relatives (no spouse or child)	12	7	7	6	7	4	5
N	139	182	251	170	225	258	293

SOURCE: Anonymized data from the census of 1921.

TABLE 2.7   Thirteen English and Welsh Communities, 1921: Residence Patterns of Elderly Females

Residence Patterns	Abergavenny	Axminster	Banbury	Bethnal Green	Bolton	Earsdon
Alone	9%	9%	14%	16%	13%	5%
Nonrelatives only	9	16	11	10	12	5
Spouse only	10	16	16	12	4	12
Spouse and others (no child)	5	4	7	3	4	5
Child with or without other persons	58	39	43	49	59	62
Other relatives (no spouse or child)	9	15	9	8	8	9
N	223	298	328	188	143	129

Residence Patterns	Morland	Pinner	Saffron Walden	Stoke	Swansea	Walthamstow	York
Alone	17%	4%	16%	7%	6%	11%	13%
Nonrelatives only	6	13	5	11	8	10	12
Spouse only	12	9	20	5	10	10	10
Spouse and others (no child)	5	4	6	5	4	4	5
Child with or without other persons	48	58	43	63	62	58	48
Other relatives (no spouse or child)	13	11	9	10	9	6	12
N	168	270	276	245	278	353	390

SOURCE: Anonymized data from the census of 1921.

It might be expected that many of these differences could be readily explained by relating them to specific features of the local economies, even if these are broadly defined as "agricultural," coal mining, and inner urban, but in practice such relationships are not easily detected. For example, although two of the industrial areas, Earsdon and Stoke, have a very low proportion of elderly men living on their own, other industrial areas such as Bolton and Swansea have only "average" proportions. Conversely, comparable (and low) proportions of elderly men living on their own occur in places that are known to be strikingly dissimilar (e.g., Stoke and Pinner). It may well be, of course, that a more detailed specification of the economic character of the areas in question, or possibly of subareas within them, would clarify the nature of the relationships between economic factors and household forms. This must await further analysis of the data. What can, however, be pointed out now is that it is in the rural communities around Saffron Walden that the family and household patterns of the elderly in 1921 took on their most "modern" look, with higher proportions of both elderly men and women living on their own, or with only their spouse, and lower proportions with nonrelatives only, or with a child, than was generally the case in 1921.

RESIDENCE PATTERNS OF THE ELDERLY AFTER 1921

Keeping track of the residence patterns of the elderly after 1921 is not a particularly easy task because of the scarcity of detailed surveys and the degree of variability in the patterns recorded in those surveys that were taken. As early as 1929, the New Survey of London Life and Labour reported that 19 percent of elderly men and 37 percent of elderly women from the London working class were living alone, percentages that for women in particular were far in excess of those in Bethnal Green only eight years earlier (Gordon 1988: 26). Yet as the Second World War ended, in another working-class population, the mid-Rhondda, just 1 percent of men and 7 percent of women over the age of 65 lived alone (Nuffield Foundation 1947: 140–141). Such a low incidence of living alone is matched among the populations enumerated in 1921 only by Earsdon in the case of elderly men and by Pinner, Swansea, Stoke, and Earsdon again in the case of elderly women (see tables 2.6 and 2.7).

To measure the pace of change in the residence patterns of the elderly in the nation as a whole, it is necessary to continue to limit the comparison to the percentage of the population who lived alone. Comparisons can then be made with the results of a national survey taken in 1945 as well as with the far better-known investigation of Ethel Shanas, Peter Townsend, Dorothy Wedderburn, and others into the living arrangements of the elderly in three Western countries in the early 1960s (Shanas et al. 1968). In

TABLE 2.8   Britain, 1921–1981: Percentage of Persons Aged 65+
Who Lived Alone

	Males	*Females*
1921	6	11
1945	6	16
1962	11	30
1971	13	36
1981	17	42

SOURCES: 1921 anonymized data on thirteen local populations from census of England and Wales 1921; 1945, calculated from national sample of the British population in Thomas 1947; 1962, national sample of the British population in Shanas et al. 1968: 186; 1971 and 1981, calculated from the national samples of the English and Welsh populations taken by the Office of Population Censuses and Surveys for the purpose of the Longitudinal Study.

table 2.8, the evidence of these two surveys as to the percentages of elderly men and women living alone in 1945 and 1962 is compared with the percentages in 1921 for the group of thirteen local populations (see table 2.4) and in 1971 and 1981 for England and Wales as a whole, derived from the samples taken for the purposes of the Longitudinal Study. Between 1921 and 1945, there was no change at all in the propensity of elderly men to live alone, while just 5 percent more women over the age of 65 lived alone in 1945 than had done so in 1921. Much more evidence of change is visible by 1962, although the degree of change in the residence patterns of both elderly men and elderly women that occurred between 1945 and 1962 was still somewhat less than that which was to take place between 1962 and 1981.

One additional perspective is possible, and that is a consideration of the residence patterns of the nonmarried elderly, as in table 2.9. The decision to study this particular group of elderly was largely dictated by the fact that it is the only group whose residence patterns can be examined through to 1981 using the population samples of the Longitudinal Study, as the way in which the data streams were defined in the study renders it impossible to determine whether married couples shared their household with other relatives or nonrelatives. Even so, to extend the perspective to 1981, a fairly basic classification of residence patterns is all that is possible, and table 2.9 is limited to showing how many elderly men and women lived with relatives, or only with nonrelatives, or alone. However, on the positive side, it should be emphasized that the nonmarried elderly are a very important group, not only because they constituted a large proportion of the total population over the age of 65 (e.g., more than four in ten of the men and two-thirds of the women aged 65+ in 1921) but because, lacking a spouse, they were particularly exposed to the risk of residential isolation.

In the late nineteenth and early twentieth century, as table 2.9 makes clear, approximately two-thirds of the elderly women and just under two-

TABLE 2.9   England and Wales, 1891–1981: Percentage of Nonmarried Persons Aged 65+ Who Lived Alone, with Nonrelatives Only, or with Relatives

		1891	1901	1911	1921	1962	1971	1981
Males	Alone	12	10	13	15	37	49	63
	Nonrelatives only	29	25	27	23	8	15	12
	Relatives	59	65	59	62	55	36	26
	N	721	767	970	1,115	303	6,681	8,209
Females	Alone	16	16	14	16	45	57	65
	Nonrelatives only	19	14	16	15	5	8	5
	Relatives	65	70	70	69	50	35	26
	N	1,474	1,540	1,953	2,224	986	24,318	27,752

thirds of the elderly men who were not currently married nevertheless lived with at least one person to whom they were related. By 1962, this proportion had fallen, but not dramatically so. The real change had occurred with a rise in the percentage of the nonmarried elderly, both men and women, who lived alone and a marked decline in the proportion living only with non-relatives. Much the greater part of the rise between 1921 and 1962 in the proportion of elderly men living alone can therefore be explained by the decline in the percentage who were in some senses already economically in-dependent in that they budgeted separately from the nonrelatives with whom they lived but lacked the wherewithal to establish their own house-holds. About a third of the change in the residence patterns of elderly women can also be explained in this way. After 1962, the situation appears to change considerably with a very spectacular fall in the percentage of both elderly men and elderly women living with relatives, particularly between 1962 and 1971, matched by a continuing expansion in the proportion liv-ing on their own. The proportions living only with nonrelatives, in contrast, appear to have drifted upward between 1962 and 1971, only to fall back again by 1981.

CULTURAL, ECONOMIC, AND DEMOGRAPHIC DETERMINANTS OF THE LIVING ARRANGEMENTS OF THE ELDERLY

At this point it is appropriate to return to the issue of whether the primary factors influencing the temporal and spatial variations in the residence pat-terns of the elderly were cultural, economic, or demographic. Both demo-graphic and economic factors have clearly had a large part to play in in-creasing in the longer term the numbers of elderly who live on their own or as couples on their own, by decreasing the frequency with which the elderly live with either nonrelatives or their children. The role of economic factors is evident in the long-term decline in the frequency of sharing a household with nonrelatives. Some of these nonrelatives encountered in the households of the elderly in preindustrial society would have been servants, but many others would have been lodgers or boarders or even unrelated people put together into one household by Poor Law authorities anxious to economize by arranging for the younger poor to care for the elderly poor (Erith 1978; Robin 1990: 208). It is often impossible to establish just how independent some of the lodgers and other unrelated people may have been of the household to which they were attached, as living spaces were so circumscribed. Over time, as the rise in living standards has allowed the standard of accommodation to be improved beyond measure, it has become much easier to see which individuals are living independently in the sense that they occupy separate accommodation. However, the lodgers and boarders of earlier times will have budgeted separately from the main household and on the definition of "independent living" ought perhaps to be judged as forming their own "households." From this perspective, therefore, some of the increase in the numbers of elderly living on their own is more apparent than real, and the role of economic forces in helping to bring about the new household forms rather less significant than might appear at first sight.

It is also interesting that the introduction of old age pensions in 1908 seemed to have little visible impact on the living arrangements of the elderly. The award of a pension, even if the initial payments were neither universal nor particularly generous (Thane 1990: 34–35), should have enabled a higher proportion of the elderly to maintain their own household. As mentioned above, this was Michael Anderson's expectation, and B. Seebohm Rowntree hinted at the existence of such a tendency in York when he compared the households of the poor in 1936 with those of the poor in 1899 (Anderson 1972: 230–231; Rowntree 1941: 114). There was no sign of this, however, when the censuses between 1891 and 1921 for the thirteen communities were analyzed (see table 2.4). A slight rise is visible from 1911 in the percentage of elderly men living alone but not in the percentage of elderly women, nor in the percentage of either elderly men or elderly women who lived "independently" in that they resided alone or only with nonrelatives. Nor is there any evidence to support Anderson's alternative suggestion that the introduction of the old age pension may have made it more feasible for sons or daughters with families of their own to offer to shelter their elderly parents in case of need (Anderson 1972: 231, quoting the statement of one pensioner circa 1912). Table 2.4 shows that although the percentage of elderly men and women living with a child did increase between 1901 and

1911, this merely continued a trend of the preceding decade that had therefore begun well in advance of the introduction of the old age pension.

Other changes in the living arrangements of the elderly are demographic in origin. Improvements in life expectancy over the past two centuries have obviously increased the proportion of those who survive through to old age, yet in the Britain of today the proportion of elderly women who live with a spouse is lower than the proportion who lived with a spouse in preindustrial rural England. The reason for this is that there has been a greater improvement in the life expectancy of females than of males. This has prolonged the period women spend as widows while ensuring that many more men than in the past have a spouse to provide care and companionship in old age. Another demographic change of possibly even greater significance for the living arrangements of the elderly is, paradoxically, the fall in fertility beginning in the later nineteenth century and the altered pattern of birth spacing within marriage. Prior to the demographic transition, women continued to bear children into their late 30s or early 40s. When parents reached the age of 65, it was entirely feasible, therefore, for them still to have unmarried children in their household without these children necessarily having to postpone unduly the date of their own marriage, or not marrying at all, unless of course one or both parents survived into extreme old age and still insisted on keeping the parental household intact and unchanged. In a present-day population, it is much less likely that the elderly will have a never-married child on whom they can rely, while the earlier cessation of childbearing results in children leaving the parental household much earlier in the life of the parents. The increase in the proportions who eventually marry (or cohabit with a partner) will simply intensify these trends.

It took some time, of course, before the fertility fall of the late nineteenth century and the early part of the twentieth century came to affect directly the lives of the elderly. That is why there is so little sign of change in family and household patterns of the elderly by 1921 (see table 2.5). No firm evidence can be produced to demonstrate how soon after 1921 the decline in the percentage of elderly living with an unmarried child may have established itself, but it was by no means over when Ethel Shanas and colleagues undertook their research in 1962 (Shanas et al. 1968: 186). According to their study, 22 percent of elderly men and the same percentage of elderly women in Britain in 1962 co-resided with a never-married child, percentages that were indeed lower but not substantially lower than had been the case for the elderly in 1921 when 38 percent of men and 32 percent of women over the age of 65 lived with a never-married child (see table 2.5).

Economic and demographic factors also undoubtedly help to account for much of the variation in residence patterns that emerges when the experience of one local community is compared with that of another. The precise impact of the factors, however, is difficult to measure. In part this is because the fertility and mortality rates to which the families of the inhabitants had been exposed are not easily calculated, as a large proportion of the adult population will not have been born in the area in which they were resident at the time of the census. In addition, however, there is the problem of identifying the likely intercorrelations between a range of economic and demographic factors, on the one hand, and the various components of the household, on the other. One example would be when a buoyant local market pushed some sections of the native population toward both earlier marriage and an earlier exit from the parental home while at the same time the improvement in the standard of living and consequent fall in mortality make it less likely that the parental home would be broken by out-migration of the children following an early parental death. In fact, what is particularly surprising is that the residence patterns of the elderly from the various populations are not more different given the differences in their economies and in the level of epidemic and endemic mortality to which they were exposed. It was established above that the population of Stoke in 1701 was in all probability considerably poorer than that of Lichfield in 1692. Their economies certainly differed as both did from those of the rural populations that were also undoubtedly healthier. E. A. Wrigley and R. S. Schofield, for example, suggest that mortality in the most sparsely inhabited rural parishes such as Hartland in Devon might be two or three times lower than that in a substantial town (Wrigley and Schofield 1983: 178–179), although the difference in the level of mortality between Lichfield and Stoke and the pooled data on the rural populations included above may be somewhat less than this as the latter did not include any community quite as remote or with such a scattered settlement pattern as Hartland. Nevertheless, in terms of the household patterns of the elderly, Lichfield, Stoke, and the rural populations appear remarkably similar. Strikingly, the 54 percent of men over the age of 65 in Lichfield who lived with a child is the same as in Stoke and just 5 percent more than did so in the rural populations. For elderly women, the range is from 37 percent in the rural populations to 46 percent in Stoke.

Much the same point can be made in connection with the thirteen populations enumerated in 1921. There is undoubtedly some variation in residence patterns between one population and another, usually somewhat greater in the case of elderly women than elderly men, but the variation is not that large given that the thirteen include some of the least healthy areas of the country, such as Stoke, as well as some low mortality populations such as Morland and Axminster (*Annual reports* of the Registrar General). There is no evidence either that any of the different local economies, whether mining, industrial, suburban, or agricultural, produced a unique family pattern. This might seem to suggest that there might be different "cultural" preferences in particular areas favoring the formation of one type of household rather than another. However, the evidence that would prove that such preferences existed and were acted upon has yet to be produced, and it seems more likely that such limited variation as there is in residence patterns does reflect the different demographic and economic circumstances of the various populations. Moreover, it is worth emphasizing that even a shared characteristic, for example, a high proportion of elderly people living alone, can occur in different demographic and economic contexts, as in the case of Saffron Walden and Bethnal Green.

Over the longer term, cultural influences may have exerted a greater impact on the sort of households that were formed. Again, however, the evidence is lacking which would establish definitely the existence of norms prescribing the residence rules for various sections of the population. By contrast with the frequent references that can be found to various forms of behavior that were deemed to be morally offensive or contrary to the natural order, such as conceiving a child out of wedlock, mésalliances, and scolding wives, little appears to have been said about when, or even whether, children should leave the parental home, or about the rights of an elderly parent to live with a child. Such norms, if they existed, therefore, must have been internalized rather than embodied in a legal code, perceived as a matter of choice by the parties immediately concerned even though their neighbors would have reacted in the same way if faced with the same situation. Laslett (1984: 364) has labeled norms of this type "noumenal normative rules," holding them applicable in particular to the process by which in England children on their marriage regularly established a household independent from that of their parents. A wider applicability, governing, for example, whether the elderly should maintain an independent household even if widowed, is also possible. Yet merely to posit the existence of such norms in one sense solves very little as Laslett himself realized. The origin of the rule system and the reason why different rules are applied in some other parts of Europe remain to be explained and could conceivably be derived from the nature of the relationship between the population and its resource base at some distant point in the past.

Also requiring explanation is why in the recent past, particularly from the 1960s, there has been the explosion in the proportion of elderly living on their own. It was suggested above that demographic change, particularly the fall in fertility earlier in the century, probably accounts for a good deal of the decline in the proportion of elderly persons residing with their children. However, it should be noted that some other investigations of the trends in family and household patterns over recent decades in a number of Western countries have concluded that not all of the trend can be explained by improvements in the standard of living and modifications to the age structure of the population (for some of the arguments, see Michael, Fuchs, and Scott 1980; Pampel 1983; Schwarz 1983). This apparent inconsistency may arise from the fact that too much of the research has focused on possible period effects, whether the primary concern is with cultural, demographic, or economic determinants of residence patterns, when cohort effects may be of equal or even greater significance. The data that would allow such hypotheses to be investigated do not exist for England, but it seems plausible that each generation that reached old age after 1945 was wealthier than its predecessor, rendering the members of these generations increasingly reluctant to disband their households to move in with their children or other relatives even in extreme old age. In countries, such as the Netherlands, with population registers that can be linked to income tax and real property records, such hypotheses could be subjected to a thorough testing (see Bulder 1993 on the Netherlands before 1940).

REFERENCES

Anderson, Michael. 1972. "Household structure and the industrial revolution: Mid-nineteenth-century Preston in comparative perspective." In *Household and family in past time,* ed. Peter Laslett and Richard Wall, 215–235. Cambridge: Cambridge University Press.

———. 1988. "Households, families and individuals: Some preliminary results from the national sample from the 1851 census of Great Britain." *Continuity and Change* 3(3): 421–438.

———. 1990. "The social implications of demographic change." In *The Cambridge social history of Britain 1750–1950.* Vol. 2. *People and their environment,* ed. F. M. L. Thompson, 1–70. Cambridge: Cambridge University Press.

Arber, Sara, and Jay Ginn. 1992. "In sickness and in health: Care-giving, gender and the independence of elderly people." In *Families and households: Divisions and change,* ed. Catherine Marsh and Sara Arber, 86–105. London: Macmillan.

Bulder, E. A. M. 1993. "The social economics of old age: Strategies to maintain income in later life in the Netherlands 1880–1940." Ph.D. dissertation, Tinbergen Institute, Erasmus University, Rotterdam.

Defoe, Daniel. [1928] 1974. *A tour through the whole of the island of Great Britain,* ed. G. D. F. Cole and D. C. Browning. London: J. M. Dent and Sons.

Duprée, Marguerite. 1989. "The community perspective in family history: The potteries during the nineteenth century." In *The first modern society: Essays in English history in honour of Laurence Stone,* ed. A. L. Beier, David Cannadine, and James M. Rosenheim, 549–573. Cambridge: Cambridge University Press.

Erith, F. H. 1978. *Ardleigh in 1796: Its farms, families and local governments.* East Bergholt: Hugh Tempest Radfort.

Fiennes, Celia. 1947. *The journal of Celia Fiennes,* ed. Christopher Morris. London: Cresset Press.

Gordon, Chris. 1988. "The myth of family care: The elderly in the early 1930s." Discussion Paper 29, Centre for Economic and Related Disciplines, London School of Economics.

Laslett, Peter. 1977. *Family life and illicit love in earlier generations.* Cambridge: Cambridge University Press.

———. 1984. "The family as a knot of individual interests." In *Households: Comparative and historical studies of the domestic group,* ed. Robert McC. Netting, Richard R. Wilk, and J. Eric Arnould, 353–379. Berkeley, Los Angeles, and London: University of California Press.

———. 1989. *A fresh map of life: The emergence of the Third Age.* London: Weidenfeld and Nicholson.

Laslett, Peter, Kenneth W. Wachter, and Robert Laslett. 1978. "The English evidence on household structure compared with the outcome of microsimulation." In *Statistical studies of historical social structure,* ed. Kenneth W. Wachter, Eugene A. Hammel, and Peter Laslett, 65–87. New York: Academic Press.

Michael, Robert T., Victor R. Fuchs, and Sharon R. Scott. 1980. "Changes in the propensity to live alone 1950–1976." *Demography* 17(1): 39–56.

Nuffield Foundation. 1947. *Old people: Report of a survey committee on the problems of ageing and the case of old people.* London: Nuffield Foundation.

Pampel, Fred C. 1983. "Changes in propensity to live alone: Evidence from consecutive cross-national surveys 1960–1976." *Demography* 20(4): 433–447.

Plot, Robert. 1686. *A natural history of Staffordshire.* Oxford: Timothy Halton.

Registrar General of England and Wales. 1837–. *Annual reports.* London: HMSO.

Robin, Jean. 1990. "The relief of poverty in mid-nineteenth-century Colyton." *Rural History* 1(2): 193–218.

Rosser, Colin, and Chris Harris. 1965. *The family and social change: A study of family and kinship in a South Wales town.* London: Routledge and Kegan Paul.

Rowntree, B. Seebohm. 1901. *Poverty: A study of town life.* 2d ed. London: Thomas Nelson.

———. 1941. *Poverty and progress: A second social survey of York.* London: Longmans, Green.

Schwarz, Karl. 1983. "Die Alleinlebenden." *Zeitschrift für Bevolkungswissenschaft* 9(2): 241–257.

Shanas, Ethel, Peter Townsend, Dorothy Wedderburn, Henning Friss, Paul Mihøj, and Jan Stehouwer, eds. 1968. *Old people in three industrial societies.* London: Routledge and Kegan Paul.

Shaw, Simeon. [1829] 1970. *A history of the Staffordshire potteries.* Hanley: privately printed; reprint, Newton Abbot: David and Charles.

Thane, Pat. 1990. "Government and society in England and Wales, 1750–1914." In *The Cambridge social history of Britain, 1750–1950.* Vol. 3. *Social agencies and institutions,* ed. F. M. L. Thompson, 1–61. Cambridge: Cambridge University Press.

Thomas, Geoffrey. 1947. "The employment of older persons." An enquiry carried out in mid-1945 for the Industrial Health Research Board for the Medical Research Council. *The Social Survey,* new series, 60(2).

Wall, Richard. 1982. "Regional and temporal variations in the structure of the British household since 1851." In *Population and society in Britain 1850–1980,* ed. T. Barker and Michael Drake, 62–99. London: Batsford.

———. 1984. "Residential isolation of the elderly: A comparison over time." *Ageing and Society* 4(4): 483–503.

————. 1987. "Leaving home and the process of household formation in pre-industrial England." *Continuity and Change* 2(1): 77–101.

————. 1989. "English and German families and the First World War." In *The upheaval of war: Family, work and welfare in Europe 1914–1918,* ed. Richard Wall and Jay Winter, 43–106. Cambridge: Cambridge University Press.

————. 1992. "Relationships between the generations in British families past and present." In *Families and households: Division and Change,* ed. Catherine Marsh and Sara Arber, 63–85. London: Macmillan.

Ward, John. 1843. *The borough of Stoke upon Trent.* London: J. W. and S. Shaw.

William Salt Archaeological Society. 1921 and 1936. *Collections for a history of Staffordshire.* 1921, London: Harrison and Sons; 1936, Stafford: J and C Mort.

Wrigley, E. A., and R. S. Schofield. 1983. "English population history from family reconstitution: Summary results 1600–1799." *Population Studies* 37(2): 157–184.

Young, Michael, and Peter Willmott. 1957. *Family and kinship in East London.* London: Routledge and Kegan Paul.

THREE

The Elderly in the Bosom of the Family: *La Famille Souche* and Hardship Reincorporation

E. A. Hammel

Perhaps the most outstanding demographic characteristic of the human species, one that may have appeared as long ago as one hundred millennia or more, is the extraordinary prolongation of life beyond the age of reproduction. There is no immediately discernible reason why animals should continue to exist beyond their reproductive span, why the forces of natural selection would favor the emergence of such survival and thus of a species that was characterized by it. Salmon, after all, are the ultimate in age-structural efficiency; the support of the elderly is no burden to their spawn.

In the absence of immediate postreproductive death, as in the example of the salmon's nuptial couch, it is not always easy to tell whether males die soon after they cease mating. It is easier to know that for females. With rare exceptions in captivity, there are apparently few examples of living, post-menopausal female primates outside the human species. Primate females, other than humans, reproduce until they die, and these deaths are apparently "natural," not only attributable to predation. Indeed, because the chimpanzee infant is breast-fed for about three years and dependent on its mother for another two or three, the last-born child of a chimpanzee almost always dies, predeceased by its mother in the first few years of its life. Not so with human females, who may nurture not only their children but their grandchildren and even their great-grandchildren for the half or more of their adult life that now falls beyond menopause. And so also with their mates, whose longevity is only modestly less but the termination of whose reproductive activity has often been as much a matter of inquiry for their spouses as for analysts such as ourselves. The prolongation of life is not simply a function of modern health care systems; it is found as well among hunter-gatherers such as the !Kung, where the expectation of life at the age of menopause is about another quarter century.

To what may we attribute this extraordinary change in primate, mammalian, and animal demography? To the existence and selective importance of culture, of course. The experience and skills of a lifetime, the knowledge of heath and meadow, the wisdom that adjudicates dispute, that forges alliances with neighbors, are not to be discarded with the cessation of genetic transmission. The elderly, defined in a Darwinian sense as those over about 50, are the first transgenetic resource bank in the animal world—a place where surplus knowledge is stored.

As with any bank, the resources of this one have to be discounted. In those ancient times when the growth of new knowledge was modest, the rate of cultural inflation was low, perhaps something like the rate of population growth.[1] The stock of knowledge was much the same for cohorts of elderly separated by many years of historical time. Even if their own learning rates were less than those of the contemporary young, there was not so much new to learn, and the knowledge of the elderly was not subject to much discounting. As the rate of knowledge production grew, the value of the knowledge of the elderly, even in the presence of their continued learning, would have to have been more heavily discounted. It would have been all they could do to keep up with those whippersnappers.

Thus, if we think of this knowledge economy and its value to the species, we may conclude that in the old days no one knew very much, but the elderly knew most of that, while in modern times, many people know much more, but the elderly know much less of it, even net of the specialization of labor and expert knowledge that diminish the relative stock of any participant, regardless of age. We can only conclude from this examination that the elderly are worth less to society than they used to be.

But we should inquire into the support structure that has enabled the elderly to contribute to the development of the species. In the old days, when they knew almost everything that anyone else did, they were supported in families and households. One does not have to travel back into the Paleolithic with Dr. Wonmug and Alley Oop to find those conditions; they are encountered in much of the less-developed world today and perhaps everywhere just a few centuries ago. The knowledge that they had, again net of specialization of labor (for what farmer was a goldsmith even in his youth?), was knowledge useful to the same group that nurtured them. Thus the elderly may never have been of much use to society at large (except in some derivative Darwinian sense by the aggregation of small familial advantages) but only to the familial and household group in which they resided. Now, even today, the elderly continue to be of value in those same contexts.[2]

So, from this reexamination, we may conclude that although it might seem that the elderly were once worth more than they are now, their value in the context of their support groups may not have changed so much, after all. It leads us to ask, in a more theoretically informed way, in what kinds of groups have the elderly been nurtured, and how much difference does it make?

SOME SYSTEMS OF HOUSEHOLD FORMATION

In the history of Europe and its derivative societies, from which comes most of our information on the history of the family and household, there have been a few primary contexts. The first of these is the so-called nuclear family, or at least its residue, in which two elderly spouses care for each other. The second is the solitary household, in which one elderly person is left to care for herself usually, less often himself. Third is the complex household, sometimes called multiple lineal, in which an elderly couple resides with one or more married children. The so-called stem family household, or *famille souche* of LePlay's notice, is a variety of these. Fourth is the arrangement in which a surviving parent lives with a married child. This last arrangement can occur when one senior surviving spouse in a multiple lineal household dies. It can also occur if on the death of one senior spouse in a nuclear household, the survivor is reincorporated into the household of a married child. In the terminology pioneered so long ago by Peter Laslett, the contrast can be seen as one between systems of the stem family household and those of reincorporation under nuclear hardship.

In this chapter, I examine the mutual effects between two plausible systems of accommodation of the elderly and different levels of mortality between two contrasting and plausible historical demographic regimes. I also examine whether we would be able to distinguish systems of family formation or regimes of demographic rates with the sample sizes ordinarily available in historical censuses.

MICROSIMULATION MODELING

The examination is carried out by computer microsimulation. This technique is useful in the exploration of theoretical relationships, especially when the relationships between components of a model of behavior are very complex, or when one's interest is in the variability of behavior. It is particularly useful in speculating about processes that occur in small samples, such as those typically encountered by historians, in which random error is an important source of differences. Computer microsimulation is extremely helpful in assessing the effects of random sampling error.

Now, microsimulation is a fairly complicated and technical business, the kind of endeavor that many scholars with an interest in family structure and the broad issues raised in my introductory remarks might find uncongenial. I apologize for the technicalities that follow, and I keep them to a minimum in the text itself, relegating what I can to the notes and to appendixes that can be obtained on request. They are necessary to keep the game honest. It is all too easy to wave one's hand with an abracadabra and a whiff of technology to amaze the uninitiated. The technicalities are here so that the initiated can have a legitimate target for criticism.

Briefly, in this microsimulation model, a population of appropriate age and sex structure is entered into a computer and subjected to some set of demographic rates and rules of household formation. The notional individuals in this population have children, marry, divorce, die, and form and dissolve households. The *demographic* events occur to individuals by chance, governed by the general set of demographic rates. In the long run, populations so subjected to random occurrence of the same rates will exhibit on average the values of those rates, and differences between them will be a function of sample size and random statistical error. This is not a trivial matter, for one of the lessons most frequently learned from such exercises is that at the sample sizes typically encountered in real historical data, it is actually quite difficult to separate true differences from purely random statistical variation.

The behavior of the notional population is rather different with respect to rules of household formation. Whereas in the simulation of demographic events, occurrences are executed by chance under a set of governing rates, the simulation of household formation is here *inflexible*. For example, if birthrates are such that on average women between the ages of 20 and 25 could expect to have one child, the simulation does not insist that every woman have exactly one child during that age span, no more, no less. Some women have none, some one, some two, and so on, but on average they have one. Conversely, if our household formation rule is that the youngest son should remain in the parental home on marriage, *every* son who marries and is not the youngest moves out, and *every* son who is the youngest and marries stays home. Using such a fixed and rigid rule, we have a terra firma for our questions and can ask what are the effects of changes in fertility and the joint survivorship of parents and children on the attainment of stem family household organization. Of course, in reality, even in a society in which stem families were ideal, not every marriage would follow the kind of rule I have described. Some younger sons would leave to seek their fortunes, some older sons would be better farmers than their younger brothers, and so on. We might like to have a flexible set of decision rules with various contingencies pertaining to the characteristics of the household and its members. Or, we might like to have a statistical distribution of decision rules, so that different principles could compete with one another for the formation of households, in just the same way that alternative demographic events like marriage and death compete for execution in the demographic part of the simulation.[3]

Why do we not treat household formation in the same, sophisticated way that we treat demographic events? Let it be clear that we have nothing against it in principle. The reason is that we have no good knowledge of the statistical distribution of decisions that lead to household formation, other than the events of birth, marriage, and death that are produced by the demographic part of the experiment. We may have historical knowledge of the statistical distribution of household types in a population, but we cannot simply use those distributions to invent decision rules. It would be an empty exercise to use results as causes. Until we acquire the detailed historical or ethnographic knowledge about the actual decision processes and contingencies in specific historical populations, we must rest with this more rigid approach. At least it provides us with a firm background against which to examine the effects of demographic variation.

When the computer has done its work of simulating demographic events and household formation, censuses are taken of the population and the households at appropriate times to learn the outcomes. This kind of electronic experimentation is carried out under the contrasting conditions of interest and for each of these, a sufficient number of times to assess the importance of sampling error.[4]

It is important to realize that such experiments are not intended to recreate a specific past. Even if one used a known historical population as the one subjected to a set of demographic rates and household formation rules, and even if one used the rates and rules appropriate to that population, the very first event to occur to the notional population would with virtual certainty *not* be the same as that which occurred to the historical population. Any individual population is unique. The knowledge we seek is knowledge of kinds of populations. What we seek is knowledge of the expectable range of outcomes for classes of populations under classes of demographic rates and classes of household formation rules, within which individual historical populations may be deemed to fall.

In this exercise we contrast two different demographic regimes, one putatively almost modern and another putatively ancient. For each of these we contrast two systems of household formation, both of them designed in principle to offer co-residence and aid to the elderly. The first demographic regime used here is that of the United States in 1900, as a fairly typical western European system at the beginning of the industrial revolution. It is here called "Late Premodern," abbreviated LPM.[5] The second is a medieval regime gleaned from historical evidence. It is here called "Medieval," abbreviated MED.[6]

The first system of accommodation of the elderly is a form of the classical stem family. In it the youngest male child of a household to marry remains at home. It is here called "stem," abbreviated S. The second system is one in which all children leave the household on marriage but in which a widowed parent, on the attainment of some specified age, rejoins the household of the youngest surviving married son. This system is here called "reincorporation," abbreviated R.

The rules of household formation require some explanation and justification. To achieve comparability between the stem and reincorporation scenarios in all but their critical differences, the kind of child whose marriage creates the stem family and the kind of child who takes the lead in reincorporating an aged parent should be the same. It would not do to have stem families formed on the basis of a son's marriage and reincorporations take place in a daughter's household, because the mortality expectations of sons and daughters are different and could not be separated from other effects. Similarly, it would not do to have stem families formed on the basis of the marriage of an oldest child and reincorporation take place in the household of a youngest child, because mortality chances vary by age. Differences between household formation rules and demographic regimes could not then be clearly attributed; the effects of demography and of household formation rules would be confounded. In this experiment we want to keep them as separate as we can.

The decisions taken were predicated largely on the intuitive ethnographic expectation that in premodern northern European societies aged parents were more likely to be reincorporated into the household of a youngest child than that of an older child. All manner of plausible reasons for this can be imagined. Sentimental ties are usually stronger between parents and younger children. Younger children have accumulated fewer conflicting social obligations than older ones. And so on. Now this expectation is in conflict with that of primogeniture, which of course obtained in some parts of Europe and under which the eldest child (usually the son) would remain on marriage to form the next generation of the stem family. Nevertheless, the decision was to standardize on the youngest children and thus on ultimogeniture.

One must also decide whether these youngest children are sons or daughters. The choice is difficult. Because stem family formation was intimately connected with inheritance of real property, parents most frequently co-resided with sons. However, there are good reasons to anticipate that elderly parents, especially mothers, might be more likely to be reincorporated in the households of their daughters than of their sons, to avoid conflicts between mothers and daughters-in-law. The choice was to opt for sons; the youngest son, in principle, remains in the parental home, and reincorporated parents in principle join the youngest son.

The rules for stem family formation are thus as follows. Sons are preferred over daughters, but if there are no sons, the youngest daughter remains. The effect of having the youngest rather than the oldest child co-reside is to elevate the proportion nuclear, as early-marrying and on the whole older children are ejected one by one, and to shorten the existence of the ultimately formed stem family households since, although younger children are less likely to predecease their parents, parents are older when their youngest child marries than when their older children do and thus more likely to die.[7]

The rules for reincorporation of widowed parents have to take into account the possibility of competition between the parents of husbands and wives and are as follows. A widowed parent seeks his or her youngest surviving ever-married child, preferring sons over daughters. If a widowed parent (A) finds an available child and has no other qualifying children but a parent (B) already resides in that household with the child, then if B has other ever-married children with whom he or she might live, B leaves to co-reside with that other child. A does not displace B if B has no other place to go. Surviving parents bereft of already co-residing children or children-in-law will seek another place to live even if they have co-residing grandchildren. If the bereft parent does not find a qualifying child but remains in the household with grandchildren, that household is then classified as a special household, namely, one without any nucleus (see below).[8]

It is also necessary to decide whether the reincorporation of widowed parents takes place immediately on widowhood or whether the parents remain independent for a time. For example, it seems strange to imagine the reincorporation of a 45-year-old widow, who might more realistically remain independent. Thus I subdivide the reincorporation scenario into two, one of early and one of late reincorporation. For simplicity, I use two critical ages at which reincorporation takes place. The first is simply the age at widowhood, whenever it occurs, which for notational convenience I here call age 0. The second is age 65, which I select somewhat arbitrarily. Any other reasonable age could have been chosen, but 65 provides a useful comparison point. The reader will later note that for purposes of symmetry, the same distinction is made in explication of stem family formation but that it has no effect under that scenario whatever.

EXPERIMENTAL RESULTS—MEANS

The average results of the simulations are presented graphically. The graphs incorporate a great deal of information in highly condensed form, so that I must spend some time decoding them.

First I distinguish between the two ages of reincorporation (widowhood and 65, abbreviated 0 and 65, respectively). Then I distinguish within each of these the two demographic regimes, Late Premodern (LPM) and Medieval (MED). Within these I distinguish the rules of household formation, stem formation as S and reincorporation as R. There are three kinds of binary distinctions being made (age at reincorporation, demographic regime, household formation), with the result that there are 2^3, that is, eight different categories of information. Thus there emerge results for each rule of household formation under LPM and MED and under both critical age constraints (0 and 65). In the graphs these are labeled LPM(0), LPM(65), MED(0), and MED(65) for Late Premodern with no age constraint, Late Premodern with critical age 65, Medieval with no age constraint, and Medieval with critical age 65. Each of these four sets occurs under the reincorporation and the stem family formation regimes. Of course, as already noted, the distinction between the two critical ages of reincorporation has no bearing on the formation of *stem family* households. It was simply more convenient in the computing work to set up the design in a completely cross-classified way, but the design gives us the additional advantage of actually doubling the sample size for the stem family scenario and allows us to see the results of purely chance variation between the inconsequentially different subsets of stem family formation, for any demographic regime, that are normally distinguished by the critical ages of 0 and 65.

The results are first presented graphically in the form of proportional distributions of households by type, out of all households in the population (fig. 3.1). Since some complex types of household occur only rarely under these systems of household formation and are of lesser theoretical interest when the focus is on the elderly, for example, fraternal joint households, I concentrate here on only four types. These are nuclear (NUC), solitary (SOLE), multiple lineal (MLN), and extended lineal (XLN).[9] The data of figure 3.1 are found in table 3.1.[10]

Let me explicate the graph. Along the horizontal axis are first distinguished four situations in which elderly parents are absent. These are nuclear families and solitaries (NUC and SOLE), each of two varieties. Then there are distinguished four situations in which elderly parents are present. These are multiple lineal and extended lineal (MLN and XLN), each of two varieties. Within each set of four (as just given) and for each household type (NUC, SOLE, MLN, XLN), there are distinguished the two basic regimes of household formation that lead to the constellations indicated. These regimes are stem (S) and reincorporation (R). Thus we see along the horizontal axis nuclear households occurring in stem family systems [NUC(S)], nuclear households occurring in reincorporation systems [NUC(R)], and so on, to extended lineal households occurring in stem family systems [XLN(S)] and in reincorporation systems [XLN(R)].

The reader will note that each of these eight combinations of household type of interest and household formation regime of origin has space for four columns in the bar graph directly above it. Thus, for example, NUC(S) has four bars above it. Each of these bars represents a different combination of demographic regime and critical age of reincorporation. Thus, as the legend shows, we have LPM(0) for Late Premodern with critical age 0 (widow-

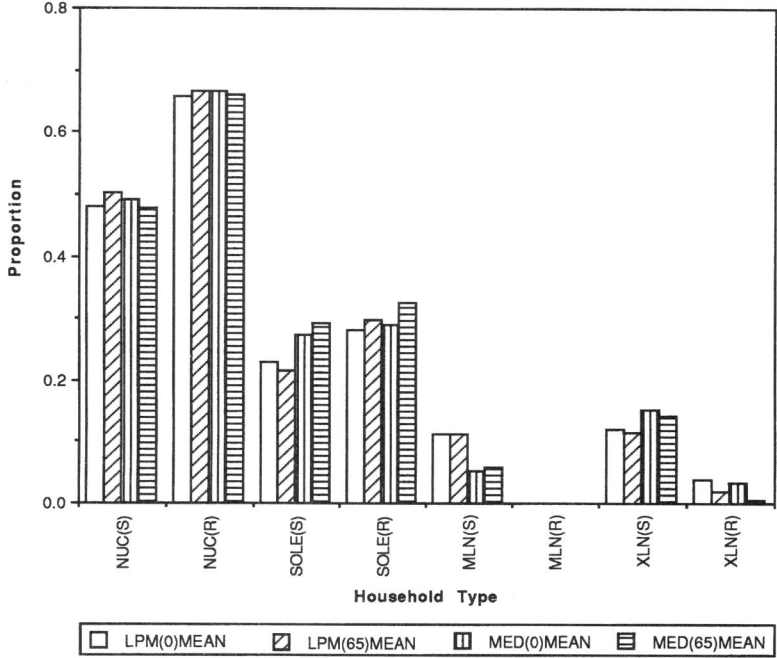

Fig. 3.1. Household proportions for all households—in the four time periods.

hood), LPM(65) for Late Premodern with critical age 65, and so on. These bars are differently patterned. LPM(0) is clear. LPM(65) is striped diagonally. MED(0) is striped vertically. MED(65) is striped horizontally. These structures and conventions enable us to compare conditions very conveniently. The reader can compare the heights of bars within one of the eight categories on the horizontal axis, for example, comparing the effects of demographic regimes within NUC(S), to see the effect of such different regimes on the formation of nuclear families in a stem family system, or across the eight categories, for example, to see whether NUC(S) or NUC(R) is more prevalent under Late Premodern conditions.

For each of the bars in the graph, the vertical axis indicates the proportion that that kind of household, under those conditions, makes up of the totality of households under those conditions. Let us first contrast the achievement of parent-child co-residence (MLN and XLN) with its absence (NUC and SOLE) across the two regimes of stem formation and reincorporation. We see that the proportion of households that are nuclear is consistently higher across all demographic regimes under a scenario of hardship reincorporation than under one of stem family formation. That is, each of the NUC(R) bars is higher than the corresponding NUC(S) bar with the same

TABLE 3.1   Proportions of Household Types by Demographic Regime and Household Formation Scenario

Type	All Households				Households of the Elderly			
	LPM(0)	LPM(65)	MED(0)	MED(65)	LPM(0)	LPM(65)	MED(0)	MED(65)
NUC(S)	0.482	0.503	0.490	0.477	0.205	0.230	0.118	0.150
NUC(R)	0.658	0.667	0.665	0.661	0.349	0.367	0.113	0.107
SOLE(S)	0.229	0.216	0.274	0.293	0.288	0.281	0.343	0.335
SOLE(R)	0.282	0.297	0.289	0.324	0.496	0.535	0.695	0.825
MLN(S)	0.113	0.112	0.053	0.058	0.183	0.168	0.083	0.093
MLN(R)	0.000	0.000	0.000	0.000	0.000	0.000	0.000	0.000
XLN(S)	0.121	0.116	0.153	0.141	0.277	0.272	0.402	0.356
XLN(R)	0.039	0.019	0.031	0.006	0.123	0.079	0.165	0.068

hatching. The same pattern holds for solitary households; each of the SOLE(R) bars is higher than its corresponding SOLE(S) bar. Conversely, the proportion of households that are multiple lineal (MLN) or extended lineal (XLN) is consistently less under reincorporation than under the stem family scenario. MLN(R) is by definition of zero occurrence, since reincorporation affects only widowed parents, and thus there can be no multiple lineal households under a reincorporation scenario. However, extended lineal households can occur under either stem or reincorporation scenarios, and all the XLN(R) bars are lower than all the XLN(S) bars.

These results show that the reincorporation scenario, which is in principle an explicit effort to include elderly parents in the households of their children, is less successful in achieving that accommodation than simple stem family formation. Why should a household formation system (R), striving to maximize the co-residence of parents and children by the explicit reincorporation of isolated parents, yield a lower proportion of such co-residence in a census? The answer is, on reflection, simple. Under a system of *stem* family formation, the number of person years a parent will spend in the household of a married child is greater than under a system of *reincorporation*, for the parent does not separate from the child and then rejoin. Thus a census is more like to capture a parent while living with a child rather than in a nuclear family after the child has left but before the parent has rejoined the child.[11] As has so often been pointed out in sensitive studies of family formation, a census is but a time slice through a process and may not reveal it.[12]

Similarly, under stem family formation rules, a widowed parent would remain with his or her *child-in-law* if the co-resident married *child* died. Under reincorporation rules, the widowed parent would rejoin a surviving married child, but not the widowed spouse of that child, if the child had been widowed before the parent.[13] Thus, under reincorporation rules, the formation of extended lineal households is depressed by those situations in which married children predecease their widowed parent.[14]

I submit that these relationships of timing and their results are perfectly obvious after they have been detected but that they were not obvious before they were exposed by these experiments.

Smaller differences are induced by changes in demographic regime (i.e., LPM vs. MED), for any system of household formation. This can be seen by comparing the heights of the bars within each block of four. Demographic regime makes almost no difference in the proportion nuclear. Under stem family rules, the Medieval demographic rates yield relatively lower proportions of stem households and higher proportions of sole and extended lineal households than the Late Premodern rates. With their higher mortality, they break up stem family households, making some people solitaries and others extensions in the households of their children. Under the reincorporation scenario, the effect of reducing the critical age of reincorporation from 65 to the actual age of widowhood gives the increase in extended lineal households that we would expect; the 0 bar is always higher than the corresponding 65 bar.

Now we shift the point of view. Up until now, the examination of the prevalence of different household types has been that of proportional representation among *all* households. Such data address questions like, What proportion of all the households in a census, under a particular demographic and household formation regime, are of Type X? But our focus can shift to inquire not how all persons in the population live but rather how the elderly live.

Figure 3.2 changes the view to that of the households of the elderly, that is, those households containing persons over age 65. Under LPM demographic conditions, the proportion of the elderly living in nuclear households is higher under the reincorporation than under the stem scenario. The result is just as it was for all households taken together (compare fig. 3.1), again because under the reincorporation scenario parents and children are separated for that period of their joint lives after the marriage of

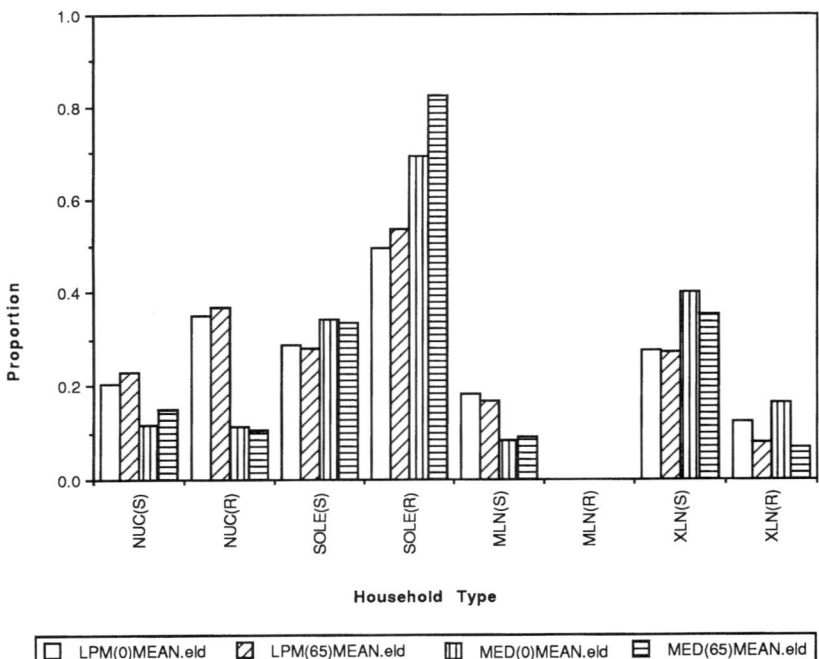

Fig 3.2. Household proportions for households of the elderly only—in the four time periods.

the child but before the widowhood of one of the parents. However, the relationship changes under MED demographic conditions, where the proportion nuclear is noticeably lower either under the S or the R regime, and nuclear structure is somewhat more likely under stem family formation rules than under reincorporation rules. Both of these features are a reversal of the pattern for all households taken together (fig. 3.1). The reason is that the higher mortality rates under MED conditions break up elderly conjugal units, lowering their level of occurrence, both in general and also during the period of parent-child separation under the reincorporation scenario. The proportion solitary is also higher under the reincorporation scenario, for the same reasons. Some widowed persons over 65 remain solitary because they have no surviving children. This circumstance is more likely under reincorporation rules because there is a chance for married children to die during the period of separation. The effects are stronger under MED demographic conditions because of the higher mortality levels. The proportion in extended households is higher under the stem than under the reincorporation scenario, again for the same reasons; co-residence is not interrupted other than by death under the stem scenario. Comparing across demographic regimes, we see that the proportion of the elderly living in stem families is lower under Medieval conditions for the same reasons of mortality, and generally the proportion in extended lineal households is higher, because one of the spouses will be more likely to have died.

These data show us that the point of view of the classification is important for interpretation. Asking in what kinds of households people live under various combinations of demographic and household regimes is different from asking in what kinds of households the elderly live. Although some patterns persist despite a change in classification, others change markedly.[15]

EXPERIMENTAL RESULTS—VARIABILITY

The estimates of household proportions achieved through these microsimulation experiments can be regarded as statistically stable because the sample sizes were so large.[16] What happens to our view of patterns and differences if sample sizes are realistically smaller? To answer this question, the large samples were used as a sampling frame, and the statistical technique of bootstrapping was employed; that is, small samples were drawn repeatedly and randomly from the large sample. In this way, without going to the trouble of running the simulations again at small sample sizes, one arrives at a good estimate of what the results would have been like if the simulations had actually been done again. Drawing samples of 100 households each 100 times with replacement produced bootstrap estimates of the means and standard errors of the means for samples of 100 households. The bootstrap means are of course almost identical to the simulation ("observed") means, and the more bootstrap trials we did (say, 1,000), the closer they would be. It is the sampling errors that are of greatest interest and based on them, the confidence intervals. We should be cautious about how we interpret a confidence interval. A confidence interval of, let us say, 95 percent does not mean that we are 95 percent confident of the result. It simply specifies a range about the sample mean within which we would expect 95 percent of a large number of sample means to fall, if we sampled repeatedly and randomly from the same population. The idea is that if the mean of one sample falls within the confidence bounds of another sample, the two samples would in 95 percent of such instances actually be from the same population and are thus not truly distinguishable. This just tells us that sometimes what looks like a difference is not a difference.

Figures 3.3 and 3.4 show, for sample sizes of 100, the range from which sample proportions of household types, under the various demographic rates and formation scenarios, could be expected to come 95 percent of the time by chance alone. Figure 3.3 is for nuclear and solitary households, and figure 3.4 is for the multiple and extended households. They are divided in this way to keep the graphs from being cluttered. The categories along the horizontal axis are different from those employed in figures 3.1 and 3.2. Because figures 3.3 and 3.4 are more complex and must show ranges of data,

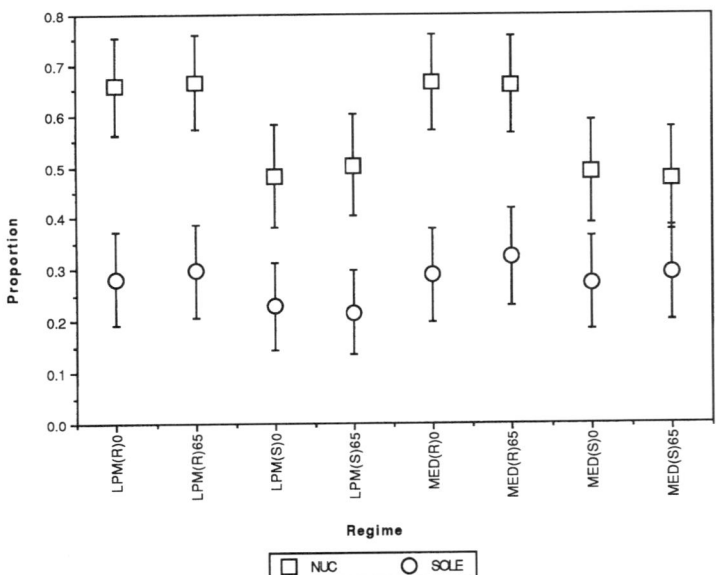

Fig. 3.3. Ninety-five percent confidence intervals for household proportions—nuclear families and solitaries.

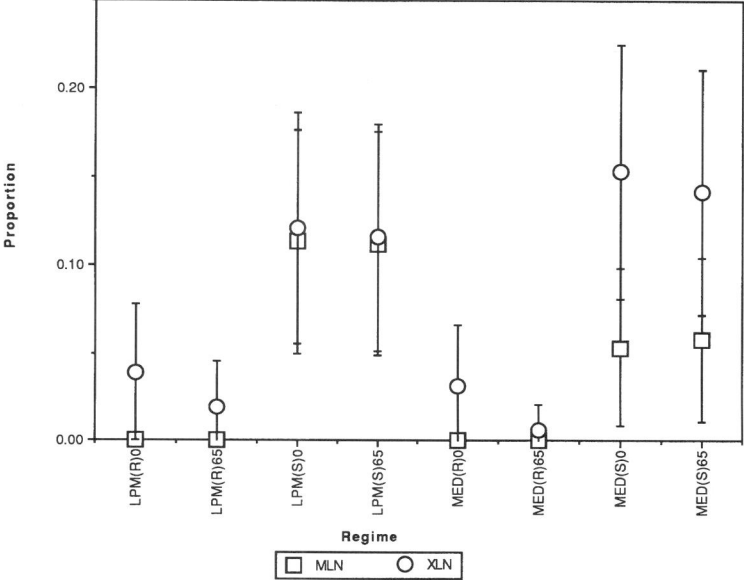

Fig. 3.4. Ninety-five percent confidence intervals for household proportions—multiple lineal families and extended lineal families.

the categories on the horizontal axis are combinations of demographic
regime and household formation rules. There are eight of these categories
in each figure. The first four are Late Premodern (LPM), and the last four
are Medieval (MED). In each set of four, the first two categories are for reincorporation regimes, and the second two are for stem regimes. For each
such pair the first member is for critical age 0, and the second is for critical
age 65. Above each category are displayed the information about two different kinds of household: NUC and SOLE in figure 3.3, and MLN and XLN
in figure 3.4. Each such display of information is represented by a bar, at the
center of which is the mean proportional occurrence of the household type,
under the stated conditions, surrounded by the 95 percent confidence interval. For example, in figure 3.3, under LPM(R)0, which means under Late
Premodern demographic regimes with a system of reincorporating elderly
parents as soon as they are widowed, the nuclear households constitute
about 66 percent of all households, and solitary households constitute
about 29 percent. We would expect the proportion of nuclear households
to fall 95 percent of the time between about 57 percent and 75 percent and
that of solitary households to fall 95 percent of the time between about 19
percent and 38 percent, in samples of 100. Of course, we know from statistical theory that if sample sizes are larger, the confidence intervals will be

narrower. Thus, if sample sizes were increased by a factor of 10 to 1,000, we would expect the confidence intervals to be reduced by a factor of the square root of 10, thus about a third of what is shown in the figure.

The question to be addressed is thus whether we could expect to be able to distinguish the demography and household formation regimes from the evidence of their results, at particular sample sizes. We would ask whether the mean for a household type under some scenario did or did not fall within the confidence interval of that same household type under some contrasting scenario. If it did not, then at these sample sizes we could use evidence of the household type proportions to argue for the presence of an underlying demographic regime, or household formation scenario, or some combination of the two. If a mean fell within the confidence interval of another regime, we could not reliably use such evidence.

In figure 3.3 we see that it is never possible, on the evidence of nuclear and solitary households, to distinguish between regimes that differ only by virtue of the critical age of reincorporation. That conclusion comes from the observation that the adjacent members of the successive pairs in the figure, such as LPM(R)0 and LPM(R)65, always show the mean of one member falling within the confidence interval of the other. Critical age of reincorporation, although it makes a difference, does not make very much difference, and that difference would be reliably detectable only at very large sample sizes, such as the totality of the simulations presented in figures 3.1 and 3.2. Although figures 3.1 and 3.2 are a reliable guide to some large universe of results, they are not a reliable guide to historical reality as we recover it in the activity of being real historians.

We further see that it is always possible even at sample sizes of 100, on the basis of the proportion of households nuclear, to distinguish between stem and reincorporation scenarios under the same demographic conditions, for example, LPM(R)0 and LPM(S)0. However, it is never possible to use the proportion solitary in the same way, for example, MED(R)0 and MED(S)0. If comparisons are made for the proportion nuclear across regimes and scenarios that differ both in their demographic regime and in their critical age, for example, LPM(R)0 and MED(R)65, the only factor that permits clear distinction is that between household formation scenarios. The stem system and the reincorporation system always give different results. However, the proportion solitary cannot be used in this way. Thus the evidence from nuclear households is a more reliable guide to underlying conditions and process than is the evidence from solitary households. The differential quality of the evidence would not have been obvious before undertaking these experiments.

The same exercise can be conducted with figure 3.4. Of course, we must ignore the proportion MLN under nonstem scenarios, since it is by definition 0. Again, by definition, under the stem scenarios it is never possible to distinguish between systems differing by age of reincorporation, for example, LPM(S)0 and LPM(S)65, because age at reincorporation is irrelevant to stem family formation.

It is usually possible from the proportion MLN to decide between the LPM and MED demographic regimes. Notice that we can only compare the stem (S) regimes and that age or reincorporation is irrelevant. Thus we should compare the error bars for the third and fourth against the seventh and eighth categories of the horizontal axis. The square plotting points that represent MLN in the seventh and eighth categories are just at the limits of the error bars for the third and fourth, while the plotting points for the latter are well outside the confidence limits for the former.

It is scarcely ever possible to distinguish between critical ages of reincorporation on the grounds of the proportion lineally extended (XLN), except under the reincorporation scenario under Medieval demographic conditions. Only in this last instance does the mean fall outside the comparable confidence interval; the open circle for XLN under MED(R)0 falls well above the upper limit of the confidence interval under MED(R)65.

It is always possible to distinguish between the reincorporation and stem scenarios on the grounds of the proportion XLN; it is always higher under stem family formation than under reincorporation rules, for the reasons already noted in the discussion of figures 3.1 and 3.2. Speaking in general, we get less reliable evidence about underlying process from observing proportions of extended and multiple households than we do from observing nuclear and solitary households; the separation of results is rather better in figure 3.3 than in figure 3.4.

DISCUSSION

The conclusion from this exercise is that demographic differences per se are only weakly influential as against differences in household formation rule systems. This is a further confirmation of conclusions reached earlier with respect to stem family formation under plausibly different demographic regimes for historical England[17] and for joint family systems under early medieval rates.[18] The results given in this chapter are also based on ordinary and expectable historical rates. The differences between these plausible rates, however, are rather substantial, with the expectation of life at birth being only about 25 under the Medieval regime but about double that under the Late Premodern one. However, we must note that mortality differences and changes in the past have rested principally on improvements in infant and child mortality, and these have less effect on stem family and reincorporation scenarios than do changes in adult mortality. The results here presented make all the more striking the situation prevailing today in many northern European and American societies, as well as in Japan, in which the

mortality rates for higher ages are sufficiently different from historical experience to provoke sharp changes in household and kinship network constitution. Even for modernizing China, we have shown elsewhere that mortality changes since traditional times have been sufficient to make it more
likely that traditional household structures can be reached and maintained
now than earlier.[19] Whereas our customary view of demographic differences
and their effects on age structure and social structure has focused on fertility and infant mortality, we see that mortality differences at higher ages can
also be productive of major effects.

These explorations led to some surprises. The first was that the two
household formation regimes could often be distinguished at relatively
small sample sizes around 100. In earlier work, devoted to the detection of
differences between stem family and nuclear scenarios without reincorporation, sample sizes of close to 200 were required. This is a welcome result
for historians, who often deal with samples not much larger than about 100.
But this helpful result holds only for the ability to distinguish regimes by examining *some* household types. For example, the required sample size necessary to distinguish each scenario from any other is only about 30 for the
proportion nuclear and between 200 and 300 for the proportion solitary under most regimes but almost 4,000 under the Medieval demographic
regime. The minimal size required for extended lineal proportions varies
between about 20 and 60. Only trivial sample sizes are needed to distinguish
rule systems on the basis of the proportion of multiple lineal households,
since they should only occur under stem family formation rules, except as
freak accidents of household recombination through remarriages. Working
historians should be prepared to follow different strategies to make their
points, depending on the household types on which they choose to focus.
All households do not give answers of the same reliability.

Also unexpected was the depression of the proportion of extended lineal households, the very goal of reincorporation as an alternative to stem
family formation, under an explicit system of hardship reincorporation.
The residue of stem families on the death of a senior member yields a higher
proportion of extended lineal households than a behavioral system that
brings the elderly back from nuclearity when widowhood leaves them solitary, because of the effects of prior mortality on married children.

CONCLUSION

This chapter began by inquiring into the contribution of the elderly to
their nurturant environment. Which social environment permits them their
greatest contribution, and what social contract facilitates both it and their
nurturance? Who should be responsible for this nurturance? The answer, if
one wants to have old Mum at the hearth, is to start early, so that she remains

longer and more continuously in the bosom of the family. From a policy point of view, George Homans's villagers of the thirteenth century had it right; they kept Mum home from the start.

What of responsibility? The contribution of the elderly is surely more to their narrow than to their broad social environment, more to the family and household than to society at large. Surely those who benefit the most from their presence should take the major responsibility for their nurturance. Now, this nurturance need not involve co-residence, and the analyses presented here are only a special case, for the historian bound to four walls by the nature of the scribblings of busybodies. In the modern era we must attend to the cellular telephone, the answering machine, and perhaps even to grandmothers who send electronic mail and faxes. But the general point is the same, even if eased by technology. The care of the elderly is less likely to be a general social burden if it can be made the responsibility of their heirs—not only of their biological descendants but of their social descendants, thus not only of their children but also of their children-in-law. The filial conjugal *estate* should carry the social debts of both of its coparceners, the younger spouses. Might we realistically expect daughters-in-law to enter with joy into such contracts?

As levels of mortality diminish, of course, the children whom Mum might rejoin through reincorporation are less likely to be widowed, so that Mum is not robbed of a locus through the death of a child and the survival only of a child-in-law. However, as mortality declines, Mum lasts longer herself. The depression of extended lineal households under a system of reincorporation is thus a function of the ratio of the survivorship of adult children to that of their parents, or in the phrase employed in macroanalytic approaches to this same problem, the size of adjacent generations. Although the situation is not precisely analogous to the effects of shifting cohort sizes in social security systems at the macrolevel, it involves, even as there, an element of intergenerational social contract. At the microlevel the situation is conditioned by the cultural fact (at least in Euro-American societies) that blood is thicker than water. The care of the elderly, under these contrasting household formation scenarios, becomes a general social responsibility where reincorporation is the rule because some social descendants may escape an obligation that could be construed as properly theirs by virtue of their survival as coparceners of the conjugal estate that had that obligation. Under the stem family formation system, they would have continued to hold it. The outcome is obvious, but like many obvious outcomes, only after the experiments.

This exercise conducted with computers and focused on a problem from the distant past indeed has a connection to the broad problems raised at the beginning of the chapter. It is, after all, culture that differentiates us from our animal forebears, and that culture with implications for attitudes between the generations and for the maintenance of the cultural stock itself is closely related to mortality systems. It is these shifting mortality systems that drive the coexistence of the generations and that demand the cultural accommodation. The world now emerging is not like the old one in which parents were never free of their children but is one in which children are never free of their parents until they are themselves old. Childhood, in the psychological sense, reaches unimagined proportions. The responsibility of women as caregivers now extends across generations in two directions, and the usually earlier demise of men unites in a curious dyad the rivals who were linked to them, one as mother, the other as wife.

NOTES

1. In the view of some, perhaps exactly the rate of population growth.

2. Rapid fluctuation in fads of child rearing may make them seem unuseful, but this is misleading. They are just a little out of phase.

3. Ruggles (1987) has made just this point.

4. A full exposition of these matters is given in Wachter, Hammel, and Laslett 1978. Details of the SOCSIM microsimulation programs are given in Hammel, Mason, and Wachter 1990. I am indebted to Carl Mason for the programming of these simulation runs.

5. I use here the demographic rates employed by Hammel, Wachter, and McDaniel (1981) in a first exploration of some of these issues, as improved by Reeves (1982, 1987) to include divorce, and further modified for this exercise to adjust for an improved marriage market algorithm. Details of these rates, as employed in this analysis, may be obtained from the author on request.

6. I use here the demographic rates employed by Hammel (1990), based on the work of Acsádi and Nemeskéri (1970), Russell (1958), Coale and Demeny (1983), and Laiou (1977), and taken as typical of a harsh premodern environment. Details of these rates, as employed in this analysis, may be obtained from the author on request.

7. More detailed specifications can be obtained from the author.

8. More detailed specifications can be obtained from the author.

9. See Hammel and Laslett 1974 for detailed definitions. Brief definitions, including those types omitted from the analysis here, are

NUC	one conjugal pair with or without children or one surviving parent with children
SPEC	no conjugal pairs
SOLE	a person living alone
MLT	> 1 conjugal pair in the same generation collaterally linked
MLN	> 1 conjugal pair lineally linked
MLTD	> 1 conjugal pair lineally and collaterally linked
XLT	one conjugal pair and an unmarried relative in the same generation collaterally linked
XLN	one conjugal pair and an unmarried relative lineally linked
XLTD	one conjugal pair and an unmarried relative lineally and collaterally linked

10. The reader will note that the proportions of the different household types do not sum to 1, because the rare types are omitted from the table. A full table of results can be obtained from the author. Similarly, the standard deviations of these proportions are not given (see the section on confidence intervals later in the text). The standard deviations of these proportions as estimated by bootstrap techniques are very close to the theoretical expectations and can be calculated as $\sqrt{\frac{pq}{N}}$.

11. We should never find multiple lineal households under a system of nuclear reincorporation, except by bizarre combinations of divorces or spousal deaths and remarriages. We did our best to prevent the occurrence of such bizarre events.

12. See, e.g., Hammel 1972, 1980.

13. This is not a very deep proposition, ethnographically.

14. Of course, one person's child-in-law is another person's child, and that second person might move in with the child, if both of the co-in-laws were widowed. Each is eligible to move in with a married child if their child survives (although only one is permitted to do so, since co-in-laws may not themselves co-reside); only one of them is eligible if the other has no surviving children. We would expect these differences in extended lineal proportions to diminish if, under stem family rules, a surviving widowed parent were ejected by a surviving widowed child-in-law. We do not implement that heartless rule, even if there are no grandchildren.

15. Much the same point can be made in the classification of households themselves. The decision that specifies the head of household for the purpose of classification is crucial to the outcome.

16. The number of households ranged from about 2,000 under MED(S) conditions to about 7,000 under LPM(R) conditions.

17. See Wachter, Hammel, and Laslett 1978.

18. See Hammel 1990.

19. See Hammel et al. 1991.

REFERENCES

Acsádi, Gyorgy, and J. Nemeskéri. 1970. *History of human life span and mortality.* Budapest: Akademiai Kiado.

Coale, Ansley, and Paul Demeny, with Barbara Vaughan. 1983. *Regional model life tables and stable populations.* 2d ed. New York: Academic Press.

Hammel, E. A. 1972. "The zadruga as process." In *Household and family in past time,* ed. Peter Laslett, 335–373. Cambridge: Cambridge University Press.

———. 1980. "Household structure in 14th-century Macedonia." *Journal of Family History* 5: 242–273.

———. 1990. "Demographic constraints on the formation of traditional Balkan households." *Dumbarton Oaks* [Washington, D.C.] *Papers* 44: 173–180.

Hammel, E. A., and Peter Laslett. 1974. "Comparing household structure over time and between cultures." *Comparative Studies in Society and History* 16: 73–109.

Hammel, E. A., Carl Mason, and Kenneth Wachter. 1990. *SOCSIM II: A sociodemographic microsimulation program. Revision 1.0: Operating manual.* Special Publication of the Graduate Group in Demography and Program in Population Research, University of California, Berkeley.

Hammel, E. A., Kenneth Wachter, and Chad K. McDaniel. 1981. "The kin of the aged in 2000 A.D." In *Aging.* Vol. 2. *Social Change,* ed. James Morgan, Valerie Oppenheimer, and Sara Kiesler, 11–39. New York: Academic Press.

Hammel, E. A., Kenneth Wachter, Carl Mason, Feng Wang, and Haiou Yang. 1991. "Rapid population change and kinship: The effects of unstable demographic changes on Chinese kinship networks, 1750–2250." In *Consequences of rapid population growth in developing countries,* 243–271. London: Taylor and Francis.

Laiou, Angeliki. 1977. *Peasant society in the late Byzantine empire: A social and demographic study.* Princeton: Princeton University Press.

Reeves, Jaxk H. 1982. "A statistical analysis and projection of the effects of divorce on future U.S. kinship structure." Ph.D. dissertation, Department of Statistics, University of California, Berkeley.

————. 1987. "Projection of number of kin." In *Family demography: Methods and their application,* ed. John Bongaarts, Thomas K. Burch, and Kenneth W. Wachter, 228–248. Oxford: Clarendon Press.

Ruggles, Stephen. 1987. *Prolonged connections: The rise of the extended family in nineteenth-century England and America.* Madison: University of Wisconsin Press.

Russell, J. C. 1958. "Late ancient and mediaeval populations." *Transactions of the American Philosophical Society,* new series, vol. 48, pt. 3.

Wachter, Kenneth, E. A. Hammel, and Peter Laslett. 1978. *Statistical studies of historical social structure.* New York: Academic Press.

FOUR

Household Systems and the Lives of the Old in Eighteenth- and Nineteenth-Century Hungary

Rudolf Andorka

Where did the elderly find a place to live in past centuries in Hungary? Or, more specifically, in what type of households did they live? This question is not of historical interest only; it is relevant for present-day social policies. Like other advanced societies, Hungary is facing the problems caused by the aging of the population. But these problems are somewhat different in Hungary. As the decline of fertility below the level of simple replacement occurred more or less a decade earlier (at the end of the 1950s) in Hungary than in western European societies, these problems became acute about a decade earlier in Hungary. And, as the welfare state is much less developed in Hungary than in most western European societies, the elderly must necessarily rely much more on help from family, kin, and other personal contacts than is the case in the West. It is therefore interesting to know how the elderly were cared for in past centuries in Hungary.

The conditions of the elderly in Hungary are also important from an international comparative perspective. Earlier historical sociological research, most notably by Peter Laslett (1977, 1983), has shown that western Europe was unique in past centuries in many demographic and social indicators and institutions, including those relating to the conditions of the old population. The famous Trieste-St. Petersburg line of John Hajnal (1965), with the "late marriage, low celibacy" eastern European pattern lying to the east, passes along the western frontier of Hungary. Hungarian historians have long focused on the question of whether Hungary belongs to western or to eastern Europe, a question given new prominence by recent political events. Neglecting here the political implications of the answer to this question, I would like to point to what is probably the most serious work on this subject, by Ernö Tárkány-Szücs (1981). Tárkány-Szücs argues that after belonging to western Europe from 1000 to 1500, Hungary slid after its defeat

in the battle of Mohacs by the Ottoman Turkish army to a special "intermediate" eastern-central European region, together with other parts of the
Habsburg empire and Poland.

It ought to be added that more recent research has shown that the demographic and social patterns in Europe were more complicated than a
simple east-west division suggests. There were variations within western Europe; most notably, southern Europe seems to have been different from the
West in many respects, while in the east the Balkans were different from Russia and the Ukraine, and there were "western" islands in eastern Europe and
"eastern" islands in western Europe, most of all in central Europe (Laslett
1983; Viazzo 1989). There are signs that Hungary itself was rather differentiated, some regions or ethnic or denominational groups being more western European and others more eastern European.

A SHORT OUTLINE OF THE DEMOGRAPHIC, ECONOMIC, AND
SOCIAL HISTORY OF HUNGARY IN THE EIGHTEENTH AND
NINETEENTH CENTURIES

The nearly two centuries of Turkish wars and occupation of the majority
of the present territory of Hungary (from 1526, the date of the battle of
Mohacs, to 1711, when the Habsburg army defeated the Hungarian army
of Rákoczí fighting for independence) caused great population loss, most
of all in the central part of Hungary, which was dominated by the Ottoman
Empire. Estimations of population size based on tax lists in 1715 and 1720
vary from 2.6 to 4 million in the territory of the Hungarian Kingdom and
Transylvania; less than one-third of that number lived in the present territory of Hungary. In the following decades of the eighteenth century, the relatively peaceful conditions and the gradual ending of the plague (the last
great epidemic was in 1738–1741) favored rapid population growth. The
first census in Hungary in 1784–1787, performed under the reign of Joseph
II, found a population of 8.1 to 8.2 million in Hungary and Transylvania, of
whom 2.7 million lived in the present territory of Hungary. Thus, the population more than doubled in about seventy years.

A civil servant made and published a calculation of the birth- and death
rates in 1777. Although these are estimations, the very high birthrate—
55.2—and the much lower death rate—40.4—support the conclusion
drawn from the census population numbers that the second half of the eighteenth century was indeed a period of very rapid population growth.

The population of the present territory of Hungary was 5 million at the
time of the next reliable census, 1870. Thus in more than ninety years, the
population had almost doubled again. The growth rate was clearly lower
than in the eighteenth century. The birthrate was 45.4 and the death rate
40.2 in 1870–1879, when regular official vital statistics began to be kept.

Thus the birthrate seems already to have begun to decline in the first half of the nineteenth century, much before the onset of industrialization, but the death rate did not improve until the 1870s.

For the decades before the 1870s, only sample studies can be used to calculate vital rates. Estimations of life tables on the basis of the data from a sample of parish registers demonstrate a life expectancy at birth of about 30 years (table 4.1). Life expectancies at the age of 30 for married males and females, who figured on the completed family sheets, could be calculated from family reconstitution studies (table 4.2). Infant mortality rates were established from parish registers used for family reconstituting (table 4.3).

TABLE 4.1   Select Indicators from Mortality Tables Calculated from a Sample of Parish Registers, 1821–1830

	Life Expectancy at Age 30 (e_{30})		Number of Survivors per 1,000 Births (l_{60})	
Category of Settlement	Male	Female	Male	Female
Villages				
Population < 2,000	31.3	28.8	251	226
Population > 2,000	32.6	30.9	258	253
Agricultural towns				
Population < 2,000	31.5	29.5	265	219
Population > 2,000	32.6	31.4	255	253
Towns having "royal right"	28.6	30.5	172	214
Total	31.6	30.8	238	242

TABLE 4.2   Life Expectancy at Age 30 of Married Males and Females in Six Hungarian Villages in the Eighteenth and Nineteenth Centuries, by Marriage Cohorts, Based on Family Reconstitutions

		Life Expectancy at Age 30 (Years)	
Village	Marriage Cohort	Male	Female
Vajszló and Besence	1791–1820	36	31
	1821–1850	35	33
	1851–1880	40	41
Alsőnyék	1760–1790	34	28
	1791–1820	32	31
Sárpilis	1752–1790	37	28
	1791–1820	34	29
Átány	1730–1789	33	29
	1790–1819	29	28
Pocemegyer	1759–1790	29	29
	1791–1820	25	28

TABLE 4.3 Some Demographic Rates Found by Family Reconstitution in Hungarian Villages

Village	Region	Ethnicity	Religious Denomination	Age at First Marriage of Women 1850–1895	Illegitimate Births (%)		Infant Mortality per 1,000 Births		Total Marital Fertility, 20–49, Marriage Cohorts of	
					1790–1820	1850–1895	1790–1820	1850–1895	1790–1820	1850–1895
Vajszló and Besence	Southern Transdanubia	Hungarian	Calvinist	19.9	1.0	4.4	282	130	4,760	2,760
Alsónyék and Sárpilis	Southern Transdanubia	Hungarian	Calvinist	17.5	0.4	4.5	188	215	3,725	2,725
Kerkáskápolna	Southern Transdanubia	Hungarian	Calvinist	19.1	5.9	7.8	168	182	4,415	2,500
Bakonya	Southern Transdanubia	Hungarian	Roman Catholic	20.5	.	.	.	.	3,595	.
Töttös	Southern Transdanubia	Hungarian	Roman Catholic	19.9	.	.	.	.	4,705	.
Velem	West	Hungarian	Roman Catholic	22.1	.	.	.	.	6,635	.
Rábakecöl	West	Hungarian	Roman Catholic	.	1.4	.	290	.	7,395	.
Bük	West	Hungarian	Roman Catholic	25.0	4.6	7.0	128	207	.	.
Bük	West	Hungarian	Lutheran	23.2	0.9	4.9	189	207	.	.
Bárna	North	Slovakian	Roman Catholic	19.5	0.2	2.3	.	225	7,795	7,375
Felsővadász	Northeast	Ruthenian	Greek Catholic	20.1	1.9	3.6	243	108	6,249	8,665
Átány	Great Plain	Hungarian	Calvinist	22.8	1.5	2.4	173	232	6,230	6,775

household structure and kin relations and caused important differences as compared to Western societies, where support for poor individuals from the collectivity was available (Laslett 1988; McIntosh 1988; Pullan 1988).

At the same time, there was a vague but deep feeling in the Hungarian peasantry until at least the first half of the twentieth century that it was appropriate for married children to help their parents in farming and to stay at least for some years with their parents in the same household. Even when the young couple built their own house, the mutual helping relationship between parents and children and between married brothers and sisters was maintained (Fél and Hofer 1969). It might be concluded that the Hungarian peasant culture favored—but did not necessarily prescribe—mutual help and common or nearby residence of parents and adult children. Thus the elderly in Hungary in the eighteenth and nineteenth centuries could usually rely on their descendants and their families, in most cases by living together with them in the same households.

Sources of Data on the Household Conditions of the Old
To study the household contexts of older people, listings of households and populations that provide ages are needed, similar to those used by Laslett (1977) for the investigation of the history of aging and the aged. Such listings are relatively rare in Hungary in the precensus decades and centuries. Only a few listings of the first census of 1784–1787 are available in different local archives (Dányi 1965). The census forms of the regular decennial censuses beginning in 1870 were largely destroyed. Therefore, to study the household context in which old people lived, we have to search for population and household listings in the local archives and in the individual parishes. Four such listings, all found in local parish archives, are used here: (1) the *status animarum* of the Roman Catholic village of Fajsz in 1762, prepared for the administration of the bishopric of Kalocsa (Barth 1975); (2) the listing of the Calvinist village of Mezőcsoknya in 1800, prepared by the local pastor to replace the parish register, which was burned together with the local church building two years earlier, giving the year of birth and marriage of each inhabitant; (3) the listing of the Calvinist village of Sárpilis in 1804, prepared by the local pastor for the administration of the department (*megye*) of Tolna in the framework of a conscription of the population of the department;[4] and (4) the listing of the Calvinist village of Kölked in 1816, prepared by the honorary principals of the local congregation, giving the age of each inhabitant (Mándoki 1971).

These listings are of varying quality. For example, Sárpilis's does not give the age of all women, so ages were determined by trying to find them in the parish register of burials. The problem of completeness, that is, of the eventual omissions, causes more serious concern. The possibility of

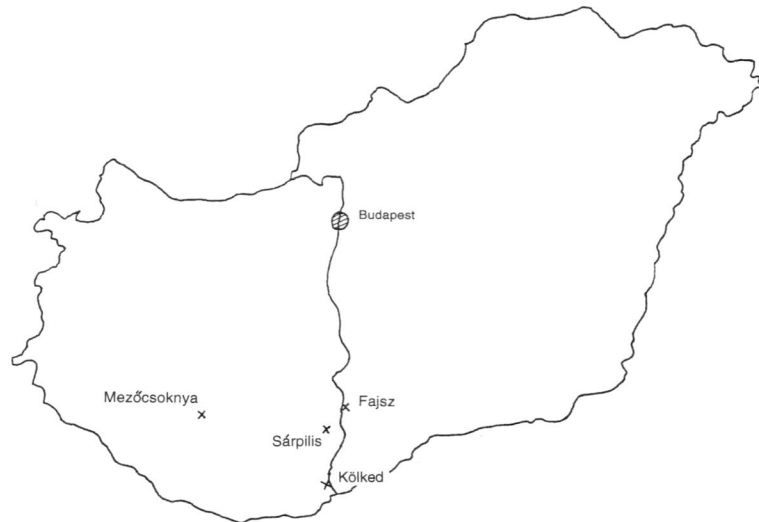

Fig. 4.1. Location of the four Hungarian villages investigated.

TABLE 4.5   Characteristics of Population Aged 60+
in Four Hungarian Villages

Village	Population Size	Number Aged 60+			Percentage Aged 60+	Sex Ratio 60+
		Male	Female	Total		
Fajsz	1,022	43	18	61	6.0	239
Mezőcsoknya	547	9	11	20	3.7	82
Sárpilis	525	19	10	29	5.5	190
Kölked	643	17	15	32	5.0	113
Total	2,737	88	52	142	5.2	163

omissions is suggested by the very high sex ratio of the populations over age 60 investigated here (table 4.5). One reason for the higher number of males over age 60 might be the shorter life expectancy of females (tables 4.1 and 4.2). The very high sex ratio in Fajsz and Sárpilis, however, cannot be explained simply by mortality differences of men and women. In the case of Sárpilis, it was possible to compare the parish registers and the listings and to verify in this way that no old women are missing from the listing of 1804. The surplus of men might be caused partly by the migration balance by sexes of the previous years. From 1792 to 1804, 45 men out-migrated and 33 immigrated, while 58 women out-migrated and 40 immigrated. Thus the loss of migration was 12 men and 18 women (not detailed by age). If the migration balance was similar in previous decades, then in addition to the higher mortality of women, the greater loss of women by out-migration might explain the very high sex ratio. No similar data are available to explain the even higher sex ratio found in Fajsz. It might be assumed that—as the listing dates from an earlier period than that of Sárpilis—the surplus mortality of women was higher.

All four listings present the names of the inhabitants and their ages ordered by households. Households are divided by serial numbers. It is, however, not absolutely clear what the serial numbers mean, namely, whether one household or one house is given under one serial number. It might be assumed, however, that the enumerators used the definition of the census of 1784–1787, according to which all those belong to one "familia" that cooks and eats together.

Usually the oldest male family head is given as the first person in the household and might be defined in consequence as the household head. In some exceptional cases, the male head of the younger family is first mentioned. Widowers seem to be treated similarly, that is, they are usually listed as household heads if they are the oldest in the household. Widows are sometimes mentioned first and are therefore defined as household heads; in other cases, they are mentioned as a family member of the household head, who is usually their son. The household position of the other members is defined in relation to the first-mentioned person of the household (e.g., spouse, child, mother of the household head).

Cotters (landless peasants) and servants are mentioned explicitly in the listings of Fajsz and Sárpilis. Two types of them were distinguished in the analysis of the data and were treated differently: (1) solitary servants and cotters, who are always assigned in the listings to households, are treated as members of these households; (2) cotters and servants having a family were treated here as separate households, even if they were assigned in the listing to another household. Ethnographic evidence suggests that these cotter and servant families cooked and ate separately. As, however, the number of cotters and servants assigned to other households was relatively small (much lower than in contemporary England), their treatment in the analysis does not influence the results very much.

As is visible from the data presented earlier in this chapter, in the case of Sárpilis, additional sources were used. A listing of the population in 1792, not containing complete age data, was used to study household structure. The comparison of the listings of 1792 and 1804 and of the parish register could be used to investigate migration and the changes of household structure. A listing of the economic resources of the households from 1793 made it possible to investigate the characteristics of households and families by social strata (Andorka and Balázs-Kovács 1986). The family reconstitution based on the Calvinist parish register made it possible to investigate the demographic characteristics and changes from 1752 to the end of the nineteenth century (Andorka 1978).

Some Data on the Economic, Social, and Demographic
Characteristics of the Four Villages

The four villages are situated near one another in a well-defined geographic and ethnographic region of Hungary, namely, southeastern Transdanubia and the opposite bank of the Danube (Fajsz). This region was not poor, the soil being fertile, but land became scarce in the second half of the eighteenth century, and the area was far from any markets and from centers of protoindustrialization. The geographic conditions—marshy areas around the Danube, lack of roads—also contributed to the isolation of the region from European and even national influences. It might be concluded that these populations lived at that time in archaic conditions.

Relatively little is known about the family economy of these four villages. A monograph on the villages of the western bank of the Danube gives more information on Sárpilis and Kölked (Andrásfalvy 1975). The economic conditions were probably similar in Fajsz on the eastern bank. The economy of these villages was dominated by the fact that, being on the floodplain of the Danube, they had relatively little arable land. In consequence they had to combine cultivation of arable lands with animal husbandry (for which purpose the meadows that were periodically inundated were very suitable), fishing, hunting in the forests and at the riverside, and long-distance transportation with horse-drawn carts. The economic register of Sárpilis in 1793, which was matched to the population listings of 1792 and 1804, as well as two similar economic registers demonstrate that these peasants had little arable land. Most households had less than one unit of land held in villenage but a relative abundance of animals (horses, oxen, cows). These fragmentary data suggest that the peasants of these villages had to employ a very flexible family economy, continuously adapting their labor supply to the sources of income open to them and expanding and reducing their productive activities according to the number of adults in the household. For example, plowing of arable land could be done either by oxen or by horses. Oxen were stronger and therefore could plow the soil deeper, but plowing with one or two pair of oxen required two adult men, because in addition to the man directing the plow, one man was needed to guide the oxen. Therefore either the number of adult males had to be adjusted to the oxen or, if only one adult male lived in the household, horses had to be used instead of oxen for plowing. It might be hypothesized that peasants sought to employ a certain household structure to utilize efficiently the possibilities of production.

The peasants of these villages were socially rather differentiated. The data from Sárpilis in 1793 illustrate the social differences: of the 85 households, 32 comprised rich peasants, having 2 or 4 oxen or 2 to 6 horses; 31 comprised middle-level peasants, having 0 to 2 horses and some cows; 11 comprised poor peasants, having no large animals; and another 11 comprised very poor peasants, not included in the listing of resources. Richer peasants tended to have larger and more complicated households.

As compared to other villages in Hungary, all four villages investigated here had larger and more complicated households (table 4.4). It is doubtful that the demographic indices of Sárpilis, calculated on the basis of family reconstitution, can be assumed to represent the historical demography of the other three villages as well.

Mortality conditions in Sárpilis can be characterized by the indicators of infant and child mortality.[5] In the period from 1792 to 1820, 382 deaths of children age 0 to 9 per thousand births occurred. The rate was somewhat higher for girls (410) than for boys (350), the opposite of the usual pattern. Similarly, the mortality of adult males was more favorable than that of adult females (table 4.6).

In the period 1752–1790, the average age at first marriage for women was 19 years, and in the period 1791–1820, it was 18.4 years. The average age of men at marriage was 24.4 and 19.9, respectively, in these periods. It is difficult to estimate the frequency of remarriage in Sárpilis, as until 1805 the marital status of bridegrooms is not given. Of the 100 marriages celebrated between 1792 and 1804, 13 involved brides who were widowed and 2 involved brides who were divorced. In the case of the 66 marriages over the next ten years, between 1805 and 1814, 18 bridegrooms were widowers, 9 brides were widows, and 1 bride was divorced. From these data, it might be guessed that remarriage of widowers was more frequent than remarriage of widows.

Sárpilis is one of the villages where signs of early birth control were observed in the marriage cohort of 1752–1790. However, marital fertility was still very high, amounting to a total fertility rate of 7,180 from the ages of 20 to 49.[6] Illegitimacy rates were low (table 4.3).

The high level of fertility and the moderate rate of mortality resulted in a high rate of natural increase. In the period from 1779 to 1803, 630 bap-

TABLE 4.6   Survival of Couples Married in Sárpilis before 1791

| Age | Percentage Attaining the Given Age | |
	Male	Female
30	100	100
40	100	89
50	91	71
60	74	50
70	46	34

tisms and 414 burials are mentioned in the parish register of Sárpilis, and the population (458 in 1792 and 555 in 1804) increased by 216 as a result of the surplus of births over deaths.

Data on migration were obtained by matching the listings of 1792 and 1804 and the parish register of Sárpilis. From a population of 458 in 1792, 103 persons out-migrated in the following twelve years. From a population of 555 in 1804, 73 persons had in-migrated during the previous twelve years. Thus part of the natural increase of 216 over those years was "discharged" from Sárpilis through a negative migration balance. This fact itself points to the difficulties caused by the high rate of natural increase for the society of Sárpilis.

The out-migration of 22 percent from Sárpilis in 1792–1804 is lower than the migration intensity from Clayworth and Cohenhoe in seventeenth-century England and Hallines in eighteenth-century France and more or less similar to the population turnover in Longuenesse in eighteenth-century France (Laslett 1977). It is, however, higher than out-migration in Pinkenhof, Latvia (Plakans and Wetherell, this volume), and Krasnoe Sobakino (Czap 1983) in nineteenth-century Russia.[7]

An important factor in both out-migration and in-migration was marriage with residents of neighboring villages. The residence of the new couple was mostly determined by the principle of living in the household or at least the village of the father of the bridegroom. A few cases were found in which the new couple resided with the father of the bride.

Another important factor in the turnover of population was the out-migration and in-migration of complete households. These households belonged to three types: (1) most were landless cotter families who frequently migrated from one place to another; (2) the households of the local Calvinist pastor, notary, and schoolteacher from time to time changed their place of work from one Calvinist village to another; and (3) two economically strong farmer households and a nuclear family component of an economically strong multiple family household out-migrated from 1792 to 1804, demonstrating that there was pressure, probably caused by land scarcity, to find new "farm niches" in less densely populated parts of Hungary.

In addition, there were some "individual" migrants. Five were found in the listing of 1804. Their demographic and social characteristics illustrate the causes of these movements. These in-migrants were the following: a 35-year-old discharged soldier who returned to the household of his father and brother; a widowed father who came to live with his married son; a widowed woman who came to live with her married sister; a 77-year-old widower (the only one who was above 60 among these individual migrants) who came with his son, who had married the daughter of a local peasant; and a widowed mother who joined the household of her married son. Thus it seems that in exceptional cases of hardship, the "reincorporation strategy" (Hammel, this volume) was utilized. Nevertheless, Plakans's hypothesis that old age or "post-labor force" migration might have been rare in preindustrial rural places in Europe seems to be confirmed by the data from Sárpilis.

All these data point to the fact that these were most probably not average Hungarian villages but villages living in archaic conditions. The findings on the conditions of the elderly should not be generalized, therefore, to the whole of Hungary, where demographic and social conditions, including the conditions of the elderly, might have been rather varied. These data nevertheless give some insight into the question of the type of household conditions in which the elderly lived in archaic Hungarian villages.

Household Composition and Household Position of the Population over Age 60 in the Four Villages

On the basis of the four listings containing age data, the indicators and tables used by Laslett (1977) were calculated and compiled. The data are compared to Laslett's.

The percentage of the population over age 60 is lower than in the English, French, German, Italian, Icelandic, and Japanese localities given by Laslett but is near those found in Austria, Estonia, and Serbia. The sex ratio is among the highest in all these places (table 4.5). The problems of the elderly, which in present-day Western societies are predominantly the problems of old women, were in these four villages about two hundred years ago predominantly the problems of old men.

The most conspicuous difference in terms of marital status between the Hungarian villages and the places presented by Laslett is the absence of single persons in the former.[8] The percentage of married men is somewhat higher in the Hungarian villages than in most places given by Laslett, while the percentage of married women is similar or somewhat lower in Hungary than in England and France but much higher than in Serbia and Japan (table 4.7). In consequence, the percentage of widows among the women is higher in Hungary than in all the English and French locals but much lower than in Serbia and in Japan.

The high sex ratio and the much higher percentage of married persons among the men than among the women over age 60 suggest that the age difference between spouses might have been important. The comparison of the ages of married men with the ages of their wives demonstrates that, indeed, more than half of the wives were ten or more years younger than their husbands (table 4.8).[9] Husbands' second marriages were distinguished only in the listing of Mezőcsoknya. Here both husbands over age 60 who had wives who were younger by more than ten years were in a second marriage.[10] It might be assumed that in the other villages, marriages involving husbands

TABLE 4.7　Proportion Married among Those Aged 60+

Village	Men (%)	Women (%)
Fajsz	81	61
Mezőcsoknya	89	9
Sárpilis	79	60
Kölked	53	27
Total	76	41

TABLE 4.8　Number of Married Men Aged 60+ by Age Groups and the Age Groups of Their Wives in Four Hungarian Villages

Age of Husband	Age of Wife									Total
	≤ 39	40–49	50–54	55–59	60–64	65–69	70–74	75–79	80+	
60–64	1	12	9	3	4	—	—	—	—	29
65–69	1	1	1	—	1	1	—	—	—	5
70–74	—	2	1	1	2	3	2	—	—	11
75–79	2	—	1	—	—	1	1	—	—	4
80+	1	1	1	1	—	1	2	1	2	11
Total	5	16	13	5	7	6	5	1	2	58

who were much older than their wives were second marriages as well. Therefore, it might be hypothesized that the relatively low proportion of widowers among the old men was due to a large extent to the fact that widowed men usually remarried, sometimes marrying much younger women.

As in the English communities presented by Laslett, most married men and women over age 60 were household heads and spouses of heads (table 4.9). The majority of widowed men were also household heads, but only about half of the widows were heads of households. Altogether, 93 percent of the men and 70 percent of the women over age 60 were household heads (table 4.10).

A closer look at the persons who were not household heads helps explain the high headship rates. Only two married men were found who were not heads of households. One of them was 93 years old and lived with his 88-year-old wife in the household of a married son. The other was an 85-year-old servant-lodger who lived with his 38-year-old wife in the household of an unrelated farmer. The two widowed men who were not heads and lived with married children were 77 and 76 years old. The two who lived in a household of nonkin were a 76-year-old lodger and a 60-year-old servant. One of the widows who was not a head lived as a servant in a nonkin-related household.

TABLE 4.9   Proportion of Persons over Age 60 Who Are Household
Head or Spouse of Head

Village	Male		Female	
	Married (%)	Unmarried (%)	Married (%)	Unmarried (%)
Fajsz	94	75	91	100
Mezőcsoknya	100	100	100	30
Sárpilis	100	100	100	0
Kölked	100	100	100	60
Total	97	81	96	52

No systematic difference could be found between the widows who were heads of the households in which their married and/or unmarried children lived and the widows who lived in households headed by their married children. Men over age 60 were not heads only in exceptional cases of old age or poverty. No clear rule is evident for women remaining heads after widowhood or giving over the headship to one of their children.

The most conspicuous difference as compared to the English communities analyzed by Laslett is that in these Hungarian villages, no person over age 60 lived in an institution, only two unmarried men and one unmarried woman lived as a servant and/or lodger in a nonkin household, and no person lived alone. It is clear that no institutions for the care of old and poor persons existed in these villages, and apparently no children were willing to let their widowed parents live by themselves. Old widowed parents either continued to live in their households together with their unmarried and married children or entered the households of married children after widowhood. Not only the parents of the household head but in some cases also the widowed mother of the head's spouse lived in the household. Comparison of the listing of 1804 and Sárpilis with the listing of 1792 indicates that widowed parents in some cases were accepted into the households of their married children, that is, the hardship reincorporation household scenario (Hammel, this volume).

Both married and unmarried old people lived much more frequently with their married children than was the case in England (table 4.10). Seventy-six percent of the men and 82 percent of the women over age 60 lived together with married children and in most cases with grandchildren. In consequence, the generational depth of the households in which old people lived was great: in 73 percent of these households, members of three generations lived together (table 4.11). Most old persons thus had everyday contact with their grandchildren, and many children had everyday contact with their grandparents.[11]

TABLE 4.10 Number of Persons Aged 60+ by Sex, Marital Status, and Household Position in Four Hungarian Villages

	Fajsz 1762		Mezőcsoknya 1800		Sárpilis 1804		Kölked 1816		Total	
Marital Status and Household Position	Male	Female	Male	Female	Male	Female	Male	Female	Male	Female
Married, household head, having in their household										
Unmarried children	7	—	3	—	—	—	—	3	10	3
Married children	6	3	1	—	9	3	6	1	22	7
Unmarried and married children	17	6	2	—	6	3	3	—	28	9
Others	3	1	—	—	—	—	—	—	3	1
Only spouse	—	—	2	1	—	—	—	—	2	1
Married, not household head, living in the household of										
Unmarried children	—	1	—	—	—	—	—	—	—	1
Married children	1	1	—	—	—	—	—	—	1	1
Unmarried and married children	—	—	—	—	—	—	—	—	—	—
Others	1	—	—	—	—	—	—	—	1	—
Not married, household head, having in their household										
Unmarried children	2	1	—	—	—	—	1	—	3	1
Married children	2	5	1	2	1	—	7	5	11	12
Unmarried and married children	2	1	—	1	1	—	—	1	3	3
Others	—	—	—	—	—	—	—	1	—	1
Not married, not household head, living in the household of										
Unmarried children	—	—	—	—	—	—	—	—	—	—
Married children	1	—	—	7	1	2	—	3	2	12
Unmarried and married children	—	—	—	—	1	1	—	1	—	2
Others	1	—	—	—	—	1	—	—	2	1
Total	43	18	9	11	19	10	17	15	88	54

TABLE 4.11   Distribution of Households by Generational Depth
in Four Hungarian Villages

Number of Generations in Household	Fajsz	Mezőcsoknya 1800	Sárpilis	Kölked	Total
1	1	1	—	—	2
2	16	4	3	4	27
3	31	14	18	24	87
Solitary servants	2	—	2	—	4
Total	50	19	23	28	120

NOTE: In Fajsz, 2 persons aged 60+ lived in two-generation households and 9 persons in three-generation households; in Mezőcsoknya, 2 persons lived in 1 one-generation household; in Sárpilis, 2 persons lived in 6 three-generation households; in Kölked, 2 persons lived in 4 three-generation households.

The other aspect of the same phenomenon is that most of the households in which old people lived were of complex structure: following the typology proposed by Laslett (1972), only 13 percent belonged to the simple family household type, 26 percent to the extended family household type, and 57 percent to the multiple family household type (4 percent were not classifiable). Of the 57 percent who lived in multiple family households, 26 percent belonged to the "stem" type, 18 percent to the "joint" type, and 13 percent to the "frérèche" type.[12] Thus the joint- and frérèche-type households, which were infrequent in Hungary and very rare in western Europe, were relatively frequent among the households of the elderly in these villages (table 4.12).

It seems that older people lived largely in extended and multiple family households. It would be premature, however, to draw the conclusion that a stem and/or joint family system was the general rule in these four villages. To understand the formation of these complicated households, the changes of household contexts of the elderly have to be analyzed.

The comparison of the listings of 1792 and 1804 gives some insight into the changes of the household context of the persons over age 60 in 1804 in Sárpilis. Five of these older persons were not found in the listing of 1792; they probably immigrated in the meantime. Two of them were widowed mothers of household heads. It might be assumed that they lived in a neighboring village before the death of their husbands and came to live after widowhood with their married sons in Sárpilis. The three others were old men who immigrated with their families.

For those found in both listings, we can distinguish the following transitions: (1) becoming a cotter or a servant; (2) living in the same simple household; (3) the household changing from a simple to a more complex pattern, in consequence of the marriage of an unmarried child; and (4) splitting of the household, the elderly parent living in 1804 in a "successor"

TABLE 4.12   Household Structure of Persons Aged 60+:
Number of Households by Type in Four Hungarian Villages

Household Type	Fajsz 1762	Mezőcsoknya 1800	Sárpilis 1804	Kölked 1816	Total
3. Simple family household					
3.a. Married couple alone	1	1	—	—	2
3.b. Married couple with child(ren)	8	3	—	1	12
3.c. Widower with child(ren)	—	—	—	1	1
3.d. Widow with child(ren)	1	—	—	—	1
4. Extended family household					
4.a. Extended upward	8	6	3	11	28
4.b. Extended downward	2	—	—	—	2
4.c. Extended laterally	1	—	—	—	1
5. Multiple family household					
5.a. Secondary unit(s) up	—	—	—	—	—
5.b.1. Secondary unit(s) down "stem"	16	4	6	5	31
5.b.2. Secondary unit(s) down "joint"	6	—	10	6	22
5.c.d. Units on one level	4	5	2	4	15
5.e. Other multiple[a]	1	—	—	—	1
6. Not classifiable (solitary servants in household of nonkin)[a]	2	—	2	—	4
Total	50	19	23	28	120

[a]The conjugal families of two married brothers and of one married son of one of the brothers living in one household.

household. There is no case of an elderly person who lived in 1792 in a complex household living in 1804 in a simple household.

One person, who was head of a simple family household in 1792, was widowed; his son married into another household, and he himself lived as a cotter in a nonkin household. A widower who lived in the stem household of his son in 1792 lived after the death of this son as a servant in a nonkin household in 1804.

One person lived as the head of the same simple family household in both years with his wife and his unmarried young children. One person lived as the head of the same stem household with his wife and the family of his married son. Two persons, an old couple, lived as heads of the same stem household with the family of their eldest son, the two younger daughters having departed to a neighboring village when they married.

Seven people—three couples and a male household head—lived in simple family households in 1792 which became stem households in 1804 as a result of the marriage of one of their sons. One male household head lived in a simple family household in 1792 which became a joint household in 1804 due to the marriage of two sons. One male household head lived in a simple family household in 1792 which became a multiple household (type 5.c.d.) after the death of his spouse and the marriage of two sons.

The remaining nine people over age 60 in 1804 lived in households in 1792 which had split by 1804 into several households. One woman had lived with her husband in a simple family household. Her husband died, one of her sons married, and she then lived with her younger son in the stem household of this married son, who was the head of the household. Meanwhile, a daughter married and entered another simple family household.

One old man lived with his wife, his younger unmarried son, and his older married son in a stem household in 1792. The married son separated and lived in his own simple family household. The younger son also married and lived with his parents, who remained household heads, in a stem household.

Two people lived in a stem household with one married son and three unmarried children. Two of the unmarried sons married between 1792 and 1804; one of them established a separate simple family household, the other remained in the household of the parents together with the oldest married son, so that the household was of a joint type (5.b) in 1804.

One male household head lived in a joint household in 1792 with two married sons. One of the married sons established a separate 3.b household, so that the original household of the head became a stem household.

One male household head lived in 1792 in a frérèche-type (5.c.d) household with the family of his younger married brother. The two families split, and the older brother lived in a simple family household, while one of the sons of his younger brother married, so that they ended up living in a stem household.

One male household head lived with his family and two younger married brothers in a frérèche household. The three families split and established separate households, the younger brothers forming simple family households, the oldest brother a stem household in which a married son lived with his parents.

Finally, a couple lived in 1792 with two married sons and the widowed sister of one of their daughters-in-law and her child in a joint household. The widowed sister died, and her son married into another household, where his father-in-law was the head. The older married son established his own separate simple family household, while the parents lived with their younger married son in a stem household.

Thus the household context of the old people changed in various ways between 1792 and 1804 under the influence of demographic events. One type of change, however, never happened: no elderly person who lived in a complex household with his or her children later lived in a simple family household, if married children were present in the villages. No clear corre-

TABLE 4.13   Co-Residence by Age and Sex in Kölked, 1816

Age	Percentage Living in Extended and Multiple Family Households	
	Male	Female
0–9	55	62
10–19	51	63
20–29	85	88
30–39	71	57
40–49	49	59
50–59	68	83
60+	89	100
All	64	67

lation could be found between the changes of these households and their economic resources (measured by the number of oxen, horses, and cows in their possession in 1793). The two households that disappeared were, however, poor.

It seems that the life of the older population was organized in a rather different way in these four Hungarian villages from that in western Europe and even in western-central Europe (e.g., Austria). Most of the old people lived in households with their married children or at least with one married child (table 4.13). They shared with them not only housing but also the costs of living. In case of need, adult children were able to care for their old parents. This resulted from a household system characterized by a large proportion of extended and multiple family households. This household system was well adapted to the economic circumstances of these villages and was supported by cultural values and norms. Nevertheless, this did not result in "perennial" multiple family households. The household structure adapted continuously—both on the micro- and macrolevel—to the changing demographic and economic conditions of the individual families and of the village community.

IMPLICATIONS FOR THE HANDLING OF CURRENT SOCIAL PROBLEMS IN HUNGARY

The conditions of the elderly population (18.7 percent of the total population was over age 60 in 1989) are problematic in several respects. As pensions are not indexed, only the lowest pensions are increased so that they do not fall below the official minimum. The older pensioners, more or less those above the age of 70, often face serious financial problems. The health conditions of the elderly are very bad; many suffer from chronic illnesses. Many old persons, especially widows, are isolated. As long as the old people continue to work after retirement in a part-time job or in the second economy, their daily life is dominated by these income-supplementing activities. When they cannot find such work, they, especially the old men, do not find rewarding and meaningful leisure activities for themselves (Andorka 1990).

The Hungarian state is not able to solve the problems of the elderly. It does not seem to be possible to assure the indexing of pensions in the framework of the present social security system. The health care system, particularly the care provided for the elderly, is considered to be of rather low quality, so that those in the medical service and the old patients themselves are very dissatisfied. The institutional homes for the elderly provide housing and care for only a small segment of the elderly population and are considered to give very poor services, so that older people and their younger family members tend to take advantage of them only in case of extreme need.

In these circumstances, families, especially children, aid their older relatives as much as possible in Hungary today. The simplest way to provide financial support, daily health care, and human contacts to the elderly is for elderly parents and their married or unmarried adult children to live together in the same household. Although the share of complex households has declined, it has remained relatively high in Hungary: in 1980, 13.5 percent of the population lived in households that might be defined as "extended," and 8.3 percent lived in "multiple family" households, following Laslett's typology (table 4.14). A survey in 1969 showed that 40 percent of the men of pensionable age (60+) and 49 percent of the women of pensionable age (55+) lived together with at least one child (Andorka et al. 1972). A comparison of the households of the elderly in the United States and in Budapest in the 1980s demonstrates that a much higher percentage of Hungarian elderly lived with adult children in the same households (Farber et al. 1990).

TABLE 4.14   Household Structure: Distributions of Persons and of Households by Type in Hungary, 1980

Household Type	Persons (%)	Households (%)
Solitary	7.1	19.6
Nonfamily household	2.6	3.4
Simple family household	68.5	63.5
Extended family household	13.5	9.2
Two-family, in vertical relation	7.4	3.8
Two-family, in lateral relation	0.1	0.1
Two-family, nonkin	0.4	0.2
Three-family	0.4	0.2
Total	100	100

All available survey data suggest that the old people living with or at least in the proximity of younger family members, usually children, have fewer income problems, are better cared for in case of illness, and are more satisfied with their human relationships and with life in general than those who do not have frequent contact with their children. The decline of the average number of children per family, the growth of the divorce rate, the decline of the rate of remarriage of divorced persons, urbanization, the high level of migration, and the small size of new dwellings in urban apartment houses all tend to diminish the cohabitation of parents and adult children, increasing the loneliness of old couples and unmarried old persons.

These are tendencies of modern life; nevertheless, it might be hypothesized that long-standing national characteristics, cultural values, beliefs, and norms continue to condition the living conditions of the older population even in advanced societies (Altergott 1988). From the data presented here, it seems that the cohabitation of elderly parents with their adult married children and the intensive help provided to elderly parents by their children are long-standing norms in Hungarian culture. It might be hoped that at least as long as the present hardships of an important part of the old population continue, their children will be willing to provide the financial help and the personal care that the underdeveloped welfare state is unable to provide.

NOTES

1. A similar tendency of growing household complexity was observed in two Italian communities: Fagagna (Laslett 1983) and Casalecchio (Kertzer 1989).

2. Originally one unit of land held in villenage, called a "serf parcel," was considered to be necessary for supporting one peasant family.

3. In the villages of German ethnicity, the households were on the average smaller, and simple family households predominated (Andorka and Faragó 1983).

4. I am grateful to Sandor Balázs-Kovács for locating and giving me access to the population listings of Sárpilis and to Laszlo Kosa for finding and giving me access to the Mezőcsoknya listing.

5. The rate of mortality of ages 0–9 is used instead of the infant mortality rate, as it is often not clear from the register whether mortality cases given as "one year old" were really somewhat below or over the first birthday.

6. Therefore, the famous "one child family system" or the "sin of Transdanubia" (Vásáry 1989) still had no influence on the conditions of the elderly in 1804 in Sárpilis.

7. When evaluating the migration rates, it is worth noting that only Pinkenhof had a larger population than Sárpilis. The other villages were smaller.

8. The absence of single persons in the population over age 60 was so surprising that the four lists were very carefully reviewed to find out whether single persons were not "hidden" among the widowed. This review, however, proved that there were indeed no single men and women over age 60 in these lists.

9. The age of several wives in the listing of Sárpilis could not be identified.

10. The husband and the wife in these two couples were aged 78 and 47 and 67 and 47.

11. Tables 4.11 and 4.12 present the distribution of households in which persons over age 60 lived (i.e., not the distributions of the persons over age 60). The notes to these tables give additional data on the households in which two old persons lived, so that the distributions of persons over age 60 can be calculated.

12. The Laslett (1972) typology is supplemented by subdividing the multiple family household (= type 5.b), secondary unit(s) down category, into stem (5.b.1) and joint (5.b.2) subcategories. In the stem households, one parental conjugal family unit and one nuclear unit of an ever-married son or daughter or his or her widowed spouse lived together. In the joint households, one parental conjugal unit and more than one unit of ever-married sons or daughters or their widowed spouses lived together.

REFERENCES

Altergott, Karen. 1988. "Daily life in later life: Concepts and methods of inquiry." In *Daily life in later life,* ed. Karen Altergott, 11–22. Newbury Park, Calif.: Sage.

Andorka, Rudolf. 1978. *Determinants of fertility in advanced societies.* London: Methuen.

———. 1988. *A családrekonstituciós vizsgálat módszerei* [The methods of family reconstitution]. KSH Népességtudományi Kutató Intézet Történeti Demográfiai Füzetek, no. 4.

———. 1990. "The role of the family in the care of the elderly in Hungary." In *Aiding and aging: The coming crisis in support for the elderly by kin and state,* ed. John Mogey, 35–48. New York: Greenwood Press.

Andorka, Rudolf, Laszlóné Babarczy, László Cseh-Szombathy, Béla Ghyczy, and András Laktos. 1972. *Az öregek helyzete és problemai* [The conditions and problems of the aged]. Budapest: Central Statistical Office.

Andorka, Rudolf, and Sándor Balázs-Kovács. 1986. "The social demography of Hungarian villages in the eighteenth and nineteenth centuries, with special attention to Sárpilis, 1792–1804." *Journal of Family History* 11: 169–192.

Andorka, Rudolf, and Tamás Faragó. 1983. "Pre-industrial household structure in Hungary." In *Family forms in historic Europe,* ed. Richard Wall, with Jean Robin and Peter Laslett, 281–307. Cambridge: Cambridge University Press.

Andrásfalvy, Bertalan. 1975. *Duna menta népének ártéri gazdálkodása Tolna es Baranya vármegyében az ármentesítés befejezéséig* [The economy in the inundated area of the population living at the riverside of the Danube in counties Tolna and Baranya until the completion of the anti-inundation works]. Szekszard: Tolna megyei Tanacs Leveltara.

Barth, Janos. 1975. "Fajsz népessége a 18. század közepén" [The population of Fajsz in the middle of the eighteenth century]. *Bacs-Kiskun megve multjabol* 1: 81–131.

Berkner, Lutz K. 1972. "The stem family and the development cycle of the peasant household." *American Historical Review* 77(2): 398–418.

Czap, Peter. 1983. " 'A large family, the peasant's greatest wealth': Serf households in Mishino, Russia, 1815–1858." In *Family forms in historic Europe,* ed. Richard Wall, with Jean Robin and Peter Laslett, 105–151. Cambridge: Cambridge University Press.

Danhieux, Luc. 1983. "The evolving household: The case of Lampernisse, West Flanders." In *Family forms in historic Europe*, ed. Richard Wall, with Jean Robin and Peter Laslett, 409–420. Cambridge: Cambridge University Press.

Dányi, Dezsö. 1965. "Városi háztartások és családok a 18.század végén, Györ, 1787" [Urban households and families at the end of the eighteenth century]. *Történeti Statisztikai Évkönyv 1963–1964* 3: 5–204.

Faragó, Tamás. 1977. "Háztartásszerkezet és falusi társadalom-fejlödés Magyarországon 1787–1828" [Structure of households and development of rural society in Hungary, 1787–1828]. *Történeti Statisztikai Tanulmányok* 3: 105–214.

Farber, Bernard, John Mogey, Ione DeOllos, and Robert A. Lewis. 1990. "Household composition among the elderly in the United States and Hungary: A comparison." In *Aiding and aging: The coming crisis in support for the elderly by kin and state*, ed. John Mogey, 11–33. New York: Greenwood Press.

Fél, Edit, and Tamás Hofer. 1969. *Proper peasants*. Chicago: Wenner-Gren Foundation.

Flinn, Michael W. 1981. *The European demographic system 1500–1820*. Brighton: Harvester Press.

Gaunt, David. 1983. "The property and kin relationships of retired farmers in northern and central Europe." In *Family forms in historic Europe*, ed. Richard Wall, with Jean Robin and Peter Laslett, 249–279. Cambridge: Cambridge University Press.

Hajnal, John. 1965. "European marriage patterns in perspective." In *Population in history*, ed. D. V. Glass and D. E. C. Eversley, 101–143. London: Edward Arnold.

———. 1983. "Two kinds of pre-industrial household formation systems." In *Family forms in historic Europe*, ed. Richard Wall, with Jean Robin and Peter Laslett, 65–104. Cambridge: Cambridge University Press.

Kertzer, David I. 1989. "The joint family household revisited: Demographic constraints and household complexity in the European past." *Journal of Family History* 14(1): 1–15.

Laslett, Peter. 1972. "Introduction: The history of the family." In *Household and family in past time*, ed. Peter Laslett, with Richard Wall, 1–89. Cambridge: Cambridge University Press.

———. 1977. *Family life and illicit love in earlier generations*. Cambridge: Cambridge University Press.

———. 1983. Family and household as work group and kin group: Areas of traditional Europe compared. In *Family forms in historic Europe*, ed. Richard Wall, with Jean Robin and Peter Laslett, 513–563. Cambridge: Cambridge University Press.

———. 1988. "Family, kinship and collectivity as systems of support in pre-industrial Europe." *Continuity and Change* 3: 153–176.

Mándoki, Lászlo. 1971. "A kölkedi népszámlálás" [The conscription of Kölked in 1816]. *Janus Pannonius Muzeum Evkonyve* 13: 215–224.

McIntosh, Marjorie K. 1988. "Local responses to the poor in late medieval and Tudor England." *Continuity and Change* 3: 209–246.

Palli, Haldur. 1983. "Estonian households in the seventeenth and eighteenth centuries." In *Family forms in historic Europe*, ed. Richard Wall, with Jean Robin and Peter Laslett, 207–216. Cambridge: Cambridge University Press.

Pullan, Brian. 1988. "Support and redeem: Charity and poor relief in Italian cities from the fourteenth to the seventeenth century." *Continuity and Change* 3: 177–208.

Tárkány-Szücs, Ernö. 1981. *Magyar jogi népszokások* [Hungarian legal folk customs]. Budapest: Gondolat.

Vásáry, Ildiko. 1989. " 'The sin of Transdanubia': The one-child system in rural Hungary." *Continuity and Change* 4: 429–468.

Viazzo, Pier Paolo. 1989. *Upland communities: Environment, population, and social structure in the Alps since the sixteenth century.* Cambridge: Cambridge University Press.

FIVE

Migration in the Later Years of Life in Traditional Europe

Andrejs Plakans and Charles Wetherell

The spatial mobility of persons in the later years of life in traditional Europe remains virtually unexplored. Although the subject should be part of research on migration and old age, the current agendas in both fields do not lend themselves to merging for several reasons. For one, historians of migration and old age focus primarily on demographically and economically "modern," "modernizing," "industrial," or "industrializing" societies, a tendency attributable to the prominence of modernization theory in early debates on aging as well as to the indisputably profound level of migration in the Western world during the last three centuries (Moch 1992). Thus historians have ignored the migration of the elderly in the *distant* past, where discussions of "traditional Europe" should properly be lodged, in part because they perceive the action to have been in the *recent* past.

For another, in mapping the demographic landscape of both traditional and modern Europe, demographers have devoted more attention to mortality and fertility than to migration generally and far more to the movements of those who were actively involved in productive labor and the search for it than of those who were withdrawing from it or had completed the process altogether (Knodel 1988; Smith 1981; Wall 1984). We also know more about the western and central parts of Europe than about southern and eastern areas, although recent changes in archival access in eastern Europe promise to rectify some of the geographic imbalance. Moreover, demographers of modern Europe have focused on older segments of populations because these became proportionately larger after the demographic transition and now generate immense concern as the population of the Western world "ages" in the twentieth century.

Although historians have found the analytical imperatives of modernization theory and the demographic realities of the modern world less compelling in recent years (Hareven 1976; Jackson and Moch 1989; Moch 1983, 1992), simply shifting attention from the recent to the distant past cannot instantly fill the void in our historical understanding of migration among the elderly in traditional European societies. A disaffection with the explanatory power of structural differences between the traditional and modern worlds (as yet temporally undefined in any meaningful way) and a preference for attitudinal change that characterizes much current re-search handicap historians of inarticulate, traditional European popula-tions. Yet major structural differences, such as those embodied in the insti-tution of serfdom, do separate the distant and more recent European past. Whether they are important to the history of the mobility of the elderly re-mains to be seen. At the very least, the meager knowledge historians pos-sess about the old in traditional Europe, particularly the migrating old, sug-gests the need to avoid simplistic or anachronistic conceptualizations. Moch's (1992) recent survey of migration in western Europe since 1650 goes a long way to correct earlier notions, but historians of the elderly still face a formidable task.

Historians dealing with the migration of older Europeans in the twenti-eth century, for example, draw heavily on labor economics and view move-ment among the elderly principally as *retirement migration* (Cribier 1974, 1982; Law and Warnes 1982). While a useful perspective for societies in which age grading is prominent, the notion seems decidedly unhelpful for traditional Europe, where withdrawal from the world of work was piece-meal and the elderly worked until infirmity or death (Plakans 1989). Any sharp contrast between the independence of the traditional and modern European aged may also need to be rethought, as has proved to be the case for the United States (Achenbaum 1978; Fischer 1977; Gratton 1986). In a study of retirement migration in contemporary France, Françoise Cribier (1974: 361) argued that "the proportion of the elderly in the population of a region, which *used to be* a function only of the birth rate and the exo-dus or in-migration of young people, *today* depends also on the actual be-havior of the elderly" (emphasis added). Cribier never says why the elderly in societies that *used to be* did not exercise as much choice, but her premise seems to be that decision-making talent marked only the better-endowed modern old.

Finally, the notion of migration itself poses analytical difficulties for any analysis of the traditional past. Geographers and demographers rou-tinely distinguish between *migration* and *mobility*. Conceptually, they base that distinction on the distance people move and on the social impact of that movement. Changing residence constitutes mobility if work, for exam-ple, remains close enough not to disrupt other social activities; it consti-tutes migration if work is not close enough to avoid disruption. Practically, however, the distinction often translates into movement across administrative boundaries, which can pose enormous strategic problems for historians forced to deal with records from separate secular or ecclesiastical divisions.

Beyond the seemingly simple yet often intractable distinction between migration and mobility, researchers also commonly differentiate among types of movement. In addition to *local* migration in which the distance moved is generally short and the accompanying level of social dislocation is low, Charles Tilly (1978: 51–57; see also Moch 1992: 16–17) distinguished among *circular* (distance unimportant, but return involved), *chain* (persisters following movers), and *career* (long-distance, no return) migration. Despite their considerable heuristic value, the underlying context of each type of migration is economic (specifically, labor markets) and so primarily useful for evaluating migration in the recent past. David I. Kertzer and Dennis P. Hogan's (1989) and Leslie Page Moch's (1992) studies of the nature and context of local, regional, and continental patterns of migration in western and southern Europe have greatly advanced our understanding of the phenomenon by showing how larger, often state induced, changes in the "fundamental structures of European economic life: landholding, employment, demographic patterns, and the development of capital" (Moch 1992: 6) affected migration. Yet if movement was always a central feature of European life, what Tilly and others term "local flows" (Tilly 1978: 63) remain the least investigated—and perhaps most common—in traditional European societies where the spatial worlds of work and community life were constrained by law and habit.

The major obstacle to a sharper image of migration in the traditional European past lies, of course, in the nature and extent of available historical sources. Few communities exist with records as extensive as Casalecchio in Italy (Hogan and Kertzer 1985; Kertzer and Hogan 1985, 1989, 1990), and therefore analysis almost always has to be data rather than problem driven. As existing studies of the more distant past make abundantly clear, refining the question to ask who moved at certain ages compounds the difficulties because of the nearly complete absence of age-specific migration information in standard historical sources such as parish registers and census enumerations. And if we pose the question in an even more specialized form to deal only with people in the later years of life, comparative opportunities narrow even further. We find, for example, that R. S. Schofield's analysis (1987) of the unique population listing for Cardington parish in eighteenth-century England deals only with the mobility of persons to about age 30 because the list permits no more; that Peter Clark's (1987) study of migration in England in the late seventeenth and early eighteenth century groups the elderly with everyone over 40; and that Jan Lucassen's study (1987) of European migrant labor in the period 1600–1900 contains no age-specific information. If the elderly appear at all in work on historical migration, it is most often as an afterthought.

A CASE STUDY: PINKENHOF, 1833–1850

Our dissatisfaction with existing work stems from our continuing investigation of an eastern European serf estate, Pinkenhof, in the Russian Baltic province of Livland, now Latvia, between 1790 and 1850 (Plakans and Wetherell 1988*a*, 1988*b*, 1988*c*, 1990, 1992). Until 1819, the peasants of Pinkenhof were serfs, and their movements across estate boundaries were severely restricted. The Peasant Emancipation Law of 1819 (Schwabe 1928; Tobien 1899) introduced personal freedom and expanded the right of movement, both of which the Livlandic nobility viewed as necessary prerequisites to a free labor market. Yet the new law did not permit absolute freedom of movement (that right was introduced gradually to different segments of the peasant population) and formally deprived the peasantry of even those usufruct rights to land they had enjoyed under the old estate regime of serfdom. In principle, peasants were free to sell their labor to the highest bidder. In reality, now landless, peasants did not move away but continued to occupy their old farmsteads in exchange for money rents. Although the population possessed both traditional and modern demographic attributes that indicate it was moving swiftly into the demographic transition (Plakans and Wetherell 1988*a*), the decades immediately following emancipation in Pinkenhof were ones of gradual adjustment and not rapid change.

The Russian Imperial head tax censuses, or "revisions of souls," for Pinkenhof, which provide detailed enumerations of the human groupings at the farmstead level from 1782 onward, reveal no massive in- or out-migration in either the pre- or the postemancipation periods, although both kinds of movement existed to varying degrees. The 1850 revision, however, was more than a simple nominal listing of 1,569 residents living on 123 farmsteads, the main estate farm, or *Hof*, and several smaller, functionally specialized places; it indicated where each of the 1850 residents had lived in 1833. Moreover, if an 1833 inhabitant had left the estate before 1850, his or her departure was noted, together with a date and a destination; if he or she had arrived since 1833, that was noted also, together with the place of origin although not always with the year of arrival. The 1850 revision, therefore, allows us to explore external migration and, to a lesser extent, internal mobility.

As in most Baltic landed estates, everyday rural life in Pinkenhof transpired on spatially separated farmsteads, not nucleated villages. Each of the 123 fixed residential farms in 1850 bore a name that recurs in estate documents as far back as the latter part of the seventeenth century. New entrants

TABLE 5.1   Age-Specific External Migration Rates,
Pinkenhof, 1833–1850

Age Cohort	Midperiod Population	Number of Migrants	External Migration Rate (CMR$_e$)
0–14	490	7	0.8
15–19	162	17	5.8
20–24	140	50	19.8
25–29	145	84	32.2
30–34	129	21	9.0
35–39	104	7	3.7
40–44	85	3	2.0
45–49	63	2	1.8
50–54	61	1	0.9
55+	93	2	1.2
Total	1,472	194	7.3

SOURCE: The Ninth Imperial Revision for Livland, Central National Historical Archive, Riga, Latvia (Baltic Microfilms, D112, Oekonomie Expedition d. Stadtkassakollegiums IV E. 4, Revisionsliste Gut Pinkenhof, J. G. Herder Institut, Marburg a.d. Lahn, Germany).

into the estate, therefore, augmented the labor force of particular farmsteads, and those who left diminished it. Correspondingly, internal mobility, including that of the elderly, took place between farmsteads, rather than between farmsteads and institutions reserved for the aging, or between a farm's main residential quarters and outbuildings set apart for the aged as was frequently the practice in central Europe (Mitterauer and Sieder 1977: 162–163). The main building of a farmstead was therefore the residential site of all members, including the aging and aged; and judging by the architecture of these buildings, the living space within could be readily adjusted to accommodate any increase or decrease in residents (Kundzins 1974; Veveris and Kuplais n.d.). As such, housing the marginally productive elderly—if indeed the elderly can be thought of in this way at all—was not a serious problem, and we have to seek the reasons for their movement elsewhere.

But Pinkenhofers did move. Between 1833 and 1850, 192 men and women left and entered Pinkenhof, for a net migration rate of −17.7. For females, the rate was 4.1 and for males, −21.7, a discrepancy attributable to a high level of conscription among males (Plakans and Wetherell 1988a). Table 5.1 displays age-specific migration rates for both males and females; figure 5.1 gives a stylized age profile.

Overall, the crude external migration rate, CMR$_e$, was 7.3, but the incidence of migration was greatest for those in their 20s (30.3) who were moving in and out of the estate to marry.[1] At the same time, the neighboring estate of Bebberbeck and others in the adjoining province of Kurland, which

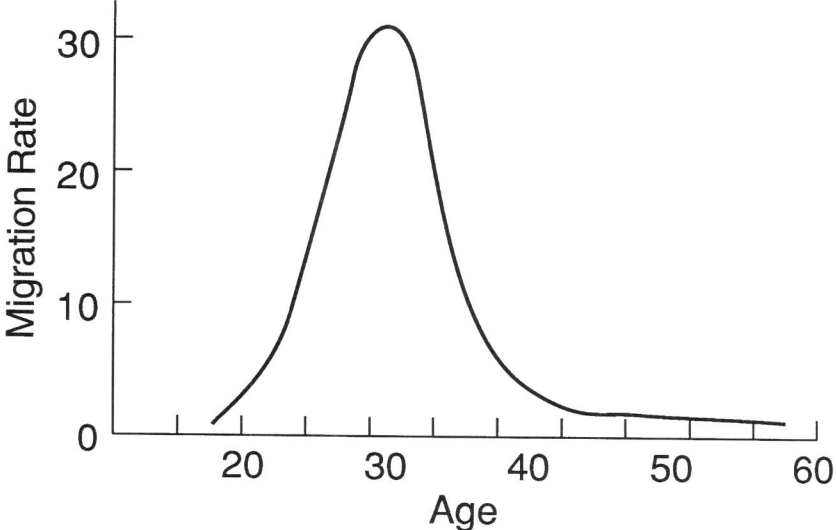

Fig. 5.1. Stylized age profile of external migrants, Pinkenhof, 1833–1850. Data from the Ninth Imperial Revision for Livland, Central National Historical Archive, Riga, Latvia (Baltic Microfilms, D112, Oekonomie Expedition d. Stadtkassakollegiums IV E. 4, Revisionsliste Gut Pinkenhof, J. G. Herder Institut, Marburg a.d. Lahn, Germany).

were the sources of half (44 of 84) of all immigrants and half (38 of 74) of all emigrants (excluding 36 conscripted males), were so geographically close to Pinkenhof that any hard and fast distinction between migration and mobility may blur the historical reality. Nonetheless, the record indicates that external migration, defined as movement across the estate's boundaries, was limited almost exclusively to young adults; for those over 40, it was virtually nonexistent.

Internal mobility is more difficult to evaluate for two reasons. First, the revision only documents the presence of a person in one farmstead in 1833 and in another in 1850; it does not record any intervening moves that might have occurred between those two years. Second, the source does not allow us to say at what ages internal migrants moved. All we know are the ages of 459 people who were at least 18 years old in 1850 and who had changed their farmsteads of residence at least once between 1833 and 1850. At the same time, it seems safe to conclude that movement within the estate—*mobility*—was much greater than movement across estate boundaries—*migration*. For one thing, the ratio of recorded internal to external moves was more than 2:1. For another, the record keepers were especially careful to document movement into and out of the estate. Indeed, 2 of the 192 migrants both entered and left Pinkenhof between 1833 and 1850. Finally, we also know that

TABLE 5.2   Hypothetical Age-Specific Internal Migration Rates and
Proportions of 1850 Population Internally Mobile, Pinkenhof, 1833–1850

Age Cohort	1850 Population	Number of Migrants	Internal Migration Rate (CMR$_i$)	Percentage of Population Mobile
18–19	76	30	21.9	35.9
20–24	139	79	31.6	56.8
25–29	136	75	30.6	55.1
30–34	125	72	32.0	57.6
45–39	106	53	27.8	50.0
40–44	104	43	23.0	41.3
45–49	85	39	25.5	45.9
50–54	72	31	23.9	43.1
55+	126	37	16.3	29.4
Total	969	459	26.3	47.4

SOURCE: The Ninth Imperial Revision for Livland, Central National Historical Archive, Riga, Latvia (Baltic Microfilms, D112, Oekonomie Expedition d. Stadtkassakollegiums IV E. 4, Revisionsliste Gut Pinkenhof, J. G. Herder Institut, Marburg a.d. Lahn, Germany).

the labor force in Pinkenhof was far from stationary and that adult farmhands and their children, who accounted for 43 percent of the population in 1850, traditionally moved about the estate on a regular basis (Plakans and Wetherell 1988*b*, 1992; Svarane 1971). Accordingly, we take the incidence of external migration in the 1850 revision to be a good reflection of the historical reality and the corresponding level of internal mobility as an absolute minimum.

Table 5.2 displays hypothetical age-specific internal migration rates for those 18 years of age and older in 1850 and figure 5.2, a stylized age profile. The age-specific rates are hypothetical and cannot be taken at face value because they reflect only movement *sometime* between 1833 and 1850 and do not represent standardized rates of mobility for persons in each age cohort. Only if the 63 peasants who were between 45 and 49 years old in 1850, for example, had actually moved while they were 45 to 49 would the reported age-specific rate be valid. Yet a crude internal migration rate, CMR$_i$, of 26.3 suggests that spatial mobility was a common experience in Pinkenhof. Indeed, table 5.2 also reveals that nearly half (47.4 percent) of the 1850 population at risk had moved at least once within the estate since 1833. We also know that internal migrants did not move very far, on the average only 2.5 kilometers. Thus local flows, although common, were short (Plakans and Wetherell 1988*a*; Wetherell, Plakans, and Wellman 1994).

The views of external and internal movement that the 1850 revision provides suggest two scenarios that define the probable extremes of the migratory experience of the elderly in Pinkenhof. Both, however, indicate low levels of movement. On the one hand, if the age profile of internal migrants

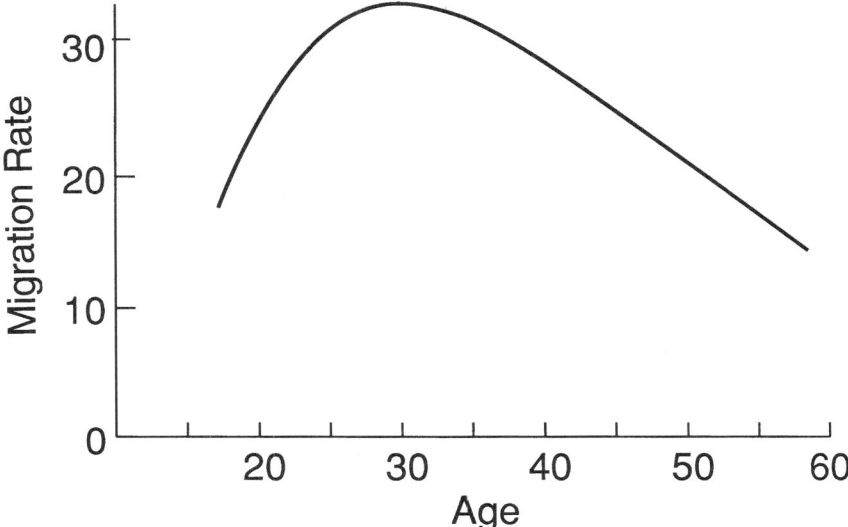

Fig. 5.2. Stylized age profile of internal migrants, Pinkenhof, 1833–1850. Data from the Ninth Imperial Revision for Livland, Central National Historical Archive, Riga, Latvia (Baltic Microfilms, D112, Oekonomie Expedition d. Stadtkassakollegiums IV E. 4, Revisionsliste Gut Pinkenhof, J. G. Herder Institut, Marburg a.d. Lahn, Germany).

that table 5.2 reveals is grossly wrong and the real pattern of internal mobility actually resembles that of external migration presented in table 5.1, then the spatial mobility of the elderly (those 55 and over) was extremely limited. Although many may have moved during their lives (and a $CMR_i >$ 25 attests to this), those moves would have taken place twenty to thirty years before they reached old age.[2] So in one scenario, the elderly rarely, if ever, moved. On the other hand, if a substantial minority of Pinkenhofers moved regularly from farm to farm in the course of their lives as nonquantitative research on these peasants maintains (Strods 1972; Svarane 1971), then the pattern of mobility that table 5.2 presents may well reflect the collective migratory experience of this particular peasant community. In this scenario, the elderly moved ($CMR_i < 20$) but still not as often as young adults ($CMR_i > 30$).

Despite the weaknesses in the record, several things seem clear about mobility and migration in Pinkenhof in the decades immediately following emancipation:

1. Most spatial movement consisted of local, short-distance moves within the estate or to neighboring estates.
2. Internal mobility was common. Perhaps half of all peasants changed their residence at least once in their adult years.

3. External migration was confined to young adults who moved largely to and from neighboring estates in order to marry.
4. Movement of those over 30 was virtually always within the estate.
5. The elderly either (*a*) moved frequently within the estate but less often than those in their 20s, 30s, and 40s or (*b*) moved very infrequently, if at all, after reaching their 30s.
6. By virtue of their number, internal migrants, far more than external migrants, created the need for any social and psychological adjustments that may have accompanied movement.

In light of these findings, it is unsurprising that mid-nineteenth-century social commentary has little to say on the subject of migration among those in the later years of life.

PINKENHOF PATTERNS IN COMPARATIVE PERSPECTIVE

Placing the migratory experience of the Pinkenhof elderly in comparative perspective poses two basic problems: one involves evidence, the other actual behavior. A logical case could be made against finding much usable information of any kind about the old in the historical sources common to traditional European societies.[3] When they did so at all, record keepers enumerated populations for specific purposes, such as assessment of taxes and labor obligations, and had little incentive to make a careful record of those persons who had withdrawn from roles that entailed such involvements. Although we have no evidence of such carelessness in Pinkenhof, age heaping of the elderly is a well-documented attribute of historical European sources.[4] Moreover, we can easily imagine that, by virtue of a growing dependency on the young, older people were increasingly less likely to cross boundaries of administrative units such as parishes, departments, estates, or provinces. Thus the likelihood of the elderly showing up in those few sources that were primarily concerned with boundary crossers diminishes even further.

At the same time, the record of external migration in Pinkenhof between 1833 and 1850 suggests a fundamental immobility among those over 55 that is not without modern parallels. In 1968 in France, for example, 86.5 percent of persons 55 and older still resided in the same commune as they had in 1962 (Cribier 1974: 362). The 13.5 percent who had moved to another commune during that period, moreover, represented a 35 percent increase over the years from 1956 to 1962. Although external migration ($_{55+}$CMR$_e$ = 144.7) among the elderly in contemporary France was much greater than in Pinkenhof ($_{55+}$CMR$_e$ = 1.2), it still suggests a basic propensity among those in the later years of life not to migrate. If less than one-fifth of the elderly in a population with access to modern transportation, communication, and information systems chose to migrate, it seems likely that in traditional societies without such systems, where mental maps extended only to the edges of landed estates, older people chose to stay close to or at the sites of their past productive labor or to the residences of their family and kin. They may still have moved, but their movements could be measured only with household-level sources that serially enumerated (at a minimum by name, age, sex, and residence) the same local population. Accordingly, the "inattention" to the elderly that Gerald N. Grob (1986: 33) argues has characterized historical migration research may in fact be a matter of definition. By focusing exclusively on migration across administrative boundaries, historians may have overlooked that domain in which most elderly in the traditional European past moved, if they moved at all. In Pinkenhof at least, mobility was limited almost entirely to the bounded community. The elderly may have been *mobile*, but they did not *migrate*.

Studies of larger patterns of migration in the twentieth-century Western world provide another point of comparison that suggests a fundamental structural difference between the recent and the distant European past. Figure 5.3A presents a stylized, three-part migration schedule for post-World War II Europe and the United States (Rogers and Castro 1986). The underlying model predicts that the rate of migration will start high but decrease rapidly in the first fifteen years of life as children (the prelabor force) move with young adult parents (the labor force). Migration will then increase sharply to its maximum levels among young adults in their 20s, peak at about age 30, and decline quickly thereafter. Rates will continue to drop until just after retirement and then will show a slight, short-lived upward turn corresponding to retirement migration (the postlabor force). Moreover, figure 5.3B reveals not only that the basic migration schedule applies to both migration and mobility but also that the incidence of local moves exceeds that of long-distance moves. In the modern world, then, (1) the level of local, intracommunity mobility is higher than the corresponding level of external, intercommunity migration, and (2) the age profile of both kinds of movers is the same. Both points allow us to place migration among the elderly in Pinkenhof in a long-term context.

First, the record of residential movement in both the modern and the traditional European past indicates that mobility invariably exceeded migration. Second, the age profile of external migration in Pinkenhof (fig. 5.2) resembles the modern European schedule (fig. 5.3A). Although Pinkenhof's external migration did not possess a prelabor force component of children, the nature of the peasant marriage market, in which brides and grooms moved at the time of marriage, would logically work to minimize the number of children involved. Consequently, we might speculate that in traditional peasant societies when young adults migrated across community boundaries, they did so without spouses or children. Third, the similar age

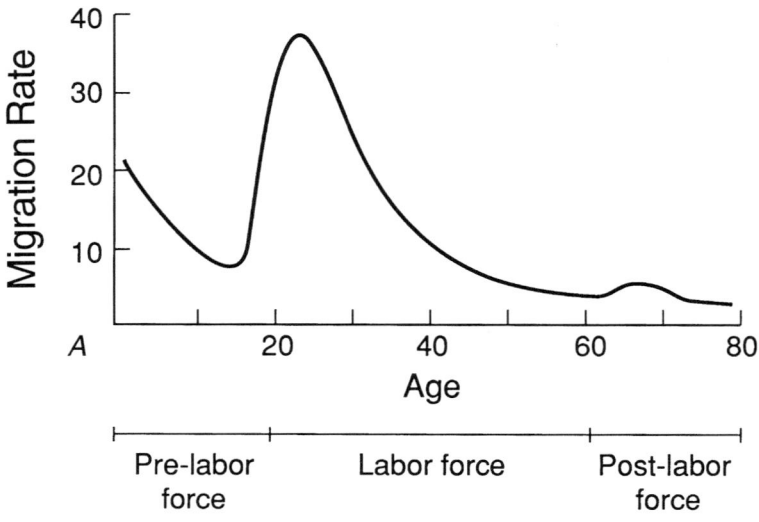

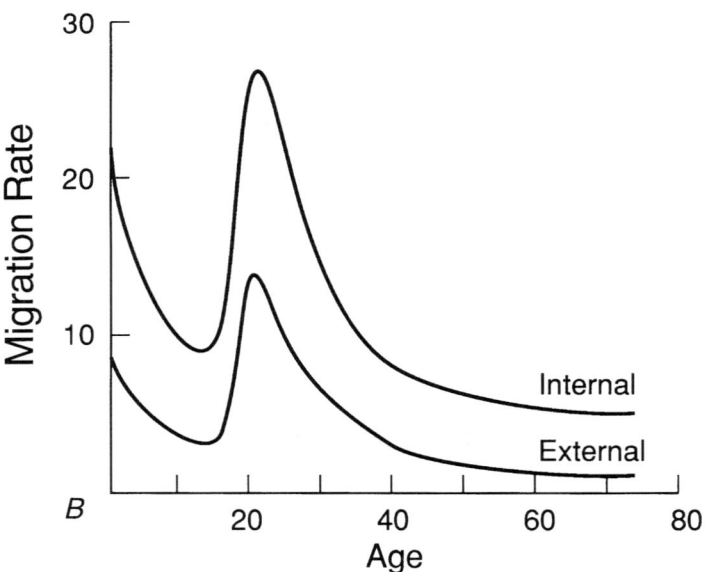

Fig. 5.3. Stylized migration schedules: *A*, generalized; *B*, external and internal. Adapted from Rogers and Castro 1986, pp. 172 and 162, respectively.

profiles of both the modern mobile and the modern migrant suggest that we have to choose between two basic interpretations of the incomplete record of internal mobility in Pinkenhof. In essence, the question is whether the migration schedule in figure 5.3A reflects the historical reality of mobility in Pinkenhof or whether the hypothetical migration schedule in figure 5.2 is a better guess. Clearly the evidence at hand does not allow us to say with any certainty. A look at the motives behind both modern and traditional European moves provides help.

The 31 percent of the population over 55 in Pinkenhof in 1850 who had moved at least once since 1833 no doubt had good reason for doing so, although their motives remain hidden from us. At the same time, we have no reason to believe that decision making by the old—and by those family members and friends whose actions would affect the old—was significantly less patterned than in contemporary populations. Cribier found that no single reason predominated among the economic, familial, and personal factors that elderly couples considered before deciding to leave Paris in the early 1970s.

> The nine most commonly stated reasons given by either partner for leaving Paris were (1) nothing to do in Paris after retirement . . . ; (2) Paris had become unbearable . . . ; (3) Paris is unhealthy . . . ; (4) did not want to go on living in a flat . . . ; (5) wanted a change of climate . . . ; (6) wanted to go back home . . . ; (7) for family reasons other than reason 6 . . . ; (8) cost of living too high in Paris . . . ; (9) eviction. (Cribier 1982: 117)

Although impossible to weigh with much precision, Cribier's respondents seemed to be concerned with family, health, housing, and leisure time. Yet they lived in a period of European history when retirement from remunerative employment had become a well-marked life course transition. They also lived in a modern, industrial society where the choices available to them were more numerous than in the traditional European past. Indeed, Imhof (1981) has argued that all life patterns involving the elderly changed entirely with the arrival of the contemporary world.

The older inhabitants of Pinkenhof, more than a century earlier, may well have shared the same concerns of housing, health, and family that Cribier's respondents voiced, but they certainly had fewer options. Their reasons for moving at all probably involved a mixture of both push and pull factors. Existing studies of estate policy toward peasant farmsteads suggest that push may have dominated. If an energetic estate owner added a particular farmstead's land to the demesne, the peasant holding would be broken up (*spridzinasana*, lit. "blowing up the farmstead") and its residents relocated. The elderly in these instances would most likely become farmhands elsewhere in the estate. Alternately, elderly persons might move to another peasant farmstead, which would receive some remuneration for serving as a kind of private retirement home, or to the *Hof.* Similar social welfare functions are well documented for other traditional European communities and certainly existed in Pinkenhof in both the pre- and postemancipation periods. On the basis of our evidence, we cannot say who actually decided that the elderly would move. Assuming a general proclivity among the elderly not to move, however, would suggest that other, younger people probably initiated discussions that led to any movement. Yet hovering over most peasant decisions, particularly those affecting the operation of the estate's farmsteads, was the estate owner, whose own concerns were not likely to have been much influenced by discomfort and anguish among elderly peasants.

What we know about eastern European peasant estates in general and Pinkenhof in particular also suggests that the different life experiences of farmstead heads and their families, on the one hand, and of farmhands, on the other, affected the mobility of the elderly. Of the 817 adults over age 20 in Pinkenhof who lived on the 119 farmsteads with identifiable heads in 1850, half (416) were heads themselves or co-resident kin. Of this privileged group, nearly two-thirds (268) resided on the same farmstead they had in 1833. Conversely, of those 401 adults who were not related to the head of the farmstead on which they lived in 1850, three-fourths (304) had moved at least once since 1833. Among the 121 peasants over age 55 in 1850 on these 119 farmsteads, two-thirds (86) had not moved since 1833. And for those 76 elderly peasants who were fortunate enough to be related to the head of one of Pinkenhof's farmsteads in 1850, 8 of 10 had not moved in the previous eighteen years. If elderly Pinkenhofers valued residential stability, and the emotional and physical support it undoubtedly brought, a kinship tie with a farmstead head clearly helped them achieve the goal (Plakans and Wetherell 1992; Wetherell, Plakans, and Wellman 1994).

For the half of the population who were farmhands, the pressure to move was far more pronounced and regular, for they faced an annual search for new employment. If a farmstead head decided his current farmhands were a drain on resources or were poor workers, he could always let them go and bargain with others to take their places (Plakans and Wetherell 1988*b*, 1992). In these situations, any change of residence by the elderly would have been involuntary if they were being dismissed and voluntary if they were being recruited from another farmstead. In either event, the elderly would move. Family-linked moves by the elderly could also be the result of married sons improving their lot by assuming headships on better farmsteads. Whether farmhands moved every year or every five or ten years, we can well imagine a cycle of movement that created enough turnover to give rise to the traditional folk view that the population of peasant estates was constantly churning.

The experiences of Pinkenhof's peasants, particularly those of farmhands and their families, suggest that the age profile of internal mobility in traditional eastern European peasant communities was fundamentally different from what it is in the modern world. Enough movement can be either documented or inferred to support the contention that the hypothetical internal migration schedule in figure 5.2 better captures the historical reality in Pinkenhof than the modern schedule in figure 5.3A. Although adults in their 20s and early 30s still moved more frequently than those in their late 30s and 40s, the incidence of mobility among middle-aged peasants was probably greater in the distant past than in the recent past. At the same time, mobility among the elderly was arguably less pronounced in traditional European societies for both structural and attitudinal reasons.

We cannot say with certainty why elderly Pinkenhofers moved, if they did at all, and their reasons may have been more numerous than we have inferred. Certainly Cribier's and other studies of contemporary populations suggest as much. Stanley H. Brandes, for example, found that in the twentieth-century Spanish village of Becedas, "as long as both elderly parents are still alive, it is considered heartless to break the continuity of their lives by asking them to leave their home. After one parent dies, however, the disintegrated nuclear unit no longer justifies the maintenance of a separate household, and the widowed individual must accommodate himself to the homes of his or her children" (1975: 110). Social customs of this kind, easily discovered by questioning living populations but impossible to glean from most traditional European historical sources, warn against oversimplifying behavior in the distant past.

It is no oversimplification, however, to note that more than two-thirds of peasants 55 and older in 1850 had not moved in the preceding eighteen years. Staying in place among the old was consistent with two general structural features of peasant communities: first, neither men nor women ever completely withdrew from farmstead labor (Plakans 1989); second, peasants had probably moved several times before they reached old age. Describing Russian peasant villages at the end of the nineteenth century, Adele Lindenmeyr (1982: 232–234) observed that old men and old women "performed essential tasks even if they could no longer work in the fields: fetching water, chopping wood, preparing food, cultivating kitchen gardens, rocking cradles, and minding children, chickens and geese." Similarly in Pinkenhof, the elderly would not have remained taskless in view of the dozens of light but important chores farmstead life entailed; and performing them maintained a link with the world of work that was rarely, if ever, severed. Because elderly Pinkenhofers were not strangers to movement, we do not have to idealize their lives to conclude that a fixed abode, more than likely with married children in the vicinity, if not on the same farmstead, was a desirable goal.

Residential stability—retirement immobility—was well within the realm of ways European peasants dealt with the elderly and something the elderly could realistically expect as a form of support. Peter Laslett's (1988) survey of this diversity—cast as an exploration of the different ways family and community acted as a support system for those who required it—need not be repeated here, but one of his observations helps to place the Pinkenhof experience in space and time.

> Old people were sustained by a whole range of expedients in which family and collectivity collaborated within the customary framework as the situation required. An important reason for this was that there was no standard situation in which the necessity of support arose, but a whole array of differing situations, differing from time to time, circumstance to circumstance, individual to individual. (Laslett 1988: 168)[5]

Pinkenhofers formed families and lived in them. Yet those families, by virtue of the traditional residential system that prevailed in the Baltic, were situated on farmsteads that often contained two or more conjugal family units with children and other relatives. Pinkenhof's "family system" could not possibly have allowed peasants to realize all their values independently, for they always had to reckon with the economic imperatives of the "farmstead system." The latter tended to feel the managerial hand of the estate owner (in the case of Pinkenhof, the city of Riga), and therefore we find it impossible to believe that mobility of the elderly was in any sense a pure expression of the values that drove either the family system, the estate owner, or the elderly themselves. Indeed, the world of Pinkenhof's peasants was less one of "perennial households" (Laslett 1988: 158ff., after Czap 1982) than one of "perennial farmsteads," which, together with the families in them, were the two "collectivities" that cooperated to provide sustenance and support to the elderly and reduce both their migration and their mobility.

Until we know more about the rural populations of eastern Europe after emancipation, we hesitate to generalize from Pinkenhof to any other part of the traditional European east, let alone all of Europe in the distant past. We would contend, however, that the record of migration and mobility in Pinkenhof provides an initial point of reference, certainly for the Baltic area and possibly for much of the European east. Indeed, movement in nineteenth-century Pinkenhof arguably reflects long-standing behavior because the structural constraints of law and imperatives of the farmstead-based agricultural regime operated well past emancipation. Pinkenhof's population was subject to restrictions typical of postemancipation eastern European societies. Peasants were no longer serfs, but, notwithstanding the free labor market philosophy behind emancipation, they were not absolutely free to move either.

The great increase of rural-to-urban and rural-to-rural migration in the Baltic did not begin until the 1870s, when it increased the region's cities and towns at an unprecedented pace (Anderson 1980; Leasure and

Lewis 1968; Winner and Winner 1984). How the elderly participated in that migration transition remains to be seen, but in the decades immediately following emancipation, elderly peasants in the main stayed put. Permanence of place was the hallmark of the traditional elderly that distinguished them from their modern twentieth-century counterparts. The phenomenon of retirement migration did not appear in all European societies with the advent of the modern world, but where it did, it clearly announced the arrival of a new feature in the history of the elderly. In Pinkenhof as in most traditional European communities, there was no retirement migration because *retirement* in the modern sense simply did not occur.

NOTES

1. The crude external migration rate, CMR_e, and the corresponding crude internal migration rate, CMR_i, are calculated as

$$\frac{\text{Number of external (or internal) migrants}}{\text{Midyear population, 1833–1850}} * 100$$

Age-specific rates, indicated as $_{55+}CMR_e$, for example, are equivalent to age-specific birth- or deathrates. Rogers and Castro (1986) employ a similar age-specific, although less intuitive, measure.

2. Our decision to view age 55 as the onset of old age is not altogether arbitrary. It does not rest on the Pinkenhofers' understandings of the beginnings of old age, to be sure, because we have not examined the qualitative evidence, such as folklore, that might reveal their understandings of age grading. However, in 1804, the provincial *Landtag* adopted a peasant law that required the creation of *Wackenbücher*, or registers of all serf labor obligations, that included age-specific categories of workers. The registers defined "able-bodied" (*arbeitsfahige*) males as those under 60 years of age and "able-bodied" females as those under 55 (Kahk 1982; Plakans and Wetherell 1992).

3. In an intriguing comment in chapter 3 in this volume, Eugene Hammel suggests that "household . . . regimes [can] be distinguished at relatively small sample sizes." If sustained, Hammel's finding may obviate, or at least reduce, the inevitable worries of historians who are forced to deal with very small numbers of the aged in single historical communities.

4. In 1850, the age heaping index, which reveals rounding of ages, was 103.8 for males and 90.5 for females; with no systematic rounding, the index would be 100 (Shyrock and Siegel et al. 1973: 1:205–206).

5. We address this larger issue of support in the context of kinship and community in Wetherell, Plakans, and Wellman 1994.

REFERENCES

Achenbaum, Andrew W. 1978. *Old age in the new land: The American experience since 1970.* Baltimore: Johns Hopkins University Press.

Anderson, Barbara A. 1980. *Internal migration during modernization in late nineteenth-century Russia.* Princeton: Princeton University Press.

Brandes, Stanley H. 1975. *Migration, kinship, and community: Tradition and transition in a Spanish village.* New York: Academic Press.

Clark, Peter. 1987. "Migration in England during the late seventeenth and early nineteenth centuries." In *Migration and society in early modern England,* ed. Peter Clark and David Souden, 213–252. London: Hutchinson.

Cribier, Françoise. 1974. "Retirement migration in France." In *People on the move: Studies on internal migration,* ed. Leszek A. Kosinski and R. Mansell Prothero, 361–373. London: Methuen.

———. 1982. "Aspects of retirement migration from Paris: An essay in social and cultural geography." In *Geographic perspectives on the elderly,* ed. A. M. Warnes, 111–137. London: John Wiley and Sons.

Czap, Peter. 1982. "The perennial multiple family household, Mishino, Russia, 1782–1858." *Journal of Family History* 7: 5–26.

Fischer, David Hackett. 1977. *Growing old in America.* New York: Oxford University Press.

Gratton, Brian. 1986. "The new history of the aged: A critique." In *Old age in a bureaucratic society,* ed. David Van Tassel and Peter Stearns, 1–29. New York: Greenwood Press.

Grob, Gerald N. 1986. "Explaining old age history: The need for empiricism." In *Old age in a bureaucratic society,* ed. David Van Tassel and Peter Stearns, 30–45. New York: Greenwood Press.

Hareven, Tamara. 1976. "Modernization and family history: Perspectives on social change." *Signs* 2: 190–206.

Hogan, Dennis P., and David I. Kertzer. 1985. "Migratory patterns during Italian urbanization, 1865–1921." *Demography* 22: 309–325.

Imhof, Arthur E. 1981. *Die gewonnenen Jahre* [The gained years]. München: C. H. Beck.

Jackson, James H., Jr., and Leslie Page Moch. 1989. "Migration and the social history of modern Europe." *Historical Methods* 22: 27–36.

Kahk, Juhan. 1982. *Peasant and lord in the process of transition from feudalism to capitalism in the Baltics.* Tallinn: Eesti Raamat Publishers.

Kertzer, David I., and Dennis P. Hogan. 1985. "On the move: Migration in an Italian community, 1865–1921." *Social Science History* 9: 1–23.

———. 1989. *Family, political economy, and demographic change: The transformation of life in Casalecchio, Italy, 1816–1921.* Madison: University of Wisconsin Press.

———. 1990. "Household organization and migration in nineteenth-century Italy." *Social Science History* 14: 483–505.

Knodel, John E. 1988. *Demographic behavior in the past: A study of fourteen German village populations in the eighteenth and nineteenth centuries.* Cambridge: Cambridge University Press.

Kundzins, Pauls. 1974. *Latvju seta* [The Latvian farmstead]. Stockholm: Daugava.

Laslett, Peter. 1988. "Family, kinship and collectivity as systems of support in pre-industrial Europe: A consideration of the 'nuclear-hardship' hypothesis." *Continuity and Change* 3: 153–175.

Law, Christopher, and Anthony M. Warnes. 1982. "The destination decision in retirement migration." In *Geographic perspectives on the elderly,* ed. A. M. Warnes, 53–81. London: John Wiley and Sons.

Leasure, J. William, and Robert A. Lewis. 1968. "Internal migration in Russia in the late nineteenth century." *Slavic Review* 27: 376–394.

Lindenmeyr, Adele. 1982. "Work, charity, and the elderly in late nineteenth-century Russia." In *Old age in preindustrial society,* ed. Peter Stearns, 232–247. New York: Holmes and Meier.

Lucassen, Jan. 1987. *Migrant labor in Europe 1600–1900: The drift to the North Sea.* Trans. Donald A. Bloch. London: Croom Helm.

Mitterauer, Michael, and Reinhard Sieder. 1977. *The European family: Patriarchy to partnership from the Middle Ages to the present.* Trans. Karla Osterveen and Manfred Horzinger. Chicago: University of Chicago Press.

Moch, Leslie Page. 1983. *Paths to the city: Regional migration in nineteenth-century France.* Beverly Hills, Calif.: Sage.

————. 1992. *Moving Europeans: Migration in Western Europe since 1650.* Bloomington: Indiana University Press.

Plakans, Andrejs. 1989. "Stepping down in former times: A comparative assessment of 'retirement' in traditional Europe." In *Age structuring in comparative perspective,* ed. David I. Kertzer and K. Warner Schaie, 175–195. Hillsdale, N.J.: Lawrence Erlbaum.

Plakans, Andrejs, and Charles Wetherell. 1988*a*. "The kinship domain in an East European peasant community: Pinkenhof, 1833–1850." *American Historical Review* 93: 359–386.

————. 1988*b*. "Unfree labor and family life in a Baltic serf estate, 1808–1816." Paper presented at the annual meeting of the Social Science History Association, Chicago, November 3–6.

————. 1988*c*. "Land and labor in a Baltic serf estate, 1809–1850." Paper presented at the annual meeting of the American Association for the Advancement of Slavic Studies, Honolulu, November 18–21.

————. 1990. "Transfer of headships in nineteenth-century eastern European serf estates." Paper presented at the annual meeting of the Social Science History Association, Minneapolis, October 18–21.

————. 1992. "Family and economy in a Baltic serf estate in the early nineteenth century." *Continuity and Change* 7: 199–223.

Rogers, Andrei, and Luis J. Castro. 1986. "Migration." In *Migration and settlement: A multiregional comparative study,* ed. Andrei Rogers and Frans J. Willekens, 157–208. Dordrecht: D. Reidel.

Schofield, R. S. 1987. "Age-specific mobility in an eighteenth-century rural English parish." In *Migration and society in early modern England,* ed. Peter Clark and David Souden, 253–266. London: Hutchinson.

Schwabe, A. 1928. *Grundriss der Agrargeschichte Lettlands* [The basic agrarian history of Latvia]. Riga: Bernhard Lamey.

Shyrock, Henry J., and Jacob S. Siegel et al. 1973. *The methods and materials of demography.* 2 vols. Washington, D.C.: Government Printing Office.

Smith, Daniel Scott. 1981. "Historical change in the household structure of the elderly in economically developed societies." In *Aging: Stability and change in the fam-*

ily, ed. Robert W. Fogel, Elaine Hatfield, Sara B. Kiesler, and Ethel Shanas, 91–114. New York: Academic Press.

Strods, Heinrihs. 1972. *Lauksaimnieciba Latvija parejas perioda no feodalisma uz kapitalismu* [Agriculture in Latvia in the transition period from feudalism to capitalism]. Riga: Zinatne.

Svarane, Melita. 1971. *Saimnieks un kalps Kurzeme un Vidzeme XIX gadsimta vidu* [Farmstead heads and farmhands in Kurland and Livland in the mid-nineteenth century]. Riga: Zinatne.

Tilly, Charles. 1978. "Migration in modern European history." In *Human migration: Patterns and policies*, ed. William H. McNeill and Ruth S. Adams, 48–72. Bloomington: Indiana University Press.

Tobien, A. von. 1899. *Die Agrargesetzgebung Livlands im 19 Jahrhundert* [The agrarian laws of Livland in the nineteenth century]. Vol. 1. Berlin: Puttkamer and Mühlbrecht.

Veveris, Ervins, and Martins Kuplais. n.d. *Latvijas Etnografiskaja brivdabas muzeja* [In the Latvian ethnographic open-air museum]. Riga.

Wall, Richard. 1984. "Residential isolation of the elderly: A comparison over time." *Ageing and Society* 4: 483–503.

Wetherell, Charles, Andrejs Plakans, and Barry Wellman. 1994. "Social networks, kinship, and community in Eastern Europe." *Journal of Interdisciplinary History* 24: 639–663.

Winner, Irene P., and Thomas G. Winner, eds. 1984. *The peasant and the city in Eastern Europe: Interpreting structure*. Cambridge: Schenkman.

SIX

Older Lives on the Frontier: The Residential Patterns of the Older Population of Texas, 1850–1910

Myron P. Gutmann

This chapter is about the role played by the moving American frontier in defining the domestic residential experiences of the families of the older population. Between 1850 and 1910, Texas had a great deal of open land, a young population, and substantial ethnic diversity. All these factors shaped the experiences of the older population. Within the state there were significant numbers of African-Americans, Mexican-Americans, recent European immigrants and their children, and white Americans who were the children of parents born in the United States.[1] The residential living arrangements of a population are the result of responses to other changes in their lives: in the case of the older population, the important turning points are the consequences of the aging of parents and children and the end of marriage through widowhood. Economic and cultural contexts shaped the nature of residential arrangements. Some older Texas couples seem to have preferred to live by themselves, while others preferred to live with a variety of other kin. Even where such a preference was held, the nature of working arrangements and the lack of property sometimes made it impossible for an older couple to gather their family around them. All this took place in the context of a growing and maturing regional population. As the regional population grew, older Texas residents had more kin nearby, which opened new possibilities for some of them to live with kin rather than with strangers.

The experience of aging in Texas occurred in a larger American context. The kinds of multiple sharecropper households described for northern Italy by David I. Kertzer and Nancy Karweit elsewhere in this volume were extremely rare in the United States, and the kinds of household arrangements they describe for widows and widowers were also rare. The population of Texas described in this chapter was a rural population that lived in small towns and on isolated farms and was employed in agriculture and in services that supported agriculture.[2] Agricultural populations have more flexibility than urban industrial populations, such as those described by Tamara K. Hareven and Peter Uhlenberg in the American Northeast, with which to accommodate the needs of an older population, and that too is part of the message of this chapter.

During the second half of the nineteenth century there were more large and complex families in the United States than there had been previously, or than there would be since.[3] Moreover, older people in the United States were far more likely than most other members of the population to be living in complex families, most notably, with their married children, with other kin, or with nonkin. That is the conclusion of the research reported here and the research of others, especially Daniel Scott Smith, who directed an important project on the older population of the United States in 1900.[4] Yet even this situation was undergoing change. The results reported here show that as lives lengthened at the end of the nineteenth century, it became possible for men and women to spend more of their later years living together as a nuclear couple, without being forced to live with their married children. In many cases, it was only after the death of one spouse that a surviving widow lived with one of her or his married children.

Later in the twentieth century the residential patterns of the older population changed yet again. Fewer of them lived in complex domestic arrangements, more of them lived with their spouses, and many more of them—especially widowed women—lived alone (Riley 1982). This isolation of the elderly is one of the great changes in residential patterns that have taken place in the twentieth century, and its implications have been the subject of a considerable amount of study (Smith 1981, 1986). Despite its importance, and despite evidence that married older Texans were increasingly likely to live by themselves, the new isolation of the elderly in the twentieth century is not the principal subject of this chapter. Rather, I want to look at developments that led up to the kind of conditions that existed at the turn of the century.

The results reported here are drawn from data collected from the 1850, 1860, 1870, 1880, 1900, and 1910 U.S. manuscript censuses for six Texas counties: Red River, DeWitt, Gillespie, Webb, Angelina, and Jack.[5] These six counties taken together reflect the range of cultural, ethnic, economic, and ecological characteristics of the rural part of the state.

Three of the counties are located in the eastern half of Texas. Red River County, in the northeast corner of the state, was among the earliest areas settled extensively by immigrants from elsewhere in the United States. It had a native-born population of whites and blacks and an economy largely dominated by the production of cotton. Angelina County, in East Texas near the Louisiana border, also had a mixed white and black population, with a cotton economy supplemented by the production of timber and sugar. DeWitt

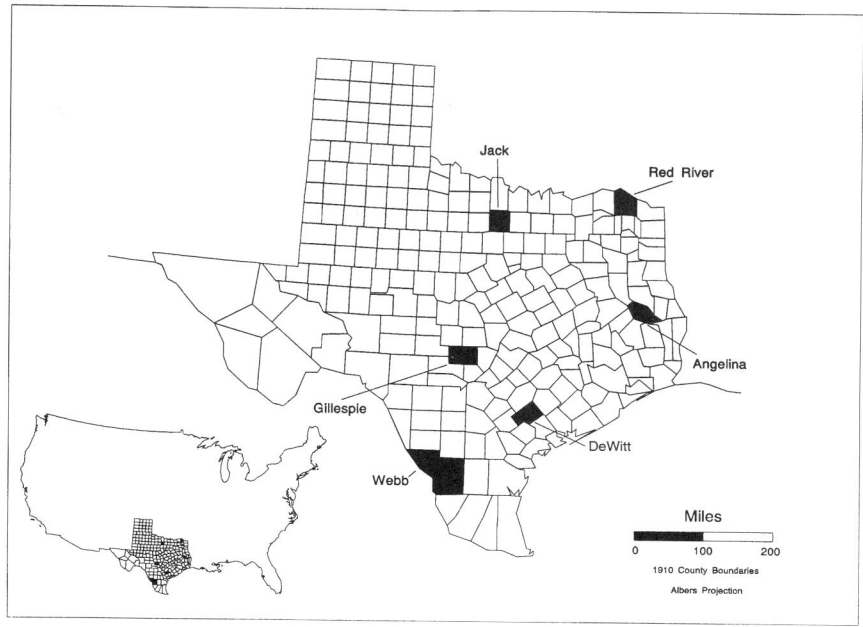

Fig. 6.1. Location of the six Texas counties analyzed.

County is located in Southeast Texas. It had the most varied population of any of the counties studied here, made up of German immigrants, native-born whites and blacks, and an increasing number of Mexicans in the early twentieth century. Its economy consisted of a mixture of cotton production and cattle ranching.

The remaining three counties are located in the central and western parts of the state. Webb County is located on the Mexican border and has as its seat the most important town in our study, Laredo. Its population was almost exclusively of Mexican origin, and it had a diverse economy of ranching and town and transportation services. Gillespie County, located in the Central Texas hills, was another haven for immigrants. Settled in 1846 by German immigrants, it remained largely German-American well into the twentieth century. Its economy was a diverse mix of agriculture and cattle, sheep, and goat ranching. Jack County was the last settled of those studied here. Located west of Fort Worth in North Texas, it was organized in 1852 and remained only scarcely settled until after 1870. With a population that consisted mostly of native-born whites, Jack County's economy was largely devoted to cattle ranching.

The data used in this chapter were collected as part of a larger project intended to study the dynamics of the rural population of Texas from 1850 to

1910.[6] A sample was drawn from each of the six counties' manuscript census returns, designed to permit us to link references to individuals from census to census and from the census to other documents.[7] The sampling proportions differed from county to county, depending on the size of the population (Gutmann and Fliess 1989). The choice of counties was made so as to overrepresent the European immigrant (especially German- and Slavic-speaking) and Mexican origin elements of the population. The analysis reported here uses data weighted to restore the actual statewide ethnic balance in each census year. Despite our efforts to be able to study subgroups within the population, we have not completely succeeded. Slaves were recorded in a separate census schedule in 1850 and 1860. While those schedules are available and could be transcribed and analyzed, the living arrangements of slaves are not readily comparable to those of the free population. We therefore have no African-American population before 1870 (there were few free blacks in Texas, and virtually all lived in cities). Our sample of Mexican-Americans includes no data for 1850 because of the difficulty of working with the census manuscripts for Webb County, as well as other largely Mexican-American areas, in that year.[8]

The results reported here include many categories of individual, spread over a number of points in time. I have attempted to organize the data so that they yield the largest amount of information while reducing the amount of confusion produced by the volume of data points and categories. The data, which cover six decennial time points from 1850 to 1910, will often be reported in three groups, each consolidating two points in time. This has the advantage of reflecting three different eras in the evolution of the population of the state of Texas. The first period, 1850 and 1860, is the antebellum era of settlement. This is the era in which the population of Texas is small, and our sample is still quite small. The second period, 1870 and 1880, is the post-Civil War era of continued settlement and accommodation to the consequences of the end of slavery. The third period is the early twentieth century, encompassing 1900 and 1910. The consolidation of data also has a secondary advantage of enlarging the number of cases in individual cells, although this advantage is mediated by a partial lack of statistical independence.[9] The strategy for data presentation divides the older population into three age groups, 50 to 59, 60 to 69, and 70 and older. This data presentation strategy avoids the more common division at age 65, because in this population the break at age 70 is the most important. The divisions prior to age 70 are made to present evenly structured groups.

FAMILIES AND HOUSEHOLDS IN AN AGING POPULATION

While there was tremendous variety in the kinds of households in which the older population lived and the kinds of relationship older residents had with the rest of their household, there are also overall patterns. Most older Texans were married, or had been married. Few had never married. For the majority who were or had been married, there was a single preferred living arrangement: they lived in nuclear households with one or more of their unmarried children. Even after their children had grown and left the home, many couples continued to live by themselves. This preference for nuclear family arrangements, consisting of a married couple or a surviving spouse and unmarried child, is unexceptional. For a number of older people, however, the nuclear family living pattern was not the only one they experienced in their later years. A large proportion of all older people spent at least some of their life in a more complex family arrangement, one in which they shared living accommodations with a married child. The older woman or man lived with a married child only after her or his spouse had died; very few married couples shared a dwelling with one of their married children and his or her spouse. Not every widowed older person had married children with whom to live, however. A significant share of older people lived away from their immediate family, either with other kin or with nonkin.

We can recast the preceding generalization in the form of a description of the stages in the residential lifetime of a married couple. While there are a number of possible scenarios, an examination of the lifetimes of many individuals in the six Texas counties reveals that most older people passed through only two or three of the stages that will be described here. In the first stage, a young couple set up a household on its own at the time of marriage, or shortly thereafter. Most, though not all, of these young couples soon had children. The husband and wife lived in this household with their unmarried children, so long as their children remained unmarried. As each child married, he or she left to set up a separate household. This stage was continued, under different conditions, after the death of husband or wife. When one spouse died, the surviving spouse continued as household head, in company with unmarried children. In Texas, this stage of household development could be a lengthy one for a widowed woman because her odds of remarrying were slight. For a man, who was much more likely to remarry, this stage often did not last long, and he returned to the beginning of the development process.

The second category in the development of family residence patterns began when the last child left the household. At that time the older couple or the surviving spouse was left alone. This "empty nest" stage was a common and probably popular alternative to other living arrangements, especially among the German immigrants in our sample who reached old age around the turn of the century. Household after household in Gillespie County in 1910 consisted of an older couple (often in their 70s) living by themselves. There was, nevertheless, an alternative to the "no children" living arrangement. The third category in the development of family residence patterns began when the couple or surviving spouse joined a married child to form a complex two- or three-generational household. This was often the final stage in the process, because it was usually only the onset of very advanced age that provoked the sharing of a residence in this way. Widowed women spent more time residing with their married children than widowed men, and both were more likely to live with married children than were older married couples.

Most older individuals in the six Texas counties passed through only two stages of residential life. In the first stage, they spent the majority of their married (and widowed) lives sharing a residence with their unmarried children. After their children left home, the parents followed only one of two alternatives. Either they lived by themselves or they shared a residence with a married child. Among the individuals captured by our research, at least, it was not common for older people to pass from living with unmarried children to living by themselves without children and then to live in their extreme old age with a married child. Cases of that sort certainly exist. William Herrington of Angelina County lived with his wife and unmarried children in 1850, when he was 50 years old. In 1860, he was still married, living with his wife but independent of his children. By 1870, at age 70, he was widowed and living with a married son. Herrington was probably dead by 1880, because we can no longer locate him in the census. The case of William Herrington is unusual, however. Far more representative is the case of Peter Alberthal of Gillespie County. Alberthal was enumerated in the census as late as 1880 (when he was 49 years old) as living with his wife and unmarried children. In 1900 and 1910 (when he is 79 years old), he is still married and living only with his wife.[10] Equally representative is Carl Barsch of Gillespie County, who was also living with his wife and unmarried children in 1880 (at age 55) but who was widowed and living with a married son in 1900 at age 75. Barsch was not enumerated in 1910 and presumably had died.

Two other alternatives were possible for the married or widowed older population. Some lived in a fourth kind of residential arrangement, with a combination of kin or with kin other than their married or unmarried children; others lived in a fifth category, with families to whom they were not related. Those who lived with nonkin were mostly servants, lodgers, boarding-house keepers, and older couples in empty nest households in which there were resident servants. These options—living with other kin or with nonkin— were more frequently taken by widowed than married individuals. Men were more likely to live with nonkin, while women were more likely to live with kin other than their children.

The five stages or categories described here were neither obligatory nor ordinal. It was not necessary for every individual or couple to pass through all five stages, and not everyone passed through the five (or fewer) stages in the order given. It was possible to skip a step, or even to double back (as in the case of a woman or man who remarried). It should be added that these categories owe a great deal to the categories of analysis for the study of households for gerontological studies devised by Ethel Shanas and her colleagues (1968).[11] I should add that for this analysis I have decided to forgo the frequently used categories published by Peter Laslett (1972). Those categories, which emphasize the structure of family households, are very useful and could be used to add illumination to this work. But they are less enlightening for this purpose than categories that emphasize the situation in which the older person is living and the people with whom that person lives.

The foregoing discussion of stages in the residential experiences of older Texans has left aside the population that never married. Not many older people in Texas were single. Fewer than 6 percent of older men and probably no more than 3 percent of older women had never married.[12] The small number of older people who never married makes their situation difficult to study in detail, but the differences between men and women are interesting. Unmarried men were more likely than women to live alone or with nonkin, while unmarried women were more likely than unmarried men to live with kin. Both unmarried men and unmarried women were more likely to live with kin in the early twentieth century than they had been in the years after the Civil War. This suggests that over time unmarried older people had more kin with whom to live as the population of Texas grew and matured.

The characteristic residential patterns just described took place in the context of an American population that has steadily aged over the last two centuries. Like the United States as a whole, the population of Texas has aged, although the older population has been smaller in Texas—as a proportion of the whole population—at every census. It is not necessarily easy to date the beginning of old age, and it is therefore difficult to choose an age at which to establish its beginning. Using age 65, a common time at which the beginning of old age is measured, table 6.1 presents results about the size of the older population in Texas and the United States, using both published census data and data from the six sample counties. It is worth repeating here that the data reported in this and other tables have been weighted to correct the overrepresentation of European and Mexican immigrants—and their children—in the data samples.[13] The population of the six counties was slightly older than that reported in published enumerations for the state as a whole.

The proportion of people aged 65 and older in Texas was substantially less than that in the United States as a whole in the mid-nineteenth century. Since then, the gap has partly closed, especially between 1870 and 1910. In 1870, the percentage of people aged 65 and over was nearly twice as large in the United States as a whole as it was in Texas. By 1910, it was only half again

TABLE 6.1   Estimates of the Older Population, 1850–1970

| | Population Age 65+ | | | Total Population (Six-County Sample) | Total Number (Six-County Sample) | | Sex Ratio: Males per 100 Females (Six-County Sample) | |
	Six-County Sample (%)	Texas (%)	United States (%)		Age 50+	Age 65+	Age 50+	Age 65+
1850	0.9	—	—	5,721	305	51	178	123
1860	1.0	—	—	13,526	815	131	141	166
1870	1.6	1.5	2.9	20,799	1,360	336	126	137
1880	1.8	1.7	3.4	37,443	2,644	664	123	126
1890	—	2.1	3.8	—	—	—	—	—
1900	2.6	2.4	4.0	31,671	2,835	817	122	132
1910	3.0	2.8	4.3	34,962	3,560	1,044	122	106
1930	—	4.0	5.4	—	—	—	—	—
1950	—	6.7	8.1	—	—	—	—	—
1970	—	8.9	9.9	—	—	—	—	—

SOURCES: Texas Historical Demography Project Database; Skrabanek, Upham, and Dickerson 1975: 7; Achenbaum 1978: 60.

as large. The population of Texas had aged disproportionately in the nine-teenth and early twentieth century for a variety of reasons. A young popula-tion entered the state during its time of great expansion, and that popula-tion had aged, producing by 1900 its first sizable older population. But another process was at work as well. The population was also aging because of the decline of mortality. Over time, the population of Texas lived longer; this too is especially noticeable by 1900. One important implication of the lengthening of the lives of older Texans after 1900 is the delay in the arrival of widowhood. While this did not occur among all groups (it is most charac-teristic of German immigrants), for those it affected the lengthening of lives contributed to a modification of living arrangements by permitting surviv-ing couples to live by themselves for a longer time after their children had grown.

The population of Texas had a smaller proportion of older inhabitants than the United States as a whole in the nineteenth and early twentieth century for a variety of reasons, but the most important was its proximity to the frontier and its relatively recent settlement. Immigrants, whether from other American states or from other countries, were younger than a settled population would have been. Texas was Mexican territory until 1836, then an independent Republic of Texas from 1836 until 1845, when it became an American state. Until the 1820s, the Mexican government had discour-aged the settlement of Americans in Texas. Only during the early 1820s did the Mexicans permit substantial immigration and colonization, and much of the state was relatively unsettled in the 1840s. The great wave of Texas settlement took place after Texas become independent of Mexico in 1836, especially after it became part of the United States in late 1845. The settlers were relatively young. The first generation of settlers, who arrived before the Civil War, aged during the second half of the nine-teenth century; it is their swelling numbers that show in the larger pro-portions of older people after 1880. Before that time, it is clear from table 6.1, the older population was very small. In our six-county data sample, the numbers are striking. There are only 51 people aged 65 and older in 1850, only 87 in 1860, and only 336 in 1870. It will be very difficult to draw unequivocal conclusions from these few individuals, especially in 1850 and 1860. Table 6.1 shows that taking the population aged 50 and older will give us substantially larger numbers, but these too are rela-tively small.

In addition to being small, the older population was distorted in at least one other way. There were more men than women. Table 6.1 also reports the sex ratio for the population aged 50 and older and for the popula-tion aged 65 and over for the six-county sample. The normal sex ratio for a total population is about 105 men for every 100 women, and the ratio tends to decline as the population ages, because of relatively higher male mortality. Yet the Texas population, because of its history of frontier immigration, continued to have a very high proportion of men.

LIVING ARRANGEMENTS OF THE OLDER POPULATION: MEN AND WOMEN, MARRIED AND WIDOWED, OLDER AND OLDEST

More older people in Texas lived with unmarried children than in any other residential arrangement. Life with unmarried children was thus the most common of the several distinct patterns and stages in which older people lived. Table 6.2 presents a breakdown of the older population in the six Texas counties into the categories of residential arrangements discussed earlier. Depending on the time period, at least two of three married people aged 50 and older and at least three of ten widows of the same age lived with their unmarried children. The remaining married older people were mostly living by themselves or with married children, with a few living with other kin and with nonkin. Widows were very likely to be living with married children or other kin and less likely to be living alone or with nonkin. Table 6.2

TABLE 6.2   Residential Living Arrangements of the Population Aged 50 and Older, Six Texas Counties

	Married		*Widowed*		*Single*	
	Women	Men	Women	Men	Women	Men
1850–1860						
Number of cases	254	481	192	171	26	19
Unmarried children	78%	84%	32%	36%	—	—
No children	10	6	4	8	0%	39%
Married children	6	4	28	23	—	—
Other kin	5	3	24	12	57	5
Nonkin	1	2	11	21	43	55
1870–1880						
Number of cases	846	1,694	901	408	39	108
Unmarried children	68%	78%	29%	37%	1%	—
No children	14	9	7	10	5	23%
Married children	8	6	33	23	10	—
Other kin	4	3	16	6	40	21
Nonkin	6	5	15	24	44	56
1900–1910						
Number of cases	1,617	2,764	1,182	408	80	190
Unmarried children	64%	72%	30%	38%	1%	—
No children	18	13	9	13	11	31%
Married children	10	7	38	24	3	—
Other kin	6	4	19	11	60	30
Nonkin	3	3	5	14	25	39

gives us a sense of the important differences between men and women and between married and widowed people.

Over the course of time, the proportion of older married individuals living with their unmarried children declined. This is one among several clear temporal themes in the results reported in table 6.2. Three other categories of residential arrangement compensate for the decline in individuals living with their unmarried children: there is substantial growth in the proportion living without children present and some growth in those living with married children (especially women) and with other kin. There are three possible explanations for this change. It is possible that the taste for parents living with unmarried children changed, either because parents no longer wanted to live with their children or because the children no longer wanted to live with their parents. It is also possible that the supply of children diminished, because of lower fertility, or the age structure of the older population changed, producing relatively more parents in the very old category (70 and older), all of whose children had married. Neither of the two demographic explanations put forward here is likely to have been the case. The older population in 1910 and earlier in Texas had experienced very little fertility decline (Fliess, Gutmann, and Vetter 1990), and the decline in older men and women living with unmarried children is characteristic of all age groups within the over-50 population. We are left with a potential change in taste and in the overall structure of communities.

In addition to changes through time, the experiences of older women were different from those of older men, and the experiences of widowed individuals were different from those of married individuals. Table 6.2 reveals that men were more likely to live with unmarried children than women, all other things being equal. This curious finding, produced by the large average difference in ages between married men and women, will be discussed in greater detail later. Women, in contrast, were more likely than men to live with married children and other kin. This is especially so for widowed women. Widowed men were more likely to live with nonkin. This last characteristic is a consequence of the quite different social and economic roles available to older men and women in nineteenth- and early-twentieth-century Texas. Older men living with nonkin were agricultural laborers; older women were more likely to be living with their families. While both older widowed women and men could work as servants, it appears that more work was available in agriculture than domestic service and that positions as domestic servants went by preference to younger women.

When we subdivide our population by age, we see another dramatic finding: a relatively high proportion of very old women and men—those aged 70 and higher—were still living with unmarried children. Table 6.3 presents the full matrix of the distribution of individuals between the categories of residential arrangements described earlier, by breaking up the population

TABLE 6.3 Percentage of the Older Population Living in Various Residential Arrangements

	Married Women			Married Men			Widowed Women			Widowed Men		
	50–59	60–69	70+	50–59	60–69	70+	50–59	60–69	70+	50–59	60–69	70+
1850–1860												
Unmarried children	86%	56%	0%	90%	75%	62%	44%	28%	7%	50%	28%	11%
No children	8	13	44	3	14	10	3	4	10	11	7	2
Married children	3	16	0	3	6	13	23	29	41	11	30	47
Other kin	1	15	56	1	5	15	22	19	38	5	17	25
Nonkin	2	0	0	2	1	0	9	20	4	24	18	15
1870–1880												
Unmarried children	77%	52%	33%	84%	71%	60%	41%	21%	15%	49%	36%	20%
No children	8	23	37	6	13	19	4	8	11	10	9	11
Married children	7	12	9	5	7	10	26	41	36	13	26	34
Other kin	3	7	9	2	3	5	14	15	24	5	5	10
Nonkin	5	6	12	3	7	6	16	15	15	22	24	25
1900–1910												
Unmarried children	75%	47%	22%	81%	68%	41%	48%	28%	41%	54%	42%	18%
No children	10	29	43	8	15	32	6	15	32	11	12	17
Married children	7	15	16	6	9	12	28	9	12	14	19	40
Other kin	4	7	14	3	4	10	14	4	10	12	9	12
Nonkin	3	2	5	3	3	5	5	3	5	10	18	12

aged 50 and older into three subgroups: those aged 50 to 59, those aged 60 to 69, and those aged 70 and older. Table 6.3 is limited to the married and widowed population, both because it is already sufficiently complex without adding single people and because the number of single individuals in any cell is quite small. The detailed information in the table shows that more than 60 percent of men 70 and older were living with unmarried children prior to 1900, and 41 percent were living with unmarried children in the 1900–1910 period. The percentages for women are lower (and zero in the very small population aged 70 and over before the Civil War) but still remarkable.

Men were more likely than women to be living with unmarried children at advanced ages because the older Texas population was characterized by large differences in ages between husbands and wives. Men aged 50 and older were, on average, more than seven years older than their wives, and the difference in ages between husbands and wives increased with age. Men aged 70 and older were on average at least eleven years older than their wives. With differences in ages between husbands and wives so large, a man in his 70s may well have had a wife in her 60s. Moreover, this older generation was one that bore virtually all of its children before any transition in fertility took place. Women bore children until after their fortieth birthday. A married woman in her 60s was likely to have unmarried children at home, and so was her 70-year-old husband.

As the proportions of the married and widowed older population living with their unmarried children declined with age and over time, older people increasingly found themselves in other residential arrangements. In the series of stages identified earlier, the second stage was the empty nest, in which the couple or a surviving spouse lived by themselves without children. The percentage of the older population living in this category is much smaller than that living with unmarried children, but we should not underestimate its importance. As married men and women reached their 60s and 70s, they were increasingly likely to live by themselves, without their children. The increase in numbers living by themselves does not compensate for the decline in the number living with unmarried children, but it contributes a lot. Already in the early twentieth century, many couples and a considerable number of widowed women and men were finding themselves in circumstances in which they lived by themselves, without children, other kin, or nonkin.

UNDERSTANDING THE ROLE OF ETHNICITY, ECONOMIC SECTOR, AND OCCUPATIONAL STATUS: A MULTIVARIATE APPROACH

Thus far the analysis reported here has emphasized the important role played by age, sex, and marital status in determining the ways in which members of the older population lived. While these demographic characteristics are significant, other characteristics of the older population and the house-holds they lived in are also worth considering. Any further information added to the analysis reported here will require a different approach from that already taken. If we need to look—as we do—at the role of ethnicity in addition to age, sex, and marital status, the tables would be so complex and the cell sizes so small as to render them impossible to interpret. We use in-stead a multivariate approach that permits conclusions to be drawn with more independent variables and smaller cell sizes.

In the special context of Texas and the data on which this analysis is based, evidence about ethnicity and occupation should be vitally important in determining the arrangements in which the older population lived. Eth-nicity is especially important because each of the four most important eth-nic groups—those of African, Mexican, and European origin and the native-born children of native parents—was likely to participate differently in the economy and to live in different kinds of communities. The recent settle-ment of the state meant that all the members of these groups were de-scended fairly recently from migrants and might be seen to shun strong commitments to the community. That, of course, was not the case. Immi-grants to Texas from other states were often likely to move on again once they arrived, and much of the Mexican-American population worked in un-stable jobs, but the African-American and German-American populations more often built stable communities.[14] This may have affected the kinds of households in which they lived, although the outcome that I will report may run counter to our intuition about the relationship of community to the res-idential experiences of the older population.

There is not much previous work on ethnic differences in household arrangements among the older population in the rural South on which to base this analysis. Daniel Scott Smith, Michel Dahlin, and Mark Friedberger (1979) examined the residential patterns of older southern blacks and whites in 1880 and 1900. These authors show the complexity involved in studying black-white differences; our four- or five-category division of eth-nicity is still more complex. Nevertheless, their conclusions are worth com-ment. Smith and his colleagues differentiate between two kinds of motiva-tion for parental co-residence with children, that based on economic production and inheritance and that based on family welfare. They show that for both blacks and whites, family welfare was more important than the alternative in producing co-residence. What this means is that few older people lived with their children so that they could share the responsibility for running a farm or other enterprise or so that they could provide inheri-tance to the younger generation. Rather, older people lived with their close kin to help support the otherwise needy, whether it was the older or the younger generation that was in need. Smith, Dahlin, and Friedberger con-clude that differences between whites and blacks existed in 1880 and 1900—

blacks were more likely than whites to provide welfare in a downward direction to children and grandchildren, for example—but that these differences were largely a function of black poverty and were less significant than the enormous change that has taken place since 1900.

Despite strong kin ties within certain groups, and despite the existence of many large and complex households, there is no evidence that any sizable ethnic or economic group in Texas chose to live in multigeneration households. Married parents lived with married children, out of choice and for reasons of economic productivity, but such cases were relatively unusual. Put another way, while there appears to have been a strong preference for co-residence with unmarried children, there was no "family economy" of co-residence in Texas which might have served to bring older parents and married children together. Rather, most co-residence of parents and married children occurred for what Smith, Dahlin, and Friedberger call "welfare" reasons: to provide for someone in need. If this was indeed the case, we should find that most co-residence took place among those who had the most need and among those who had the greatest resources. We can get an idea of propensities to needs and resources in different ethnic groups by looking at overall occupational patterns within different groups.

The principal ethnic groups in Texas each had a distinct pattern of economic participation. Table 6.4 presents evidence for 1860, 1870, and 1900 on the economic activities of the households in which our sample population lived. The data represent the economic and ethnic characteristics of household heads, but the numbers represent the total population, because each individual in the population is given the ethnic and occupational characteristics of the head.[15]

A majority of each ethnic population (except the Mexicans) lived in a household in which the head held a farm occupation, but the internal structure of those farm occupations differed from ethnic group to ethnic group. The European origin population largely consisted of farm-owning households. While the native white population had a majority of farm-owning households, it also had a very significant number of farm tenants.[16] The African-American population was at the opposite end of the farmer-tenant continuum from the Europeans. In both 1870 and 1900, the majority were farm tenants, while a minority were farmers or farm laborers. Among farming Mexicans the distinctive feature is the large proportion of farm laborers. In these generally rural communities, there was nonetheless a significant part of the population that worked outside of agriculture. The differences between ethnic groups are predictable. African-Americans and Mexican-Americans were most likely to hold unskilled nonfarm occupations, while the Europeans and native whites were the most likely to be involved in white-collar work. In all groups there were a significant number of

TABLE 6.4 Occupation Distribution of Households by Ethnicity

	African		European	
	N	%	N	%
1860				
Farm				
Farmer	—	—	720	63
Tenant	—	—	28	2
Laborer	—	—	23	2
Nonfarm				
White collar	—	—	76	7
Skilled	—	—	183	16
Unskilled	—	—	77	7
No occupation	—	—	42	4
Total	—	—	1,149	—
1870				
Farm				
Farmer	202	4	848	54
Tenant	3,629	65	56	4
Laborer	1,017	18	10	1
Nonfarm				
White collar	8	0	173	11
Skilled	42	1	272	17
Unskilled	289	5	127	8
No occupation	416	7	76	5
Total	5,603	—	1,562	—
1900				
Farm				
Farmer	1,232	19	2,552	69
Tenant	3,041	48	250	7
Laborer	923	15	67	2
Nonfarm				
White collar	146	2	343	9
Skilled	128	2	249	7
Unskilled	522	8	46	1
No occupation	348	5	205	6
Total	6,339	—	3,712	—

Mexican		Native		Other	
N	%	N	%	N	%
40	8	4,566	36	239	60
0	0	2,297	18	14	4
42	8	2,487	20	3	1
21	4	1,037	8	51	13
98	20	739	6	28	7
271	54	607	5	23	6
32	6	949	7	39	10
504	—	12,682	—	397	—
21	3	4,520	44	281	64
20	3	2,011	20	26	6
224	30	443	4	0	0
26	4	1,133	11	53	12
86	12	544	5	47	11
220	30	526	5	16	4
144	19	1,125	11	19	4
742	—	10,303	—	441	—
80	6	7,190	42	432	29
109	8	5,460	32	245	16
482	35	754	4	135	9
68	5	1,635	10	238	16
172	13	752	4	178	12
301	22	582	3	133	9
155	11	830	5	142	9
1,367	—	17,204	—	1,503	—

households in which the head held no occupation; this was especially the case among Mexicans.

It is best to concentrate our attention first on the farming part of each ethnic population. Farm owners were more likely than farm tenants or laborers to have had the resources required for a multigenerational household. Farm tenants may have been constrained by tenancy contracts to limit the number of residents on the farm, so as to ensure its profitability (Ransom and Sutch 1977). On this basis we might assert that the German-origin population, which consisted almost totally of farm owners, had the greatest resources with which to support co-residence of parents with married children but probably also the least need. African-Americans and Mexican-Americans, however, had the fewest resources combined with the greatest potential need. Native whites were somewhere between these other groups, but their majority of farm owners within the farm population leads us to place them closer to the European origin population than to the Mexican-American and African-American populations. Turning to the nonfarm population, it was less likely to support co-residence than the farming population, a combination of overall wealth and space in which co-residing parents and married children could live. The ethnic distribution of nonfarm occupations is distinctive, confirming ethnic status in nineteenth- and early-twentieth-century Texas: Mexican-Americans and African-Americans in lower status occupations, and native whites and European origin whites in the higher status occupations.

The goal of the multivariate analysis of the determinants of domestic arrangements for the older population is to bring together in a single model a number of independent variables. From a variety of independent variables we should be able to see the range of influences that cannot be seen using contingency tables and also to be more sensitive to the interaction of variables so that we see genuine effects. The dependent variables are taken from the method of categorizing the family arrangements of the older population, so that we can see the determinants of living with unmarried children, for example, or the determinants of living without children present. Given the categorical dependent variables, I have chosen a logit regression approach.[17] I report this approach with three different dependent variables: whether or not the older person is living with unmarried children (table 6.5); whether he or she is living without children or others present (table 6.6); and whether he or she is living with one or more married child (table 6.7).

The models are estimated from a database of 12,549 men and women aged 50 and older in one or more of the six censuses we have transcribed for the period from 1850 to 1910.[18] The independent variables place the occurrence in a time period (1850–1860, 1870–1880, or 1900–1910), categorize the age of the older person (50–59, 60–69, or 70+), and measure sex,

TABLE 6.5   Logit Model: Living with Unmarried Children as
Dependent Variable

Variable	Coefficient	Odds Ratio
Time period[a]		
Period 1 (1850–1860)	0.2390	1.2700**
Period 2 (1870–1880)	0.1075	1.1135**
Age group[b]		
60–69	−0.8814	0.4142**
70+	−1.7543	0.1730**
Sex and marital status[c]		
Married females	−0.6056	0.5458**
Widowed males	−1.4405	0.2368**
Widowed females	−1.8108	0.1635**
Single females	−5.7685	0.0031**
Single males	−6.6135	0.0013**
Nonfarm occupation (head)	−0.1194	0.8874
Ethnicity[d]		
African-American	−2.8035	0.0606**
East European	0.1288	1.1374
Mexican-American	−0.4726	0.6234**

NOTE: Log likelihood = −6754; number of cases = 12,549; $\chi^2(13)$ = 3607.10, p ≤ .0001.
[a]1900–1910 is the reference period.
[b]50–59 is the reference group.
[c]Married males are the reference group.
[d]Native American and Other are the reference groups.
*p ≤ .01.
**p ≤ .001.

marital status, the occupation of the head of the household, and the ethnic group of the older person. All of these variables are categorical. When there are more than two categories in a categorical variable used in logit regression, the variable must be converted to a group of variables, each of which has a value of zero or one. One of these variables is not used in the analysis and is considered the reference. The coefficients for the variables included in the equation then describe the situation relative to the eliminated category.

The most important set of categorical variables included in the analysis in this way combine sex and marital status. Rather than use one variable for sex (male vs. female) and several variables for the three categories of marital status (single, married, widowed/divorced), I combined sex and marital status into six categories and treated married males as the reference category. The other important categorical variable was ethnic group, from which I created four new variables, with individuals born in North America of North American parents, plus the residual "other" category, the reference groups.

TABLE 6.6   Logit Model: Living without Children as
Dependent Variable

Variable	Coefficient	Odds Ratio
Time period[a]		
Period 1 (1850–1860)	−0.4802	0.6186**
Period 2 (1870–1880)	−0.2534	0.7762**
Age group[b]		
60–69	0.8223	2.2758**
70+	1.2157	3.3728**
Sex and marital status[c]		
Married females	0.5037	1.6548**
Widowed males	−0.2739	0.7604*
Widowed females	−0.8973	0.4077**
Single females	−0.5499	0.5770
Single males	1.1700	3.2219**
Nonfarm occupation (head)	0.9184	2.5054**
Ethnicity[d]		
African-American	0.3104	1.3639**
East European	0.4465	1.5628**
Mexican-American	0.3386	1.4030*

NOTE: Log likelihood = −4167; number of cases = 12,549; $\chi^2(13)$ = 834.58, p ≤ .0001.
[a]1900–1910 is the reference period.
[b]50–59 is the reference group.
[c]Married males are the reference group.
[d]Native American and Other are the reference groups.
*p ≤ .01.
**p ≤ .001.

In all three of the logit models reported here, the overall results are significant. The tables report the overall results of the analysis, plus the coefficient for each variable included. In addition, I report the odds ratio, which is the coefficient exponentiated, because the exponentiated value of the coefficient can often be more easily understood than the coefficient itself. For categorical variables, the exponentiated coefficient is the ratio of the odds of a value in the stated group to that of the reference group. For example, the value of 8.1 for the exponentiated coefficient for widowed females means that widowed females were slightly more than eight times as likely to be living with married children as were married men (the reference group), all other things being equal. With the exception of the coefficients for single females in two of the three models, the basic independent variables reporting age, sex, and marital status were predictable and significant. Age group, for example, predicted a lower likelihood of living with unmarried children as people aged and a higher likelihood of living alone or with married children as people aged. The same set of conclusions can be extended

TABLE 6.7 Logit Model: Living with Married Child as
Dependent Variable

Variable	Coefficient	Odds Ratio
Time period[a]		
Period 1 (1850–1860)	−0.2862	0.7511**
Period 2 (1870–1880)	−0.1388	0.8704
Age group[b]		
60–69	0.6121	1.8443**
70+	1.0247	2.7862**
Sex and marital status[c]		
Married females	0.4448	1.5601**
Widowed males	1.3535	3.8708**
Widowed females	2.0896	8.0813**
Single females	−0.1859	0.8303
Single males	−1.8019	0.1650**
Nonfarm occupation (head)	−0.7195	0.4870**
Ethnicity[d]		
African-American	−0.3144	0.7303**
East European	−0.2323	0.7927**
Mexican-American	0.1869	1.2055

NOTE: Log likelihood = −4359; number of cases = 12,549; $\chi^2(13)$ = 1572.16, p ≤ .0001.
[a]1900–1910 is the reference period.
[b]50–59 is the reference group.
[c]Married males are the reference group.
[d]Native American and Other are the reference groups.
*p ≤ .01.
**p ≤ .001.

from the contingency tables presented earlier in this chapter to these logit models. Similarly, the conclusions we drew about changes over time are confirmed by the multivariate models reported here. As time passed, older people were less likely to live with unmarried children and more likely to live alone or with married children, all other things being equal.

The results about economic sector reported in tables 6.5, 6.6, and 6.7 show that older people who lived in households headed by someone in the nonfarm sector were slightly less likely to be living with unmarried children, rather less likely to be living with married children, and quite a bit more likely to be living alone or with a spouse than those who were living in a farm sector household. These results are consistent with what we should expect. A set of alternative models involving five occupational categories was also attempted, and the results of that analysis did not improve on the results based on a simple farm versus nonfarm categorization.[19]

The results for different ethnicities help us go beyond what was revealed by simpler approaches and allow us to speculate about possible cultural differences in the approach to family life for older people. When compared with the reference group, European immigrants and their children were more likely to be living with unmarried children, more likely to be living without children, and less likely to be living with married children. African-Americans were less likely to be living with unmarried children, more likely to be living without children, and less likely to be living with married children. Finally, Mexican-Americans were less likely to be living with unmarried children, more likely to be living without children, and more likely to be living with married children, when compared with the reference group. We can put these conclusions in another way and then use these findings to go on to more general conclusions. In all this we need to remember that the results are expressed with reference to the native-born population of native parentage. Compared to that group, the European immigrants and their children (many of whom would have reached age 50 by 1910) were more "nuclear" in their residential preferences and practices. The Europeans were more likely to live with unmarried children and more likely to live alone or merely with their spouse than the reference group. By contrast, the Mexican-Americans were more "extended" in their residential preferences and practices, when possible. They were more likely to live with married children but also more likely to live alone or with a spouse. The African-Americans might be described as "disenfranchised." They were less likely to be living with children than any other group. Whether this is due to their inability to support larger households given their financial condition or whether this is a consequence of their greater propensity to live outside normal family situations, either as servants or lodgers, remains to be seen.

The ethnic differentials in the living arrangements of the older population lead to at least one speculation that is worth putting forward here. Research we have done about out-migration from these counties suggests that the European origin population was very likely not to leave, especially when compared to the other groups described here (Gutmann et al. 1990). White natives and African-Americans were in an intermediate group, white Mexican-Americans were most likely to have emigrated or died between any two censuses. One conclusion this suggests is that by the turn of the twentieth century, at the latest, Euro-Americans in Texas had a well-developed local set of kin contacts, especially married children. There was no need for their parents to co-reside with married children, because a significant group lived nearby which might offer greater support than a single co-residing family could.

CONCLUSION

Like the rest of the population in America and many other Western nations, a large majority of older Texans lived in nuclear family households with spouse and unmarried children. Rural Americans in the Southwest did not participate—or wish to participate—in a family economy in which several generations shared economic resources and a residence. Despite that conclusion, a significant number of older Texans lived with married children, and a growing number over time lived alone or merely with a spouse and not with children or other kin. I have emphasized two kinds of transitions away from the normative life in which the older person lived with a spouse or unmarried children. For older couples who both survived until their last child had left the family household and for some widows, life alone was increasingly common by the turn of the twentieth century. For widows and a small proportion of surviving couples, life with a married child was possible, although it was not as common.

That older couples in small towns and the countryside increasingly lived away from unmarried or married children by the turn of the twentieth century is one of the principal conclusions of this chapter. In good part, their ability to live by themselves was a consequence of longer lives. Unlike older widows, who may not have been able to maintain even a small household on their own, older couples could live by themselves. The fact that as the frontier filled in they were more likely to have had a number of children nearby and thereby a standby welfare system probably also made it easier. Most important, however, was perhaps a growing sense even a century ago that the generations were better off if they did not share a residence. Although the analysis here is too dependent on evidence from censuses and too filled with unresolved complexities to be absolutely sure of its implications, it is nonetheless suggestive of the values of both the older population and their children. By the early twentieth century, conditions were beginning to be right for separate residence to work. If this is the case, then we see as early as 1900 the origins of the late-twentieth-century tendency for the elderly to live isolated lives.

The differences between ethnic groups in Texas add subtleties and complexity to our analysis of the changing ways in which the older population lived. There is little evidence that anyone in Texas lived in complex households as part of a household economy that combined generations to maximize economic productivity or guarantee inheritance.[20] There were differences between ethnicities, but they seem to have been the consequence of different economic conditions rather than of different value systems. Both poverty and prosperity led older couples not to live with their married children, and this was the case for the African-American and the European origin populations. The European—mostly German—population was kin oriented and prosperous. They could have supported co-residence if they had a strong propensity to do so. They did not, because they appear to have been little inclined to share a residence with their married children until widowhood and because they had the economic resources and the standby kin resources to avoid co-residence. The African-Americans, however, may have had more need but certainly had less resources with which to support co-residence. The older population was more likely to live alone.

The Texas counties studied in this chapter are near or just behind the moving American frontier between 1850 and 1910, and we expected their proximity to the frontier to affect the living arrangements of their older inhabitants. Was that the case? The major impact of the frontier was in the overwhelmingly agricultural economic structure and in producing a youthful population that aged relatively rapidly when compared with the population of the United States as a whole. The agricultural characteristic of these rural counties certainly contributed to the large proportion of older and widowed women who lived with their married children or with other kin. This was offset for older men and couples, however, by the availability of land, so that younger and older generations did not need to share property.[21] The aging of the population probably contributed to some sense of increasing complexity of households, but the process is difficult to study because there may have been several things going on at once: aging, which created more need for complex households as well as a longer-lived population and the availability of more kin to live with over time, and the beginning of the tendency for the older generation to wish to live alone.

NOTES

This research has been supported by Grant R01 HD23693 from the National Institute of Child Health and Human Development and by grants from the University of Texas Project Quest and the University Research Institute of the University of Texas. I am grateful to my collaborators, Kenneth Fliess, John Vetter, and Jane Zachritz, for advice about how to proceed on a difficult subject. Thomas Pullum gave me invaluable advice on logit regression. I am also grateful to the numerous individuals who have worked on this project and who have contributed to the creation of an extraordinary and effective body of data.

1. Unfortunately, it is not possible to ask the same questions for the American Indian population or for the African-American population before the end of slavery.

2. The exception is the population of Webb County, which is dominated by the small city of Laredo. Laredo had a more varied economy.

3. There is a considerable background literature about residential arrangements in the United States in the nineteenth and early twentieth century. Unfortunately, not enough of it deals with rural, as opposed to urban, populations. For the best general overview and a novel interpretation, see Ruggles 1987.

4. See Smith 1979, 1984, and 1986; and Smith, Dahlin, and Friedberger 1979.

5. For an overview of the project, see Gutmann and Fliess 1989. For methodological considerations, see Holmes and Gutmann 1989, Gutmann and Holmes 1988, and Gutmann et al. 1989.

6. For an example of other work in this project, see Gutmann 1991.

7. The sampling scheme involves taking a sample of households headed by individuals whose surnames begin with certain letters of the alphabet, in order to be able to link from document to document. See Vetter 1990 for a discussion of the representativity of this method. The linkage techniques used are described in Vetter, Gonzalez, and Gutmann 1992.

8. Webb County existed by 1850, but it was enumerated together with other Rio Grande Valley counties, in which most of the Mexican-American population lived.

9. The sample was designed to maximize the possibility of linking individuals between census years, so there is some likelihood that an individual sampled in the 1870 census would also be sampled in the 1880 census. By combining 1870 and 1880, the likelihood that all the cases in the combined sample are independent of each other is reduced. This problem is minimized by the low level of linkage obtained in all but the German-American population (Gutmann et al. 1990) and by the fact that we divide the population into ten-year age groups. Thus persons aged 65 in 1870 would be aged 75 in 1880, and they would be found in different cells in most of our analyses.

10. Whether he would have lived with a child at the very end of his life is open to question. His living only with his wife at age 79 is a clear sign of a preference for living alone, especially in a strong kinship community such as Gillespie County.

11. In this we follow the work of Smith (1979) and Smith, Dahlin, and Friedberger (1979). Like Shanas and colleagues, we give priorities to some residential arrangements, in the event more than one occur simultaneously. First, the categories used here give preference to close kin over more distant kin or nonkin. Second, the categories give preference to residence with married children over all others and to residence with unmarried children over all remaining possibilities. Thus, if an individual lives with a spouse, an unmarried child, and a married child, he or she would be placed in the category of living with a married child. If an individual lives with an unmarried child, a spouse, and other kin, the appropriate category would be "unmarried child." The literature is vague about whether widowed children are considered married or unmarried. Here they are treated as unmarried.

12. These figures are drawn from the Texas historical demography project database, described above. Smith (1979: 287) reports results about the marital status of men and women in the United States as a whole in 1900. His results are similar to those reported here for men but higher than those reported here for women. Women in Texas were probably more likely to have married, because sex ratios were different in Texas in the nineteenth century than in the whole United States, improving the likelihood of women marrying.

13. A proportional weight is applied to each case so that for the total sample for any year the proportion in each ethnic group in the sample population is the same as that for the state as a whole as reported in census publications. In general, the weights for the European and Mexican origin populations are less than one, and those for all other groups are somewhat greater than one. No other corrections have been applied to the data.

14. For differential migration once they arrived in Texas, see Gutmann et al. 1990.

15. This was accomplished by weighting each household head by the size of the household he headed. If instead of all residents of the sample counties we look to

the economic activities of the households of the older population, the pattern is little different from that in table 6.4. In all ethnic groups the proportion of people aged 50 and older living in farm owner households and living in no occupation households is greater than in the population as a whole.

16. In 1860 and 1870, tenants were defined as those who were enumerated as farmers but who reported no real property. In 1900, tenants were those who were enumerated as farmers but who declared themselves as renters in the question about home ownership or rental. Also, see Houdek and Heller 1986 and Ransom and Sutch 1977.

17. For an explanation of such approaches, see Agresti 1990. The analysis was done using the logit program of the STATA statistical analysis package.

18. A small number of people appear more than once in this database, in those cases where a person stays in the sample after age 55 for two or more censuses. We have not corrected for the lack of independence this implies, because we estimate that fewer than 10 percent of the cases are individuals who appear more than once. The logit estimation procedure makes use of the data weights we have used elsewhere in the analysis reported here.

19. The categories were (1) farmer or farm tenant, (2) farm and nonfarm worker, (3) white-collar worker, (4) skilled craftsperson, and (5) no profession. The farmer and farm tenant category was used as the reference. These categories were significant for models in which living alone and living with unmarried children were the dependent variables but not for one in which living with married children was the dependent variable. Where they were significant, the three occupational categories (numbers 2, 3, and 4 above) had roughly similar values and similar signs. They were positively related to living alone and negatively related to living with unmarried children.

20. An analysis of ages of heads of household of extended and multiple households showed that the most likely age of head was under age 35 and that in most cases, the co-resident kin was the sibling of the head and not the parent.

21. The role played by property ownership and its passage can be studied using our cross-references linking census data to property tax data and linking census data across time periods. Those data are exceptionally complex, and we have not yet gotten far enough in the underlying project to exploit them for the study of property transfers from generation to generation.

REFERENCES

Achenbaum, W. Andrew. 1978. *Old age in the new land: The American experience since 1970.* Baltimore: Johns Hopkins University Press.

Agresti, Alan. 1990. *Categorical data analysis.* New York: John Wiley and Sons.

Fischer, David Hackett. 1978. *Growing old in America.* Oxford: Oxford University Press.

Fliess, Kenneth H., Myron P. Gutmann, and John E. Vetter. 1990. "The creation of Mexican-American fertility patterns." Paper presented at the annual meeting of the Population Association of America, Montreal, Canada, May.

Gutmann, Myron P. 1991. "Denomination and fertility decline: The Catholics and Protestants of Gillespie County, Texas." *Continuity and Change* 5: 391–416.

Gutmann, Myron P., and Kenneth H. Fliess. 1989. *How to study southern demography in the nineteenth century: Early lessons of the Texas Demography Project.* Austin: Texas Population Research Center Papers, no. 11.11.

Gutmann, Myron P., Kenneth H. Fliess, Amy E. Holmes, Amy L. Fairchild, and Wendy Teas. 1989. "Keeping track of our treasures: Database management for historical research." *Historical Methods* 22: 128–143.

Gutmann, Myron P., and Amy E. Holmes. 1988. *The Texas census data system.* Madison: Wisc-Ware.

Gutmann, Myron P., John E. Vetter, Kenneth H. Fliess, and Gregory Joslyn. 1990. *Staying put or moving on? Ethnicity and persistence in Texas from 1850 to 1910.* Austin: Texas Population Research Center Papers, no. 12.03.

Holmes, Amy E., and Myron P. Gutmann. 1989. "Four 'nos': A data entry system for class projects." *The History Teacher* 21: 439–467.

Houdek, John T., and Charles F. Heller, Jr. 1986. "Searching for nineteenth-century farm tenants: An evaluation of methods." *Historical Methods* 19: 55–61.

Laslett, Peter. 1972. Introduction. In *Household and family in past time,* ed. Peter Laslett, 1–90. Cambridge: Cambridge University Press.

Ransom, Roger L., and Richard Sutch. 1977. *One kind of freedom: The economic consequences of emancipation.* Cambridge: Cambridge University Press.

Riley, Matilda White. 1982. "Aging and social change." In *Aging from birth to death,* ed. Matilda White Riley, Ronald P. Abeles, and Michael S. Teitelbaum, 11–26. Boulder: Westview Press.

Ruggles, Stephen. 1987. *Prolonged connections: The rise of the extended family in nineteenth-century England and America.* Madison: University of Wisconsin Press.

Shanas, Ethel, Peter Townsend, Dorothy Wedderburn, Henning Friis, Poul Milhøj, and Jan Stehouwer. 1968. *Old people in three industrial societies.* New York: Atherton Press.

Skrabanek, R. L., W. Kennedy Upham, and Ben E. Dickerson. 1975. *The older population of Texas.* College Station: Texas Agricultural Experiment Station.

Smith, Daniel Scott. 1979. "Life course, norms, and the family system of older Americans in 1900." *Journal of Family History* 4: 285–298.

———. 1981. "Historical change in the household structure of the elderly in economically developed societies." In *Aging: Stability and change in the family,* ed. Robert W. Fogel, Elaine Hatfield, Sara Bikiesler, and Ethel Shanas, 91–114. New York: Academic Press.

———. 1984. "Modernization and the family structure of the elderly in the United States." *Zeitschrift für Gerontologie* 17: 13–17.

———. 1986. "Accounting for change in the families of the elderly in the United States, 1900–present." In *Old age in a bureaucratic society: The elderly, the experts and the state in American history,* ed. David Van Tassel and Peter N. Stearns, 87–109. New York: Greenwood Press.

Smith, Daniel Scott, Michel Dahlin, and Mark Friedberger. 1979. "The family structure of the older black population in the American South in 1880 and 1900." *Sociology and Social Research* 63: 544–565.

Vetter, John. 1990. "The Texas Project letter sample." Working paper, Frontier Demography Project, Population Research Center, University of Texas at Austin.

Vetter, John E., Jesus R. Gonzalez, and Myron P. Gutmann. 1992. "Computer-assisted record linkage using a relational database system." *History and Computing* 4: 34–51.

Wall, Richard, with Jean Robin and Peter Laslett, eds. 1983. *Family forms in historic Europe*. Cambridge: Cambridge University Press.

SEVEN

A Home of One's Own: Aging and Home Ownership in the United States in the Late Nineteenth and Early Twentieth Century

Michael R. Haines and Allen C. Goodman

An essential aspect of aging is the provision for food, shelter, and general economic well-being later in the life course. In closer-knit and less mobile societies, great reliance can be placed on kinship ties and relations of reciprocity and exchange between kin and other community members. In more mobile and rapidly changing environments, the elderly must often be more self-reliant. Consequently, individuals and families accumulate wealth for the anticipated slowdown or cessation of work. This wealth can take a variety of forms, both real and financial, but a principal one has been a home.

Home ownership has been central to the hopes and aspirations of American families. For many Americans, a home was—and remains—the major source of real property holding, especially as the society became more urban and less agricultural. Before the creation of large-scale, comprehensive pension plans, homes were the principal repository of all wealth for older urban individuals and households. Even today the "savings of the elderly are primarily in the form of housing" (Wise 1989: 2). In addition to providing more secure housing services, owner-occupied homes could be a source of income from rentals, boarding, and lodging. This was often of considerable importance later in the life course, especially for widows. Over the life course, mortgages have provided a means to accumulate savings in real property. It is an example of a life course phenomenon in which decisions made early in life have a major impact in later years.

It has become ingrained in American culture that a "home of one's own" is part of the aspiration for the good life—the "American dream" (Morris and Winter 1978; Perrin 1977; Rossi 1980). Home ownership has acquired important symbolic value. As John Adams (1987: 18) notes,

The equity in owned housing represents the dominant financial asset of the typical household in America, where 64 percent own the houses they live in. Buying a house is usually the most important financial commitment that a family makes, and for many households—perhaps most—housing decisions are highly emotional and intensely personal. . . . Housing has multiple hidden meanings . . . status, position, power, and personal identity.

Further, Peter Rossi and Anne Shlay (1982: 30) have noted,

American preferences for homeownership and for the spatial segregation of homeowners from renters appears to be so general that they can be regarded as norms deeply embedded in American values. . . . Owning one's home is viewed widely as a measure of achievement, as part of the American dream.

Historically, home ownership has been "one of the basic elements of satisfactory middle class life" in the United States (Warner 1962: 157). It was of importance to both native-born and immigrant workers (Kirk and Kirk 1981). Possession of property, especially homes, seemed desirable as a stabilizing and conservative influence, reinforcing thrift, industriousness, occupational and geographic stability, good citizenship, and other virtues, as well as providing a sense of status and economic security (Kirk and Kirk 1981: 473–475; Tygiel 1979: 92–93).

One manifestation of these aspirations is that home ownership, or at least a fair chance at it, is likely to increase with age. Increasing age may serve as a proxy for increasing income and/or wealth. Allen Goodman (1990) discovers, however, that even when income, housing prices, and other sociodemographic variables are controlled, age still has a positive and significant impact on the probability of home ownership. This impact may also indicate acceptance of and ability to meet the social norms that characterize home ownership.

One might ask whether this relationship occurred historically. What were the implications of the patterns of age and home ownership? It is the goal of this chapter to explore the issue for the United States in the period from the Civil War to the 1930s.

American society has unquestionably aged since the middle of the nineteenth century. In 1850, the proportion of the population aged 60 and over was 4.1 percent. This had risen to 6.4 percent in 1900 and 8.5 percent by 1930. In 1989, the proportion of those aged 60 and over had doubled again to 18.9 percent (U.S. Bureau of the Census 1975: Series A, 119–134; 1991: table 22). A combination of a positive relationship of home ownership and aging with a rising share of the elderly in the population has resulted in a greater share of housing wealth held by the older population. In 1900, about 17 percent of all nonfarm owner-occupied dwellings were owned by households with heads aged 65 and over. This had risen to over 26 percent in 1987 (table 7.2; U.S. Bureau of the Census 1991: table 1285). This has meanings for residential mobility and patterns of co-residence. Are the elderly more or less likely to co-reside with children of their own or rent? Does ownership convey great financial independence and bargaining influence with family and society?

When the nation was predominantly agrarian, a home usually went along with ownership of the farmstead. By the time of the 1890 U.S. census (the first to ask direct questions about housing), almost 48 percent of all dwelling units were owner occupied (see table 7.1).[1] Predictably, the ownership rate was lower among nonfarm households (37 percent) than among farm households (66 percent). For an earlier period, Lee Soltow has estimated for 1850 that about 50 percent of all dwelling units were owner occupied. This had changed little by 1870, when about 51 percent were owned by their occupants. In addition, an ownership differential similar to that found in 1890 applied between farm (65 percent owner occupied) and nonfarm (38 percent owner occupied) households (Soltow 1975: table 2.5). Indeed, there seem to have been few changes in home ownership incidence over the latter half of the nineteenth century.

By 1970, the national proportion of home ownership had risen to about 63 percent, with 62 percent among nonfarm households and 80 percent among the relatively small number of farm households. Since that time, the overall ownership rates have remained roughly stable at about 63 to 64 percent (see table 7.1). Much of the increase in home ownership rates has, however, taken place since 1940. Given the precipitous fall in the share of farm households, the increase must be explained almost entirely by the change in home ownership among urban households.

Among urban workers, lower rates of home ownership have been observed in the past. Only about 18 percent of worker families in the U.S. Commissioner of Labor Survey of 1889–1890 were home owners (U.S. Commissioner of Labor 1890, 1891), as compared with about 37 percent for all nonfarm households in the 1890 census (table 7.1). By 1901, this had risen to 19 percent for a survey of 25,440 urban families in thirty-two states and the District of Columbia (U.S. Commissioner of Labor 1904). This rate has converged toward the national average as the United States has urbanized and as relative worker incomes have grown.

By international standards, the United States has had relatively high levels of owner occupancy. For example, in the 1889–1890 survey of worker households just mentioned, 1,735 European households (in Belgium, France, Germany, Great Britain, and Switzerland) were also sampled. In contrast to the American home ownership rate of 18 percent, that among the European workers was only about 7 percent (and only 2 percent in Great Britain and 5 percent in France). By the middle of the twentieth century when the nonfarm ownership rate was 61 percent for the United States in 1960, it was 50 percent for Belgium (1961), 33 percent for urban France (1962), 13 percent for urban Germany (1961), 26 percent for urban Sweden (1965), and 43 percent for urban England and Wales (1961) (United Nations 1973: table 203). The greater abundance of land in the United

TABLE 7.1 Home Ownership Rates: Total, Nonfarm, and Farm, United States, 1890–1987

Year	Total			Nonfarm			Farm		
	Units[a]	Owned[a]	%	Units[a]	Owned[a]	%	Units[a]	Owned[a]	%
1890	12,690	6,066	47.80	7,923	2,924	36.91	4,767	3,143	65.93
1900	15,429	7,205	46.70	9,780	3,567	36.47	5,649	3,638	64.40
1910	19,782	9,084	45.92	13,672	5,245	38.36	6,110	3,838	62.82
1920	23,811	10,867	45.64	17,229	7,041	40.87	6,581	3,826	58.14
1930	29,322	14,002	47.75	22,917	10,550	46.04	6,405	3,452	53.90
1940	34,855	15,196	43.60	27,748	11,413	41.13	7,107	3,783	53.23
1950	42,826	23,560	55.01	37,105	19,802	53.37	5,721	3,758	65.69
1960	53,024	32,796	61.85	49,458	30,164	60.99	3,566	2,633	73.84
1970	63,450	39,885	62.86	60,351	37,393	61.96	3,095	2,492	80.52
1980	80,390	51,795	64.43						
1987	90,888	58,164	64.00						

SOURCES: U.S. Bureau of the Census 1975: Series N, 238–245; 1991: table 1283.
[a]In thousands.

States played a role, but more recent settlement (allowing for property acquisition by a wide variety of the population) and cultural values were also important. During the late nineteenth and early twentieth century, a relatively high rate of asset accumulation was characteristic of the United States generally in contrast to industrializing European nations (Ransom and Sutch 1989). These phenomena granted the possibility of greater independence in attaining security in old age.

As noted, home ownership has constituted a significant part of asset acquisition over the life cycle. For example, in 1988, equity in owner-occupied homes was 43 percent of total household net worth in the United States (U.S. Bureau of the Census 1991: table 759). One group of economic models aimed at explaining savings uses life cycle accumulation behavior (e.g., Modigliani 1988). The models hypothesize that households and individuals in the middle of the life course save in the form of both financial (e.g., pensions) and real assets (e.g., homes) for expected retirement in the later years of the life course. In this connection several authors have recently noted that housing wealth contributes to the interesting phenomenon of continued positive accumulation among many elderly and retired persons, even in the form of housing (see Ai et al. 1990; Feinstein and McFadden 1989; Kotlikoff 1989: 78–79; Stahl 1989; Venti and Wise 1989, 1990).

Housing also constitutes an important component of consumer budgets, a factor of importance to the elderly on retirement incomes. In the later nineteenth century, housing and housing operations took up to between one-fifth and one-fourth of all consumer spending. This had risen to almost 30 percent by the 1980s (U.S. Bureau of the Census 1975: Chap. G; 1991: table 706). Even though housing costs tend to decline for the elderly (Stahl 1989), the issue of owning one's dwelling can bear significantly on the security of residence in old age.

Age is an explanatory variable for demographers, economists, and others using or testing life cycle models of saving and accumulation (Kotlikoff 1989; Modigliani 1988). It would seem that studies of the age pattern of home ownership would be more common. It appears that they are not, especially historically.[2] The aim of this chapter is to provide a preliminary historical overview of the relationship of aging and home ownership from the late nineteenth to the early twentieth century, a period of rapid growth in ownership, to suggest some means of describing these data more concisely, and to examine some of the implications for the later life course of the rising and changing incidence of home ownership over time.

DATA AND SOURCES

Table 7.2 provides a summary of the data and sources used here. These by no means exhaust potential sources. In particular, Soltow (1975) and oth-

TABLE 7.2 Age Patterns of Home Ownership in the United States, 1865–1930

	New York Counties Sample, 1865[a,d]			U.S. Commissioner of Labor Survey, 1889–1890[a]			U.S. Census, 1900[a,e]		
Age Group	Total	Owners	%	Total	Owners	%	Total	Owners	%
Below 25	59	4	6.78	291	12	4.12	658	54	8.21
25–29	196	42	21.43	1,010	102	10.10	1,374	205	14.92
30–34	240	52	21.67	1,192	181	15.18	1,787	413	23.11
35–39	263	81	30.80	1,155	194	16.80	1,869	573	30.66
40–44	237	87	36.71	1,021	201	19.69	1,708	604	35.36
45–49	252	100	39.68	839	183	21.81	1,352	553	40.90
50–54	180	82	45.56	582	144	24.74	1,225	547	44.65
55–59	160	59	36.88	356	88	24.72	887	451	50.85
60–64	135	51	37.78	221	65	29.41	744	409	54.97
65–69	78	31	39.74	82	17	20.73	544	330	60.66
70+	95	41	43.16	33	11	33.33	667	447	67.02
Total	1,895	630	33.25	6,782	1,198	17.66	12,815	4,586	35.79

U.S. Census, 1890[b]

Age Group	Total	Owners	%
Below 25	412,708	55,644	13.48
25–29	949,514	184,980	19.48
30–34	1,159,634	316,756	27.32
35–39	1,119,561	361,977	32.33
40–44	967,557	363,420	37.56
45–49	865,962	360,222	41.60
50–54	749,591	338,202	45.12
55–59	536,246	269,172	50.20
60+	1,162,200	673,298	57.93
Total	7,922,973	2,923,671	36.90

U.S. Census, 1930[c]

Age Group	Total	Owners	%
Below 25	1,266,066	130,869	10.34
25–34	5,878,711	1,516,341	25.79
35–44	7,082,391	3,142,403	44.37
45–54	5,743,244	3,201,077	55.74
55–64	3,680,822	2,396,679	65.11
65–74	1,880,969	1,361,618	72.39
75+	561,223	424,288	75.60
Total	26,093,426	12,173,275	46.65

SOURCES: *Seven New York Counties Sample, 1865*: Five percent sample of seven New York counties (Allegany, Dutchess, Montgomery, Rensselaer, Steuben, Tompkins, and Warren) from the manuscript of the 1865 New York State census. *U.S. Commissioner of Labor Survey, 1889–1890*: U.S. Commissioner of Labor (1890, 1891). The sample consists of 6,809 households of workers in nine industries (bar iron, pig iron, steel, coke, bituminous coal, iron ore, cotton textiles, woolen textiles, and glass) in 24 states of the United States. *U.S. Census, 1900*: Tabulations from the public use sample of the 1900 U.S. census of 101,438 individuals. *U.S. Census, 1890*: U.S. Bureau of the Census 1896: table 77. *U.S. Census, 1930*: U.S. Bureau of the Census 1933: table 35.

[a]Male and female heads of households.
[b]Males and females.
[c]Male heads of household only.
[d]Nonfarmers only.
[e]All persons living in homes; farms excluded.

ers have worked with sample data on real and personal property holdings from the U.S. census manuscripts for 1850, 1860, and 1870. Roger Ransom and Richard Sutch (1989) and their colleagues are studying savings behavior in America since the late nineteenth century and are making use of the many state labor department surveys that provide data on wealth and home ownership. There also exist national public use samples of the federal censuses of 1910, 1940, and 1950 (as well as later) which provide opportunities to tabulate and analyze housing tenure status by household head's age and other characteristics.[3]

The sources utilized here were readily available to the authors as microdata (i.e., the sample of upstate New York counties in 1865; the 1889–1890 U.S. Commissioner of Labor Survey; and the 1900 U.S. census public use sample) or were obtained from the published volumes of the 1890 and 1930 censuses. Although the federal census has systematically collected data explicitly on home ownership since 1890, relatively little has been published along the dimension of the age of the household head. The censuses of 1890 and 1930 were exceptions. (Note 1 discusses the issue of attribution of ownership and household headship.)

HOME OWNERSHIP AND THE LIFE COURSE, 1865–1930

Some of the basic results from table 7.2 are reproduced in figure 7.1, which gives the age-ownership profiles for the sample of seven New York counties in 1865, the 1889–1890 U.S. Commissioner of Labor Survey, the 1900 census public use sample, and published data from the 1930 U.S. census.[4] It is important to note that these results apply to urban and rural nonfarm households. The 1865 New York data are tabulated only for heads of household who were not farmers. The actual question asked in the New York census was, however, whether the individual owned land, so the results (like those from the federal censuses of 1850–1870) are not strictly comparable to those for later dates when explicit questions were posed on renter or owner-occupancy status of the household. The 1889–1890 survey clearly applied only to industrial, mostly urban, working-class households. The 1900 U.S. census public use sample tabulations were done only for heads of household who owned or rented homes or dwellings and not farms.[5] The tabulations from published data for 1890 and 1930 excluded farm households.

There was, not unexpectedly, an upward shift in the age-ownership relationship among urban and rural nonfarm households in the United States from at least the late nineteenth century. The low level of home ownership in the sample of industrial workers in 1889–1890 is also evident, as compared to national census data for 1900 (or 1890) or even the New York data for 1865. This was partly due to the more urban residence of these workers. Results from the U.S. census of 1890 (fig. 7.5, below) demonstrate that ur-

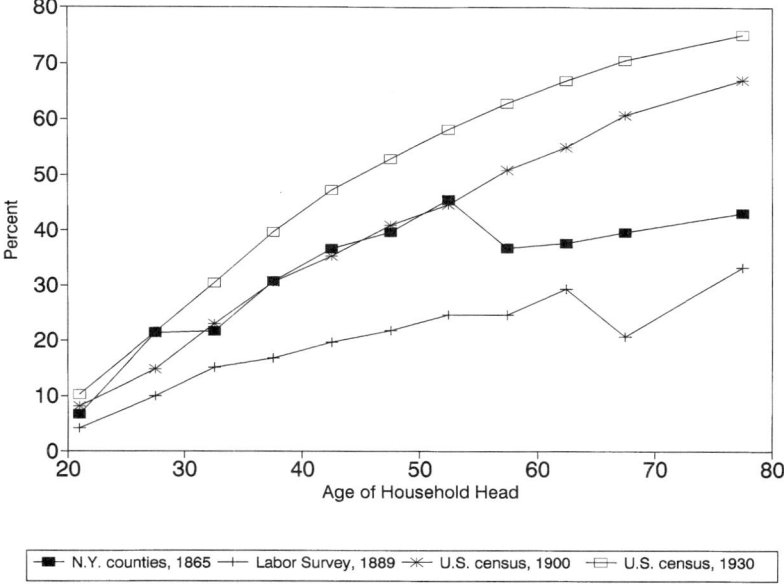

Fig. 7.1. Home ownership, by age, 1865–1930.

ban areas had lower ownership rates than rural areas and the larger the urban area, the lower the ownership rate. The lower rate for workers was also
due to lower incomes relative to the urban middle and upper classes.

Another notable feature in figure 7.1 is the contrast between the smooth
upward progression of ownership by age in the national data for 1900 and
1930 (as well as for 1890, as seen in fig. 7.4, below) in comparison with the results for New York State in 1865 and for the 1889–1890 survey data. The curves
for the latter two data sets tend to flatten out, or even decline, at older ages.
This may be seen more dramatically in figures 7.2 and 7.3. It is interesting to
point out that similar shapes for the censuses of 1850, 1860, and 1870 were
generated by Soltow (1975: 29, chart 2.1) when he plotted the proportion
of free adult males having real estate or total real and personal estate.

It appears that the age pattern of property holding changed in the late
nineteenth century from one that peaked in middle age to one that peaked
late in the life course. It is a most interesting result. It seems that in New
York State in the mid-nineteenth century (as well as in Soltow's national
samples for 1850–1870) and among urban working-class families in the late
nineteenth-century maximum, home ownership was achieved by about age
40 to 50. That is, there was no greater ownership late in the life course than
in middle age. This had changed by the turn of the century for the population as a whole. With the consistent upward movement of the age-ownership

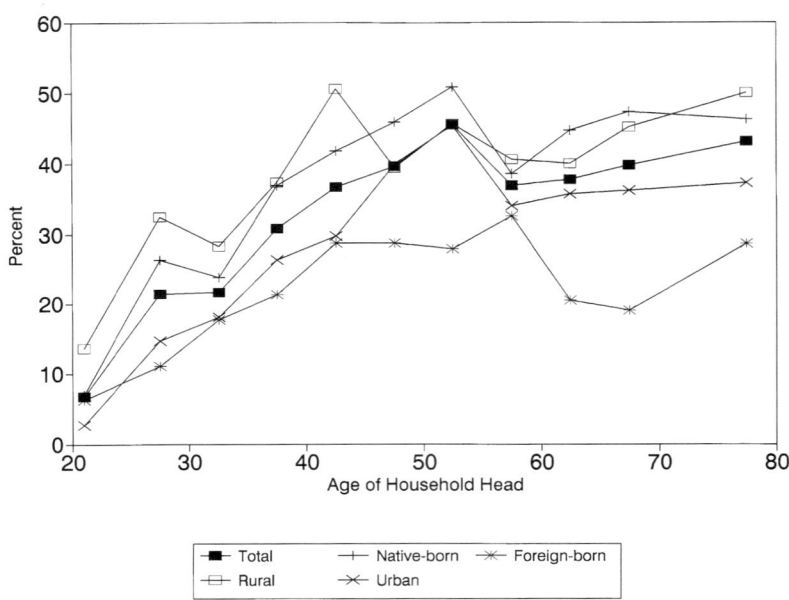

Fig. 7.2. Urban, rural, native-born, foreign-born, and total home ownership, by age, N.Y. counties sample, 1865.

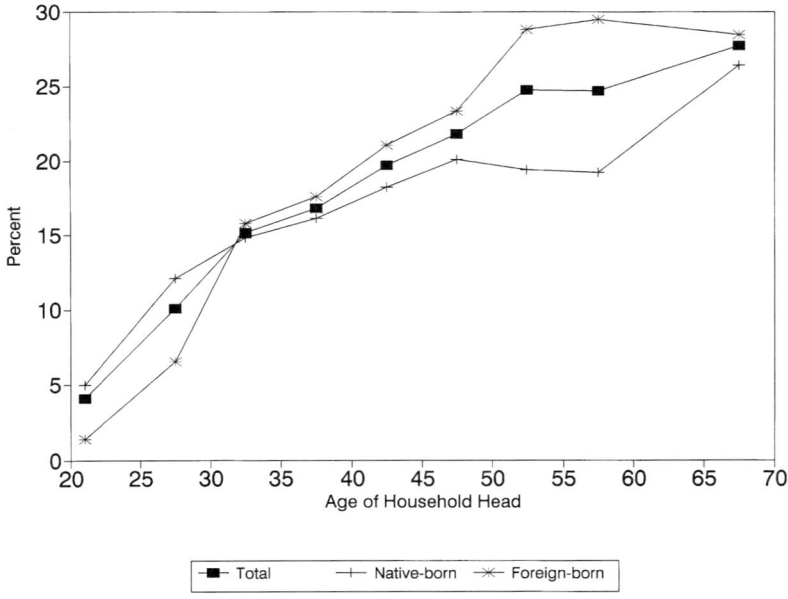

Fig. 7.3. Native-born, foreign-born, and total home ownership, by age, U.S. labor survey, 1890.

profiles from the 1890, 1900, and 1930 censuses and with the upward shifts in those profiles, it is clear that individuals were able to continue acquiring homes (on a net basis) right into their 60s and 70s. Looking from census to census, it is also apparent that this was true for the same age cohorts over time as well as across age groups at a point in time. Age was proving to be no barrier to the achievement of this part of the American dream. Increasingly, wealth in the form of homes was characteristic of the later years of the life course.

More detailed information from the five data sets is plotted in figures 7.2 through 7.9, which provide a variety of dimensions of the age-ownership profiles. Several salient aspects appear. Urban ownership rates were lower than nonfarm rural rates.[6] This was true in 1865 New York (fig. 7.2) and in the country as a whole in 1890 (fig. 7.3), 1900 (fig. 7.6), and 1930 (fig. 7.8). Within the urban population, the results for 1890 (fig. 7.4) demonstrate that smaller cities (population between 50,000 and 250,000) had higher ownership rates than larger cities (with populations above 250,000). A plausible explanation is that the higher population densities of larger cities raised land values, which, in turn, increased housing prices, reduced ownership rates, and raised the profitability of building and maintaining multiple family rental properties. Current evidence for 1960, 1970, and 1980 indicates that ownership rates continue to be lower in (denser) central cities

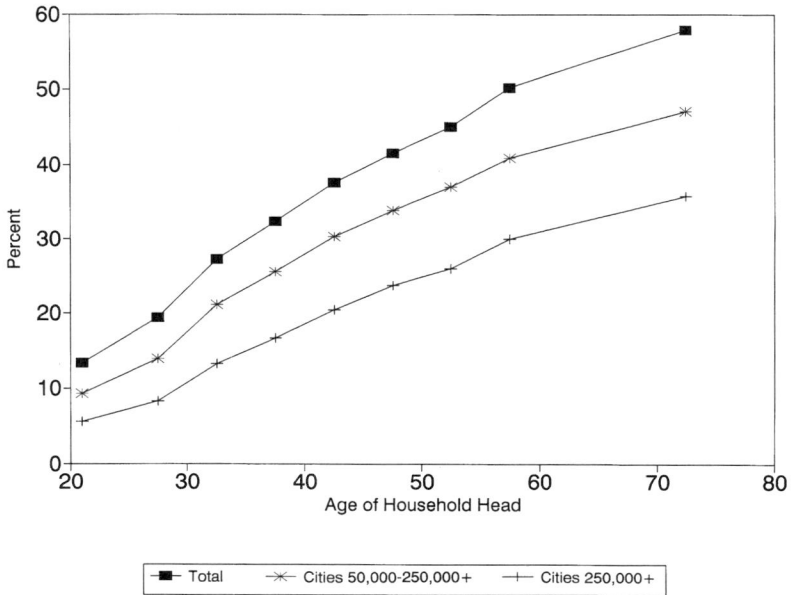

Fig. 7.4. Urban home ownership, by age, U.S. census, 1890.

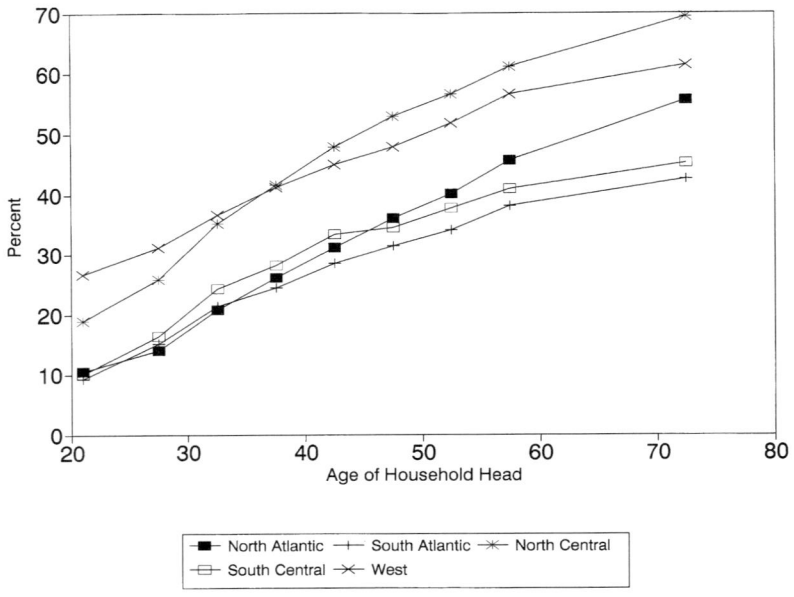

Fig. 7.5. Home ownership, by age and region, U.S. census, 1890.

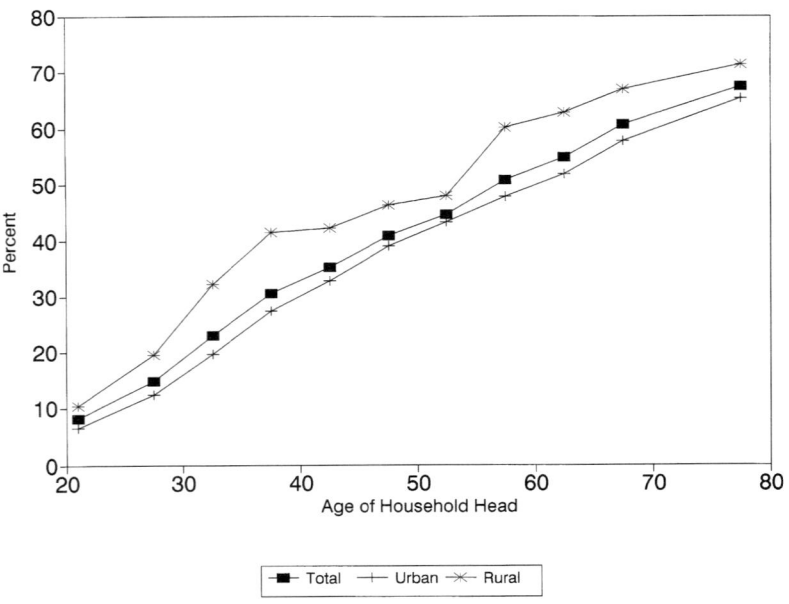

Fig. 7.6. Urban, rural, and total home ownership, by age, U.S. census, 1900.

than the remainder of the standard metropolitan statistical areas (SMSAs) and higher outside of SMSAs than within (Adams 1987: 53, table 3.14).

Historically, there were also ownership differentials by nativity and race. Certainly differences in residence and income accounted for some of this. For example, many blacks had lower incomes but lived in rural areas where ownership rates were higher. Many white immigrants lived in large urban areas, most often in central cities where ownership rates were lower. But cultural and other factors may have played a role. Immigrant peasants often viewed property as a sign of social mobility but also as a means of reducing risk in an uncertain economic environment (Bodnar 1985: 180–183). Higher home ownership rates among working-class Irish immigrants have been seen as a consequence of land hunger carried from Europe, with children's earnings used to achieve this goal at the expense of their education (Thernstrom 1964: 154–157). The evidence on this is not clear (Bodnar 1985: 182), but there were a variety of factors, such as specific area of origin, duration of residence in the United States, region and place of residence, occupation, and income, that interacted with race and ethnicity to produce the observed patterns.

For the sample of New York counties in 1865, foreign-born whites had consistently lower ownership incidence than the native born (fig. 7.2). This was still true for the nation as a whole in 1900 (fig. 7.7), although the differences by age were much smaller. The nativity differential in home ownership rates for urban and rural nonfarm whites had virtually disappeared by 1930 (fig. 7.9), indicating that, on this dimension, immigrants were assimilating and eventually sharing in this promise of American life. In addition, this advantage was achieved within a generation. Tabulations from the 1900 public use sample and published data from the 1930 census show that when nativity of parents is considered, there were only small differences in home ownership between native whites with native parents and second-generation immigrants (native whites of foreign or mixed parentage).

Interestingly enough, the home ownership curves for native versus foreign born exhibited a crossover in the 1889–1890 labor survey (fig. 7.3), with the foreign born having had lower home ownership incidence up to age 30 and higher rates thereafter. A breakdown of the data for specific nativity of household head shows that this was due especially to German and Irish immigrants. It should be noted, however, that many migrants were more likely to live in regions of the country (such as the Midwest) where home ownership was more common and that they also had different incomes, occupations, and family compositions. Nevertheless, multivariate analysis of this data set has indicated that the ethnic differentials do not entirely disappear when differences in incomes, residence patterns, industries, occupations, ages, and family composition are taken into account. German migrants were significantly more likely to own a home than the native born,

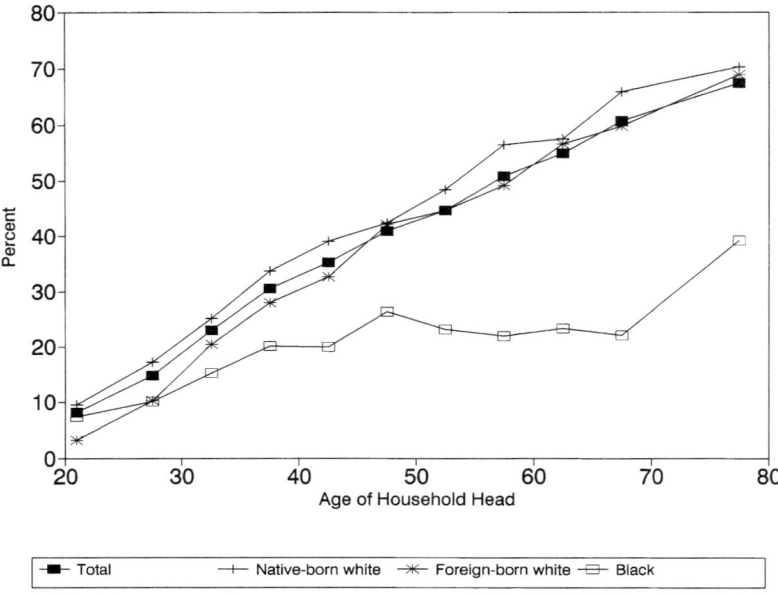

Fig. 7.7. Home ownership, by age and race, U.S. census, 1900.

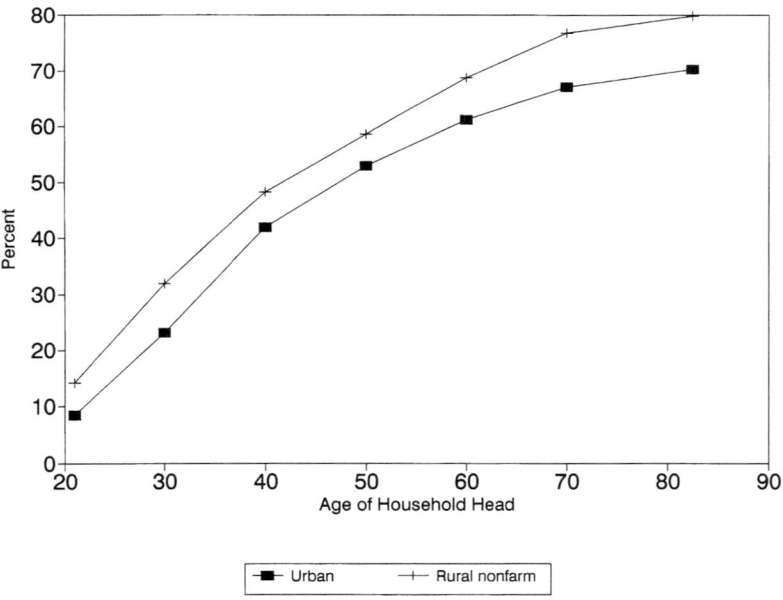

Fig. 7.8. Urban and rural nonfarm home ownership, by age, U.S. census, 1930.

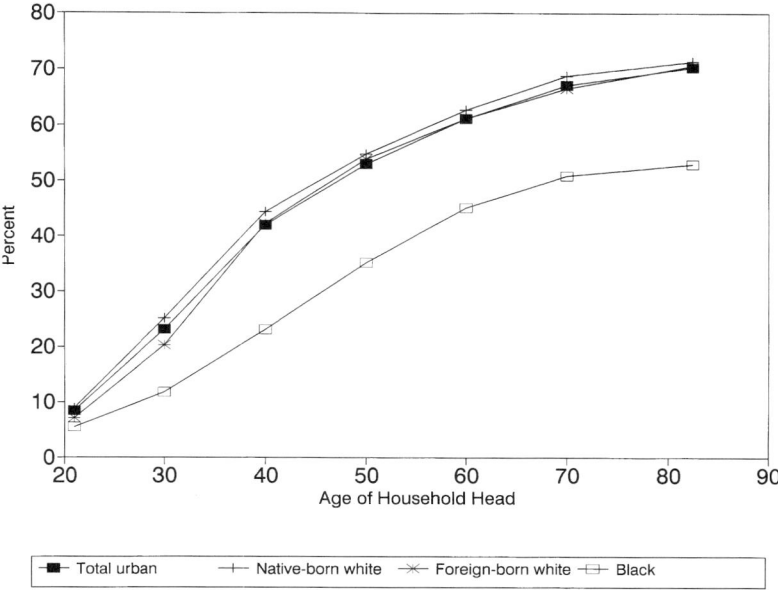

Fig. 7.9. Urban home ownership, by age and race, U.S. census, 1930.

while Canadian and British migrants were less likely (Haines and Goodman 1992). The same analysis also revealed a strong and significant nonlinear relation of age to the probability of home ownership.

In contrast, differentials by race did not disappear over this period. Data from the 1900 (fig. 7.7) and 1930 (fig. 7.9) censuses point to systematically lower ownership rates for urban and rural nonfarm blacks relative to whites, both immigrant and native born. In 1900, the nonagricultural black population only attained an ultimate ownership rate of about 20 to 25 percent, and this was achieved by about age 40. Indeed, the age pattern resembled that of the white population in the middle of the nineteenth century rather than around 1900. It also looked a good deal more like that of the industrial workers in the 1889–1890 survey.

Perhaps this should also not be too surprising, since there existed a number of confounding elements. Average income, occupational attainment, and socioeconomic status of the black population was low relative to the native white population and most immigrant groups, and there were also specific barriers to property acquisition in many areas, limiting opportunities for ownership as well as creating residential segregation. For example, for 1880 in Philadelphia, the proportion of adult males listing occupations as unskilled was 78.4 percent among blacks, 48.7 percent among Irish immigrants, 16.6 percent among German migrants, and 20.4 percent among all native whites (including second-generation migrants). By 1930, 56 percent of adult blacks were classified as laborers or in domestic and personal service, as opposed to 19.7 percent for foreign-born whites and 8.5 percent for native whites. Blacks also had the highest indexes of residential segregation in both 1880 and 1930 (Hershberg et al. 1981: 468, 471, 475).

The urban black age-ownership profile had become steeper and more regular by 1930 (fig. 7.9), but it still lay below that of the white population. While both native and foreign-born urban whites had attained 50 percent ownership rates by ages 45 to 54 and experienced increases for older age cohorts, urban blacks had barely achieved this by the last years of the life course.

Another dimension that was tabulated in the published data for 1890 was region of residence, some results for which are given in figure 7.5.[7] While it does not seem intuitively apparent that regional differences should exist, in 1890, the highest rates of nonfarm home ownership were found in the Midwest (the North Central Region) and the West, with the lowest in the South (the South Atlantic and South Central regions). New England and the Middle Atlantic states (the North Atlantic Region) were intermediate.

Differences between the regions in levels of urbanization and income account, in part, for this. For example, in terms of nonagricultural income per worker in 1900, the West was unquestionably the highest ($803), with the North Atlantic and North Central regions intermediate (at $630 and $650, respectively) and the South the lowest (with $223 and $225 in the South Atlantic and South Central regions) (calculated from Easterlin 1957). This would have promoted the high ownership rates in the West and North and the low rates in the South. However, the higher incidence of large cities in the Northeast and generally greater level of urbanization there relative to other regions would have depressed its ownership rates.[8] Regional differences have persisted, but the relative positions have changed. In 1983, for instance, the Midwest still had the highest incidence of owner occupancy (69.1 percent), followed by the South (67.4 percent), the Northeast (60.4 percent), and the West (59 percent) (U.S. Bureau of the Census 1985: table 1308).

One additional piece of information is available and was tabulated by age for the published census data in 1890 and the public use sample for 1900—the extent of mortgage indebtedness for owner-occupied homes.[9] Tabulations of the percentage of owner-occupied dwellings having a mortgage encumbrance reveal that the age pattern showed a generally downward incidence of mortgaged property with increasing age as individuals and families were able to attain full ownership over the life course. But the age group below 25 years had a lower incidence than the two or three next oldest groups (up to ages 35 or 40). This might have been due to inheritance, that is, a larger portion of the youngest home owners having obtained their property unencumbered via bequest. If such properties were inherited from parents or other older persons, the chance of their being unencumbered was greater. Home ownership thus played a role in intergenerational mobility.

Urban home owners were also more likely to have had mortgages than their rural nonfarm counterparts. This probably reflects higher urban site values as well as more developed mortgage capital markets in cities. In addition, there were substantial regional differences in mortgage incidence. A much higher proportion of homes were mortgaged in the Northeast and Midwest as compared with the South and the West. It is known that the South and the West had considerably higher interest rates, on average, especially relative to the Northeast in this period (Davis 1965; James 1978: chap. 1; Snowden 1987), which would have tended to reduce mortgage incidence, reduce site values, and/or discourage ownership. Finally, foreign-born whites were more likely than native whites to have mortgaged property, especially in the middle years of the life course. This likely reflects less inherited property and less wealth overall. Blacks seem to have had least access to the mortgage markets, although the number of cases is too small to permit reliable inferences.

Given the large amount of information about home ownership and age along a number of dimensions in the tables and figures developed here, efforts to condense and summarize these data are indicated. Some of these results are given in table 7.3. Several measures easily suggest themselves: ownership rates earlier and later in the life course (i.e., percent owners age 25–34 and percent owners at older ages—60 and over, 70 and over, 75 and over), as well as the overall ownership rate and an age-standardized ownership rate.[10] It turns out that age standardization does not greatly change things for the native white population or the overall rural or urban populations. The ownership rates for blacks and foreign-born whites are generally increased by standardization because of their somewhat younger age structure relative to the overall, predominantly native white, population.[11]

The last two columns of table 7.3 present elasticities of ownership with respect to age. These are simply the percentage changes in the probability of home ownership for a 1 percent change in age. They are evaluated at ages 30 and 60. They are calculated by fitting a statistical function (in this case, a logit) to the age-ownership profiles and then calculating the elasticities at these two points.[12] In general, it may be said that the propensity to acquire a home at these two moments in the life course increased over time, was higher in urban than in rural areas, was higher in larger cities and in the Northeast (in 1890), increased with age up until about 1900 and thereafter diminished with age, was generally higher among the foreign born relative to the native white population, and rose for the younger black population in the early twentieth century. It is evident that property acquisition was becoming more accessible for the younger population in the twentieth century as well as for the black population as a whole. The substantial appetite of younger immigrants for real property is also supported. The reduced likelihood of acquiring property at older ages by 1930 is interesting. It reflects

TABLE 7·3   Summary Measures of Home Ownership, United States, 1865–1930

	Percent Owners				Elasticity of Ownership	
	Aged 25–34	Upper Aged[a]	Overall	Age Standardized[b]	Age = 30	Age = 60[c]
N.Y. counties sample 1865		(70+)				
Total	21.56	43.16	33.25	32.46	0.552	0.882
Native born	25.00	46.25	37.90	37.04	0.504	0.789
Foreign born	14.86	28.57	23.30	22.48	0.488	0.836
Rural	30.19	50.00	39.19	38.58	0.329	0.563
Urban	16.61	37.25	29.39	28.74	0.701	1.096
U.S. labor survey, 1889–1890		(60+)				
Total	12.85	27.68	17.66	19.22	0.815	1.375
Native born	13.57	26.40	15.94	17.84	0.635	1.146
Foreign born	11.63	28.44	19.72	20.10	0.902	1.430
U.S. census, 1890		(60+)				
Total	23.79	57.93	36.90	37.63	0.839	1.051
Cities 50,000+	13.94	40.47	24.02	24.72	0.887	1.294
Cities 250,000+	11.13	35.82	20.32	20.97	0.938	1.417
Cities 50,000–250,000	18.03	47.13	29.34	30.11	0.843	1.164
North Atlantic	17.84	55.64	32.98	32.56	1.017	1.289
South Atlantic	18.31	42.60	26.89	28.37	0.755	1.095
North Central	31.08	69.30	46.34	47.26	0.837	0.904
South Central	20.46	45.34	29.22	31.42	0.740	1.055
West	34.27	61.40	44.05	45.39	0.562	0.710

		(70+)				
U.S. census, 1900						
Total	19.55	67.32	35.80	36.16	1.157	1.226
Urban	16.75	65.19	33.63	33.62	1.228	1.484
Rural	26.21	71.29	41.47	43.00	1.018	1.063
Native-born white	21.77	70.19	38.06	39.17	1.158	1.273
Native-born parentage	16.62	68.85	39.48	39.27	1.124	1.250
Foreign-born parentage	12.54	39.22	33.76	38.70	1.301	1.385
Foreign-born white	22.45	70.72	37.07	34.53	1.276	1.452
Black	20.26	62.50	18.49	20.19	0.757	1.339
U.S. census, 1930		(75+)				
Urban						
Total	23.20	70.18	43.07	43.14	1.117	0.957
Native-born white	25.21	71.36	43.57	45.00	1.103	0.924
Native-born parentage	25.26	71.37	42.61	44.36	1.083	0.929
Foreign-born parentage	25.11	71.32	45.58	46.25	1.144	0.914
Foreign-born white	20.36	70.59	47.33	42.63	1.069	0.900
Black	11.87	52.94	24.67	27.76	1.419	1.580
Rural nonfarm						
Total	31.98	79.79	50.85	50.37	1.005	0.597
Native-born white	33.37	80.36	51.33	51.52	0.981	0.670
Native-born parentage	32.28	79.82	49.40	50.09	0.986	0.703
Foreign-born parentage	39.25	83.34	59.97	57.76	0.912	0.532
Foreign-born white	36.41	85.31	62.98	55.04	0.875	0.518
Black	17.42	56.13	31.78	34.08	1.152	1.218

[a]Upper age group is given at the top of the column for section.
[b]Standardized to the age structure of all household heads in 1900.
[c]For 1890, elasticity at age 57.5.

the flattening out of the curves and an apparent upper limit to ownership incidence late in the life course.

CONCLUSION

Overall, examination of the relation between age and property acquisition—in this case, home ownership—seems a fruitful area for further historical research. The importance of home ownership (often unencumbered by a mortgage) to individuals and households late in the life course has become increasingly evident. Homes are a source of more secure shelter as well as a means of providing potential income (from rentals, boarding, and lodging) and collateral for borrowing. Home ownership likely conveys greater independence for the elderly.

For the American case, there were changes in both the shape and level of the age-ownership profile over time. The basic data also revealed differentials by nativity, race, rural-urban residence, city size, and region. Since roughly the middle of the nineteenth century, it has become more likely at all ages that a household would live in a home of its own but particularly later in the life course. This is reflected in the upward shift and the greater steepness of the age-ownership profile. Increasingly, immigrants and the black population began to participate in this process. This aspect of the "American dream" was becoming a reality for many but by no means all. As the society has aged and, given the positive relationship of ownership to age, a greater share of American homes are now owned by the elderly (over 26 percent in 1987, up from 17 percent of nonfarm households in 1900). This is clearly an important aspect of today's economy and society, but an understanding of its historical evolution is important as well.

NOTES

The authors wish to thank the participants of the Breckenridge Conference on the Historical Demography of Aging for a number of helpful comments. A longer working paper published by the National Bureau of Economic Research is available from the authors on request.

1. There are measurement issues concerning how the ownership information was elicited in the American census. In 1890, the enumerator's question was, "Is the home you live in hired, or is it owned by the head or by a member of the family?" The question for the 1910, 1920, and 1930 censuses was explained to enumerators as follows:

> *Home owned or rented.*—This question is to be answered only opposite the name of the *head* of each family. If a dwelling is occupied by more than one family, it is the home of each of them, and the question should be answered with reference to each family in the dwelling. If the home is *owned,* write opposite the name of the head of the family "O."

If the home is *rented,* write "R." Make no entries in this column for the other members of the family. . . . *Owned homes.*—A home is to classed as *owned* if it is owned wholly or in part by the head of the family living in the home, or by the wife of the head, or by a son, or a daughter, or other *relative* living in the same house with the head of the family. It is not necessary that full payment for the property should have been made or that the family should be the sole owner. (U.S. Bureau of the Census 1979: 30, 46)

The basic philosophy was to identify owner-occupied units, generally ignoring precisely who in the household owned the unit. This viewpoint has continued up to the present. In the past, ownership was attributed to the head of household. Thus it is possible that an aged person might have been given headship out of deference or respect, while not actually owning the dwelling. Similarly, a younger (and usually male) relative might have been attributed headship while the property was actually owned by an elderly parent. It is probable that these effects largely offset each other, but there remain real issues of measurement.

2. For some significant exceptions, see Venti and Wise 1989, 1990; Feinstein and McFadden 1989; Stahl 1989; Ai et al. 1990.

3. A national sample of the 1880 U.S. census is being prepared at the Social History Research Laboratory at the University of Minnesota. The ultimate goal is to sample the 1850–1870 censuses as well as the 1920 census.

4. The results from the 1890 U.S. census were omitted from figure 7.1 because they were very similar to the data from the 1900 census public use sample. The 1930 U.S. census data had to be interpolated to the five-year age categories of the other data sets.

5. The 1900 U.S. census asked four questions on ownership: "Owned or rented," "Owned free or mortgaged," "Farm or home," and "Number of farm schedule" (U.S. Bureau of the Census 1979: 34). The tabulations of the public use sample were done only for those heads of households who replied that they owned or rented homes. Those who owned or rented farms were excluded.

6. Other data not presented demonstrate the highest rates among the rural farm population.

7. It is possible to reconstruct this from published state- and city-level data in 1930. Tabulations can also be done from the various public use samples.

8. The Northeast (North Atlantic Region) was 59 percent urban in 1890, as compared to 33 percent in the Midwest, 16 percent in the South (South Atlantic and South Central regions), and 37 percent in the West (U.S. Bureau of the Census 1975: Series A172, 178–179).

9. The 1890 census also has information on the amounts of mortgage principal and interest rates, unlike the 1900 census, which only has information on whether the property was mortgaged or held free and clear. It is truly unfortunate that the enumerators' manuscripts of the 1890 census have been lost.

10. Direct standardization was done using the age structure of all heads of household in 1900.

11. An experiment was done to design a measure of the mean age at home ownership similar to John Hajnal's (1953) singulate mean age at first marriage. Unfortunately, the results appear to be very sensitive to the precise age categories used. The best that can be said is that the mean age of home ownership was rising from the late nineteenth century, along with the mean age of the population. The mean

age at home ownership for the overall nonfarm population calculated in this way rose from 33.3 years in 1890 to 39.3 years in 1900 to 43.7 years in 1930.

12. This approach imposes some structure on the age-ownership profiles and allows parameters from the structure to describe the data. A simple solution for this is a logit, whose basic formulation is

$$\ln[P_j/(1 - P_j)] = \beta_0 + \beta_1 AGE_j + e_j$$

where ln is the natural logarithm, P_j is the probability of owning a home for the jth age group $(0 < P < 1)$, β_0 is the constant, β_1 is the slope with respect to age, AGE is estimated mean of the jth age group, and e_j is an error term. The estimation was done using weighted least squares and a minimum chi-square criterion for fitting. The procedure used was glogit in STATA with aggregated (grouped) data. Since the age-ownership curves are clearly nonlinear, the logit specification is a means to attempt linearization. In addition, it transforms a variable (P) from one bounded at 0 and 1 to one bounded at $-\infty$ and $+\infty$ and also has certain other desirable statistical properties (Maddala 1983: chap. 2).

The results suggest some increase in the steepness of the age-ownership profile from the mid-nineteenth century up to about 1900 and then rough stability between 1900 and 1930. The cohort phenomena that had led to the flattening out of the age-ownership profile in the middle of the nineteenth century had dissipated by the early twentieth century. The elderly in successive age cohorts began to be more likely to own property, which should not be surprising given earlier results. (When more complete data sets from successive censuses are assembled, a full cohort analysis can be done.) The upward shift in the curves between 1900 and 1930 (seen in fig. 7.1) is direct evidence of that cohort effect. The increased regularity of the age-ownership relation is accounted for by measures of goodness of fit—the adjusted R-squared values and F-ratios increase from the 1865 New York State and 1889–1890 survey data to the census data for 1890, 1900, and 1930. The differentials previously observed within censuses are not, however, immediately apparent in the slopes. In 1900, the black population definitely had a flatter profile, resembling those for 1865 New York and the 1889–1890 U.S. Commissioner of Labor Survey, but this difference had disappeared by 1930. Rural-urban and nativity differences in the slopes of the logits were not large after 1900, however. The major result remains the increased steepness of the age-ownership relation in the twentieth century.

The elasticity of ownership with respect to age is defined as

$$\epsilon_{px} = (\delta P/\delta X)(X/P) = (\beta_1 e^Z X)/((1 + e^Z)^2 P) = \beta_1 X(1 - P)$$

where ϵ_{px} is the elasticity of ownership (P) with respect to age (X), and $Z = \beta_0 + \beta_1 X$ is from the logit equation.

REFERENCES

Adams, John S. 1987. *Housing America in the 1980s*. New York: Russell Sage Foundation.

Ai, Chunrong, Jonathan Feinstein, Daniel McFadden, and Henry Pollakowski. 1990. "The dynamics of housing demand by the elderly: User cost effects." In *Issues in the economics of aging*, ed. David A. Wise, 33–82. Chicago: University of Chicago Press.

Bodnar, John. 1985. *The transplanted: A history of immigrants in urban America.* Bloomington: Indiana University Press.

Davis, Lance E. 1965. "The investment market, 1870–1914: The evolution of a national market." *Journal of Economic History* 25: 355–399.

Easterlin, Richard A. 1957. "State income estimates." In *Population redistribution and economic growth: United States, 1870–1950,* eds. Simon Kuznets and Dorothy S. Thomas, I:703–759. Philadelphia: American Philosophical Society.

Feinstein, Jonathan, and Daniel McFadden. 1989. "The dynamics of housing demand by the elderly: Wealth, cash flow, and demographic effects." In *The economics of aging,* ed. David A. Wise, 55–86. Chicago: University of Chicago Press.

Goodman, Allen C. 1990. "Demographics of individual housing demand." *Regional Science and Urban Economics* 20: 83–102.

Haines, Michael R., and Allen C. Goodman. 1992. "Housing demand in the United States in the late nineteenth century: Evidence from the Commissioner of Labor survey." *Journal of Urban Economics* 31: 99–122.

Hajnal, John. 1953. "Age at marriage and proportions marrying." *Population Studies* 7(3): 111–136.

Hershberg, Theodore, Alan N. Burstein, Eugene P. Ericksen, Stephanie W. Greenberg, and William L. Yancey. 1981. "A tale of three cities: Blacks, immigrants, and opportunity in Philadelphia, 1850–1880, 1930, 1970." In *Philadelphia: Work, space, family, and group experience in the nineteenth century,* ed. Theodore Hershberg, 461–491. New York: Oxford University Press.

James, John A. 1978. *Money and capital markets in postbellum America.* Princeton: Princeton University Press.

Kirk, Carolyn T., and Gordon W. Kirk, Jr. 1981. "The impact of the city on home ownership: A comparison of immigrants and native whites at the turn of the century." *Journal of Urban History* 7: 471–498.

Kotlikoff, Laurence J. 1989. *What determines savings?* Cambridge: MIT Press.

Maddala, G. S. 1983. *Limited-dependent and qualitative variables in econometrics.* New York: Cambridge University Press.

Modigliani, Franco. 1988. "The role of intergenerational transfers and life cycle savings in the accumulation of wealth." *Journal of Economic Perspectives* 2(2): 15–40.

Morris, E. W., and M. Winter. 1978. *Housing, family, and society.* New York: John Wiley and Sons.

Perrin, C. 1977. *Everything in its place: Social order and land use in America.* Princeton: Princeton University Press.

Ransom, Roger L., and Richard Sutch. 1989. "Two strategies for a more secure old age: Life-cycle saving by late-nineteenth-century American workers." Paper presented at the Summer Workshop of the Development of the American Economy Project, National Bureau of Economic Research, Cambridge, Massachusetts, July 17–21.

Rossi, Peter H. 1980. *Why families move.* 2d ed. Beverly Hills, Calif.: Sage.

Rossi, Peter H., and Anne B. Shlay. 1982. "Residential mobility and public policy issues: 'Why families move' revisited." *Journal of Social Issues* 38(3): 21–34.

Snowden, Kenneth A. 1987. "Mortgage rates and American capital market development in the late nineteenth century." *Journal of Economic History* 47(3): 671–691.

Soltow, Lee. 1975. *Men and wealth in the United States 1850–1870.* New Haven: Yale University Press.

Stahl, Konrad. 1989. "Housing patterns and mobility of the aged: The United States and West Germany." In *The economics of aging,* ed. David A. Wise, 93–115. Chicago: University of Chicago Press.

Thernstrom, Stephen. 1964. *Poverty and progress: Social mobility in a nineteenth-century city.* Cambridge: Harvard University Press.

Tygiel, Jules. 1979. "Housing in late nineteenth-century American cities: Suggestions for research." *Historical Methods* 12(2): 84–97.

United Nations. 1973. *Statistical yearbook, 1972.* New York: United Nations.

U.S. Bureau of the Census. 1896. *Eleventh census of population, 1890: Report on farms and homes: Proprietorship and indebtedness.* Washington, D.C.: Government Printing Office.

———. 1933. *Fifteenth census of population, 1930: Population.* Vol. VI. *Families.* Washington, D.C.: Government Printing Office.

———. 1975. *Historical statistics of the United States: Colonial times to 1970.* 2 vols. Washington, D.C.: Government Printing Office.

———. 1979. *Twenty censuses: Population and housing questions, 1790–1980.* Washington, D.C.: Government Printing Office.

———. 1985. *Statistical abstract of the United States: 1986.* Washington, D.C.: Government Printing Office.

———. 1991. *Statistical abstract of the United States: 1991.* Washington, D.C.: Government Printing Office.

U.S. Commissioner of Labor. 1890. "Part III. Cost of Living." In *Sixth annual report of the Commissioner of Labor, 1890.* U.S. Congress, House of Representatives, House Executive Document 265, 51st Cong., 2d Sess. Washington, D.C.: Government Printing Office.

———. 1891. "Part III. Cost of Living." In *Seventh annual report of the Commissioner of Labor, 1891.* U.S. Congress, House of Representatives, House Executive Document 232, 52d Cong., 1st Sess. Washington, D.C.: Government Printing Office.

———. 1904. "Cost of living and retail prices of food." In *Eighteenth annual report of the Commissioner of Labor.* Washington, D.C.: Government Printing Office.

Venti, Stephen F., and David A. Wise. 1989. "Aging, moving, and housing wealth." In *The economics of aging,* ed. David A. Wise, 9–48. Chicago: University of Chicago Press.

———. 1990. "But they don't want to reduce housing equity." In *Issues in the economics of aging,* ed. David A. Wise, 13–29. Chicago: University of Chicago Press.

Warner, Sam Bass, Jr. 1962. *Streetcar suburbs: The process of growth in Boston, 1870–1900.* Cambridge: Harvard University Press.

Wise, David A. 1989. "Overview." In *The economics of aging,* ed. David A. Wise, 1–7. Chicago: University of Chicago Press.

PART THREE

Widowhood

EIGHT

The Impact of Widowhood in Nineteenth-Century Italy

David I. Kertzer and Nancy Karweit

The historical demography of aging has come only slowly to southern Europe. As elsewhere, historical demographic study has concentrated heavily on problems of fertility, marriage, and, to a lesser extent, migration, all of which have focused attention on youths and young adults. Indeed, even the study of mortality, which might be expected to lead to a special concern with the older segment of the population, has instead been dominated here, as elsewhere, by a focus on the youngest of the young, the death of infants.

The one historical demographic field that has shed some light on the lives of the older segment of the population is the study of household composition. This field has expanded tremendously in Italy over the past fifteen years, influenced in no small part by the work of Peter Laslett (1972) and associates of the Cambridge Group for the History of Population and Social Structure. Yet, even here, systematic work on the lives of the elderly is rare. More important, life course studies that examine the dynamics of household processes for the older segment of the population are almost nonexistent. This is in contrast with work done farther north in Europe, where concern for inheritance systems and problems of peasant retirement have generated a lively literature on later life transitions in co-residential arrangements (Berkner 1972; Gaunt 1983; Plakans 1989).

What makes the study of the co-residential careers of older Italians of special interest—beyond what it tells us of Italian society itself—is the variation in household forms found in Italy. While parts of Italy were characterized by nuclear family systems, large portions of the peninsula were marked in the past by an entirely different family system, involving the co-residence of two or more related nuclear families in a single household. The implications of such a co-residential system for the later life course in general and widowhood in particular are great. For the aging individual living in a nuclear family household in which children leave home at marriage, old age may mean increased isolation and increasing difficulties in economically sustaining the household. Loss of a spouse in such a context can be disastrous, leaving the individual entirely alone.[1]

At the other extreme, in a multiple family household system, such as characterized the sharecropping zone that occupied much of central and a good part of northern Italy, aging does not entail increased isolation, nor does widowhood leave the individual on her or his own resources. As practiced in Italy, this system meant all sons might bring their brides into their parental home. New households were formed not at marriage but on the dividing up of multinuclear households when these became too large to be supported on a single agricultural holding or when tensions among the constituent units led to a breakup.[2] In such a setting, aging meant not a diminishing number of co-residents but an increasing number. Moreover, loss of a husband, for example, did not mean a household without men to take on the male household roles, nor did loss of a wife mean the absence of women to perform the roles assigned to women in the household economy.

This, anyway, is the theory. Just how this system worked as far as the older population is concerned has been little studied. We undertake such a study here, considering at the same time some of the factors that must be included in any larger theory of aging and co-residence. These factors include political economy, demography, gender systems, and culture.

We examine the interrelationship of these forces through the study of a single community, Casalecchio di Reno, lying just outside the city of Bologna. Casalecchio is of interest because it had long been dominated by a sharecropping economy but, in the period in question, 1861–1921, began to be transformed by the spread of capitalism, industrialization, and urban life. Our period of study is also of interest because it is one that saw the beginning of the demographic transition, with the fall of both mortality rates and birthrates. In short, Casalecchio not only illustrates the workings of the multiple family co-residential system associated with sharecropping Italy but also provides a window for looking at the effect the demographic and economic changes associated with "modernization" had on the co-residential lives of the older population.

CASALECCHIO DI RENO

The commune of Casalecchio lies just outside what for centuries had been the rural belt surrounding the walled city of Bologna, in Emilia-

Romagna, located in north central Italy. It had long been part of the classic sharecropping area that extended south through Tuscany, the Marches, and Umbria. Landowners lived in the cities and let their land out in small parcels to sharecropping households, either directly or through middlemen. The produce was split (often evenly) between landowner and sharecropper.

A contract bound the entire sharecropping family; emblematic was the fact that landowner consent was required before a family member could marry. Since landowners stood to gain by maximizing the number of adults on each farm, hence maximizing their half of the produce, households composed of more than one kin-related family were the rule. Indeed, the sharecroppers followed the cultural norm of patrilocal postmarital residence quite closely, with sons (not just a single son) bringing their brides into their natal household and daughters joining their husbands' households at marriage (Kertzer and Hogan 1988).

A sharp rise in the rural population in the Bologna area that began in the late eighteenth century, combined with the move by landowners to place more land on a wage labor basis, resulted during the nineteenth century in a surplus rural population that could not be absorbed into the sharecropping sector (Bellettini 1981). This population was funneled into both agricultural and nonagricultural wage labor. Thus the late nineteenth century and early twentieth century were a watershed period, when wage labor began to replace sharecropping as the backbone of the rural economy (Masulli 1980; Sereni 1968).

Casalecchio reflects these patterns; its population swelled from 2,400 to 6,000 in the six decades from 1861 to 1921. At the beginning of this period, when Bologna had just been liberated from papal state rule and made part of the unified Italy, a majority of the Casalecchio population worked directly in agriculture, and 70 percent of these were sharecroppers. But changes were already evident, for the largest textile factory in the province had just been established in Casalecchio, employing large numbers of women, children, and men. By the end of the sixty-year span, slightly over one-fourth of the workforce was in agriculture, with another one-half composed of nonagricultural wage laborers, alongside a growing number of small merchants and artisans.

That this was also a period of demographic transformation is evident from both mortality and fertility rates. The crude death rate in Casalecchio sank steadily, from 30 per thousand annually in the 1870s to 17 per thousand by the early 1920s. As elsewhere, this was due in good part to a decline in infant mortality rather than to greater life expectancy for adults. The proportion of all deaths occurring to children under age 5 sank from 45 percent in 1869–1883 to 23 percent in 1904–1918.[3] Over these six decades, fertility also began its decline, with crude birthrate sinking from about 35 in the first portion of this period to about 21 by the end.[4]

CO-RESIDENCE IN CASALECCHIO

In looking at the households in which the people of Casalecchio lived in this period, the sharecropping legacy stands out clearly. In 1871, 40 percent of the population lived in households containing two or more nuclear family components (i.e., multiple family households), virtually the same as those living in nuclear family units (43 percent). An additional 13 percent lived in extended family households, that is, those containing some kin beyond the nuclear family but not containing two nuclear units.[5] A half century later, the situation had changed, though not dramatically. The rise of the proletarian sector led to an increase in the proportion of people living in nuclear family households (52 percent) and a decline in the proportion living in multiple family units (31 percent). The proportion living in extended family households remained virtually unchanged (14 percent).[6]

These communitywide figures, though, mask the fact that in the sharecropping sector, multiple family households continued to dominate (76 percent of those living in sharecropper households lived in multiple family units in 1871, compared to 71 percent in 1921). By contrast, among the agricultural and nonagricultural wage workers, nuclear family households had always constituted a majority, though substantial proportions lived in extended and multiple family households.[7] Indeed, given life course considerations, we could not say without further examination whether or not older widows and widowers lived with their married children among the proletarian population.

A DEMOGRAPHIC PROFILE OF WIDOWHOOD

Given the higher mortality rates pertaining in the past and, consequently, the greater variability in age at death, it is reasonable to assume that widowhood was less exclusively bound to old age in the past than it is today. Illustrative are the calculations of James Smith (1984: 433), who compares England's preindustrial population with England in 1981. Of women who became widowed in preindustrial England, 20 percent did so before reaching age 45, and another 45 percent became widowed before age 65. In contrast, in contemporary England, very few (2 percent) are widowed before age 35, and only 21 percent more are widowed before age 65. While 77 percent of English women widowed in 1981 became widows only after age 65, the corresponding proportion for the preindustrial period is only 35 percent.[8]

Thanks to our reconstruction of the Casalecchio population, we are able to look at the timing of widowhood more directly than is permitted either

TABLE 8.1   Age at Widowhood, by Sex and Period, Casalecchio

	Men			Women		
Age	1865–1889	1890–1914	1915–1921	1865–1889	1890–1914	1915–1921
16–39	17%	13%	17%	16%	15%	33%
40–49	24	11	18	22	19	13
50–59	21	24	24	26	27	21
60–69	22	32	14	27	29	23
70+	15	20	27	9	11	10
N	123	157	78	198	225	113

SOURCE: Casalecchio population register.

by census-based methods or by those employing simulation. In table 8.1 we show the results, divided into three periods: 1865–1889, 1890–1914, and 1915–1921. The first of these corresponds to the most traditional of our periods, in which the agricultural sector of the economy remained dominant and birth and death rates remained high. The second period is one of accelerating demographic, economic, and political changes. We separate this from the third period, which saw the disruption caused by the First World War and by the flu epidemic of 1919.

In our first period, we see a relatively flat curve for widowhood, especially for men. Forty-one percent of the men who lost their wives had done so before age 50, while 38 percent of the women widowed became widows before they turned age 50. Only a little over a third of the incidents of loss of spouse occurred to men and women over age 60. The second period sees the expected trend for men, though, curiously, such a trend is not evident for women. The proportion of incidents of men becoming widowed before age 50 sinks from 41 percent to 24 percent, but for women this proportion declines only slightly, from 38 percent to 34 percent. To some extent, this pattern may be attributable to a reduction in the marital age gap, yet this reduction by itself is too modest to explain much. It is also tempting to speculate that the reduction in the mortality of young adults in this period benefited women disproportionately, presumably through a decline in mortality associated with childbirth. This remains to be verified.

The effects of the First World War and the flu epidemic that followed it are evident when we look at the period 1915–1921. The impact of the war is seen clearly from the skyrocketing rates of young women's widowhood, with a third of all the widows being drawn from women under age 40, twice the proportion found in the earlier periods.

Looking at age at widowhood alone cannot tell us how large a proportion of the population was composed of the widowed and how these were dis-

TABLE 8.2   Percent of Population Widowed, by Age, Sex,
and Census Year

| | Aged 18–35 | | Aged 36–49 | | Aged 50+ | |
Census Year	Men	Women	Men	Women	Men	Women
1861	2%	2%	5%	8%	18%	37%
1881	0	1	6	7	22	38
1911	0	1	2	8	18	36
1921	1	3	4	9	18	34

SOURCE: Casalecchio manuscript censuses.

tributed by age. For this view, we turn to the manuscript censuses to see if we can find any historical trends. Table 8.2 breaks down the population of Casalecchio by sex and into three age groups: 18–35, 36–49, and 50+. We look at four censuses over the period 1861–1921.[9]

Looked at in this way, we find that few young adults (ages 18–35) were widowed. It should be recalled that mean age of first marriage for men was 27 and mean age of first marriage for women 23 to 24. Under 10 percent of both men and women aged 36–49 were widowed in any of our census years, although the proportion of women of this age group who were widowed was always higher than that of the men. Strikingly, the decline in mortality that occurred in these sixty years did not result in any change in proportion widowed for those over age 50. Indeed, no changes in these proportions are evident from 1861 to 1921.

There are some reasons to suppose that there should be a direct relationship between declining mortality and declining proportions of people over 50 who are widowed. First of all, as the expectation of length of life for those of marital age extends beyond 50, one would expect a higher proportion of those above age 50 to have a living spouse. This especially holds where, as is generally the case, the transition to lower adult mortality results not only in an increased mean life expectancy but also in a decrease in the variation found in age at death. Countervailing forces might include an increase in the disparity between male and female age at death, but this is not normally associated with this early period.

One factor, however, that must be considered in any analysis of this type is propensity toward remarriage. The likelihood that a widow or widower would remarry shrank by roughly a half over our period and especially affected the younger widowed population. It would thus appear that the decline in proportion of the widowed we might have expected from the declining adult mortality rate was counterbalanced by a decline in the rate of remarriage. The older population of Casalecchio was, as a result, just as likely to be widowed in the first two decades of the twentieth century as they had been in the mid-nineteenth century. Before turning directly to an analy-sis of the impact of widowhood on co-residence, then, we first pause to look at the effect of remarriage.

REMARRIAGE

The fate of the widowed is directly tied to the prevalence of remarriage. Yet studies of remarriage still remain underdeveloped (J. Smith 1984: 435), de-spite the notable contribution made by the publication in 1981 of *Marriage and remarriage in populations of the past* (Dupâquier et al. 1981). A few basic patterns are clear, however: (1) widowers almost everywhere are more likely to remarry than widows; and (2) the younger the individual at widowhood, the more likely he or she is to remarry. This pattern extends beyond Europe to North America (e.g., Keyssar 1974). Typical are the results from early eighteenth-century France, where Jacques Dupâquier found 80 percent of men widowed in their 20s remarrying compared to 67 percent of the women, sinking by age 40 to 49 to 52 percent of men and 20 percent of women (in Hufton 1984: 357).

We expect political economic factors to influence rates of remarriage in different places and different periods. For example, Jacek Kochanowicz (1983: 162) explained that in the Polish feudal economy of the eighteenth century, "if a farm was without some elements of its manpower, it ceased to be fully productive. Therefore, the lord required widowers and widows, and especially the latter, either to remarry or to leave the plot."

That there may be an important family economic component in deter-mining rates of remarriage may be inferred from regional differences in re-marriage rates in Italy itself. Massimo Livi Bacci's (1981: 357) study of re-marriage in the 1880s found much higher rates prevailing in the south than in the center, at least for those who were widowed before age 50. This is provocative, for it goes against the received wisdom concerning southern Italian culture. According to this view, on losing her husband the widow dons black clothes, wearing these as a sign of devotion to her husband's memory for the rest of her life. Yet 49 percent of southern Italian women widowed before age 50 remarried, compared to only 28 percent of the women in central Italy. We concur with Livi Bacci's tentative explanation for this sharp difference: in central Italy, the sharecropping economy, with its large, multiple family household, provided security for the widow, who was not left alone with her children. In contrast, the nuclear family household that prevailed in much of southern Italy placed greater pressure on widows (and widowers) to remarry.[10]

Italy's pattern of remarriages in the nineteenth century, taken as a whole, was similar to that found in other western European countries, including England and France (Livi Bacci 1981: 348). One important trend found in

nineteenth-century Italy was a continued decline in the tendency to remarry, as measured by the proportion of marriages involving one or more
previously married individuals. Athos Bellettini (1981: 260), for example,
reports that the proportion of marriages in Italy involving at least one previously married individual sank from 19.4 percent in 1864–1870 to 13.8 percent in 1891–1900. In both periods, almost twice as many men remarried as
did women.[11]

In Casalecchio over the period 1865–1921, we count 361 men whose
wives died and 539 women whose husbands died. Of course, the older the
couple, the more likely one of them was to die. However, 16 percent of
the widowers and 20 percent of the widows were under age 40 when their
spouse died, with a total of 33 percent of the widowers and 39 percent of the
widows under age 50. It was thus not uncommon for a person to lose his or
her spouse while still caring for dependent children.

Remarriage was not common in Casalecchio, and in keeping with the
Italy-wide pattern, it became even less common over the years.[12] In the earlier period (1865–1882), 12 percent of all marriages involved at least one
widow or widower, while by the latter period (1897–1921), this had sunk to
5 percent. Widowers were more likely to remarry than widows; in fact, remarrying widowers outnumbered remarrying widows by 3:1 in the nineteenth century and by 2:1 in the twentieth century.

Italian men also waited less time before remarrying than did Italian
women. In the mid-1880s, for example, almost one-fifth of all Italian widowers who married did so within six months of the death of their wives,
and another one-fifth did so within the next six months. By contrast, widows were considerably more restrained, with widow remarriage within six
months of a husband's death extremely rare (0.5 percent). Such rapid widower remarriage, however, was not as common in the Bologna area, including Casalecchio, presumably due to the household economic system
described above.

Of the 110 men who remarried in Casalecchio from 1865 to 1921, almost
half (46 percent) were still in their 20s or 30s. Yet only 16 percent of the men
who lost a wife in Casalecchio did so while they were under age 40. This provides strong, though only indirect, evidence of the relationship between age
and propensity to remarry. Put differently, only 58 men in this age category
became widowers in this period, while 51 widowers in this age category remarried. By contrast, while 303 men over age 40 lost their wives in these
years, just 61 men over age 40 remarried.

Although widows were much more likely to remarry if they were in their
20s or 30s (indeed, 52 percent of all widows remarrying were in this age
range), even young widows had only limited remarriage possibilities. Indeed, while 539 women became widows in Casalecchio in these years, there
were only 70 widows who remarried.

For the great majority of women who lost their husbands, widowhood would be their lot for the rest of their lives. Even those who lost a husband at an early age, although much more likely to remarry than older widows, seldom remarried. This reflects a cultural bias against widow remarriage, together with a social system that provided, through kin co-residence, a means for widows and widowers to survive without remarrying. By contrast, there did seem to be the general expectation that men who were widowed early should remarry, and such remarriages were not hard to arrange.[13]

It is likely that the propensity for remarriage among older widowers was linked to their economic and household positions, but the relationship here is complex. The well-off sharecropper, for example, might be a good bet for attracting a spouse, despite his age and widowed status. But, living in a multiple family household, he was under much less pressure to remarry, even if he had young children, for he was surrounded by female kin. Indeed, the other women of the household might not look favorably on the prospect of a new female authority figure among them. However, the poor proletarian widower might have a difficult time surviving without a wife, especially if he had small children; yet he was much less desirable as a spouse.

THE IMPACT OF WIDOWHOOD ON CO-RESIDENCE

With all the studies of household composition in the European past that have appeared over the past two decades, rather few have considered the impact of widowhood on the surviving spouse's co-residential circumstances. The issue, though, is of considerable importance, not only for understanding the social meaning of widowhood in the past and not only for understanding more about the lives of other people but also for understanding the very nature of the household system. Just as the moment of marriage is a key component in defining household formation systems, so, too, is the moment when the marriage is broken. Where marriage entails the formation of a new household, for example, we may still find extended family units as a regular part of people's life course co-residential experiences if taking in one's widowed parent is the norm. Thus, we need to avoid an exclusive focus on marriage as the diagnostic element of household systems. One implication of this is that rather than simply dividing household systems in Europe into nuclear, stem, and joint, based on postmarital residence rules, we need to consider the complication added by rules governing the residence of the widowed.

Perhaps the most active setting for work on the impact of widowhood on co-residence has been England. Here the issues have not only been framed in demographic terms but have also been related to debates over the Poor Laws, with their controversies over where the family's responsibilities end and the community's or state's begin (J. Smith 1984).

Laslett (1977: 199–200) concludes that in preindustrial England the loss of a spouse entailed no change in household arrangements for the survivor, though the whole remaining family might move to another community. It is striking, however, that evidence from mid-nineteenth-century Preston reveals another pattern. Looking at widowers and widows over age 65, Michael Anderson (1971: 140) finds that 50 percent of the former and 41 percent of the latter lived with a married child, compared to just 15 percent and 17 percent of married men and women, respectively. He finds a similar pattern in his agricultural village sample (ibid.: 84). If this represents a change from the preindustrial pattern, it would be instructive to know just when, how, and why this change took place. Jean Robin's (1984) finding of a high proportion of elderly living with kin in nineteenth-century Colyton brings into question Laslett's earlier generalization. The lack of separate data on the widowed in Robin's study, however, makes conclusions here difficult.

Studies of the co-residence of widows and widowers in Italy are only now getting under way and focus largely on the situation of women (Palazzi 1990). Yet the Italian case is an interesting one given the prevalence of complex family household arrangements in much of Italy. Insofar as people live not in nuclear family households but in larger households surrounded by various kin, we would expect the co-residential impact of widowhood to be considerably reduced. In particular, loss of one's spouse would not entail isolation, nor would it have the same economic impact on the household unit.

A first view of where the widowed population of Casalecchio lived and how they differed from people who were still married is provided in table 8.3. There we look both at 1881 and 1921, comparing widows and widowers over age 50 with their married counterparts of the same age. In both years, a slight majority of the married men and women lived in simple family households, while around two-fifths lived in multiple family households. Fewer than 10 percent of the married men and women lived in extended family households. In comparing 1881 with 1921, what is striking is the lack of change in household arrangements of older married adults during a period of dramatic economic, social, political, and demographic change.

Compared to those still married, the widowed were much more likely to live in extended family households, largely at the expense of simple family co-residence. The changes associated with "modernization" and urbanization did not bring about any notable increase in the proportion living by themselves or in nonfamily situations (a proportion that, in total, hovers around a tenth for both widows and widowers). The lesser proportion generally living in multiple family households can be attributed to the impact of spousal death on households consisting of two conjugal nuclei. Using the standard typology, this has the effect of transforming a multiple family household into an extended family household.

TABLE 8.3   Co-Residence of Casalecchio Population over Age 50,
Married versus Widowed, by Sex, 1881 and 1921

	1881		1921	
	Married	Widowed	Married	Widowed
Women				
Solitary and no family	—	8%	—	12%
Simple family household	54%	19	52%	22
Extended family household	9	38	6	43
Multiple family household	41	34	42	22
N	123	84	321	185
Men				
Solitary and no family	0%	11%	1%	13%
Simple family household	54	32	57	19
Extended family household	9	21	6	38
Multiple family household	37	37	36	30
N	185	57	418	103

SOURCE: Casalecchio manuscript censuses.

Another view of the co-residential situation of the widowed is provided in table 8.4, which looks at the relationship of widows and widowers to the head of the household in 1881 and 1921. Again, we find rather little change over time. Most widows live not as household heads but in households headed by a son, generally a married son. A woman is many times more likely to live in her married son's household than in the household of her married daughter. This, by the way, contrasts with the picture painted in nineteenth-century England by Anderson (1971: 56), who found that two-thirds of all widows who lived with married children lived with a married daughter. Robin (1984) found a similar pattern of residence with married daughters rather than married sons in nineteenth-century Colyton. Clearly, in this part of Italy we are dealing with a strongly patrilateral system, and this system affected not only postmarital residence choices but also choices of residence for those who became widowed.

The influence of gender on the impact of widowhood is clear from a comparison of the widows and widowers in table 8.4. Before widowhood, the large majority of women had been the wife of the household head and, with him, codirector of the household. For most of these women, widowhood meant loss of this status, as they became—at least formally—dependents of their sons. The lines of authority between the widow and her daughter-in-law in such situations remains one of the most pressing questions of historical inquiry on widowhood in this part of Italy. The impact of losing a spouse was quite different for a man, for in the great majority of cases, losing one's

TABLE 8.4   Relationship to Household Head of Casalecchio
Widows and Widowers over Age 50, 1881 and 1921

	1881	1921
Widows		
Head	16%	25%
Mother of head	50	54
Mother-in-law of head	8	9
Other kin	13	5
Nonkin	13	7
N	84	185
Widowers		
Head	79%	74%
Father	7	13
Brother	5	2
Other kin	2	5
Nonkin	7	6
N	57	103

SOURCE: Casalecchio manuscript censuses.

wife did not mean any formal change in household status. He remained, as he was, a household head.

The database we have compiled for the Casalecchio population allows us to take a more direct look at the impact of loss of one's spouse on household arrangements. We created a file consisting of all those whose spouse died while they were living in Casalecchio at any time during the period 1865–1921. Identifying the household in which they lived at the time of the spouse's death, we asked what impact the death of the spouse had on household composition. We retrieved household composition six months before the death and compared it with household composition six months later. The results are shown in table 8.5.

The majority of women lived in simple family households before widowhood. Death of a husband had the immediate effect of leaving the widow in a household by herself in one-fifth of the cases. Other relatives came to join the household of the widow in only 6 percent of the cases, while 16 percent of the widows (with any co-resident children they may have had) left Casalecchio within six months of the husband's death. The other important co-residential situation in which women found themselves on the eve of their widowhood was in multiple family households (in which 36 percent of the women lived). Husband's death here rarely meant either the immediate departure of the household from Casalecchio or the formation of a simple family household (presuming the departure of the widow). In 69 percent of the cases, in fact, the household continued to have two or more

TABLE 8.5   Impact of Widowhood on Housebould Composition, Casalecchio, 1865–1921

Household Composition Six Months after Widowhood	Household Composition Six Months before Widowhood					
	Simple	Extended	Multiple	Other	Total	N
Women						
Moved	16%	9%	2%	19%	10%	56
Solitary	21	—	—	10	12	65
No family	0	—	—	5	0	2
Simple	57	13	5	52	36	194
Extended	2	74	25	10	14	74
Multiple	4	4	69	5	27	147
Total	56%	4%	36%	4%		
N	299	23	195	21		538
Men						
Moved	9%	—	3%	16%	6%	23
Solitary	20	—	—	16	11	39
No family	1	—	—	—	0	2
Simple	67	—	4	32	37	134
Extended	2	94%	24	10	15	56
Multiple	2	6	69	21	30	109
Total	50%	5%	40%	5%		
N	184	17	144	18		363

SOURCE: Casalecchio population register.

simple family nuclei within it, while in one-fourth of the cases the death meant the widow was left living simply with one of her married children's (almost always a son's) family in an extended family unit.

A look at the men whose wives died reveals that the sex of the deceased had very little effect on the impact of widowhood on household composition. Death of a husband more commonly resulted in the departure of the remaining household from Casalecchio in a short period of time, but, otherwise, there is very little to distinguish the co-residential impact of widowhood for men and women.

How frequently loss of a spouse meant emigration from the community of residence is a question that has seldom been studied empirically, either in Italy or elsewhere. We look into this question in Casalecchio, considering differences both by sex and age at widowhood.

As seen in table 8.6, where we show proportion of widows and widowers who leave Casalecchio within one year of widowhood, loss of a husband was more likely to lead to the widow's emigration than was loss of a wife in the

TABLE 8.6   Proportion Leaving Casalecchio within 1 Year
of Widowhood, by Age and Sex, 1865–1921

	Men		Women	
Age	%	Total N	%	Total N
16–39	9	55	22	102
40–49	5	61	16	100
50–59	17	83	17	136
60–69	16	88	16	144
70+	17	71	37	54
Total	13	358	20	536

SOURCE: Casalecchio population register.

case of the widower (20 percent of the women left within a year of widowhood, compared with 13 percent of the men). Interestingly, the most pronounced gender differences are found for the young and the old, with those widowed at ages 50 to 69 showing no gender difference at all in propensity to migrate. In the case of the young widows and widowers, this might be attributable to patrilocality, with the widow and her young children returning to live with family members in her own community of origin. The young widower, by contrast, would be likely to seek the help of his own kin, who would tend to live in Casalecchio. Why the oldest widows should be so much more likely to leave Casalecchio on the death of their spouse than men who are widowed at the same age is less readily explicable.

A fuller view of the likelihood of emigration for widows and widowers is provided through survival analysis, which is not limited simply to a single year following widowhood and which takes into account the effects of death of the survivor.[14] These results reveal a clearer pattern of age differences in emigration among both widows and widowers and also allow us to compare the propensity of emigration of men and women on widowhood with the propensity of their married counterparts in the population.

Figure 8.1 simply divides all those who experienced widowhood by age, looking at their cumulative survival, that is, the proportion over time remaining in Casalecchio, controlling for death and the end of the period of observation (1921). We note here no difference in tendency to emigrate between the two youngest age groups (16–39 and 40–49 at widowhood) but a progressively sharp increase in migration propensity among the next two groups (aged 50–59 and 60+).

This in itself may tell us nothing about the impact of widowhood on propensity to emigrate, since the results could simply reflect underlying age-specific migration rates in Casalecchio. We thus needed to identify an ap-

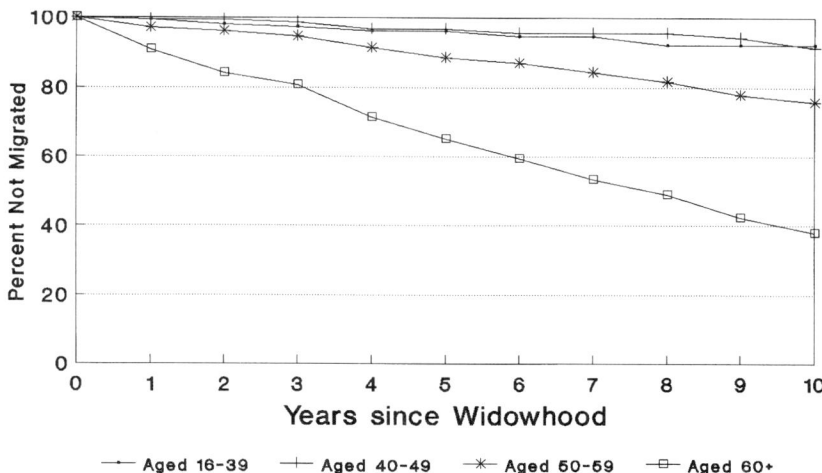

Fig. 8.1. Migration, by age widowed, 1865–1921: Cumulative survival after widowhood (Total N = 906).

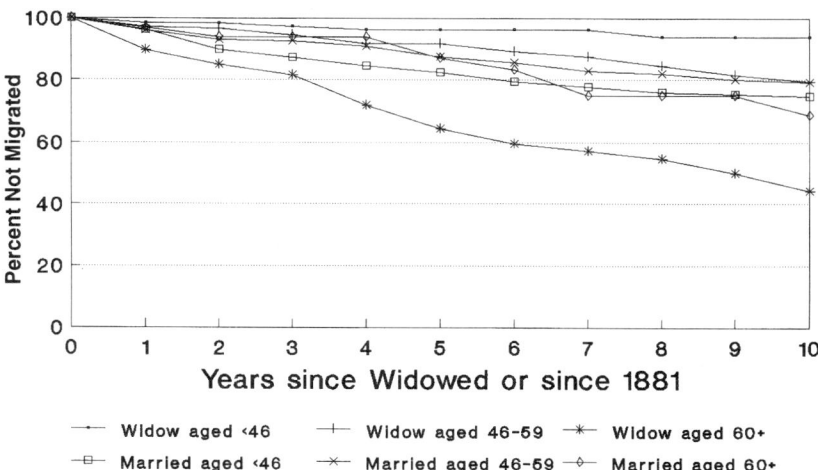

Fig. 8.2. Migration following widowhood for women versus migration of married women after 1881, by age: Cumulative survival.

propriate control group to see if the experience of widowhood itself affected migration propensity. We took all those in the 1881 census who were married, following them over time to see when, and if, they migrated.[15] The results are shown in figures 8.2 (for women) and 8.3 (for men). The most striking result here is that older widows (over age 60) are considerably more

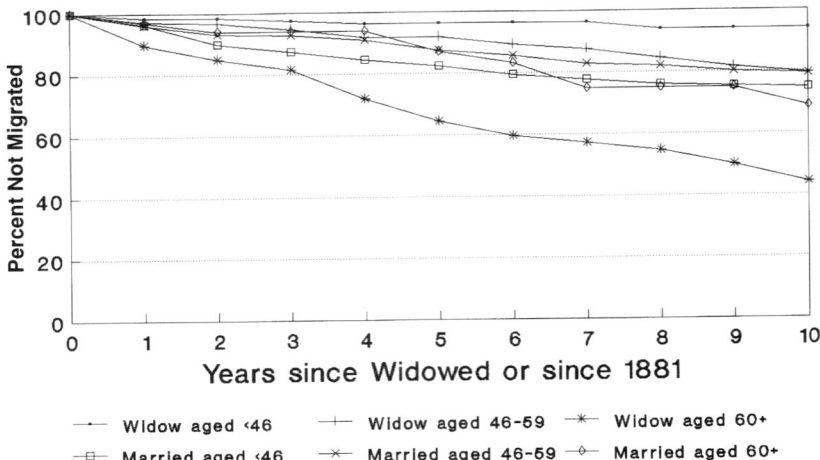

Fig. 8.3. Migration following widowhood for men versus migration of married men after 1881, by age: Cumulative survival.

likely to emigrate than are older married women. Moreover, age differences in migration propensity among married women are minor compared to the substantial differences found among women who are widowed.

To test the significance of these relationships, we employed the Lee-Desu statistic comparing survival curves. No significant difference (p < .10) in survival curve was found among the three age groups of married women. By contrast, among those who were widowed, all relationships were significant.[16] Identical results were found for the men, with no difference in emigration propensity for married men among the three age groups yet significant relationships found for those who were widowed. Loss of a spouse for older people—whether men or women—meant a significantly greater prospect of departure from the community than that faced by their married age-mates.

CONCLUSION

Understanding the impact of widowhood in the past presupposes an understanding of the workings of household systems. We would expect that insofar as different household systems prevailed, differences would be found in the impact of widowhood on people's lives. Unfortunately, research on the interaction of such systems with widowhood is not yet well developed.

Theoretical explication of the relationship between household system and widowhood requires an understanding of the influence of demographic, gender, political economic, and cultural forces. Demographic forces affect both age at widowhood and proportion who are widowed, and we would expect changes in such demographic elements as mortality rates and age at marriage to affect the prevalence of widowhood. Yet as we have seen in the case of Casalecchio, the interaction of demographic elements can be complex. Thus, for example, changing remarriage rates complicate the secular trends that would be expected to result from declines in mortality.

Differences between men and women in the impact of widowhood have thus far not been well studied historically, with the exception of remarriage, where the much greater tendency of males to remarry is now well established. Gender differences can be seen in Casalecchio in the greater likelihood of women to be widowed and in that, for women, loss of spouse meant a decline in formal household status, while it did not for men. Yet here we enter into the difficult terrain of the relationship between formal positions of authority and actual power relations. In a multiple family household, a husband's death meant being replaced as wife of household head by one's daughter-in-law. Yet it is not clear what this meant in practice for the older woman's ability to influence household decisions.

Political economic forces clearly have a great deal of influence on the social implications of widowhood. We have pointed out the apparent influence of economic differences between southern and central-northern Italy on the remarriage rates of the widowed. In this case, it seems that such forces outweighed the presumably greater cultural constraints on remarriage found in southern Italy. More generally, the prevalence of multiple family households in central Italy is the product of the political economy of sharecropping, a system that has great implications for the lives of widows and widowers.

Yet we cannot discount the role of cultural norms regarding proper behavior, not only insofar as remarriage is concerned but also with respect to the obligations people felt toward widowed parents and parents-in-law. Richard Smith (1984: 425) has made this point with respect to Britain in the past, and the situation in Casalecchio bears him out. First of all, we have seen that the tremendous economic, political, and demographic changes of the six decades under consideration did not result in equally dramatic changes in the co-residential circumstances of the widowed. Even though by 1921 sharecroppers had become only a minority of the population, two-thirds of the widowed over age 50 still lived with extended kin. Moreover, the patrilateral principle that predominated, again associated with a sharecropping family economy, continued to guide co-residential decisions of the widowed even after proletarianization. The tendency to live with a married daughter rather than a married son, documented for parts of nineteenth-century Britain, is simply not found in this part of Italy.

The rise of proletarianization and the slow demise of a sharecropping household system that offered special support to the widowed population (as to the older population in general) thus did not necessarily lead to the co-residential abandonment of the widowed. However, the sharecroppers' large, multiple family household had offered special protection to the widowed, and the same degree of protection would be hard to duplicate in a proletarian family economy, at least until the economic position of the wage workers would itself improve substantially.

NOTES

1. A further factor relevant here is age at marriage, historically high in western Europe, which affects the age of the widow(er)'s children at the time of widowhood. See R. Smith 1984: 424–425.

2. On the dynamics of the sharecropper household in Italy, see Barbagli 1984 and Kertzer 1984, 1989.

3. For a fuller analysis of mortality in Casalecchio, see Kertzer and Hogan 1989: 62–65.

4. A detailed analysis of fertility changes and fertility differentials in Casalecchio in these years is provided in Kertzer and Hogan 1989: 157–173.

5. Here we make use of the household composition typology described by Hammel and Laslett (1974).

6. Demographic and economic data on the Casalecchio population are drawn from the Casalecchio database. This consists of a reconstruction of the approximately 19,000 individuals who ever lived in Casalecchio during the period 1865–1921, plus the inclusion of individuals who appeared in the 1861 census. Data sources include manuscript censuses, the population register, annual household tax registers, conscription registers, and other sources. For a full description, see Kertzer and Hogan 1989: 189–208.

7. The agricultural wage laborers actually showed an increasing likelihood of living in multiple family arrangements over this period, passing from 14 to 36 percent. The nonagricultural wage laborers maintained a constant 18 to 20 percent multiple family proportion in these years. For more details, see Kertzer and Hogan 1989: 53–57.

8. The view that widowhood commonly affected younger women in the preindustrial past is disputed by Keyssar (1974), on the basis of his study of Woburn, Massachusetts, in the eighteenth century. Simulation methods are employed by Bongaarts (1989) to examine the impact of changing rates of mortality, remarriage, and divorce on the proportion of people widowed by age in the United States in 1800, 1900, and 1980.

9. No census was taken in Italy in 1891, and the 1901 manuscript census forms were not retained by the communes.

10. On household dynamics in southern Italy in the past, see Da Molin 1990.

11. In the period 1864–1870, 8.6 percent of the marriages in Italy involved a widow, while 15.2 percent involved a widower. In the period 1891–1900, the figures were 6.2 percent and 11 percent, respectively.

12. Much of this discussion of remarriage in Casalecchio is adapted from Kertzer and Hogan 1989: 145–146.

13. Of the 61 widowers over age 40 who remarried, 74 percent married women who had never previously been married.

14. The procedure also takes into account other forms of right censorship, most notably, the end of our period of reconstitution in 1921. For the use of these methods in historical migration research, see Hogan and Kertzer 1985. For other historical family applications, see Alter 1988 and Kertzer and Hogan 1989.

15. This procedure did not take into account subsequent changes in marital status. Thus, in fact, by the time many of these individuals emigrated, they may well have become widowed. The result of this procedure is to underestimate any difference in migration propensity between the widowed and the married.

16. For those widowed at ages 16–45 vs. 46–59, p < .005; for those widowed at ages 16–45 vs. 60+ and 46–59 vs. 60+, p < .0001.

REFERENCES

Alter, George. 1988. *Family and the female life course: The women of Verviers, Belgium, 1849–1880.* Madison: University of Wisconsin Press.

Anderson, Michael. 1971. *Family structure in nineteenth-century Lancashire.* Cambridge: Cambridge University Press.

Barbagli, Marzio. 1984. *Sotto lo stesso tetto: Mutamenti della famiglia in Italia dal XV al XX secolo* [Under the same roof: Family changes in Italy from the fifteenth to the twentieth century]. Bologna: Il Mulino.

Bellettini, Athos. 1981. "Les remariages dans la ville et dans la campagne de Bologne au dix-neuvième siècle" [Remarriages in the city and the countryside of Bologna in the nineteenth century]. In *Marriage and remarriage in populations of the past,* eds. J. Dupâquier, E. Hélin, P. Laslett, M. Livi Bacci, and S. Sogner, 259–272. New York: Academic Press.

Berkner, Lutz. 1972. "The stem family and the developmental cycle of the peasant household: An eighteenth-century Austrian example." *American Historical Review* 77: 398–418.

Bongaarts, John. 1989. "The demographic determinants of the duration and incidence of widowhood." In *Later phases of the family cycle,* eds. E. Grebenik, C. Höhn, and R. Mackensen, 55–65. Oxford: Clarendon Press.

Da Molin, Giovanna. 1990. "Family forms and domestic service in southern Italy from the seventeenth to the nineteenth centuries." *Journal of Family History* 15: 503–528.

Dupâquier, Jacques, E. Hélin, P. Laslett, M. Livi Bacci, and S. Sogner, eds. 1981. *Marriage and remarriage in populations of the past.* New York: Academic Press.

Gaunt, David. 1983. "The property and kin relationships of retired farmers in northern and central Europe." In *Family forms in historic Europe,* ed. Richard Wall, Peter Laslett, and Jean Robin, 249–280. Cambridge: Cambridge University Press.

Hammel, Eugene A., and Peter Laslett. 1974. "Comparing household structure over time and between cultures." *Comparative Studies in Society and History* 16: 73–103.

Hogan, Dennis P., and David I. Kertzer. 1985. "Longitudinal approaches to migration in social history." *Historical Methods* 18: 20–30.

Hufton, Olwen. 1984. "Women without men: Widows and spinsters in Britain and France in the eighteenth century." *Journal of Family History* 9: 355–376.

Kertzer, David I. 1984. *Family life in central Italy, 1880–1910*. New Brunswick: Rutgers University Press.

————. 1989. "The joint family household revisited: Demographic constraints and household complexity in the European past." *Journal of Family History* 14: 1–15.

Kertzer, David I., and Dennis P. Hogan. 1988. "Family structure, individual lives, and societal change." In *Social structures and human lives*, ed. Matilda W. Riley, 83–100. Newbury Park, Calif.: Sage.

————. 1989. *Family, political economy, and demographic change: The transformation of life in Casalecchio, Italy, 1861–1921*. Madison: University of Wisconsin Press.

Keyssar, J. 1974. "Widowhood in eighteenth-century Massachusetts: A problem in the history of the family." *Perspectives in American History* 8: 83–119.

Kochanowicz, Jacek. 1983. "The peasant family as an economic unit in the Polish feudal economy of the eighteenth century." In *Family forms in historic Europe*, ed. Richard Wall, Peter Laslett, and Jean Robin, 153–166. Cambridge: Cambridge University Press.

Laslett, Peter. 1972. "Introduction: The history of the family." In *Household and family in past time*, eds. Peter Laslett and Richard Wall, 1–89. Cambridge: Cambridge University Press.

————. 1977. *Family life and illicit love in earlier generations*. Cambridge: Cambridge University Press.

Livi Bacci, Massimo. 1981. "On the frequency of remarriage in nineteenth-century Italy: Methods and results." In *Marriage and remarriage in populations of the past*, ed. J. Dupâquier, E. Hélin, P. Laslett, M. Livi Bacci, and S. Sogner, 347–362. New York: Academic Press.

Masulli, Ignazio. 1980. *Crisi e trasformazione: Strutture economiche, rapporti sociali e lotte politiche nel bolognese (1880–1914)* [Crisis and transformation: Economic structures, social relations, and political struggles in the Bologna area (1880–1914)]. Bologna: Istituto per la Storia di Bologna.

Palazzi, Maura. 1990. "Female solitude and patrilineage: Unmarried women and widows during the eighteenth and nineteenth centuries." *Journal of Family History* 15: 443–460.

Plakans, Andrejs. 1989. "Stepping down in former times: A comparative assessment of retirement in traditional Europe." In *Age structuring in comparative perspective*, ed. D. Kertzer and K. W. Schaie, 175–196. Hillsdale, N.J.: Lawrence Erlbaum.

Robin, Jean. 1984. "Family care of the elderly in a nineteenth-century Devonshire parish." *Ageing and Society* 4: 505–516.

Sereni, Emilio. 1968. *Il capitalismo nelle campagne (1860–1900)* [Capitalism in the countryside (1860–1900)]. Turin: Einaudi.

Smith, James E. 1984. "Widowhood and ageing in traditional English society." *Ageing and Society* 4: 429–449.

Smith, Richard M. 1984. "The structured dependence of the elderly as a recent development: Some sceptical historical thoughts." *Ageing and Society* 4: 409–428.

NINE

The Demography of Widowhood in Preindustrial New Hampshire

Daniel Scott Smith

THE MALTHUSIAN-FRONTIER REGIME

In recent years, scholars in several fields have revived interest in the fundamental relationship between resources and population and the consequences for social institutions of population growth and density (Lee et al. 1988; Wrigley and Schofield 1981). Instead of being a minor adversary of Marx, Malthus now stands as an important figure in the history of thought (Dupâquier, Fauve-Chamoux, and Grebenik 1983). Certainly, emphasis on this connection is appealing to students of the first two centuries of American historical demography and family history. Frederick Jackson Turner ([1894] 1961) developed the implications of a low labor-to-land ratio in his frontier theory, which organized major features of the American historical experience. In Malthusian terms, the American case represents an extreme: land abundance, labor scarcity, and a very high rate of natural population increase. In contrast to rapid demographic expansion, rates of per capita economic growth before the nineteenth century were irregular over the short run and quite modest over the long run (McCusker and Menard 1985; Smith 1980).

Several important eighteenth-century American commentators also used a framework that linked cheap land and migration to the frontier to early and universal marriage and consequently to high rates of natural increase. Drawing on these writings, Malthus himself ([1798] 1960) cited the rapid population growth in America as an exceptional outcome that still illustrated his general rule that environmental constraints limited the possibility of positive rates of demographic expansion.

Without doubt, the Malthusian-frontier framework provides a parsimonious first approximation to the interpretation of major features of early

American history (Smith 1980). This investigation extends the theme to women (Guttentag and Secord 1983; Thompson 1974) and to the phenomenon of widowhood, a particularly interesting status because it is open to the radically divergent impacts of the frontier. A low labor-to-land ratio can lead to high wages and ownership of land for laborers, assuming they are free to make choices. This same economic environment is, however, associated historically with the institutions of slavery and serfdom. If land is cheap and labor expensive, those who want others to work for them must take away their economic choices (Domar 1970). This is the economic base of the American paradox of the coexistence of the two extremes—slavery for blacks and virtually unlimited autonomy for white farmers.

Legally, widows, unlike married women, enjoyed the right to be independent actors. The scarcity of women that is reflected in a high sex (male to female) ratio on the frontier could, all else equal, aid widows in two ways: by increasing the prospects for an advantageous marriage and by allowing for continuing economic autonomy as widows. Thus a favorable frontier effect would be apparent in a higher rate of remarriage for widows and a higher proportion of householders among those who remained widows compared to those in nonfrontier areas.

THE CASE OF BELKNAP'S NEW HAMPSHIRE

To explore this subject, New Hampshire supplies both a suitable setting and the best available data for the period before 1790 in America. It was the only colony in British North America to tally widows in its census. In both 1767 and 1773, towns returned to the colonial government the numbers of unmarried women, married women, and widows in the nonslave population. Additionally, the numbers of female householders and population data from the first census and information on the share of taxes of each New Hampshire town in 1790 were added to this data set.[1]

While census data document the incidence and covariates of widowhood, three data sets constructed from the published probate records of colonial New Hampshire wills provide evidence concerning the economic and familial context of widowhood (New Hampshire 1913–1941). The first data set contains limited information for all of the testators whose wills were probated (N = 1,455), while the second records the sparse published evidence concerning the administration of the property of those persons who died intestate (N = 1,886). The third data set records more detailed information for all women's wills up to the year 1771 (N = 93) and a same-size sample of men's wills that were recorded immediately following those for women. Unfortunately, no information on the rates of remarriage for widows is currently available.

New Hampshire provides an appropriate case for the study of the ramifications of a low population-to-land ratio for widowhood. On the northern New England frontier, its population increased more than twenty-three-fold between 1700 and 1790, expanding from about 6,000 to nearly 142,000 people, an astounding annual growth rate of 3.5 percent. From 1767 to 1790, demographic increase was even more rapid—4.3 percent per year, from a total of 52,720 in 1767. Because of the expansion of land in settled towns at a yearly rate of 3.2 percent, density only increased from 16.7 to 21.5 persons per square mile, a rate of 1.1 percent per annum.[2]

In the first history of the state (1784–1792), Jeremy Belknap, a minister at Dover for two decades, outlined the basic elements of the demographic system operative in eighteenth-century New Hampshire.

> Land being easily obtained, and labour of every kind being familiar, there is great encouragement to population. A good husbandman, with the savings of a few years, can purchase new land enough to give his elder sons a settlement, and assist them in clearing a lot and building a hut; after which they soon learn to support themselves. The household is generally given to the youngest son, who provides for his parents, when age or infirmity incapacitates them for labour. An unmarried man of thirty years old is rarely to be found in our country towns. The women are grandmothers at forty, and it is not uncommon for a mother and daughter to have each a child at the breast, at the same time; nor for a father, son and grandson, to be at work together in the same field. Thus population and cultivation proceed together, and a vigorous race of inhabitants grows up, on a soil, which labor vies with nature to render productive. (II:196–197)

Belknap attributed rapid population growth to both natural and "adventitious" causes, the latter adjective referring to migration. Noting the surge into the colony after the defeat of the French in Canada in 1760, he also shrewdly observed that movement from old to new towns *within* New Hampshire augmented growth by keeping the age at marriage low.

> Where land is cheap, and the means of subsistence may be acquired in such plenty, and in so short a time as is evidently the case in our new plantations, encouragement is given to early marriage. A young man who has cleared a piece of land, and built a hut for his present accommodation, soon begins to experience the truth of that old adage, "It is not good for man to be alone." Having prospect of increasing his substance by labour, which he knows himself able to perform, he attaches himself to a female earlier than prudence would dictate if he had no such a prospect. Nor are the young females of the country averse to a settlement in the new plantations for they could quickly be employed in dairying which always falls to their lot and is an object of their ambition, as well as interest. (II:178)

It is, of course, anachronistic to apply the "Malthusian-frontier" label to these remarks, since Belknap wrote before Malthus. Although Belknap and others collected data on mortality and argued that America had lower death rates than Europe, they did not emphasize the weakened positive check of mortality. Instead, late-eighteenth-century American authors stressed the inverse relationship between density and net migration flows as the key equilibrator of the demographic-economic system. They were population geographers concerned with the distribution and redistribution of people over space (McCoy 1987: 228; Zagarri 1987).

Belknap (1792: 213, 215–216) also took note of institutional factors that suggest that older males did not play as central a role as middle-aged men. Postrevolutionary state laws recognized a decline in activity associated with the aging process for men. A poll tax of ten shillings per head, equivalent to that paid on ten acres of arable land, applied only to males between the ages of 18 and 70. Men over age 60 were not required to be militarily prepared, either in the active militia or training band (for men between ages 16 and 40) or the reserves or alarm list (for men between ages 40 and 60).

Certainly, Belknap's emphasis on rapid demographic increase and density-dependent migration accurately captures important features of the New Hampshire experience. While not referring to Belknap, Darrett Rutman (1975: 283–284) has detailed his contentions statistically. Among settled agricultural towns, for example, density in 1767 accounted for 73 percent of the variation in population growth rates in those towns between that year and 1790.

PATTERNS IN CENSUSES

The sequence of land availability, high nuptiality, very high fertility, and a steeply sloping age distribution is evident in the indicators in table 9.1. This table compares New Hampshire in the late colonial period, the state and the country as a whole in 1790, and averages for English localities before 1800. For example, the entire difference in mean household size between England and America can be attributed to a difference of one person in the number under age 15 per household. Since children have essentially zero probability of heading a household, they can contribute only to increasing average household size. The difference in age structure is also evident among the elderly. In 1767 and 1773, New Hampshire had half the proportion of males over age 60 compared to the proportion in the English population in 1771 (Wrigley and Schofield 1981: 529, table A3.1).

Difference in the incidence of widowhood between England and America is also striking, a fact with several implications. Although detailed information on householding rates by age, sex, and marital status is lacking, it is

TABLE 9.1   Comparison of Characteristics of Populations and Families in New Hampshire in 1767, 1773, and 1790, the United States in 1790, and England from 1599 to 1796

	New Hampshire			United States	England
Category	1767	1773	1790	1790	1599–1796
Males per 100 females	104.2	102.9	101.1	103.3	91.3
Males under age 16/total males	.480	.499	.491	.495	—
Percent population age 15+	—	—	—	52	65
Percent females widowed	5.3	4.4	—	—	8.7
Percent females over age 15 widowed	10.2	8.5	—	—	13.4
Percent females married	32.8	33.3	—	—	32.1
Percent females over age 15 married	63.0	64.0	—	—	49.4
Percent widows of ever-married	13.9	11.7	—	—	21.3
Percent females single	61.9	62.3	—	—	59.2
Percent females over age 15 single	26.7	27.5	—	—	37.2
Mean household size	—	—	5.88	5.70	4.75
Widows/household	.154	.128	—	—	.216
Female heads/females over age 15	—	—	.026	.053	.111
Female heads/all heads	—	—	.038	.076	.201

SOURCES: Smith 1992*a*; Wall 1981: 304, table 1; Wrigley and Schofield 1981: 529, table A3.1.

virtually certain that the share of widows in the female population is responsible for the fraction of females who are householders. In the United States in 1900, postmarried women (including divorced and married–spouse-absent) were forty-one times more likely (51.4 percent vs. 1.2 percent) to be household heads than other women (married–spouse-present and never-married) over age 16 (table 9.2). In preindustrial England, the female householder rate (female householders per females over age 15) was twice the American rate and four times the New Hampshire rate in 1790, a gap that is due to the combination of the differences in the age distribution of the widowed and headship rates by marital status, as well as the relative incidence of widowhood.

Geographic variations in the incidence of widowhood in late colonial New Hampshire and female householding in the state in 1790 fit into the Belknapian framework. In table 9.3, the related indicators of population density and age of the town serve as a simple expression of that view. The effect of a town's age may be understood in two ways. Demographically, it captures the effect of declining sex ratios and increasing population, as new towns were disproportionately settled by younger males. Economically, it

TABLE 9.2　Householding Rates, by Sex, Age, and Marital Status,[a] for the United States in 1900

Age Group	Males			Females		
	Married	Widowed	Single	Married	Widowed	Single
16–24	89.0%	9.4%	2.9%	0.1%	9.8%	0.9%
	(985)	(85)	(7,444)	(2,682)	(245)	(5,845)
25–34	95.0	19.5	11.0	0.1	35.4	4.4
	(4,670)	(425)	(3,034)	(5,415)	(513)	(1,764)
35–44	98.1	39.8	22.4	0.1	68.0	10.5
	(4,842)	(492)	(1,095)	(4,342)	(681)	(627)
45–54	98.9	54.5	26.7	0.0	72.2	16.1
	(3,433)	(505)	(420)	(2,680)	(842)	(323)
55–64	98.7	55.2	42.6	0.1	56.8	23.0
	(1,981)	(413)	(202)	(1,456)	(935)	(178)
65+	93.9	43.4	34.7	0.2	39.2	28.0
	(1,275)	(656)	(118)	(623)	(1,249)	(107)
Total	96.6	41.9	8.9	0.1	51.4	3.5
	(17,186)	(2,576)	(12,313)	(17,198)	(4,465)	(8,844)

Population Aged 16+

	Married	Widowed	Single	Married	Widowed	Single
U.S. 1900	49.6%	7.4%	43.0%	56.4%	14.6%	29.0%
New Hampshire 1767	63.5	—	—	65.6	10.6	23.8
New Hampshire 1773	64.6	—	—	68.5	9.0	22.4

SOURCES: Public use sample of the 1900 census; Rossiter 1909: 149–151, tables 76 and 77.
NOTE: Figures in parentheses are base N's for the adjacent percentages.
[a]In 1900, married category limited to married–spouse-present; widowed includes divorced and married–spouse absent.

serves as a modifier of density, indicating the length of time in which residents of a town had a chance to develop its economic potential. Thus a younger town with the same density as an older one would have more potential for future population growth. These two indicators account for about half the variation in the widowhood rate in the colonial censuses and even more of the variance in the proportion of females over age 16 who headed households and in the fraction of households headed by women in 1790. With the exception of the adult sex ratio and the tax evaluation per poll, the independent variables are substantially intercorrelated.

Table 9.4 details how New Hampshire towns differed by density groups that were constructed by Charles Wetherell (1977) through a hierarchical clustering procedure. The expected number of widows in each town in 1790 was computed based on the relation of the widowhood rate to age and density in the colonial censuses. The householder rate for widows was then calculated as the ratio of the actual number of female householders counted

TABLE 9.3   Regressions of Town Age and Density on Adult Widowhood Rates in 1767 and 1773, Female Householder Rates and Ratios in 1790, and Headship Rate of Widows in 1790

Dependent Variable	Town Density[a]	Town Age	Adjusted R^2
Percent widows, 1767	.0236	.0417	.51
	(.0058)	(.0084)	
with other variables[b]	.0709	.0399	.64
	(.0157)	(.0096)	
Percent widows, 1773	.0244	.0353	.44
	(.0057)	(.0086)	
with other variables[c]	.0251	.0330	.66
	(.0047)	(.0074)	
Female householding, 1790			
rate	.0160	.0159	.58
	(.0022)	(.0029)	
ratio	.0280	.0348	.67
	(.0036)	(.0046)	
Widow householding, 1790			
rate, using 1767	.0554	.0663	.13
relationship[d]	(.0261)	(.0330)	
rate, using 1773	.0378	.0661	.07
relationship[d]	(.0301)	(.0381)	

NOTE: Figures in parentheses are t statistics.
[a] Each town weighted by its share of the female population over age 16.
[b] Also significant at p < .05 were the sex ratio over age 16 and tax evaluation per poll.
[c] Also significant at p < .05 were the sex ratio over age 16, a dummy variable whose value is 1 for the seven towns with nonagricultural opportunities, and a dummy variable whose value is 1 for the largest town, Portsmouth.
[d] The number of widows in each New Hampshire town was estimated using the regression of age and density to the percent widowed of females over age 16 in the colonial censuses.

in the printed listings of heads of families in 1790 to the expected number of widows. Because this method assumes that only widows were household heads, it provides an upper bound on the widowed householder rate.

Two observations from the 1790 data are worth emphasizing. First, the fraction of widows who were householders in New Hampshire in 1790 was remarkably low—27 percent, based on the 1767 relationship, or just over half the figure for American widows in 1900 (see table 9.2). Since the age-specific householder rate for widows was curvilinear, peaking in the 45–54 age group in 1900, the older age distribution of the widowed population in that year probably cannot account for much of the apparent change from the New Hampshire rate in 1790 to that of the United States in 1900. By comparative standards, this is a major difference. In 1840, of the widows of

TABLE 9.4 Variations among New Hampshire Towns in 1767, 1773, and 1790, by Density Group

Population per Square Mile	N (towns)	Density	Mean Age	% of Total Population	% of Widows	% Females over Age 16 Widowed
1767						
Nonagricultural	6	306	139	18	31	19.4
60+	11	70	83	19	22	11.2
38–59	11	47	78	15	16	9.6
20–35	10	28	51	14	14	12.1
9.01–18	17	12	35	17	12	7.2
≤9	39	5	13	16	6	3.2
Average	94	41	46	—	—	7.6
1773						
Nonagricultural	6	138	143	13	27	14.4
60+	11	71	87	14	21	11.6
40–57	11	48	85	11	12	9.1
17–37	23	26	44	26	22	8.0
10.5–16.9	21	14	29	18	11	9.9
≤10.49	64	5	11	18	7	4.2
Average	136	24	38	—	—	7.2

Population per Square Mile	N (towns)	Density	Mean Age	Female Householder Rate	Female Householder Ratio	Estimated on 1767 % Females over Age 16 Widowed	Estimated on 1767 Widowed Householder Rate
1790							
Nonagricultural	7	180	160	6.2	9.3	16.2	37.1
57+	11	63	103	4.0	7.0	11.6	35.4
36–56	30	43	70	3.1	5.2	9.9	31.7
19–35	58	27	43	1.9	2.7	8.4	23.0
10–18	42	14	26	1.3	1.7	7.4	18.0
0–9	47	5	17	1.0	1.2	6.9	16.1
Average	195	29	47	2.0	3.0	8.6	26.3

NOTE: The female householder rate equals the number of female household heads divided by the female population age 16 and older; to calculate the latter, it was assumed that the number of females under age 16 was identical to the number of males under 16. The female householder ratio equals the number of female household heads divided by the total number of household heads.

Revolutionary War pensioners, some 22.5 percent of those over age 75 were householders, a figure not much below that of 28.8 percent for the same age group in 1900 (Smith 1981: 107).

One should not, however, jump to the conclusion that there was a major change in the first fifty years of the Republic. Given that the New Hampshire female householding rate was only half of that for the nation in 1790 (2.6 percent vs. 5.3 percent; see table 9.1), it would appear that the discrepancy needs to be located in the peculiarities of the population of the Granite State in 1790. One possible explanation is that New Hampshire was still relatively unsettled in the year of the first federal census. Its low female householding rate could thus be attributed either to its extreme frontier condition or to consequences of its relatively barren agricultural environment.

Second, the householding rate for widows is related to the stage of demographic development in 1790 as measured in terms of density. Portsmouth, the one genuinely urban place despite its small population of under 5,000 persons, stands out most dramatically. In that city, 46 percent of widows headed households, compared to about one-third of all seven nonagricultural towns and rural towns with densities above 36 persons per square mile. In contrast, in towns with densities under 19, only one-fifth of widows were householders.

PATTERNS IN THE PROBATE RECORDS

Evidence from the probate records corroborates the Malthusian-frontier patterns that were detected for widows and female householders in the New Hampshire censuses (see table 9.5). First, women made up a relatively small share, 6.7 percent, of those who probated wills; the average elsewhere was 7.4 percent. It should come as no surprise at this point that more than twice the proportion of probated English wills (19.1 percent for five studies) were written by women (Shammas 1989: 138, 140). Economic autonomy is the theme joining the phenomenon of female householding to that of owning property that could be disposed of in a will (Smith 1992a: 424–436). The average inventoried wealth of women leaving wills was only 28 percent of that of male testators. An even smaller fraction (3.1 percent) of intestate decedents whose estates were inventoried were women, and they owned only 1.7 percent of the total wealth of all inventoried New Hampshire decedents, a considerably lower fraction than elsewhere in America; the mean in the studies cited above was 5.4 percent.

Because of uncertainty about the trend in the sex ratio, it is not possible to say if the fraction of women decedents who left wills changed over time. The figure was higher before 1700 (8 percent) and after 1760 (9 percent) than in the intervening six decades (6 percent). The proportion of women dying after age 25 who left wills was tiny at all times, between 1 and 2 percent of adult female decedents.

TABLE 9.5   Incidence and Wealth of New Hampshire Testate and
Intestate Men and Women

					Wealth (adjusted £)[a]		
			With Inventory				Coefficient of
Probate Record	N	%	%	N	Median	Mean	Variation
Wills							
Men	1,357	93.3	52	710	213.2	339.1	1.60
Women	98	6.7	34	33	60.5	96.2	0.90
Both	1,455	100	51	743	207.2	328.9	1.62
Administrations							
Men	1,820	96.5	77	1,407	97.0	174.4	1.48
Women	66	3.5	68	45	56.6	115.8	1.35
Both	1,886	100	77	1,452	95.0	172.6	1.48
Both records							
Men	3,177	95.5	67	2,117	128.6	229.6	1.68
Women	164	4.5	47	78	58.5	107.8	1.23
Both	3,341	100	66	2,195	126.1	225.4	1.69

[a]Wealth figures were adjusted by using the exchange rates in McCusker 1978. For the period
until 1700: 138–139, table 3.1; for 1701–1739: 151, table 3.3; for 1740–1764: 153–154, table
3.4; for 1768–1771: 142, table 3.1. I am indebted to Gloria Main for pointing out the confusing mixture of currencies used between 1765 and 1767; inventories in this three-year period were omitted.

Since women generated such a small share of the records of the probate
courts, it is important to focus on patterns in the records produced by their
husbands, who could shape the extent of economic security and possibility
of autonomy that their widows could enjoy. Overall, only 43 percent of male
decedents found in the probate records left wills, and this fraction represents one-fourth of the males over the age of 25 estimated to have died
(columns 7 and 8 of table 9.6). Of the latter total, 35 percent had their estates administered and 29 percent had inventories taken (columns 10 and
9). Assuming that the events of writing a will and having the estate administered or inventoried were independent, the Chandra Sekar-Deming
method yields the estimate that some of the decedents not appearing in the
probate records (one-fourth of the total, as seen in columns 11 and 12) may
be assumed to be similar in characteristics to those actually present in these
documents (see notes to table 9.6). The residual category includes decedents who presumably were young, unmarried, and without much property
and who, therefore, did not write wills or have their estates administered or
inventoried. It would appear that the fraction of testators is higher after
1750, but this inference depends on the assumptions of a constant death
rate over the entire period and an absence of a shift in biases in estimating

the population at risk to be probated. In particular, the probate records appear to be most nearly complete in coverage during the decade of the 1750s.

Under colonial New Hampshire intestacy law, the probate court appointed an administrator of the estate of the deceased person. The widow was entitled to one-third of the proceeds of each parcel of real estate and one-third of the personal estate. By law, the eldest son received double the share of each of the other children who, regardless of sex, inherited equally. Despite the law, there are instances of what appears to be equal division of land among all the intestate's children. Care was taken by those doing the division not to spoil the property by dividing it into segments too small to sustain a viable enterprise. In these cases, the court would require one of the heirs to compensate his siblings monetarily in exchange for their share of the property, although this transaction was not entered into the probate records.

From table 9.7, columns 3 and 4, it would appear that the widow, if one existed, was usually appointed to administer the estate. For this tendency, the large differential between the poorest and richest wealth category (39 percent vs. 74 percent) is, in all likelihood, due to the fact that richer men were older and more likely to be married. Similarly, wealthier men were more likely to be testate than poorer men (table 9.7, columns 1 and 2), and persons outside the core area of settlement were especially likely to be intestate. Men on the frontier were more likely to be younger, unmarried, and without property.

The lower fraction of widows being appointed administrators in the seventeenth century is probably attributable to the higher incidence of bachelors among men who died intestate in that period than in the next century. Those writing wills rarely expressed the reasons for doing so. On occasion, the testator invokes the norm of harmony among heirs as a reason for making a provision. One presumes that wills were more necessary to preserve equity in cases where some of the children had already received the major portion of their bequest and others had not. That one motivation for a man to write a will was to put someone other than the widow in charge is suggested by the negative impact of the presence of an adult son on the incidence of widows named as executors of their husbands' wills (34 percent vs. 62 percent; table 9.7, columns 6 and 7).

Differences remain among the categories in the analyses that control for the influence of other factors. Indeed, with the exception of the prediction of whether a widow would be named executor of the will of her husband, the strength of each factor is barely reduced by the inclusion of others. Only in the analysis of the incidence of women executors is a direct life course variable available—the presence or absence of an adult son. A more refined indicator of the composition of each decedent's surviving kin might well reduce the remaining differences among temporal, locational, wealth, and occupational categories. However, as in the analysis of female householders in

TABLE 9.6 Estimated Coverage of Male Decedents over Age 25 in New Hampshire Probate Record

| Period Probated | Testate (1) | Intestate[a] | | Estimated Omitted[b] | | Estimated Adult Male Deaths[c] (6) |
		With Inventory (2)	With Administration (3)	No Will or Inventory (4)	No Administration or Inventory (5)	
–1699	138	110	192	73	127	567
1700–1729	179	238	290	168	204	840
1730–1749	289	290	342	292	344	1,416
1750–1759	374	433	480	320	355	1,004
1760–1771	377	442	516	329	385	1,367
Total	1,357	1,513	1,820	1,182	1,415	5,194

	% Testated[d]		% Intestate[e]		% Estimated Omitted[e]		Estimated % Residual (13)
	Of Probated (7)	Of Total (8)	With Inventory (9)	With Administration (10)	No Will or Inventory (11)	No Administrator or Inventory (12)	
–1699	42	24	19	34	13	22	19/43
1700–1729	38	21	28	34	20	24	20/30
1730–1749	46	20	20	24	21	24	31/38
1750–1759	44	37	43	48	32	35	−20/−12
1760–1771	42	28	32	38	24	28	6/16
Total	43	26	29	35	23	27	12/22

[a]The number of intestates with inventories (col. 2) is a subset of the total whose estates were administered (col. 3).

[b]The number omitted (cols. 4 and 5) was estimated using the Chandra Sekar-Deming method that assumes the independence of leaving a will and having the estate inventoried or administered (Shryock and Siegel 1973: 834–836).

[c]The number of adult deaths was estimated using Model North Level 14 mortality (life expectancy at birth of 49 years) and a rate of natural increase of 30 per 1,000 in order to give an upper bound to probate coverage. A guess about the sex ratio was converted into the assumption that males over 25 comprised 21% of the total population before 1700, 20% between 1700 and 1729, 18.6% between 1730 and 1749, 18.1% between 1750 and 1759, and 17.9% after 1760. The average date of each subperiod is 1678, 1717, 1742, 1756, and 1765; for the entire sample, the mean was 1742. Total population estimates are from Rossiter (1909: 9).

[d]Col. 7 equals col. 1 divided by the sum of cols. 1 + 3; col. 8 equals col. 1 divided by col. 6.

[e]Col. 9 equals col. 2 divided by col. 6; col. 10 equals col. 3 divided by col. 6; col. 11 equals col. 4 divided by col. 6; col. 12 equals col. 5 divided by col. 6; col. 13 equals 100% minus the sum of cols. 8, 10, and 12, or 100% minus the sum of cols. 8, 9, and 11.

TABLE 9.7 Multiple Classification Analyses of Incidence of Testation, of Apparent Widows Appointed as Administrator for Intestate Male Decedents, and of Widows Named as Executors by Testate Husbands

Category	All Probated % Testate			Administrations % Widows[a] as Administrator			Wills % Widows as Executors		
	N (1)	Unadjusted (2)	Adjusted (3)	N (4)	Unadjusted (5)	Adjusted (6)	N (7)	Unadjusted (8)	Adjusted (9)
Wealth group[b]									
No inventory	1,149	62[c]	63	413	38	42	480	50	49
Poorest 20%	437	15	17	353	39	39	33	52	44
Low-mid 20%	439	25	25	319	54	53	67	39	36
40–70%	656	36	35	413	66	66	191	40	41
Top 30%	660	50	49	322	76	74	273	41	42
Eta and beta		.35	.34		.29	.27		.10	.09
Period proved									
–1699	349	43	55	192	37[d]	44	103	60	50
1700–1729	486	39	48	290	57	54	142	61	54
1730–1749	667	46	46	342	55	54	223	50	48
1750–1759	884	44	43	480	63	61	287	35	40
1760–1771	955	44	35	516	50	52	289	37	40
Eta and beta		.05	.13		.16	.10		.21	.10
Place of residence[e]									
Portsmouth	635	43	42	334	61	62	168	69	55
Other nonagricultural	587	42	42	320	58	55	174	54	52
Rockingham	1,201	51	51	581	60	57	475	38	42
Scots-Irish	141	62	65	49	41	37	62	18	21
All other	777	30	31	536	43	48	165	41	43
Eta and beta		.18	.17		.16	.12		.27	.16

	N			N			N		
Occupation[f]									
Elite	296	54	53	137	53	52	118	43	46
Artisans	330	54	55	150	63	59	138	56	53
Mariners	185	32	36	125	55	53	39	76	56
Farmers	1,053	51	53	513	54	54	424	31	37
None given	1,477	35	34	895	53	54	325	55	50
Eta and beta		.18	.20		.05	.03		.26	.14
Sex									
Male	3,177	43	42	—	—	—	—	—	—
Female	164	60	66	—	—	—	—	—	—
Eta and beta		.07	.10	—	—	—	—	—	—
Adult son present									
No	—	—	—	—	—	—	369	63	62
Yes	—	—	—	—	—	—	550	33	34
Probably	—	—	—	—	—	—	125	42	44
Eta and beta	—	—	—	—	—	—		.28	.26
Mean (Total N)	(3,341)	43.5		(1,820)	54.2		(1,044)	44.8	
Multiple R²		.190			.114			.179	

[a] Counted as widows were all women with the same surname as the deceased; most were referred to as widows.

[b] Wealth groups defined for combined samples of wills and administrations.

[c] Since the inventory was a major part of the administration of an intestate estimate, this figure should be regarded as an artifact of the difference between type of probate records.

[d] The percentages of widows renouncing the administration in the five periods were 3, 7, 5, 12, and 3.

[e] Residence: Included in the nonagricultural group are the towns of Dover, Exeter, Gosport, New Castle, Rye, and Seabrook. The Rockingham category includes towns not in that county in the previous two groups. In the Scots-Irish group are the towns of Londonderry and Peterborough.

[f] Occupation: In the elite group are gentlemen, professionals, and merchants. Shopkeepers are grouped with artisans, laborers with mariners. Yeoman are the largest group of farmers. Occupations were much more likely to be reported in wills than in the administrations of the intestate.

the census materials, the Malthusian-frontier framework provides a good first approximation but not the complete story.

The most compelling evidence of the need for a more complex framework comes from two communities, Londonderry and Peterborough, that were settled by Scots-Irish immigrants. As was the case for Scots-Irish settlers in colonial New Jersey (Landsman 1985: 155–159), a looser understanding of kinship prevailed in the two towns. As if they sought to avoid the impact of the New Hampshire intestacy statute, decedents in these communities were more likely to leave wills, probate judges were less likely to appoint widows as administrators, and married men seldom chose their wives to execute their wills.

Other differences in table 9.7 also seem quite plausible in terms of variations of normal practice in the operation of family economies. Farmers were particularly unlikely to name their widows as executors of their estates, a pattern more common in nonagricultural towns and occupational groups. It was easier, for example, for a widow to continue the enterprise of an artisan than it was for her to manage a farm household.

The demographic evolution of New Hampshire is apparent in the higher fraction before 1700 of male decedents without an adult son (table 9.8). However, throughout the colonial era, more than three-fourths of men whose wills were probated left a widow. The more marked trend in table 9.8 is not demographic. After 1730, married men with adult sons were much less likely to name their wives as executors. After 1750, this proportion increases for men who had no adult sons. Over time, a wife was less likely to be named the sole executor of her husband's will (final two columns of table 9.8). The trend over the course of the eighteenth century to deny women this important role has been found in other studies of colonial wills (Shammas, Salmon, and Dahlin 1987: 59–60, table 2.12). It would seem that the probate court resisted this trend, continuing to name the widow as the administrator in more than three-fifths of the cases of intestacy during the 1750s (table 9.7, columns 5 and 6). However, as the notes to table 9.7 indicate, widows declined to serve in 12 percent of the cases during that decade, allowing the court to appoint a son or some other person. As no reasons are given for refusal to serve, one can only speculate that both widows and their children in intestacy cases were affected by the same change in values that led men to prefer their sons to their widows as executors of their wills.

Women in eighteenth-century New Hampshire had limited opportunities for autonomy, and their disadvantage was especially marked in the countryside. Legal autonomy was, of course, nearly impossible for married women. Only 3 of the 93 women's wills were written by a wife, while husbands wrote 83 percent of the men's wills (table 9.9). Widows wrote nearly 90 percent of those generated by women. They were only half as likely as

TABLE 9.8   Patterns in Wills of Male Decedents in New Hampshire before 1771

Period Proved	N	Without Wife	Without Adult Son	Excluding Wife as Executor			Wife Only as Executor		Son Named Executor	
				Total	Without Adult Son	With Adult Son	Total	With Adult Son	Total	With Adult Son[a]
–1699	138	25%	46%	40%	36% (45)	43% (58)	45%	31%	27%	49%
1700–1729	179	21	41	39	26 (51)	46 (91)	31	21	35	60
1730–1749	289	23	38	50	31 (77)	60 (146)	32	20	40	64
1750–1759	374	23	33	65	45 (95)	74 (192)	19	8	49	73
1760–1771	377	23	36	66	39 (101)	76 (188)	23	13	47	73
Total	1,357	23	37	55	37 (369)	65 (675)	28	16	42	68

NOTE: Figures in parentheses are the number of cases.
[a]Includes those who named a minor son as executor.

TABLE 9.9 Comparison of New Hampshire Men and Women Will Writers, in Portsmouth and Elsewhere (matched sample)

Category	Women			Men			p^b
	Portsmouth	Elsewhere	Total	Portsmouth	Elsewhere	Total	
Marital status	(40)	(52)	(92)	(15)	(77)	(92)	.001
Widowed	95%	85%	89%	13%	12%	12%	
Single	3	11	8	7	5	5	
Married	3	4	3	80	83	83	
Used seal	12 (41)	8 (52)	10 (93)	27 (15)	17 (78)	18 (93)	.14
Literacy	37 (40)	33 (51)	35 (91)	92 (12)	62 (77)	66 (89)	.001
Revokes previous will or adds codicil	46 (41)	29 (52)	36 (93)	53 (15)	42 (78)	44 (93)	.37
Mentions physical state	(41)	(52)	(93)	(15)	(78)	(93)	.42
None	20	23	21	13	18	17	
Good health	2	4	3	7	5	5	
Aged (any note)	17	8	12	7	6	6	
Other debility	61	65	64	73	71	72	
Male executors	84 (37)	90 (49)	87 (86)	55 (15)	74 (77)	71 (92)	.01
Male witnesses	73 (41)	90 (52)	82 (93)	93 (15)	94 (78)	94 (93)	.01
Son present	53 (41)	69 (52)	62 (93)	80 (15)	87 (78)	87 (93)	.001
Adult son	49 (41)	63 (52)	57 (93)	47 (15)	76 (74)	71 (89)	.05
Daughter present	59 (41)	71 (52)	66 (93)	66 (15)	81 (78)	79 (93)	.07
Son(s) and daughter(s) present	(17)	(33)	(50)	(10)	(64)	(74)	.01
Favors son(s)	29	48	42	60	72	70	
Favors daughter(s)	18	24	22	0	5	4	
No preference	53	27	36	40	23	26	

	(41)	(52)	(93)	(15)	(78)	(93)	[b]
Bequests to[a]							
Extended kin	66	71	69	33	36	35	.001
Substantial	43	54	49	13	22	20	.001
Nonkin	24	19	22	20	9	11	.07
Charity	5	6	5	13	3	4	.99
Property left to widow				(12)	(64)	(76)	
More than one-third				50	48	49	.99
Same or less than one-third				33	27	28	
Unclear				17	25	24	
Terms of endearment for							
Wife	14 (29)	20 (39)	18 (68)	91 (11)	92 (64)	92 (75)	
Child	20	13	13	15 (13)	33 (69)	30 (82)	.10
Other	12 (41)	13 (52)	13 (93)	20 (15)	10 (78)	12 (93)	.99

NOTE: Figures in parentheses are the total number of cases.

[a] Extended kin category includes all persons designated as related except spouses and children. The largest group is grandchildren, especially those of deceased children.

[b] Significance level of difference between men and women.

men to sign their names to their wills (35 percent vs. 66 percent) and to attach a seal to their testament (10 percent vs. 18 percent).

Their families were also different. In their wills, only three-fifths of the women mentioned a son and two-thirds a daughter, compared to 87 percent and 79 percent, respectively, for men. Their pattern of bequests was also markedly different, often due in part to the absence of children. Women were twice as likely as men to give to someone other than immediate nuclear kin (69 percent vs. 35 percent) and to unrelated persons (22 percent vs. 11 percent). Women with children were a bit less likely to refer to them in terms of endearment than were men, confounding notions of a greater sentimental maternal than paternal attachment to children (table 9.9). Love was focused on dependents. One New Hampshire minister warned his wife that "Her Bowells [are] more likely to yearn towards Her children [from her first marriage], then theyrs toward theyre mother" (Will of Seaborn Cotton of Hampton, May 20, 1684; New Hampshire 1913: 276). Nearly all husbands (92 percent) referred to their wives as "beloved," "dearly beloved," and so on, since wives, unlike children, were permanently dependent.

Certain elements were, however, common to the wills of both men and women. As in New England generally, very few (5 percent) made a charitable bequest. Judging by the terms used in the preamble of the will to describe physical state, debility (indicated by such phrases as "sick" or "sick and weak"), not old age, prompted both to write their wills. Although the date of death of the testators is not known, exactly a year passed on average between the dating of the will and its arrival in probate court. And for nearly two-fifths, the will finally probated was a revision of a previous document.

In the matched will sample, the distinctive features of Portsmouth stand out. An astonishing 43 percent of wills written by women in New Hampshire came from that city compared to 16 percent of wills produced by men, a phenomenon consistent with the high householding rate for widows in the city in 1790. Inventoried Portsmouth women were wealthier than their rural counterparts, a difference not apparent for men, although urban women were not more literate than their rural counterparts. Portsmouth women, however, were not more likely than rural women to make bequests beyond the immediate family (to extended kin and nonkin). For both urban men and women, there is a hint of more egalitarian treatment of sons and daughters, a pattern that has been glimpsed elsewhere in New England (Ditz 1986).

SUMMARY

The frontier in American history did represent an increase in freedom for some—but not for all. Using indirect evidence from census materials and probate records, this chapter has outlined central features of the phenomenon of widowhood in New Hampshire in the eighteenth century. Because of the high fertility and nuptiality of the Malthusian-frontier demographic regime, there were relatively few widows and older persons in the population, especially in the low-density, recently settled areas.

On balance, the frontier does not pass the tests of increasing opportunities for widows (see Main 1989). It is possible that remarriage rates were higher on the frontier. Yet since these rates usually fall precipitously with age (Smith 1989), the low ratio of widows to married women may be entirely the result of a younger age structure and an earlier age at bereavement. Widows were less likely to be householders in frontier areas than in longer-settled rural areas.

One may possibly interpret the greater role played by seventeenth-century widows as a positive impact of the frontier. In the absence of adult sons or other kin who could be trusted, this interpretation suggests that husbands in early New Hampshire had to rely more on their wives. However, widows of men with surviving adult sons were less likely to be named executors in wills written just before the revolution than in the early decades of settlement. That is, controlling for one important demographic consequence of the early frontier environment, a change is still apparent.

The cross-sectional evidence yields a clearer verdict for the negative impact of the frontier on widows. Both the patterns in the incidence of female householding in the late-eighteenth-century census data and the evidence from the probate records point to a lesser role for widows on the frontier. Increasingly over time, and outside of the more commercial towns (especially Portsmouth), widows had relatively little autonomy, being less likely to serve as the executors of their husbands' wills and less likely to head households in 1790. Rather, widows were typically made dependents of their sons, which usually involved the transmission of ownership and control of the farm. While such an arrangement provided security for widows, at the same time it limited their autonomy. It was in the city, whether because of the nature of economic activity or because of more favorable attitudes, that widows enjoyed greater possibilities for autonomy.

Reconciliation of the apparent conflict between the temporal and cross-sectional patterns probably requires the introduction of an additional variable. With the limited data available in this analysis, such an additional factor cannot be established. Possibly, the reduced role of the widow in the execution of her husband's estate may be traced to a change in attitudes with respect to gender deriving from the waning of the Puritan emphasis on the centrality of the married couple in the family. However, the declining tendency of probate court judges to appoint widows as administrators was not so marked as the decreasing tendency of husbands to name their wives as executors. This is surprising, since one would expect judges to apply a normative standard, while husbands' decisions would be based more on spe-

cific circumstances. Better qualitative information on changes in the func-
tioning of the family economic enterprise in the century before the American Revolution also might resolve the paradox. Finally, the trend in these
New Hampshire data toward a lesser role for widows may point to a larger
problem of change in family history. Many phenomena, seemingly rooted
in the particularities of a time and place, exhibit parallel patterns in dis-
parate parts of the early modern Euro-American world.

NOTES

I am much indebted to Terry Ann Nissly for research assistance on the New
Hampshire probate records.

1. The original schedules are not extant. Also returned by towns were the numbers of unmarried men from age 16 to 60; married men from age 16 to 60; boys aged
16 years and under; men aged 60 years and upward; and male and female slaves
(Rossiter [1909] 1966: 149–151, tables 76 and 77). The first federal census of 1790
only recorded information on white males under and over age 16, white females, all
other free persons, and slaves; the extant manuscript returns have been published
(U.S. Bureau of the Census 1907). Tax data for 1790 are from Belknap (1970):
II:226–242. I am indebted to Charles Wetherell for a machine-readable copy of the
colonial censuses of 1767 and 1773 and the 1790 U.S. census returns for New Hampshire towns.

2. The figures are as follows:

		Settled Towns		Density per Square Mile	
Year	Population	Number	Area	In Towns	Statewide[a]
1767	52,720	94	3,151	16.7	5.9
1773	73,097	136	5,022	14.5	8.1
1790	141,899	195	6,587	21.5	15.8

[a]New Hampshire = 8,981 square miles.

REFERENCES

Belknap, Jeremy. [1784–1792. 3 vols.] 1970. *The history of New Hampshire*. Reprint of
    the 2-volume 1831 edition. New York: Johnson Reprint Corporation.
Coale, Ansley, and Paul Demeny. 1966. *Regional model life tables and stable populations*.
    Princeton: Princeton University Press.
Ditz, Toby L. 1986. *Property and kinship: Inheritance in early Connecticut, 1750–1820*.
    Princeton: Princeton University Press.
Domar, Evsey D. 1970. "The causes of slavery or serfdom: A hypothesis." *Journal of
    Economic History* 30: 18–32.

Dupâquier, J., A. Fauve-Chamoux, and E. Grebenik, eds. 1983. *Malthus past and present*. New York: Academic Press.

Guttentag, Marcia, and Paul F. Secord. 1983. *Too many women? The sex ratio question*. Beverly Hills, Calif.: Sage.

Landsman, Ned C. 1985. *Scotland and its first American colony, 1683–1765*. Princeton: Princeton University Press.

Lee, Ronald, D., W. Brian Arthur, Allen C. Kelley, Gerry Rodgers, and T. N. Srinivasan, eds. 1988. *Population, food and rural development*. Oxford: Clarendon Press.

McCoy, Drew R. 1987. "James Madison and visions of American nationality in the confederation period: A regional perspective." In *Beyond confederation: Origins of the Constitution and American national identity*, ed. Richard Beeman, Stephen Botein, and Edward C. Carter II, 226–258. Chapel Hill: University of North Carolina Press.

McCusker, John J. 1978. *Money and exchange in Europe and America, 1600–1765*. Chapel Hill: University of North Carolina Press.

McCusker, John J., and Russell R. Menard. 1985. *The economy of British America, 1607–1789*. Chapel Hill: University of North Carolina Press.

Main, Gloria. 1989. "Widows in rural Massachusetts on the eve of the revolution." In *Women in the age of the American Revolution*, ed. Ronald Hoffman and Peter J. Albert, 67–90. Charlottesville: University Press of Virginia.

Malthus, Thomas Robert. [1798] 1960. *An essay on the principle of population, as it affects the future improvement of society*. New York: Modern Library.

New Hampshire. 1913–1941. *Provincial and state papers*, vols. 31–39. *Probate records of the province of New Hampshire*, vols. 1–9. Manchester: State of New Hampshire.

Rossiter, W. S. [1909] 1966. *A century of population growth from the first census of the United States to the twelfth, 1790–1900*. New York: Johnson Reprint Corporation.

Rutman, Darrett B. 1975. "People in process: The New Hampshire towns of the eighteenth century." *Journal of Urban History* 1: 268–292.

Shammas, Carole. 1989. "Early American women and control over capital." In *Women in the age of the American Revolution*, ed. Ronald Hoffman and Peter J. Albert, 134–154. Charlottesville: University Press of Virginia.

Shammas, Carole, Marylynn Salmon, and Michel Dahlin. 1987. *Inheritance in America from colonial times to the present*. New Brunswick: Rutgers University Press.

Shryock, Henry S., and Jacob S. Siegel. 1973. *The methods and materials of demography*. Washington, D.C.: Government Printing Office.

Smith, Daniel Scott. 1980. "A Malthusian-frontier interpretation of United States demographic history before c. 1815." In *Urbanization in the Americas: The background in historical perspective*, ed. Woodrow W. Borah, Jorge Hardoy, and Gilbert A. Stelter, 15–24. Ottawa: National Museum of Man.

———. 1981. "Historical change in the household structure of the elderly in economically developed societies." In *Aging: Stability and change in the family*, ed. Robert W. Fogel, Elaine Hatfield, Sara B. Kiesler, and Ethel Shanas, 91–114. New York: Academic Press.

———. 1989. "Inheritance and the social history of early American women." In *Women in the age of the American Revolution*, ed. Ronald Hoffman and Peter J. Albert, 45–66. Charlottesville: University Press of Virginia.

————. 1992*a*. "Female householding in late eighteenth-century America and the problem of poverty." *Journal of Social History* 28 (Fall 1994).

————. 1992*b*. "Change and continuity in the meanings of family and household." *Population and Development Review* 18: 421–456.

Thompson, Roger. 1974. *Women in Stuart England and America*. London: Routledge and Kegan Paul.

Turner, Frederick Jackson. [1894] 1961. "The significance of the frontier in American history." In *Frontier and section: Selected essays of Frederick Jackson Turner*. Englewood Cliffs, N.J.: Prentice-Hall.

U.S. Bureau of the Census. 1907. *Heads of families at the first census of the United States taken in the year 1790: New Hampshire*. Washington, D.C.: Government Printing Office.

Wall, Richard. 1981. "Women alone in English society." *Annales de démographie historique* 16: 303–317.

Wetherell, Charles. 1977. "A note on hierarchical clustering." *Historical Methods Newsletter* 10: 109–116.

Wrigley, E. A., and R. S. Schofield. 1981. *The population history of England, 1541–1871*. Cambridge: Harvard University Press.

Zagarri, Rosemarie. 1987. *The politics of size: Representation in the United States, 1776–1850*. Ithaca: Cornell University Press.

TEN

Transition to Widowhood and Family Support Systems in the Twentieth Century, Northeastern United States

Tamara K. Hareven and Peter Uhlenberg

Adult life in the early twentieth century in the United States occurred in a context of high mortality, low divorce, economic dependence of married women on their husbands, and almost nonexistent public welfare measures to support dependent persons. Because of high mortality and low divorce, women surviving past midlife commonly experienced widowhood (Uhlenberg 1978). Economic dependence of married women on their husbands meant that widowhood would involve a dramatic transition in the life course of women (Chudacoff and Hareven 1978, 1979). The lack of social welfare programs meant that the state or other agencies in the public sector would not assume much responsibility for the economic support of widows. Under these conditions widows had to develop particular strategies for coping with the challenges thrust on them by their husbands' deaths.

Young women who were socialized in the early twentieth century had the opportunity to observe the coping strategies employed by widows in their families and used these models in formulating their expectations of how their own futures might unfold. By the time these women actually experienced widowhood later in their lives, however, the social environment was remarkably different. Each of the contextual variables mentioned above changed significantly over the lifetime of these women: mortality declined, divorce increased, economic independence of women increased, and social welfare measures expanded. The experiences of widowhood for women born in the early 1900s would have been considerably different from those of other widows they observed, therefore, during their childhood.

In this chapter we examine changes in the life course positions of widows, their status and their support networks, among several cohorts of white American women over this century. To trace changes in the transition to widowhood across the twentieth century, we employ two diverse but complementary data sets. Quantitative data are drawn from the public use samples of the U.S. census, and qualitative life history data are drawn from extensive interviews conducted in Manchester, New Hampshire (Hareven 1982). From an analysis of the public use samples from the 1910, 1940, and 1970 U.S. censuses we gain cross-sectional perspectives on labor force participation and living arrangements of widows at different time periods. To increase compatibility with life history data from Manchester, New Hampshire, our population sample from the census is restricted to white women living in the Northeast, excluding New York City.[1] The census variables of particular interest, in addition to work and household composition, are the widow's age and the number of living children she had.

The qualitative data source comes from extensive life history interviews with three cohorts of men and women from Manchester, New Hampshire, whose combined lives span the period from the 1880s to the present. Hareven and her associates collected rich retrospective life histories from these respondents in the period 1980–1985. Their three- to four-hour interviews of each person (repeated three times) include memories of childhood, family relations, and the status of older family members and their caring strategies and support networks in the later years of life, as well as of the milieu within which they formulated their childhood expectations regarding their future lives. These interviews also include accounts of personal experiences of widowhood occurring later in the century. By weaving together demographic data from the censuses and the detailed life experiences of selected individuals, we hope to gain a better understanding of how women experienced and perceived the transition to widowhood in the twentieth century.[2]

INCIDENCE OF WIDOWHOOD

Considerable change in age-specific incidence of widowhood has occurred over this century. The prevalence of widows among ever-married women at various ages in 1910, 1940, and 1970 is shown in figure 10.1. Widowhood during young adulthood was relatively uncommon in 1910. About 13 percent of ever-married women aged 35–39 had experienced the disruption of their first marriage, and 7 percent were classified as currently widowed. After age 45, the ratio of widowed to ever-married women grew rapidly. About one-fifth of ever-married women aged 50 in 1910 were widows, but more than half of those aged 65–69 were widows.

As mortality rates declined over the twentieth century, the incidence of widowhood decreased at every age (fig. 10.1). For example, the proportion of widows among ever-married woman aged 35–39 declined by 50 percent between 1910 and 1940, and by 1970, only 2 percent were in this category. In each time period examined here, the incidence of widowhood rises with

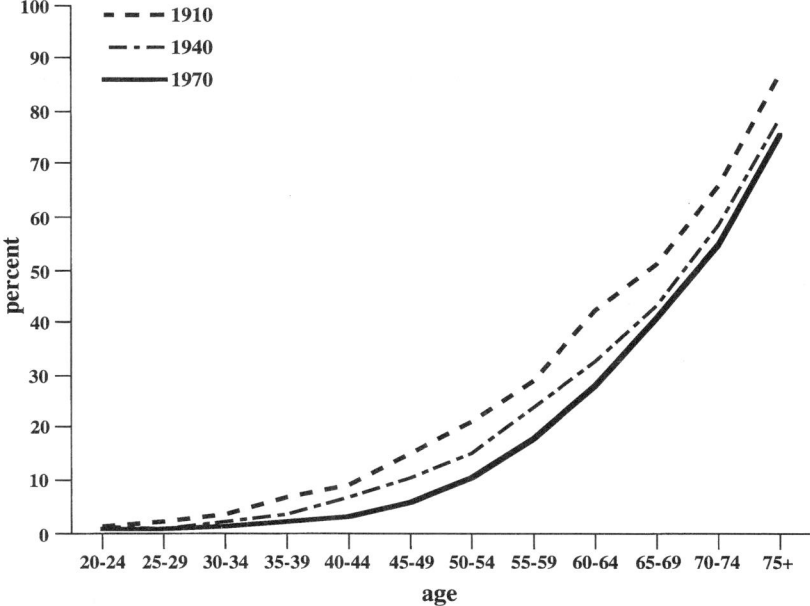

Fig. 10.1. Ever-married white women in the northeastern United States who were widows, by age: U.S. census, 1910, 1940, and 1970.

age. Increasingly over time, widowhood became associated with later life. In 1940, widowhood did not become the modal experience until around age 70, and by 1970, the tipping point was well past age 70.

A woman's life course position at the time she loses her husband clearly has important implications for her experience as a widow. To be a young widow is different from being an old widow, and being a widow with children is different from being a childless widow, young or old. These two life course variables—age and number of children at the time of becoming a widow—are available from census records, and analysis begins with these two factors. How did age and number of children affect the work experience and living arrangements of widows in different historical time periods? After exploring these issues in the census data, we integrate these patterns of working and living arrangements with the available qualitative data from the ethnographic materials.

YOUNG WIDOWS

Since widowhood early in life has not been common in the twentieth century, young widows have been forced to cope with an unexpected life course transition. A substantial proportion of women widowed before age 40 escaped this status by remarrying. About as many women aged 20–39 in 1910 were in second or higher-order marriages as were in the widowed state, suggesting that half or more of all young widows remarried. The proportion remarrying among the cohort born around 1910 was probably even higher since age-specific remarriage rates increased over most of this century. (The low divorce rate leads us to assume that most of these second marriages followed the death of a spouse, rather than divorce.) Among women aged 30–34 in 1940, 5.3 percent were in higher-order marriages, while only 3.4 percent were either widowed or divorced. An examination of census data on remarried women reveals that their living arrangements and work experiences were very similar to women of comparable ages in first marrying. Thus young women who escaped widowhood by remarriage probably reestablished lives not very dissimilar to those of married women.

The lives of young widows who did not remarry, however, were quite different from those of either never-married or married women in 1910. (See table 10.1 data on young widows.) Compared with the never married, widows more frequently headed their own households, especially if they had children. Over two-thirds of the young widows with more than one child maintained separate households. Young widows were much more likely than married women to reside in their parents' households. Among women aged 20–39 with two or more living children, 22 percent of widows but only 4 percent of married women lived with parents.

Interestingly, young widows were no more likely to head their own households in 1940 than were their counterparts in 1910. Indeed, a larger proportion of young widows with children were living with parents in 1940. Statistics for 1940 are based on a relatively small sample, 68 widows, but there is a plausible explanation for why a larger proportion of young widows may have lived with parents at this time. A larger proportion of young widows had parents with whom they could potentially live. Decreasing mortality meant that more young adults had surviving parents, and fewer widows in 1940 were foreign born without parents living in the United States. By 1970, despite the fact that more parents were potentially available for co-residence, most young widows with two or more children (almost 90 percent) were heads of their own households, and only 4 percent lived with parents. Norms of independent living had prevailed.

A clear indication of the precarious economic circumstances encountered by young widows in 1910 is their high labor force participation rate recorded in the census. Reflecting the strong norm censoring mothers working outside the home, only 5 percent of married women with children were in the labor force. By contrast, over 60 percent of the widows with children were recorded as gainfully employed. The great majority of these widows held low-status jobs classified as machine operators or service workers.

TABLE 10.1 Distribution of Widowed Women in the Northeast Aged 20–39: Occupational Status and Relationship to Household Head, by Number of Children, 1910, 1940, 1970

	No Children			1 Child			2+ Children		
	1910	1940	1970	1910	1940	1970	1910	1940	1970
Occupation									
Not in labor force	30.9%	25.4%	20.4%	39.5%	25.7%	36.4%	38.5%	58.6%	44.3%
White collar	12.7	21.9	57.4	11.6	22.1	33.9	12.6	15.3	29.4
Blue collar	56.4	52.7	22.2	48.8	52.2	29.7	48.9	26.1	26.3
Relationship									
Head	29.1	27.7	70.4	38.4	29.4	75.4	68.1	63.6	88.5
Daughter	25.5	44.4	13.9	34.9	47.1	15.3	15.6	24.2	4.3
Sister	3.6	0.0	8.3	5.8	0.0	3.4	5.2	3.0	1.2
Boarder/lodger	25.5	11.1	0.9	7.0	5.9	0.0	3.0	3.0	0.6
Other	16.3	16.7	6.5	13.9	17.6	5.9	8.1	6.1	5.4
Total N	55	18	108	86	17	118	135	33	323

The proportion of widows with two or more children in the labor force was down to about 40 percent by 1940, when slightly larger numbers of married women tended to be in the labor force. This drop in employment of young widows with children reflects their increasing ability to support their families without working outside of the home. In 1970, when the norm against mothers working had relaxed greatly, the proportion of young widowed mothers who were in the labor force was still below the 1910 level. This drop in employment also could reflect the increasing difficulty that widows had in finding child care.

Because the experience of widowhood early in life was uncommon, not many of the Manchester, New Hampshire, respondents fell in this category. The experiences of the few young widows with children in this industrial community who did not remarry, however, are revealing. Consistent with expectations from the census data, these widows tended to head their own households and work in the textile mills. Those who did not have kin available to help with child care often placed their children in the St. Pierre Orphanage, which served as a surrogate day care center. In some cases, the mothers picked up the children after work; in other cases, they left the children there for extended periods and took them home on holidays and weekends only (Hareven 1982).

Hester Smith, for example, who came from Vermont to Manchester at age 17 to work in the mills, was widowed after two and one-half years of marriage and was pregnant when her husband died. She took a job as a weaver, which her deceased husband's former boss offered her when she came to pick up her husband's last paycheck. Because she needed money and her family could not help her, she worked at this job until two weeks before she had the child. Her mother took care of her when she gave birth and then took the baby with her back to the farm so that Hester could work in a shoe factory. The child eventually became too active for Hester's mother, and Hester had to take the child back. She had difficulty finding baby-sitters but finally found the St. Pierre Orphanage in Manchester and kept her daughter there until she was 10, after which she took her along to the factory. During her early widowhood, Hester received help from her brother, Vernon, who had also come to work in the shoe factory in Manchester. Vernon had taken care of Hester when she was a little girl and once saved her from drowning.

Hester never remarried, and her subsequent life provides an example of one woman's evolving survival strategy. In her old age, she was cared for by her grandson and his wife. Her daughter, who did not finish high school, worked in a shoe factory until she married. On marriage, Hester's daughter and her husband moved into Hester's upstairs tenement. Her daughter lived with her "as long as she needed [a roof over her head]," but Hester was not involved with child care. The daughter had a district nurse to take care of her babies. Later Hester's granddaughter and her husband moved into her apartment. Hester, however, preferred to live alone and finally asked them to leave.

In her old age, Hester made an agreement with her grandson and his wife that they would inherit her house in exchange for taking care of her. After the couple divorced, they both continued to take care of Hester and she willed one-half of the house to each of them. She named her grandson executor of her will, and he alone was to inherit her summer cottage in New Hampshire. "She [the grandson's former wife] brings me to the store. And if I'm sick he'll [the grandson] take care of me. And they are supposed to take care of me when I'm sick; not send me to the hospital or in a rest home. Take care of me here! And they get the property equally when I'm dead."

The life course patterns of women who became widowed in the later years of life were considerably different from those of young widows who never remarried. Women widowed in old age later in this century were supported by their husbands' incomes during their marriages and possibly by pensions after their husbands' death. They also benefited from services and supports provided by their husbands through their lives, which served as important resources in their later years of life. Women widowed at a younger age who never remarried brought fewer resources into old age, because they had to work single-handedly while raising children. Older widows, who had not been employed, found reentry into the labor force difficult. Younger widows who already had jobs had the advantage of continuing a "career" after their husbands' death.

Younger widows who never remarried may have formed more intensive kinship ties and support networks over their life course, because they depended on kin assistance much more than married women. Married couples often tried to maintain some independence, while widows needed more intense relations with their kinship networks to survive. Women who were widowed at a younger age thus could rely in their old age on assistance from kinship networks with whom they had engaged in reciprocal relations over their life course.

MIDDLE-AGED WIDOWS

Widowhood was a relatively common status for middle-aged women in 1910: almost one-third of the ever-married women aged 55–59 were widows. These middle-aged widows were less likely to participate in the labor force than younger widows, but they worked more often than married women of any age. Half of the widows with one child or no child were gainfully employed, while 30 percent of those with two or more children had jobs (see table 10.2). Similar to younger widows, those who participated in the labor force were concentrated in lower-status occupations. Further, it seems likely that some of the jobs that middle-aged widows could obtain, such as work-

TABLE 10.2 Distribution of Widowed Women in the Northeast Aged 40–59: Occupational Status and Relationship to Household Head, by Number of Children, 1910, 1940, 1970

	No Children			1 Child			2+ Children		
	1910	1940	1970	1910	1940	1970	1910	1940	1970
Occupation									
Not in labor force	45.3%	45.5%	29.5%	51.0%	48.8%	31.5%	69.5%	69.4%	34.9%
White collar	6.5	19.7	40.2	9.5	17.1	38.5	4.7	6.9	35.0
Blue collar	48.2	34.8	30.3	39.5	34.1	30.0	25.8	23.7	30.0
Relationship									
Head	42.9	52.5	82.0	56.7	61.4	80.8	75.7	78.2	86.7
Daughter	10.0	8.8	4.8	7.1	3.6	3.5	2.8	2.0	1.6
Mother	2.3	2.5	1.2	14.8	15.7	7.7	12.6	11.4	7.5
Sister	11.2	10.0	6.1	6.2	7.2	3.4	1.5	3.0	1.7
Boarder/lodger	16.5	5.0	1.7	5.7	2.4	1.0	2.4	1.3	0.4
Other	17.1	21.3	4.2	9.5	9.6	3.6	5.0	7.4	2.1
Total N	170	80	756	210	83	909	675	298	3,019

ing as maids and taking in laundry, may have been underrecorded in the census. Widows aged 40–59 in 1910 also were more likely than younger ones to head their own households, although more than 10 percent of these middle-aged widows were co-residing with a child who was household head.

While the likelihood of being widowed had decreased by 1940, middle-aged widows in 1940 were remarkably similar to their 1910 counterparts in labor force behavior and living arrangements. Both in 1910 and 1940, 70 percent of the widows with two or more children were not in the labor force, and 75 percent were heads of their own households. After 1940, however, major changes occurred in the characteristics of middle-aged widows. By 1970, only one-third of the middle-aged widows with children were not gainfully employed, and the occupational status of those who were in the labor force had improved markedly. Further, more widows in 1970 maintained their own households, and fewer were living with parents or other relatives. These changes after 1940 may reflect the growth of the welfare state, the increasing acceptance of gainful employment for mothers, and changing norms about independent living.

Remarriage among middle-aged widows in the United States has not been common, but a surprisingly large number of women in the Manchester interviews reported having remarried in their middle age and even in their 60s. This pattern suggests the importance of considering community-level variations in life course transitions. Widowers in the right age range appear to have been available in Manchester. They were actively seeking marriage partners, because they could not conceive of living alone and taking care of themselves. It is also possible that strong kinship ties and ethnic community networks, centered on churches and ethnic clubs, provided men and women with opportunities to meet partners and facilitated the remarriage of widows. In many cases, the second spouse was someone the widow had already known for many years or someone to whom she was remotely related.

Of course, many of the widows did not remarry, some claiming that this was a deliberate choice. Several of the middle-aged widows interviewed in Manchester indicated that they had come to like their independence and their social life. Others either had experienced a bad marriage and were anxious about repeating the experience or had spent a considerable portion of their middle age nursing a sick husband and did not want to fall back into a similar situation. Still others claimed they had been too devoted to the memory of their husbands to contemplate replacing them.

Since these data are based on retrospective interviews, one cannot be entirely sure whether the women who claimed a preference for not remarrying had actually encountered a viable choice and rejected it or whether they were using this explanation as a rationalization. In some cases, caretaking daughters preferred that their mothers remarry. Lucille Spiro (born 1917), for example, was frustrated with her mother's preference not to remarry, and she felt that she had facilitated her mother's choice by providing her with a comfortable existence in her old age. Lucille speculated that had she not supported her mother financially, her mother might have made an effort to remarry.

Childless widows were more likely to work and less likely to be household heads than widows with surviving children, both in 1910 and 1970. One might expect widows with no surviving children to have work and household arrangements similar to those of the never-married women, since both groups were without a husband and children. But this was not the case. Compared with the never married, childless widows in 1910 were twice as likely to live as boarders in other people's households and only half as likely to live with parents or siblings. In 1970, the never-married women were five times more likely than childless widows to live with parents and twice as likely to live with other kin.

The greater tendency of the never-married women to live with kin than to board with unrelated individuals may reflect the fact that some of these women established co-residence with kin earlier in life—a pattern that persisted into later life. Alternatively, it may have been the result of the fact that they had initially lost their opportunity to marry because they stayed in the parental household to take care of younger siblings or aging parents. Childless widows also tended to be employed in more inferior jobs compared with the never married, probably indicating the disadvantage of reentering the labor force in middle age. These findings hint at the possibility that childless widows, more than any other category of widows, may not have fit comfortably into existing work and residential arrangements preferred by women.

OLDER WIDOWS

Throughout the twentieth century, widowhood has been an expected status for women in the later years of life. This does not, however, imply homogeneity among older widows. Economic status, kinship networks, and age all significantly influence the experience of widowhood in old age. Some older women worked to support themselves, but labor force participation was always much less common among those aged 60–69 than among the middle-aged (table 10.3). Further, employment rates declined sharply with age among older widows, so that relatively few (less than 10 percent) of those past age 70 continued to work. A minority of older women were able to live comfortable lives without working because of substantial economic assets brought into old age. The great majority, however, looked to kin as an important source of support. This was especially true earlier in this century before social security entered the picture.

TABLE 10.3 Distribution of Widowed Women in the Northeast Aged 60+: Labor Force Status and Relationship to Household Head, by Age and Number of Children, 1910, 1940, 1970

	No Children			1 Child			2+ Children		
	1910	1940	1970	1910	1940	1970	1910	1940	1970
In labor force									
60–69	29.4%	18.6%	37.3%	20.1%	22.4%	36.3%	14.2%	13.1%	31.5%
70–79	10.5	11.1	10.4	6.6	0.0	11.1	6.8	4.6	6.8
80+	3.3	20.0	4.5	1.9	0.0	4.2	3.0	1.8	3.0
Relationship									
60–69 Head	52.1	65.7	83.2	48.8	53.5	76.0	54.3	65.3	75.7
Mother	2.5	4.3	1.6	34.8	20.7	14.8	37.3	24.3	18.6
Sister	6.7	10.0	7.1	1.8	5.2	4.6	1.1	1.9	1.8
Boarder	10.1	2.9	1.1	4.9	12.1	0.5	3.0	2.3	0.5
Institution	3.4	2.9	2.0	3.1	0.0	1.9	0.0	0.8	1.7
Other	25.2	14.3	5.1	6.7	8.6	2.2	4.3	5.4	1.7
70–79 Head	51.2	55.6	79.2	41.2	47.6	68.0	49.1	49.8	63.6
Mother	4.7	4.8	1.9	45.6	42.9	22.0	44.1	39.5	27.9
Sister	9.3	11.1	6.0	2.6	3.2	2.6	0.5	3.4	1.7
Boarder	9.3	7.5	1.5	4.4	3.2	0.6	2.9	2.3	0.5
Institution	4.7	9.5	6.8	0.9	1.6	4.3	0.5	2.3	4.7
Other	20.9	11.1	4.7	5.3	1.6	2.5	2.9	2.7	1.6
80+ Head	40.0	26.7	58.1	30.8	38.9	43.7	38.4	35.8	41.7
Mother	10.0	13.3	3.5	46.2	44.4	32.8	57.3	45.9	38.4
Sister	6.7	6.7	5.9	0.0	0.0	2.6	0.0	6.4	1.3
Boarder	13.3	6.7	1.4	7.7	5.6	0.9	0.6	4.6	0.9
Institution	10.0	13.3	23.3	1.9	5.6	16.0	0.6	5.5	14.8
Other	20.0	33.3	7.8	13.5	5.6	4.1	3.0	1.8	2.9
Total N	235	148	3,006	330	139	3,251	1,088	629	11,986

Among older widowed mothers in 1910, only two types of living arrangements were common. More than 90 percent of these widows were either the head of a household (which usually contained a child or other relative) or the mother of the household head. At ages 60–69 more were head than mother of head, while at the oldest ages the ranking was reversed. In other words, the likelihood of living as a dependent in a child's home increased as widows moved into the latest stage of old age. By 1970, more than three-fourths of widowed mothers aged 60–69 were heading their own households, and a majority of these were living alone. As was true earlier, the proportion living in a child's house increased with age. But a new pattern is apparent by 1970: a significant proportion (15 percent) of widowed mothers past age 80 were living in nursing homes.

Compared to widowed mothers of similar ages, older childless widows have experienced greater diversity in living arrangements. Childless widows were similar to mothers in their propensity to head their own households, but they lacked the option of living with a child. Consequently, more childless widows lived with siblings, in boardinghouses, in institutions, and in other arrangements. Over time, the proportion of childless widows living with a sibling has remained fairly constant, while the proportions heading their own household and living in institutions has grown at the expense of other options. It is noteworthy that by 1970 almost one-fourth of childless widows past age 80 were living in nursing homes.

A theme that repeatedly came up in the interviews with older widows and older people in general was their insistence on maintaining as much autonomy as possible, expressed in heading their own household. This was the overwhelming preference of older couples, and it persisted for women after they lost their husbands. Widows, even more than widowers, preferred to live alone rather than to be a dependent in someone else's home. To maintain this kind of autonomy, they desired to live near kin. This is illustrated by Lois Bell (born 1901) who moved back to Manchester from Ohio eleven years after her second husband died. Her brother in Manchester, who was about to have an operation, encouraged her to come home. "They didn't want me out up there alone." Her nieces and other family members also encouraged her to come back. By the time she returned to Manchester, her brother had died.

The preference for maintaining household headship raises two questions related to living arrangements of older widows. First, what strategies did widows who headed their own households employ to maintain these households? Second, among widows with children, did the number of living children affect living arrangements? One might anticipate that as the number of children increased, the odds of living with a child would increase. After examining census and ethnographic data to shed light on these questions, we explore in greater detail the residential patterns of widows.

Number of Children and Living Arrangements of Older Widows

Was there a positive association between the number of children an older widow had and the likelihood that she received assistance from a child? Using a sample of census manuscripts from the 1900 U.S. census, Daniel Scott Smith (1979) examined the relationship between the number of living children an older widow had and the likelihood that she was living with a child. He reports two intriguing results. First, over three-fourths of the older widows who had children were living with a child. Second, the probability of a widow living with a child in her later years of life was not much affected by the number of surviving children she had. He concludes that "the motive of old age insurance did not require high fertility from nineteenth-century American women—one child was nearly as good as five" (294).

In the 1910 census public use sample we have slightly more than twice as many cases as Smith had from the 1900 sample. Our sample is limited, though, to the Northeast. Similar to Smith's findings, in our data from the 1910 census, we find that over three-fourths of all older widows were living with children (table 10.4). The cultural norm for adult children to support their aging parents, especially widowed mothers, was very strong to produce this level of conformity.[3] In contrast to Smith's findings, our analysis shows that the number of living children was a relevant factor from widows in 1910. The likelihood of a widow living with a child increased from 62 percent for those with one child to 78 percent for those with two to four children and to 89 percent for widows with five or more children. Expressed in another way, the likelihood of not having a child reside in the same household was three times greater for widows with just one child than for those with five or more.

Further detail (see table 10.4) shows what accounted for the positive relationship between number of children and probability of co-residence with

TABLE 10.4   Living Arrangements of Widows Aged 65+, by Number of Surviving Children, 1900 and 1910

| Number of Children | Living with Child | | | | Not Living with Child | | |
| | 1900[a] | 1910 | | | 1910 | | |
	Total	Total	Head	Not Head	Total	Head	Not Head
1	78.9%	62.2%	20.5%	41.7%	37.8%	22.4%	15.4%
2	71.8	78.4	30.7	47.7	21.5	14.9	6.6
3	77.6	77.5	29.7	47.8	22.5	13.7	8.8
4	81.5	77.6	32.8	44.8	22.4	12.7	9.7
5+	88.9	89.2	47.6	41.6	10.8	6.7	4.1

[a]From Smith (1979).

a child. The primary effect of having more children was to increase the odds that a widow would head a household that contained a child. A widow with one child was as likely as one with five or more to be living in a child's household (42 percent in both cases), but a widow with one child was less than half as likely to head her own household in which a child resided (21 percent vs. 48 percent). Having more children apparently provided greater opportunity for a widow to maintain her own household, because it increased the likelihood of finding an acceptable child who would live with her. Having a child in the household to provide auxiliary help was critical for an older widow's ability to retain greater independence.

The life history data for Manchester reveal a pattern that could not be identified from cross-sectional data alone. Even though elderly parents or widowed mothers usually co-resided with *one* child, some moved from one child to another, thus using the assistance offered by several children. Co-residence with children frequently involved reciprocal relations, where the widowed parent also met the needs of the child (Hareven and Adams 1994). In some cases, widowed mothers were invited to join a child's household to provide child care and then were asked to go and help another child when they were not needed any more. Anna Landry (born 1909) recalls her widowed grandmother being shuttled between the homes of several children. Her grandmother was widowed at a very young age. At that time "they did not have the programs that they have now for old people. So my grandmother was jumping from one child to the other. . . . Her daughters, her sons—one would keep her six months, and then somebody else would keep her six months. Like they'd go and get her if one needed her. Like if somebody was sick."

In other cases, a widowed daughter or son with young children moved in with her or his widowed mother to obtain child care. Robert Miller (born 1903), whose wife died and left him with five children, moved back into his mother's home after his father died. He paid his mother for caring for his children. At the time they moved into his mother's house, there were still two unmarried brothers and one sister living with her. Eventually, the three siblings left. Following his remarriage, Robert and his children moved out again after five years.

In 1970, the likelihood of living in various household arrangements still varied by number of children an older widow had (table 10.5). The proportion of older widows living in a child's household increased from 23 percent of those with one child to 35 percent of those with five or more. Also, the likelihood of a widow living in an institution or in a household headed by someone other than a child tended to decrease with the number of children a woman had (except that institutionalization was unexpectedly lower for those with one child than for those with two children). In general, the

TABLE 10.5   Living Arrangements of Widows Aged 65+, by Number of Surviving Children, 1970

Number of Children	Head	Institution	Mother of Head	Other Relative of Head	Nonrelative of Head
1	63.6%	6.7%	23.3%	4.5%	2.0%
2	61.2	9.4	24.5	3.1	1.9
3	60.4	6.5	28.1	3.5	1.5
4	57.5	6.2	32.6	2.0	1.7
5+	57.3	5.3	34.9	1.8	0.5

data for 1970 point to the important role that children continue to play in the lives of older widows.

Older Widows as Household Heads

Throughout the twentieth century most older widows seem to have preferred the autonomy associated with maintaining a separate household. A surprising number were able to achieve this goal. A substantial majority of older widows in recent years have been household heads, but even in 1910 half of the widows over age 50 lived in households they headed. Age, however, was related to the likelihood that a widow in 1910 would head the household in which she resided. Among widows aged 50–54, 65 percent were household heads. This proportion declined continuously with age, so that 50 percent of those aged 65–69 were heads, and only 37 percent of those over age 80 were heads. This observed age pattern suggests that as widows grew older, their resources and physical abilities to maintain a household declined, forcing them to adopt other living arrangements.

Three potential means by which an older widow might maintain headship of a household can be identified from the census data: (1) have someone else (usually a child) share the housing, (2) work outside the home, and (3) combine work with shared housing. A fourth category consists of widows who lived alone and were not in the labor force. The distribution of older widows across these four categories at different times is shown in table 10.6. In 1910, 84 percent of the older widows who maintained their own household had someone else living with them. In other words, very few older widows were living alone. Sharing the household was the only apparent strategy used by 72 percent of the widows, while 12 percent combined this strategy with working. Only 3 percent lived alone and supported themselves by working. This leaves 12 percent who neither worked nor shared their living space with others.

TABLE 10.6   Distribution of Widowed Household Heads: Strategy for
Support, by Age, 1910, 1940, 1970

	Aged 55–64			Aged 65+		
Strategy	1910	1940	1970	1910	1940	1970
Share house only	70.0%	67.5%	18.1%	71.9%	59.8%	24.6%
Work only	4.7	5.8	36.4	3.4	2.4	8.8
Share house and work	17.5	12.1	23.7	12.3	2.4	3.3
Neither	7.8	14.6	21.8	12.4	35.4	63.3

There is no direct evidence regarding how the 12 percent of older widowed heads of households who neither worked nor shared their residence
maintained this position. The very small proportion of widows with five
or more children who lived alone suggests that adult children rarely pooled
resources to support a widowed mother in her independent residence.
Some of the widows who neither shared housing nor worked may have had
sufficient assets to permit this independence. However, since living alone
without gainful employment was most common among the very old (over
80) who were childless, it seems that most often this was the result of a lack
of alternatives.

A huge shift occurred between 1910 and 1970 in widows' patterns of
household headship (table 10.6). Work outside the household did not become more common, but the frequency of sharing a house or apartment
with others dropped precipitously. Older widowed heads of household were
four and one-half times more likely to live alone in 1970 than in 1910 (72.1
percent vs. 15.8 percent). The most significant factor accounting for this
change may have been the growth of the social security system, which increasingly made it possible for older widows to achieve the economic independence they desired. This does not imply, however, that kin relations declined in importance, as the following life history accounts make clear.

Ethnographic Detail on Residential Patterns of Older Widows

Solitary Residence.   As the cohorts born in the early twentieth century
aged, older widows who were able to live independently generally lived
alone, preferably near one or more of their children. In Manchester as in
most other American urban communities, the pervasive residential pattern
developed by the middle of the century was that of a nuclear household and
of a separate residence for the family of procreation from the family of origin. The older generation rarely resided with their married adult children
in the same household. Elderly widows who were able to cope on their own
usually resided in proximity to their children, sometimes in the same build-

ing, but not in the same household if they could help it (Chudacoff and Hareven 1978; Hareven 1982).

Ernestine Schmidt (born 1904), for example, lost her husband at age 61 after a serious illness. She and her husband had both worked in a shoe factory. Ernestine stopped working to take care of her husband during his illness and did not return to work after his death. When Ernestine and her husband were first married, they moved into an apartment in the home of her husband's parents. She continued to live there for fifty-one years and was still there at the time she was interviewed. Her children helped make her comfortable in the apartment by giving her furnishings and by decorating it. During World War II, Ernestine converted parts of the building into additional apartments by installing kitchenettes. Her daughter lived in one of them after she married. At the time of the interview, another daughter of Ernestine's who was divorced was living in one of the apartments with her five children.

For the majority of people interviewed and for the population in general, "intimacy from a distance" seemed to be the preferred formula for the interaction of married adult children with their aging parents. When a mother who was living at a distance from her children was widowed and was still able to take care of herself, the children often moved her into a nearby apartment, sometimes in the same building. On other occasions, a child moved near a widowed mother. Gladys Spencer (born 1900) and her husband, for example, moved into the same building with her widowed mother. Initially, her grandfather lived in one apartment and her mother in another. Gladys took over her grandfather's apartment after his death. "It was my grandfather's house. My grandfather built it when my mother was 6 years old, and she lived here just about all of her life. When my grandfather died, my mother inherited the house, so it was empty upstairs, and they said, 'Would you consider selling your place and coming back?' My sister and brother were not located anywhere around here, and I knew that if it had become a problem it was easier to live in the house than to travel all the time. . . . It was a big decision from having your own place to going back to renting, . . . but it has worked out."

The ideal model of residence for an aging widow can be seen in the Duchamp family. Solange Duchamp's mother moved into the upstairs apartment in the building in which the parents of Solange's husband (Guy, born 1928) lived.

> Course my mother lives alone and I feel that with Mom and Dad D. downstairs, of course, they have always been good friends anyway, and since we've been married it's like she's in the family and when I come home from work, oh, once twice and you know . . . sometimes during the week, I'll drop by and I'll visit upstairs and I'll visit downstairs. Everybody's there all at once, and sometimes I'll come in and my mother will come down, or they'd come upstairs

or anything, and talk and it's reassuring so that everybody cares so much for each other in this household, that if anything happens upstairs I know that I don't have to worry that Mom and Dad D. downstairs would call, or vice versa. If anything happened downstairs, my mother would call. So it is a worry-free type of situation.

Children, usually daughters, frequently visited their widowed mothers, provided various forms of assistance, and involved them in the family's social activities. Often several siblings shared the responsibility of caring for a widowed mother. Lucinda and Andrew Johnson (born 1914) together with their siblings cared for their widowed mothers. The couple lived with Andrew's parents while they had young children. After Andrew's father retired and their children had grown, they moved out and bought a home of their own next door, where they still lived at the time of the interview. Andrew's widowed mother lived next door with her daughter and rented out one apartment. Lucinda's mother, who was widowed when Lucinda was 10 years old, lived in her later years of life with Lucinda's sister, and Lucinda often took care of her. After her father's death, Lucinda and her brother boarded with various families and also stayed in the St. Pierre Orphanage while her mother worked as a live-in housekeeper. During the war Lucinda delayed her marriage and stayed with her mother until her brother returned from the service.

Proximity to their widowed mothers was a major consideration in children's choice of residence. Some children moved near their mother after she was widowed or when she needed frequent assistance but was still capable of living alone. After women were widowed for some time, they developed a style of interaction with adult children. Even though the nature of that assistance changed as the widow aged, the precedent for assistance from their children had already been established earlier. Older women who were newly widowed and therefore confronted with sudden needs had to develop new patterns of interaction with their children. In some cases, this led to negotiations among siblings as to who should take on the main responsibilities of care for their widowed mother.

Residence in a Child's House.   An older widowed mother in 1910 could not be guaranteed a place in a child's household, but the odds were very good that she would reside in such a place. This was especially true if she had several children. Widowhood almost never meant living alone, and for most women, it meant living with a child. While this arrangement became less common later in the twentieth century, some of the women who were socialized in the values of kin assistance did have their widowed mothers move in with them. Their experiences shed light on the dynamics of the transition to widowhood.

In Manchester, adult children interviewed in the early 1980s co-resided with aging parents only under circumstances of extreme duress. When a widowed mother was too frail to live alone and needed help with daily activities and regular health care, a daughter generally took the mother into her household. The greatest problem of adjustment in caring for an aging mother in the home of a child, especially if she was ill, fell on the child, usually a daughter. A daughter usually took her mother into the household with the consent of her husband. But while men primarily provided financial assistance and sociability, women carried the major burden of daily care (Hareven and Adams 1994). This pattern is consistent with the care responsibilities of the middle generation found by Elaine M. Brody (1981) in her studies of caretakers of aging parents in contemporary society.

Most married women in Manchester worked in the textile mills, in shoe factories, or in service industries. They were caught in the double bind between caring for an aging parent in the household and meeting their family responsibilities. Caretaking daughters reported marital conflicts resulting from the necessity to combine working full-time outside the home, spending a great deal of time caring for a live-in parent, and carrying on their own household responsibilities. Some women worked during the day and cared for their chronically ill widowed mothers at night. The care for an elderly parent in the household became particularly difficult when it coincided with illness or problems in the caretaking daughter's family.

Suzanne LaCasse Miller (born 1916) exemplifies the "life cycle squeeze" that many daughters experience. She held two jobs while caring for her sick husband and for her mother in the household. She was married in 1941 and had four children. During her childbearing years she worked intermittently in the smaller textile mills that opened in the empty buildings of the Amoskeag Mills just before World War II. In addition, she worked at Dunkin' Donuts. Because of her husband's illness, Suzanne was the main support for her family. Suzanne's father and her older brother both died in 1955; her younger brother died two years later. After Suzanne's father's death, her mother moved in with Suzanne, the only surviving child in Manchester. The mother did not want to move to another town, an hour drive from Manchester, where Suzanne's sister lived. As Suzanne put it, "She wanted to stay here in [Manchester] cause her friends were here." Initially, Suzanne's mother provided child care, but in her last years she was sick. "And I'd have to run home from the job and get her to the hospital, get her into oxygen. She didn't want anybody else." In 1964, during the same year her mother became ill, Suzanne's husband died. Two years later, Suzanne's mother died and her last daughter married and left home.

Care for an aging parent in a child's home thus exacted a high price from the caretaking child and her spouse. Some of the daughters who took in an aging parent had to give up their full-time jobs or replace them with part-time and less satisfying work. Such changes in the wife's career often deprived the family of the supplementary income necessary to own a home or provide a better education for their children. If the caretaking lasted for several years, it affected the couple's opportunity to save and prepare for their own retirement. In cases in which the widowed mother could be left alone for part of the time, a daughter often tried to juggle a career and care for a parent. Sometimes daughters commuted over considerable distances to maintain a balance between their obligations to their own family and their parents' needs.

The most consistent pattern of assistance was that of one child assuming the main responsibility of caring for the aging widowed mother. In many instances, other children contributed to the effort through financial support, by visiting, or by taking turns keeping the parent in their home. This practice was consistent with patterns of care in contemporary society (Brody 1981, 1985; Cantor 1983). As in the case of Lucinda Johnson, for example, when Lucinda's mother lived in the house of one child, other children took her into their homes to stay for shorter periods. Usually, however, one child carried the primary responsibility for parental care and tried to mobilize and coordinate the efforts of the other children, as the need arose. This often required extensive trade-offs and negotiations among the children.

This role of "parent-keeper" was not always accomplished without strain. Role strain was intensified by the doubling of responsibilities that a widowed daughter faced in taking care of her widowed mother (Ory 1985; Scharlach 1987). Aurore Houle (born 1909), for example, lived alone as an older widow. At the time of the interview she still managed most of her own house repairs, but when she injured herself while wallpapering, her brother-in-law helped her by taking her to treatments. Aurore had seven brothers and sisters, three of whom were adopted. After her husband's death, Aurore moved into the building where her mother lived. Initially, Aurore took care of her widowed mother but then moved her into her sister's apartment because Aurore's job kept her "on the road all week." Eventually her mother went to a nursing home.

Aurore's widowed aunt took her grandmother in when she became blind and senile. She was cared for by hired help during the day and by her daughter at night. Another of Aurore's uncles came to help, because her aunt could not get any sleep. Eventually Aurore's father's brothers, who were still living in Quebec, decided to bring the grandmother back to Canada and place her in a nursing home there. "The reason they didn't want to put her in here, there was not French speaking here. . . and she couldn't speak a word of English. So in Canada, my father had two brothers that lived close to the nursing home, and one of them was married. So they figured that was the best place for her."

Widowed mothers at times "selected" the favorite child to reside with, even if that child was geographically distant. Some moved to another community to live with the preferred child. When Anna Charboneau Lessard (born 1928) and her family moved to New York City to manage an apartment building, her mother lived first with Anna's sister in Manchester. "Then she came up to me and asked me if she could live with us." The mother moved to New York and took care of Anna and her husband's four children. Sandra Kazantakis Wall (born 1921), who lived with her second husband in Maryland, brought her mother from Manchester after her father died, even though other siblings lived in Manchester. "She said, 'I want to come and live with you.'" Her mother lived with Sandra for the last five years of her life. "Dick [Sandra's husband] was very good to mother, and she loved him like a son. . . . In fact, she liked him better than some of her children sometimes."

In both cases, the mother's choice of the geographically distant child was related to earlier life experiences. Sandra was particularly close to her mother, but she eloped with her first husband at age 20. As she followed her husband in the military, she lived in various places overseas and in the United States and adopted a son in Germany. Over the years, she returned home from time to time when she had marital problems. "My mother and father, yes! that was the home, that was my life, and that's where I found the answers—at my mother and father." In 1959, after her husband was killed in a plane crash in Alaska, Sandra and her adopted son moved back to her parents' home in Manchester, where she lived until she remarried and moved to Maryland.

Adult Child's Residence in Mother's House.   As in the case of Sandra Kazantakis Wall, another form of co-residence was one in which the caretaking daughter lived in the widowed mother's household. The presence of a caretaking daughter in a household headed by a widowed mother could be the result of one of two possible circumstances: the daughter's return to her mother's household or the continued residence of the daughter in the parental home. In some cases, after the daughter was widowed or divorced, she moved back into her mother's household and remained there to care for the mother. Joan Riley (born 1914), who returned from Providence, Rhode Island, to live with her mother after her husband's death, explained why she never married again. "I had my mother to take care of. She came first because she was getting along in years and she had to have somebody." Geraldine Charboneau became a nurse and never married. "When her mother got ill she took care of her mother for years. Her mother wasn't feeling good for many years, but then she finally got bedridden and she was sick for about twenty years." On some occasions adult children moved back into their mothers' home for child care after being widowed or divorced.

Antoinette Dubois Chauvin first lived alone after being widowed, but then she invited her divorced daughter to move back home. "She was divorced and she was living in Manchester and had her own home. Got to the point where she was so depressed, having a big house and not too much income. And then she started to work here in Goffstown. After a while I said, 'Get rid of your house!'" At the same time Antoinette wished her daughter would marry again and live her own life. "At her age she should have her own home and her own things. . . . She should be having a normal life with children." Antoinette did not depend exclusively on assistance from her daughter. Her sisters and brothers and brothers-in-law were extremely helpful to her, especially in the maintenance and repair of the house. "They all pitched in; all they could. It was the thing to do. If I am stranded here, my sister will come for me." Her grandchildren also help her. In addition, she maintains a network of friends, all of whom are widowed. They used to go out together, but now that they have aged, they communicate mostly by telephone.

Some daughters never left the parental household. On rare occasions a daughter married and brought her husband into her parents' home. Other daughters continued to reside with their parents because it was expected that the youngest daughter would remain at home and take care of aging parents in their later years. Such daughters were pressured by their parents not to marry. Frank Kaminski's (born 1921) 73-year-old sister did not marry because her salary as a shoe factory worker was needed to help the family keep their home from being foreclosed during the depression. Long after their father's death, this sister, who was by then frail herself, continued to live with and care for their mother, who was in her late 90s. The family considered new arrangements but failed. "They were thinking of having my other sister take care of them. In the meantime, that sister's husband died, and she was bedridden. So she can't do it anymore. So, you know, that took care of that solution to the problem." Lucille Martineau Grenier (born 1915) was 48 when she married for the first time. Her husband was a 62-year-old widower, a father of five married children. Lucille reported that her 68-year-old mother was upset about the marriage "cause her right arm was gone. . . . I was living with her and I provided for her until I got married. She expected to have me for the rest of her life." Lucille put her mother in a nursing home because she was "really sick." Later, when her husband became sick, Lucille requested that her husband's children put him in a nursing home as well. Both died shortly after entering the home.

The Nursing Home.   The nursing home was not an option for widows in 1910, but it became the option of last resort later in this century. Children committed a parent to a nursing home only if the parent was chronically ill, required constant care, or was demented. The nursing home was the only solution for widowed mothers whose children lived in another town. Most elderly parents who went to a nursing home did so during a final period of chronic illness and died shortly thereafter. According to their testimony, children who lived in Manchester visited their parents regularly in nursing homes, often on a daily basis. Daughters did laundry, provided haircuts, bought delicacies, and took the elderly parent on "outings." If the children lived in a distant community, the visits were less frequent, and day-to-day care was left to a local child.

Even though nursing homes had come into existence in most urban communities by the late 1960s, there was still a stigma attached to having a parent institutionalized. The people interviewed in Manchester, without exception, felt compelled to offer an excuse or justification for sending a parent to a nursing home. The theme that parents had entered a nursing home on their own initiative, presenting their children with a fait accompli, recurred in the children's retrospective narratives. Mary Grzwinski Petrowski (born 1918), for example, who put her 82-year-old widowed mother in a nursing home after she was unable to live alone, said she had done so "simply because she [her mother] requested it." Mary claims that her mother did not want Mary to quit work because of her. "She didn't want to live with us; she felt we had our own life to live, and she said, 'Why don't you put me in a nursing home.' And so we did." Mary was the oldest of three children. Her father died in 1944, at the same time her daughter was born. She and her widowed mother lived in the same building. "I lived upstairs; my mother lived downstairs. So when I was teaching, my mother took care of my daughter." Later her mother stayed with a relative she had raised as a daughter. After this adopted daughter died, the mother was not able to live alone any more. Her mother stayed in the nursing home for six months until her death. "But it was her choice, because I was going to take a year off [from teaching school]. My mother was very intelligent, she was very independent, and she felt 'this is your life and why should you stop working just to sit with me.'" Had Mary stopped working, her and her husband's plans for retirement would have been financially jeopardized. Mary claimed to have visited her mother three times a day and every weekend until she died.

Most of the children in their 50s or 60s whom we interviewed felt guilty and apologetic about having sent an elderly parent, especially a widowed mother, to a nursing home. The common pattern was one of taking a widowed mother into their own home. As evidenced above and as is consistent with a large body of contemporary research, however, taking care of a chronically ill elderly mother placed the caretaking daughters under great stress (Brody et al. 1988; Tobin and Kulys 1981).

CONCLUSION

It is not at all surprising to find from census data that the prevalence of widowhood at every age declined over the twentieth century. It is worth noting, however, that the percent decline in widowhood at younger ages was much greater than the decline in old age. This is significant because the timing of widowhood in the life course significantly shapes adaptations in later life. Young and middle-aged widows generally had children to support, and many solved this challenge by remarrying. Among those who did not remarry, a large majority at each date were able to maintain their own households. To accomplish this, younger widows developed highly interdependent kin support networks. As these widows moved into later life, they carried with them well-established networks and did not have to rely heavily on their children. By contrast, women who were widowed in the later years of life had to build up new support networks and had to adjust to relationships with relatives on whom they had not depended significantly in the past. They were likely, therefore, to rely more on their children than on other kin.

From both the census data and the life history interviews, it is clear that widows generally tried to maintain autonomy and control over their own lives. Survey data in recent years reveal that older widows prefer to maintain a separate residence, and a majority are able to do so. Before the emergence of social security and other pension programs, few older widows were able to live alone. Nevertheless, even in 1910, half of all older widows were listed as head of the household in which they lived. The primary strategy to accomplish this was having others, preferably children, share the housing. From the interviews we find that over time more and more widows were able to live separate from their children. Most often, these older widows were able to survive in this fashion by living in proximity to an adult child. If the parents had not lived near that child prior to the father's death, the transition to widowhood would also involve moving closer to a child who could provide care.

When older widows were not able to head their own households, by far the most common arrangement has been to live in the home of a child. As one might expect, the odds of this arrangement occurring were affected by the number of children an older widow had. Throughout this century, the more surviving children an older widow had, the more likely it was that she lived with a child. Among older women who were not household heads in 1910, for example, 27 percent of those with one child were not residing in a child's home, compared to only 9 percent of those with five or more children.

Circumstances that led a widow to make the transition from being the head of a household to being the mother (or mother-in-law) of the head cannot be determined from census data. But from the interviews it is clear that such dependence on children became especially critical if the widowed mother's health was impaired, if she was frail and chronically ill, and if she needed regular or frequent care. The principal caretaking child was usually designated earlier in the mother's life. The caretaking child worked out the specific arrangements through complicated negotiations with their mother and other siblings. If one child took a widowed mother into the household, other children were expected to share in various tasks of support, especially in times of acute illness or crisis. Such arrangements among siblings were not, of course, always negotiated smoothly (Hareven and Adams 1994).

It was not uncommon for a co-resident caretaking child to be the youngest daughter who had never left home. In these cases that daughter was fulfilling the script that called for the last daughter to remain in the parental home to care for her aging parents. Another path leading to co-residence, as noted above, was when a child (usually a daughter) moved into the widowed mother's house following her divorce or becoming a widow. A variety of other arrangements also occurred, probably as a result of negotiations among all of the relevant parties. The household economy that resulted from co-residence did not have the widowed mothers strictly on the receiving end of assistance. As long as their health permitted, they engaged in reciprocal relations with their children, often providing assistance in child care and housekeeping.

In the first half of this century, few older widows had the economic resources required to live alone. Thus childless widows often turned to their own siblings for assistance. If their siblings were also frail and old, they tried to make arrangements with nieces or nephews or with surrogate kin. Since these arrangements were not always possible, a relatively large proportion of childless widows in the early 1900s ended up in boardinghouses. As these gradually disappeared over time, an increasing number of older childless widows who could not care for themselves entered nursing homes. By 1970, almost one-fourth of the childless widows over age 80 were in nursing homes.

The household arrangements and support systems of older widows were not dramatically different from those of elderly couples, especially among the frail elderly or among couples in which one was chronically ill. But widows lacked the most primary source of caregiving, namely, a spouse. For widows, therefore, patterns of dependency and need for kin support were more intense than those of an elderly couple where one partner could still provide the necessary support.

NOTES

The interview and demographic data on Manchester, New Hampshire, were gathered and analyzed by Tamara Hareven with the support from Research Grants 5R01 A602468 and 5R01 A606441 from the National Institute of Aging (NIA). Hareven is grateful to the NIA for their generous support and to Kathleen Adams for her help in managing the interviews in Manchester and the kinship analysis. Both authors are grateful to Cheryl Elman for her valuable assistance with the analysis of the public use sample of the 1910 federal census and to Rona Karasik for her valuable bibliographic and editorial assistance.

1. Sampling strategies for the three public use samples (PUS) differed: the 1910 PUS is a 1-in-250 sample of census manuscript schedules, the 1940 PUS is a 1-in-100 sample of households and group quarters (sampling weights are used to get a representative sample of individuals), and the 1970 PUS is a 1-in-20 sample of census records. It was possible to exclude residents of New York City from the 1910 and 1940 samples but not from the 1970 sample. We excluded residents of New York City because of the atypicality of New York City's population.

2. Data on the Manchester cohorts in this chapter were based on a longitudinal historical data set that Hareven constructed for the parents' cohort and on which Family Time and Industrial Time is based (Hareven 1982). She linked this historical data with a new data set on the children's cohorts, which she generated from intensive interviews, demographic histories, work histories, and migration histories of the children's cohort during the period 1981–1985. The real names of people discussed or quoted in this paper have been substituted with invented names.

3. While most elderly widows lived with an adult child, most adults did not live with a widowed mother. Under mortality conditions existing around the turn of the century, only 40 percent of the mothers alive at age 35 would still be living at age 75. For every 100 mothers over age 70, there were 352 living children. Thus even if all older mothers lived with a child, only about 10 percent of all adults would ever have a 75-year-old mother living with them ($1/3.52 \times 0.4 = 0.11$).

REFERENCES

Antonucci, Toni C., and Hiroko Akiyama. 1987. "Social networks in adult life and a preliminary examination of the Convoy model." *Journal of Gerontology* 42(5): 519–527.

Brody, Elaine M. 1981. "Women in the middle and family help to older people." *The Gerontologist* 21(5): 471–480.

———. 1985. "Parent care as a normative family stress." *The Gerontologist* 25(1): 19–29.

Brody, Elaine M., Morton H. Kleban, Christine Hoffman, and Claire B. Schoonover. 1988. "Adult daughters and parent care: A comparison of one-, two- and three-generation households." *Home Health Care Services Quarterly* 9(4): 19–45.

Cantor, Marjorie H. 1983. "Strain among caregivers: A study of experience in the United States." *The Gerontologist* 23(6): 597–604.

Chudacoff, Howard P., and Tamara K. Hareven. 1978. "Family transitions and household structure in the later years of life." In *Transitions: The family life and the life course in historical perspective,* ed. Tamara K. Hareven, 217–244. New York: Academic Press.

———. 1979. "From the empty nest to family dissolution: Life course transitions into old age." *Journal of Family History* 4: 59–63.

Depner, Charlene E., and Berit Ingersoll-Dayton. 1988. "Supportive relationships in later life." *Psychology and Aging* 3(4): 348–357.

Hareven, Tamara K. 1982. *Family time and industrial time: The relationship between the family and work in a New England industrial community.* Cambridge: Cambridge University Press.

Hareven, Tamara K., and Kathleen Adams. 1994. "The generation in the middle: Cohort comparisons in assistance to aging parents in an American community." In *Aging and generational relations over the life course: A historical and cross-cultural perspective,* ed. Tamara K. Hareven. Berlin: Walter de Gruyter.

Heinemann, Gloria D., and Patricia L. Evans. 1990. "Widowhood: Loss, change, and adaptation." In *Family relationships in later life* (2d ed.), ed. Timothy H. Brubaker, 142–168. Newbury Park, Calif.: Sage.

Lewis, Jane, and Barbara Meredith. 1988. *Daughters who care: Daughters caring for mothers at home.* New York: Routledge.

Lopata, Helena. 1979. *Women as widows: Support systems.* New York: Elsevier.

Ory, Marcia G. 1985. "The burden of care." *Generations* 25 (Fall): 14–18.

Scharlach, Andrew E. 1987. "Role strain in mother-daughter relationships in later life." *The Gerontologist* 27 (5): 627–631.

Smith, Daniel Scott. 1979. "Life course, norms, and the family system of older Americans in 1900." *Journal of Family History* 4: 285–289.

Tobin, Sheldon S., and Regina Kulys. 1981. "The family in the institutionalization of the elderly." *Journal of Social Issues* 37 (3): 145–157.

Uhlenberg, Peter. 1974. "Cohort variations in family life-cycle experiences of U.S. females." *Journal of Marriage and the Family* 36: 284–292.

———. 1978. "Changing configurations of the life course." In *Transitions: The family and the life course in historical perspective,* ed. Tamara K. Hareven, 65–95. New York: Academic Press.

PART FOUR

Retirement and Mortality

ELEVEN

The Impact of Aging on the Employment of Men in American Working-Class Communities at the End of the Nineteenth Century

Roger L. Ransom and Richard Sutch

At the end of the nineteenth century, one out of every three males in the U.S. labor force relied on a wage-earning job as their principal source of economic support and long-term security.[1] For working-class families in the cities, this dependence on wage employment posed a growing challenge as the head of the household grew older. The older worker found it increasingly difficult to support himself and his immediate family from wage income. Perhaps the most important factor contributing to this problem is the tendency with advancing age for health and physical ability to decline. As a consequence, the economic productivity of the worker declined and his daily wage fell after he passed "middle age." In the absence of formal arrangements to offset the effects of this decline in productivity, workers were obliged to look for alternative arrangements to maintain their purchasing power as they became older.

The prospect of declining productivity—with its concomitant decrease in wage earnings—was a bleak one for the fraction of the population who knew no other occupation than industrial wage labor. So long as the industrial wage system paid employees their current marginal product, employers had no incentive to terminate the employment of older workers with the firm, and the reduced wage offered by employers could be expected to reduce the supply of labor forthcoming. However, if wages tended to be sticky, then older workers would be increasingly overpaid, and this would give the employer an incentive to discharge the worker or at least to minimize the number of days the older worker would be employed. Either way, the incomes of older workers would be reduced.

All of this was not lost on workers, who clearly recognized that their economic situation would ultimately deteriorate. Workers anticipated the problem and tried to accumulate assets during their peak earning years to draw upon later. They also sought to make new arrangements with their employer to ensure greater job security. In this way, labor markets gradually evolved long-term (often implicit) contracts that underpaid younger workers, over-paid older workers, provided security of employment, and set a predeter-mined age for retirement. Yet we know surprisingly little about how these arrangements, which offer a considerable degree of economic security for older workers today, emerged in the United States over the past century.

In this chapter, we look to the period just prior to the turn of the century, before many of the features taken for granted today had evolved. We use census data and a series of surveys of working-class households taken in the 1890s by state bureaus of labor statistics to examine the situation of older workers. Our attention is drawn to four general aspects of labor arrange-ments at that time.

1. The phenomenon of voluntary retirement from the industrial labor force was already firmly in place by 1900. By that time workers were aware of the threat of dependency in old age, and many had accumu-lated sufficient assets to quit work at ages ranging from 55 to 65.
2. Not all workers were able to retire. Our survey data provide consider-able support for the hypothesis that many older workers moved to less demanding jobs as they aged. In an earlier study we termed this phe-nomenon *downward occupational mobility* (Ransom and Sutch 1986*a*).
3. There seems little doubt that this life cycle deskilling of workers is mir-rored in the returns to labor. One of the most striking features of the labor markets to emerge from our examination of the data is a hump-shaped profile of income and earnings that shows up across a wide va-riety of locations.
4. The decline in earnings was not only a result of lower daily wages. An examination of the days lost to various causes clearly suggests that older workers also experienced a different pattern of employment and that this pattern was related to both sickness and involuntary un-employment, on the one hand, and a greater consumption of free time, on the other.

RETIREMENT AT THE END OF THE NINETEENTH CENTURY

The propensity of older American men to retire from the labor force after the age of 60 is well documented and well studied for the period following World War II. Until recently, however, information on the pe-riod before 1940 was sketchy. In the absence of statistical data, the com-mon belief shared by economists and historians was that retirement was virtually unknown at the beginning of the twentieth century, made its appearance shortly after 1900, and then gradually increased in the years

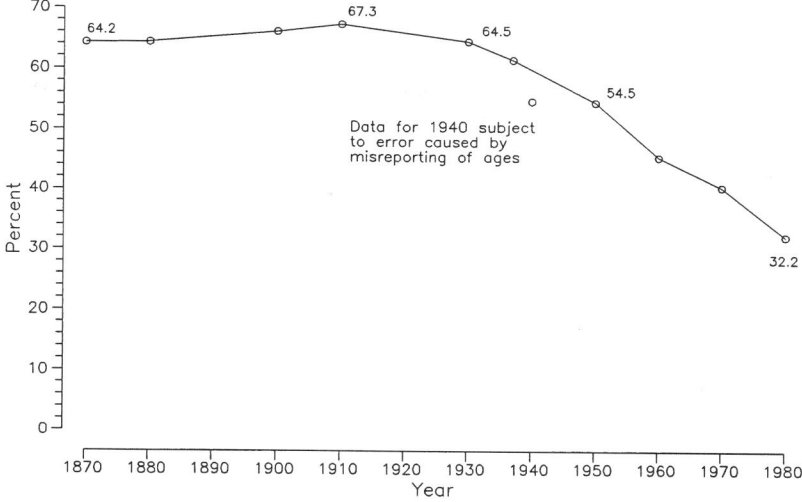

Fig. 11.1. Labor force participation, males aged 60 and over, 1870–1980.

leading up to 1940.[2] We challenged this view, compiling new evidence on labor force participation for the period from 1870 to 1940 which suggests that retirement was common throughout the entire period and that retirement rates were stable before they began a marked increase in the late 1930s.[3]

Figure 11.1 summarizes our present view of the trend in labor force participation for men 60 and over for this period. Retirement was not unusual at the turn of the century; in 1900, the probability of eventual retirement for a 32-year-old man was more than 35 percent. Indeed, national retirement rates for males were about the same in 1870 (35.8 percent) as they were in 1930 (35.5 percent). The propensity to retire began a remarkable ascendancy sometime in the late 1930s or early 1940s and has continued steadily throughout the postwar period.[4]

An examination of the impact of aging on the employment of men around the turn of the century presents a unique research opportunity to reexamine the causes and role of retirement at a time when social security benefits did not exist and few company pensions were vested in the worker. Retirement in this era was largely financed from savings accumulated while working.[5] The relatively high proportion of older males who remained at jobs in the late-nineteenth-century labor market suggests that the experience of these men was rather different from that of the current generation of retirement-aged men. Here we will explore that experience using as our guide a rich body of data collected at the end of the nineteenth century by state governments interested in examining the working conditions in the United States.

THE SURVEYS OF WORKING-CLASS HOUSEHOLDS

In 1869, the Commonwealth of Massachusetts established the first state bureau of labor statistics in an effort to collect and present statistical data on the conditions of labor to the state legislature. Under the direction of Carroll D. Wright, who became chief in 1873, the Massachusetts bureau pioneered the canvassing of households to collect data on the occupation, wages, demographic characteristics, and working conditions of "ordinary workers." Wright insisted that all of the data collected had to be made available for these surveys to have scientific respectability and political influence. Accordingly, in the *Sixth Annual Report* for 1875, the Massachusetts bureau published all of the data from each of the 397 individual responses to a survey taken the previous year.[6] The success of the data-collecting efforts and the political impact of the published reports prompted other states to follow Massachusetts' lead and create similar agencies dedicated to the collection of survey data on working conditions. These state bureaus conducted numerous surveys of workers in the late 1880s and in the early to mid-1890s, and, following Wright's example, each individual response was published in the *Annual Reports*.[7]

While the range of issues dealt with by the bureaus varied from state to state, it is clear that economic and social issues prominent at the time that the surveys were taken shaped the questions being asked. Every survey included questions on working conditions that provide data on occupation, hours worked, wage rates, and in many instances, the number of years of tenure with the employer and within the occupation. Most surveys included several questions dealing with immigration (place of birth, place of parents' birth, years in the United States, funds on arrival), union membership, and newspaper subscriptions. Concern over unemployment produced detailed questions into the amount of time "lost" from work and the reasons for lost time. Finally, there was an evident concern about the ability of working-class households to meet their expenses, which led to questions about income, expenses, and ownership of assets such as houses, life insurance, and bank accounts. These economic data are combined with demographic information on the age of the worker and the size of his or her family and the number of dependents.

These surveys, together with the various "special reports" prompted by the depressed conditions in the 1890s, provide an extraordinary window through which economic historians can examine the economic and social situation of workers at the end of the nineteenth century. Yet until very recently, when the advent of microcomputers made it feasible to put these data into machine-readable form, the rich volume of data contained in these state reports remained largely untapped by researchers.[8] In 1989, we began, in collaboration with Susan Carter, a systematic attempt to create a machine-readable database of microeconomic data extracted from a selected subset of the more than one hundred separate reports published between 1874 and 1900.[9]

This chapter draws on the responses reported by male workers in ten surveys of working-class households conducted between 1884 and 1896 by the states of Maine, New Jersey, Michigan, Iowa, Kansas, and California. The broad features of the surveys are summarized in table 11.1. Three of the surveys (California, Maine, and Kansas) canvass workers in a large number of occupations and industries across the entire state; the others concentrate on specific industries or occupations within a state. Taken together, these surveys represent a total of 38,776 responses by male workers to questions covering a wide range of topics relating to working conditions.

Our primary focus is on workers in manufacturing. Retirement was primarily an urban nonagricultural phenomenon. Farmers and rural workers in general were less likely to retire, or at least less likely to report themselves without an occupation.[10] However, to provide an occasional comparison, we have also drawn on data from a Michigan canvass of farmworkers taken in 1895.[11]

We should note at the outset several features of these surveys that affect the scope of our analysis. First is the fact that because the bureaus canvassed

TABLE 11.1   Worker Surveys Used in This Study

| | | | Number of Respondents | | |
Date	State	Description	Total	Men	Women
1890	Maine	Manufacturing workers in 33 towns	1,084	1,012	72
1888–1890	New Jersey	Workers in 6 industries[a]	12,821	12,821	0
1888	Michigan	Stone and clay workers[b]	719	719	0
1889	Michigan	Furniture industry workers	5,419	5,203	216
1893	Michigan	Railroad employees	6,051	6,051	0
1894	Michigan	Farm laborers	7,900	5,600	2,300
1895	Michigan	Hack and bus line employees	1,950	1,950	0
1895	Michigan	Owners of hacks and drays	1,250	1,250	0
1884	Iowa	Teachers	347	181	166
1884–1887	Kansas	Manufacturing workers in the state	1,165	1,165	0
1892	California	Workers in San Francisco	3,493[c]	2,824	634
Total			42,199	38,776	3,388

[a]Glassmaking, pottery, hat making, and iron mining were covered throughout the state. The building trades and printing were covered in Essex County and the cities of Trenton, Elizabeth, Paterson, and Jersey City.
[b]Fire clay, slate, coal, grindstones, gypsum, and stone.
[c]The gender of 35 respondents was not recorded. These 35 workers were excluded from the analysis.

only those workers who are in the labor force, older workers who have left the workforce for any reason will not be included.[12] Also evident from the data of table 11.1 is the absence of female workers from most of these surveys. Except in a few cases (such as the survey of "domestic farmworkers" in Michigan) in which they explicitly targeted female laborers, the bureaus focused their efforts on men. However, the absence of data on female workers should have a relatively small impact on our analysis of older workers, since at this time the female labor force comprised primarily young, unmarried women (Goldin 1990). Finally, any generalizations from these data must also take into account the rather arbitrary collection of cities and towns included in the surveys and must recognize that these are *cross-sectional*, not *longitudinal*, data.

EVIDENCE OF DOWNWARD OCCUPATIONAL MOBILITY

We begin by examining the age distribution of the workers canvassed in seven surveys mentioned in table 11.1. In all these cases, the intent of those conducting the survey was to obtain a representative sample of workers who fell within the scope of the different investigations. In Maine, Michigan, and California, the questionnaires were administered in person by agents trained for the job. In Kansas and Iowa, questionnaires were distributed through the mail. While little is said about the process by which workers were located and their cooperation secured, we have no reason to believe that a conscious bias for or against including older workers was present. Nevertheless, it is clear that all seven surveys overrepresent workers in their 20s and 30s and have surprisingly few workers over the age of 55. In figure 11.2, the age distributions of respondents are presented as smoothed polynomials in age.[13] The age distribution of all employed men derived from the 1900 census of the U.S. population is shown on the graph to provide a calibration of the distributions from the state surveys.[14]

We offer two explanations for the relative shortage of older workers in these surveys compared to the United States as a whole. First, all the surveys plotted in figure 11.2 concentrated on the nonagricultural population of cities and towns. We believe that retirement rates were likely to be much higher there than in rural districts and on farms. Second, since these surveys concentrated on manufacturing and building trades, we suspect that the age distributions reflect the impact of downward occupational mobility. As workers aged they left (or were fired from) the higher-paying—but also more physically demanding—jobs in these sectors and took lower-paying, lower-status, and less demanding jobs in other sectors. In an earlier article, we called this phenomenon "on-the-job" retirement (Ransom and Sutch 1986*a*). We presented evidence from the censuses of 1870, 1880, and 1900 to indicate that this type of age-related deskilling was a common late-nineteenth-century

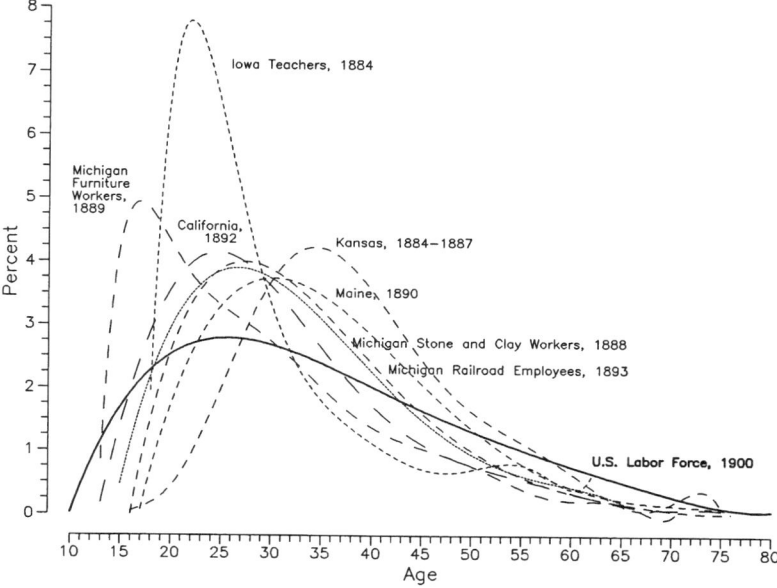

Fig. 11.2. Age distribution of respondents: Seven state labor surveys and the U.S. census.

phenomenon. Downward occupational mobility is perhaps even more evident in the age distributions from the four industry-specific surveys included in figure 11.2. The surveys of stone and clay workers and furniture industry workers from Michigan and the survey of Iowa teachers all reveal a marked deficit of older male workers relative to the 1900 standard. While the teaching profession may well be a special case, we suggest that the absence of older workers in the two Michigan surveys is largely explained by the departures produced by downward occupational mobility.[15]

DECLINE OF INCOMES AND WAGE RATES WITH AGE

Part of the explanation for the downward occupational mobility revealed by the surveys of industrial workers is suggested by the earnings profiles we have derived from these data. Figure 11.3 presents the income profiles from eight of the data sets. Each distribution shows a hump-shaped pattern, with a tendency for annual incomes to fall markedly at older ages.[16] If this cross-sectional view can be taken as a reflection of the actual or expected experience of a worker as he aged, then the declining returns from industrial employment may well have helped induce an occupational change. There is only very limited longitudinal evidence available to test whether or not we

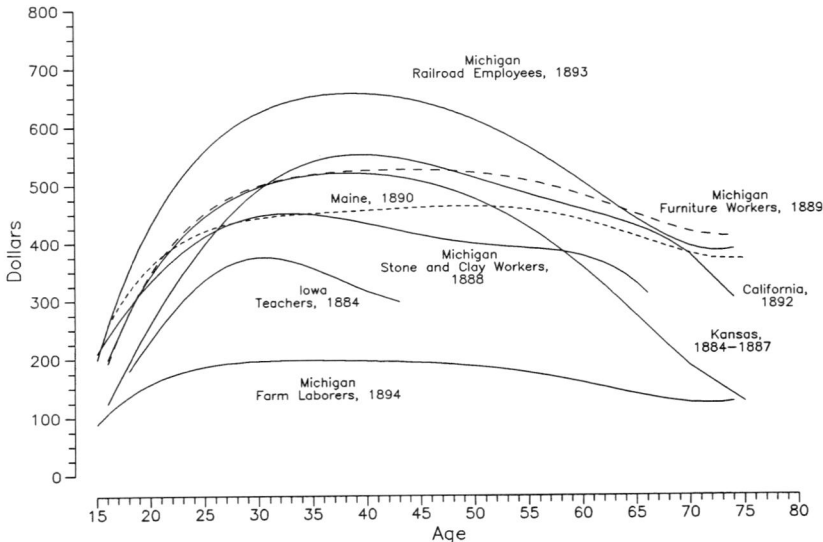

Fig. 11.3. Age profile of annual earnings: Eight state surveys.

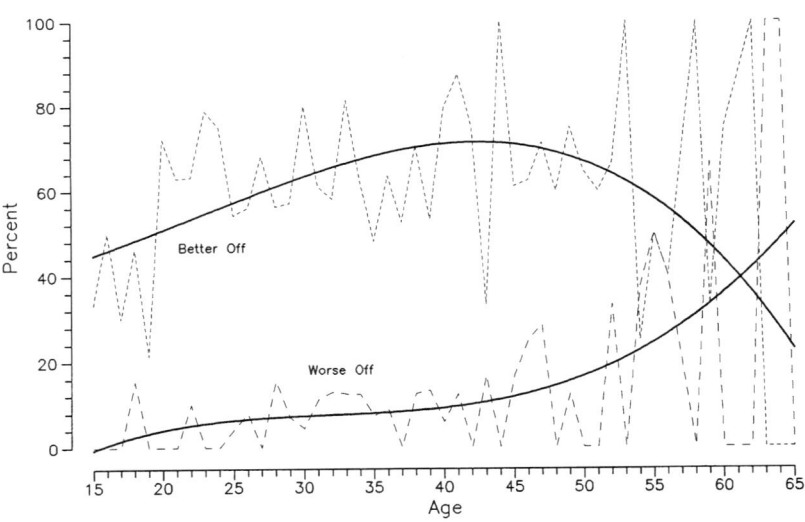

Fig. 11.4. Perception of current economic well-being relative to five years earlier, Michigan stone and clay workers, 1888.

may safely infer this impact of aging from cross-sectional data. However, two of the surveys, the Michigan stone and clay workers in 1888 and the Michigan survey of railroad employees in 1893, did ask workers whether they were better or worse off (in economic terms) in the year of the survey than they had been five years earlier. The proportion of negative answers for the stonecutters is plotted by age in figure 11.4. After about age 45, the proportion of negative answers rises sharply, suggesting that a substantial fraction of the older workers in this industry had indeed experienced a recent decline in their annual earnings. The proportion of workers reporting no change falls continuously. The data for the Michigan railroad workers, which is a much larger sample published five years later, is presented in figure 11.5. The pattern is similar to that of the stonecutters, although economic conditions had clearly deteriorated.[17] If anything, figure 11.5 suggests that declining income for railroad workers began even before the age of 40, confirming the impression given by the cross-sectional data of figure 11.3.

The decline in earnings as workers aged was produced through the combination of two separate phenomena. First, daily wage rates fell with age after reaching a peak that occurred in some occupations as early as when the workers reached their late 20s. Second, the number of days workers worked for pay during the year fell as workers aged. We first turn our attention to the cross sections of wage rates revealed in our data sets. Figure 11.6 presents the age profiles of daily wage rates reported by the workers in the sep-

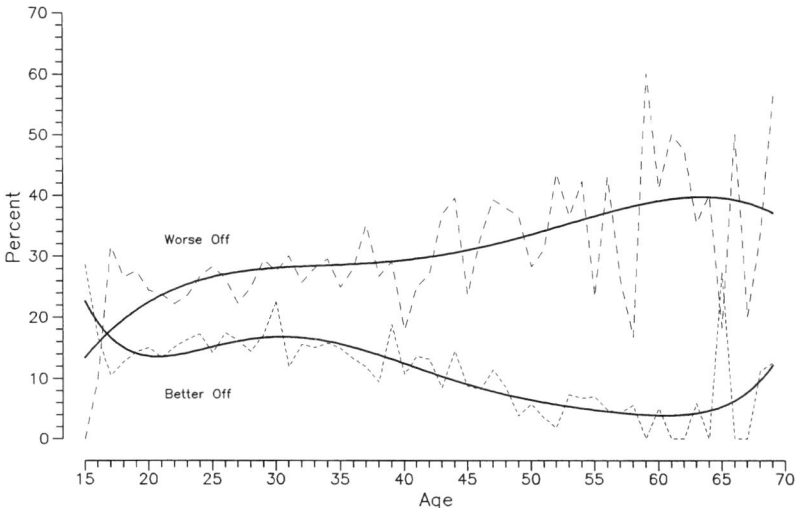

Fig. 11.5. Perception of current economic well-being relative to five years earlier, Michigan railroad employees, 1893.

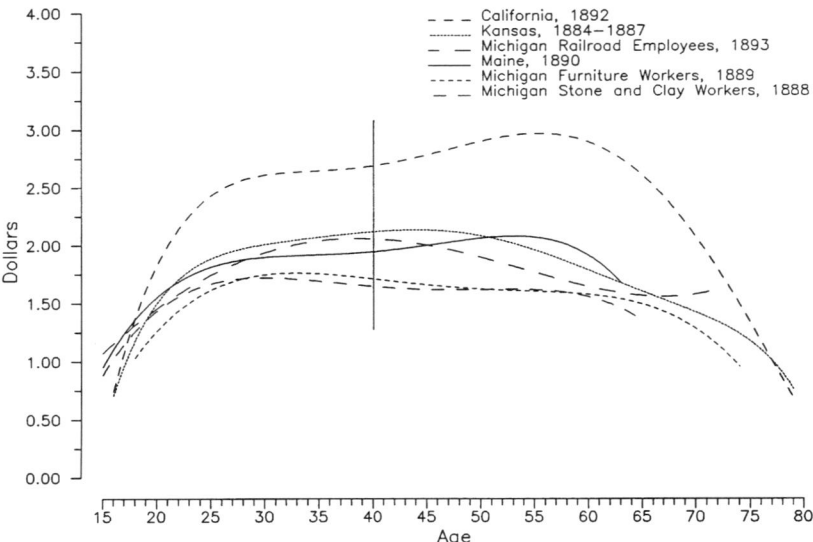

Fig. 11.6. Age profile of daily wage rates: Six state surveys.

arate surveys. If we assume that these labor markets were largely free from the long-term implicit contracts that characterize modern labor markets, then an obvious reason for older workers to be paid less than younger workers is that their physical productivity was lower. Many of these jobs required physical strength, agility, good eyesight, and other attributes that in many workers would deteriorate with advancing age. Thus, employers were likely either to reduce the daily wage without changing the worker's occupation or to move workers to less demanding but also lower-paid jobs.

The decline in income and wages evident in figures 11.3 and 11.6 could not have been wholly unanticipated by the workers. The demands of industrial jobs were such that most men could foresee the time when they would no longer have the strength, endurance, or agility to maintain the level of productivity consistent with the standard wage. This being the case, some sort of "strategy" had to be devised to meet the challenge of economic insecurity that faces older wage earners.[18]

A novel investigation into the duration of the "trade life" of working men conducted in New Jersey between 1888 and 1890 by that state's Bureau of Statistics of Labor and Industries provides striking evidence that this was so. The investigation was predicated on the assumption that after working at a given occupation for a number of years, the worker would begin to "decline" at his job. To ascertain the effect of occupation on the length of a man's working life, the New Jersey bureau conducted a survey of journeymen asking for their age and occupation, the age they began to work at their present trade, and (if they had reached it) the age when they began to decline. All together the bureau surveyed nearly thirteen thousand employed men over the age of 20 in six industries. The surveys were tabulated and the results published in three successive volumes of the bureau's *Annual Report* (New Jersey 1889, 1890, 1891).

In four industries (glassmaking, pottery, hat making, and iron mining) workers were apparently identified by their employers and were approached by bureau agents who administered the questionnaire. For the building trades and printing, workers were identified in a house-to-house canvass conducted during the early hours of the evening in the county of Essex and in the cities of Trenton, Elizabeth, Paterson, and Jersey City (New Jersey 1891:173). Table 11.2 gives the distribution of those sampled by occupation and estimates the survey coverage. Although tabulations were presented in

TABLE 11.2   New Jersey Survey of Selected Occupations, 1889–1891

Occupation	Number Surveyed	1890 U.S. Census Enumeration	Percentage Coverage
Building trades[a]			
Carpenters	2,732	21,191	12.9
Painters	1,235	9,439	13.1
Bricklayers and masons	1,022	6,767	15.1
Plumbers	661	3,085	21.4
Hat makers	2,577	6,137	42.0
Miners of iron ore[b]	1,269	1,380	92.0
Potters	1,122	3,801	29.5
Glassmakers	1,040	4,298	24.2
Printers	462	3,375	13.7
Total	12,120	61,075	19.8

SOURCES: New Jersey 1891: 178; U.S. Census 1890, vol. 1, pt. II: 324–332, table 79; U.S. Census 1890, vol. 7, *Mineral Industries:* 17.

[a]Stonecutters were also included in the New Jersey investigation (701 were surveyed). However, no data were reported on the age stonecutters began to decline. We assume that for some reason these data were not tabulated. Given the way the reports are presented, an alternative interpretation is that none of the stonecutters had yet begun to decline (New Jersey 1891: 192). Including, rather than excluding, stonecutters would make little difference to the overall results.

[b]The 1,269 miners "embrace all the workmen engaged in the mining of iron ore in the State, but do not include engineers, blacksmiths, common laborers, or those employed about the mines in handling the ore" (New Jersey 1890: 359). The U.S. Census of Mineral Industries distinguishes between employees of iron mines "above ground" (492) and those "below ground" (1,380). Only the belowground employees are included in the comparison made here. The census figures are higher than the N.J. Bureau of Statistics enumeration. Possibly this is because the census figures include all workers, while the New Jersey survey included only males aged 21 and over; also, the New Jersey figures probably exclude miners engaged in "prospecting" (New Jersey 1890: 360), while the census figures presumably do not exclude them.

TABLE 11.3   Proportion of Journeymen Aged 60+ and Percentage of Journeymen "in Decline," Selected Occupations, New Jersey, 1889–1891

Occupation	Percent Aged 60+	Percent Beginning to Decline	Average Age of Decline
Building trades	0.8	9.5	39.8
Hat makers	2.0	14.7	36.6
Miners of iron ore	3.1	7.1	44.6
Potters	0.6	8.6	38.3
Glassmakers	0.9	24.7	39.8
Printers	0.4	21.2	36.6
Total	1.4	12.0	38.9

SOURCES: New Jersey, 1889: 114–115, table 3 summary; New Jersey 1890: 380, table 2; New Jersey 1891: 178; 199–200, table 2; 201, table 3.

exhaustive detail, no clear summary statement was provided by the New Jersey officials. Two statistics calculated in the reports, the percentage of workers beginning to decline and the average age reported for the onset of decline, are given in table 11.3.

The relatively low percentage of journeymen who were still working at these skilled jobs at age 60 or over suggests that many workers left these occupations before reaching 60. It is not possible from these data alone to determine the reason older workers left their trade. Among the possible causes are retirement (including retirement due to disability or illness), downward occupational mobility, or death.

The percentage of workers who reported that they had begun to decline at their trade is remarkably high. For glassmakers, it was one quarter of all workers. Those who felt they had already begun to decline were asked to report the age at which they first noticed their difficulties. The average response is given in the table. For the entire sample, it was 38.9 years. This measure, however, will be biased downward as a measure of the typical age of peak productivity because it includes only workers who have already begun to decline. Other things equal, a worker prone to an early age of decline will be more likely to have passed this climacteric at the time of the New Jersey canvass than a worker prone to a late decline. As a result there will have been an oversampling of journeymen who began to decline at young ages and an undersampling of the age of decline of the hardy. Another possible objection to the average age of decline reported in the table is that it is based on the recollection of the worker. Such retrospective dating is notoriously inaccurate.

Several measures that eliminate both the type of downward bias mentioned above and the problems associated with the retrospective question are presented as an alternative in table 11.4. All these measures rely on the

TABLE 11.4   Estimating the Age of Peak Productivity,
New Jersey Journeymen, Selected Occupations, 1889–1891

Occupation	By Age 56	By Age 60	By Age 66	Singulate Mean	Half-Life
	Percentage in Decline				
Carpenters	33.0	51.9	70.8	56.8	59.0
Painters	54.1	67.1	80.0	50.9	53.4
Bricklayers and masons	37.0	49.8	62.5	55.9	59.6
Plumbers	26.7	a	a	a	b
Printers	64.3	a	a	49.6	51.9
Glassmakers	74.2	81.5	88.9	45.9	45.2
Hat makers	49.2	a	a	48.9	b
Miners of iron ore	48.1	61.2	74.4	55.1	55.2
Potters	77.4	a	a	46.7	45.2
Unweighted Total	47.5	55.9	64.2	52.7	56.0

NOTE: a indicates that sample size was too small for reliable estimate, b that proportion in decline was less than 50 percent.

notion of a synthetic cohort that experiences at each age demographic events at the same rate that workers of that age reported in the cross-section sample. Thus the only information used is the response (yes or no) to the question, "Have you begun to decline at your trade?" The first three columns of the table report the percentage of workers who had already entered their decline by various ages. Column 4 presents the singulate mean age of decline calculated using the synthetic cohort method of John Hajnal (1953). The last column gives the cohort's "half-life," the age at which one-half of the members of the synthetic cohort have begun to decline. Table 11.4 suggests that the typical age for the onset of decline would be in a man's early 50s.

The measures in table 11.4, however, would be unbiased estimates only if the mortality experience of those who began their decline was the same as for those who had not. In this case, "mortality" refers to any reason to cease work, including retirement and job changes as well as death. However, it is quite likely that workers who had begun to decline at their trade were more likely to leave their job than those who had not. The impact of this effect on the synthetic cohort measures will be to bias them upward. Thus we can conjecture that the "true" age of decline lies somewhere between the lower-bound estimates of table 11.3 and the upper-bound estimates of table 11.4. Since the impact of differential mortality will also bias the figures of table 11.3, the truth probably lies closer to the figures in that table where the two biases work to offset each other. The value of the New Jersey data lies not so much in our ability to use it to precisely measure the age at which industrial productivity peaked for a late-nineteenth-century worker as in the fact that it stands as strong evidence that young workers actually anticipated a decline in their vitality, productivity, and income in late life.

THE NUMBER AND CAUSES OF DAYS WORKED

We noted at the outset that a major reason for the decline of workers' incomes as they aged was that older men worked and were paid for fewer days each year than their younger counterparts. Figure 11.7 presents the age profile of the number of days worked for the Kansas and Maine surveys, together with the number of months worked in two of the Michigan surveys.[19] Both distributions exhibit a remarkable decline from a peak of over 250 paid days averaged by workers in their 30s to approximately 220 paid days worked by men in their 60s. While the number of months worked by Michigan stone and clay workers and Michigan farm laborers probably reflects seasonal fluctuations due to inclement weather, it is clear that older workers were employed for fewer months than workers in the prime age group.

In several of the surveys the number of days lost is classified by one or more general causes: layoff, illness, and voluntary time off. In figure 11.8 through 11.10, we present some summary statistics on days lost by cause that illustrate the extent to which older workers were compelled by illness or unemployment to work fewer days. Figure 11.8 displays the age profiles for

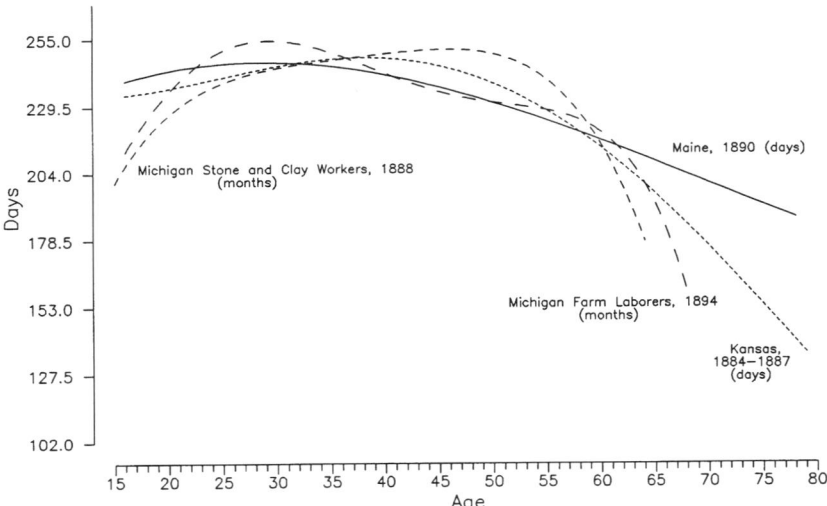

Fig. 11.7. Age profile of number of days or months worked: Kansas, Maine, and Michigan.

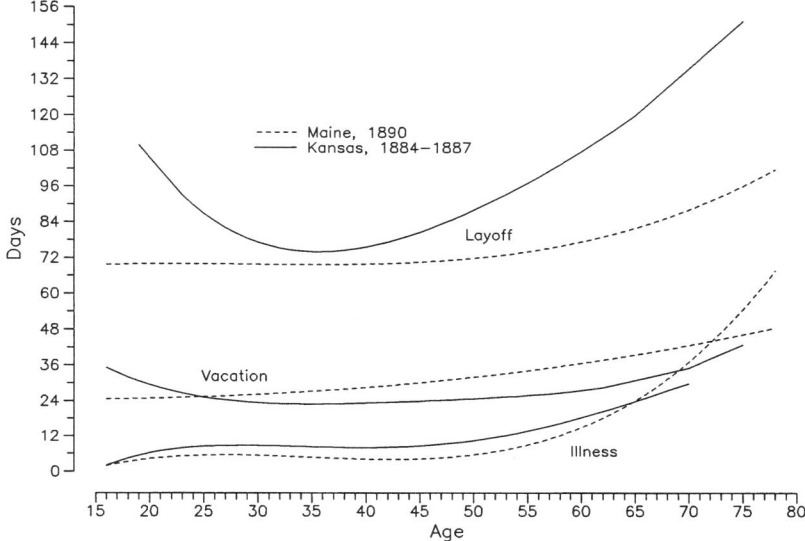

Fig. 11.8. Age profile of days lost from work, by cause: Kansas and Maine.

days lost in the Maine and Kansas surveys due to illness, lack of work, or vacation. Time lost from all three causes rises with age for both surveys, with the increases in layoff and illness among older workers being particularly pronounced. Figure 11.9 presents the days lost to illness or lack of work by employees of hack and bus lines in Michigan and owner-operators of hacks and drays. While both surveys show a pronounced upward trend with age, it is interesting to note that the self-employed lost more time to illness and lack of work at all ages than did employees. It appears that at least in this industry, self-employment did not provide protection against the problem of lost time. Finally, we note that the effect of illness appears to be as significant among farmworkers as it was for the urban labor force. Figure 11.10 presents the proportion of Michigan farmworkers reporting time lost due to illness according to age.

That illness rises with age is not surprising and reinforces the conclusions we drew from the New Jersey data on physical decline. That employers should single out older workers when layoffs were required is somewhat more surprising given modern labor market institutions that tend to protect older workers with seniority. However, if paternalism or nascent internal labor market institutions tended to prevent wage rates from falling as productivity declined, employers would have had an economic incentive to practice age discrimination when selecting workers for reduced days. It is also possible that employers tended to favor younger men who had young

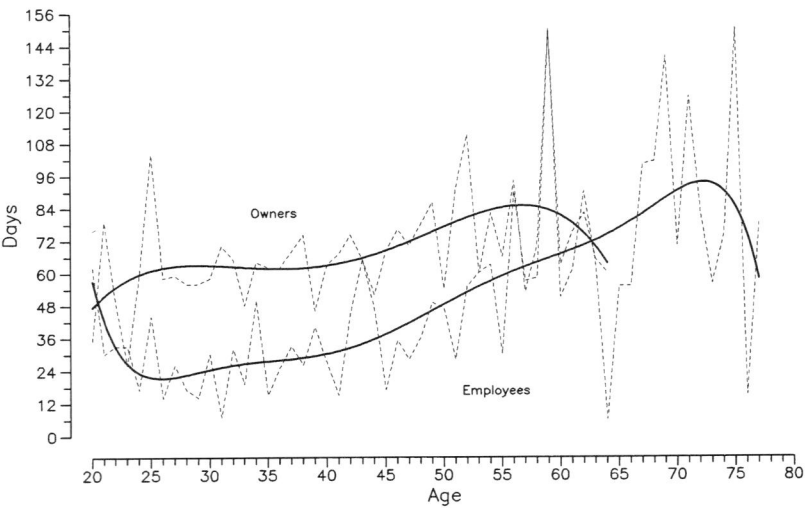

Fig. 11.9. Age profile of days lost from work due to illness or lack of work, hack and bus line employees and self-employed owners of hacks and drays, Michigan, 1896.

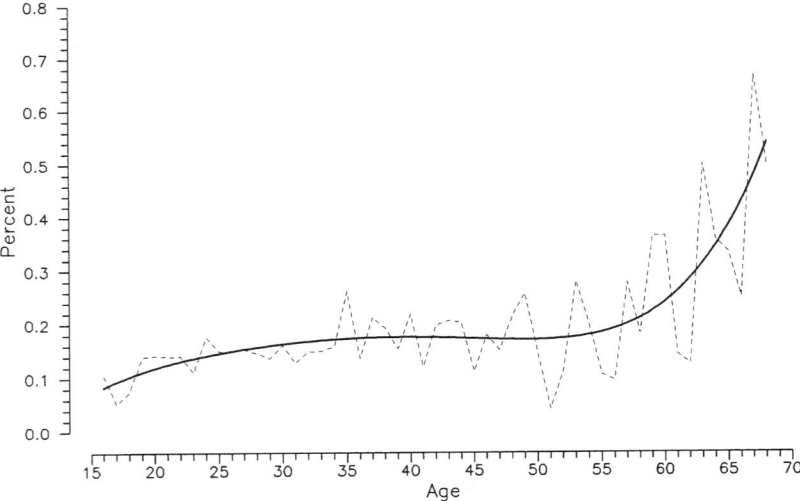

Fig. 11.10. Proportion of workers reporting illness, by age, Michigan farm laborers, 1894.

Fig. 11.11. Age profile of days taken from work for vacation, California, 1892.

children to support than older men whose children were grown and might even be in a position to support them.

The fact that vacation time increases with age can be interpreted in two ways. Perhaps some workers reported time lost as voluntary when it was induced by fatigue or illness. It is also possible that older workers were able to "afford" more leisure time because of their success in building a stock of assets when they were younger. If so, we can think of vacation time as a form of partial or phased retirement. We note in this regard that the number of days taken as vacation time by older workers is greater than that taken by younger workers when one looks only at the distribution of those reporting some vacation time. Figure 11.11 presents this comparison for the California workers.

CONCLUSION

The analysis behind the findings reported in this chapter is descriptive and the results still somewhat provisional. Nevertheless, we find the profiles of wages, earnings, and time lost by age drawn from these rather diverse samples highly suggestive and intriguing. For all of the surveys we examined, both income and annual earnings of men aged 50 or older were distinctly less than those of men aged 30 to 45. We believe that the lower income reflected an industrial wage system that was based on physical productivity, which declined as the worker moved past middle age. The decline of in-

come of older workers, together with the discovery that the incidence of lost
time rose dramatically for workers above the age of 45 or 50, reflected this
decline in productivity. That time lost and incidence of illness increased
with age is hardly surprising. However, the higher number of "days lost" suggests that older workers who did not have either a family-based form of economic security or assets accumulated over their lifetime were at substantial
risk in the labor markets of the late nineteenth century. Because of this, the
problem of economic security among older workers at the turn of the century was a major concern to working-class Americans.

A key question for economic historians in all this is whether the age profiles we examined in this chapter are reflective of a situation in which workers were able to anticipate their declining economic position and plan for
retirement in old age through life cycle saving or whether this was a world
in which older workers were caught in a vicious economic squeeze. The answer to that question is not apparent from the data presented above. However, there is considerable evidence that for a significant fraction of families
in these surveys, a substantial portion of income was being saved during the
middle of the life cycle, that assets were being accumulated by a majority of
workers, and that late-life dis-saving was common. For those who succeeded
in saving enough over previous years, retirement or substantially reduced
work effort in late life became an option whether or not their health deteriorated. Of course, retired men were not in the samples of working families used as the basis for our analysis in this chapter. The estimates of labor
force participation in 1900 and 1910 leave little doubt, however, that a sizable fraction of men did retire.

APPENDIX: ESTIMATING THE AGE PROFILE OF VARIABLES
IN THE LABOR SURVEYS

The age profile curves in the figures presented in this chapter are smoothed
polynomials derived from the raw data. To illustrate how these curves are
generated, we present two examples of this technique as it was applied to
determine the smoothed curves on age distribution of workers in Kansas
(fig. 11.2) and the age profile of wages in Kansas (fig. 11.5). Figure 11.A1
presents the age distribution for the Kansas survey. In addition to the fitted
line, we present the actual values for each age, which are then connected by
a dashed line. Figure 11.A2 presents the raw data and a smoothed polynomial for daily wage rates in the Kansas survey. Each dot in the figure
represents one (or more) worker. The smooth line is a seventh-degree polynomial fit through those points using ordinary least squares regression techniques. Figure 11.A3 plots the same smooth curve as a dashed line and for
comparison also plots a jagged line connecting the mean wage rate for each
age. The standard error about each respective mean is also represented by

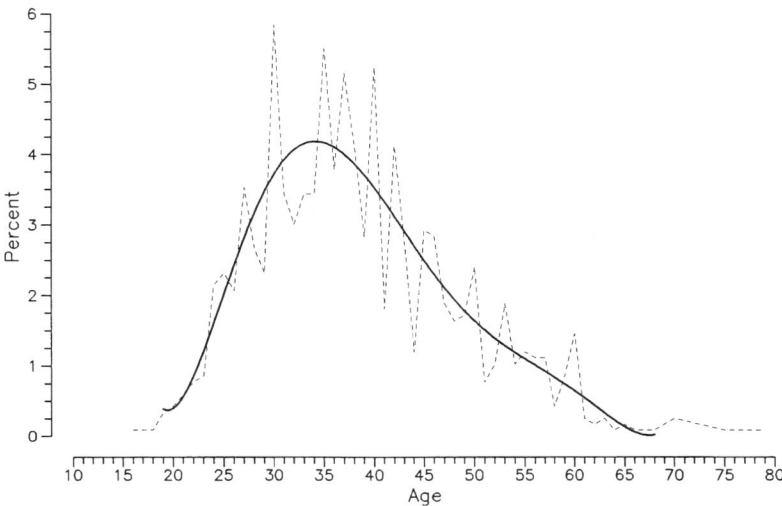

Fig. 11.A1. Age distribution of respondents, Kansas, 1884–1887: Fitted line and actual values.

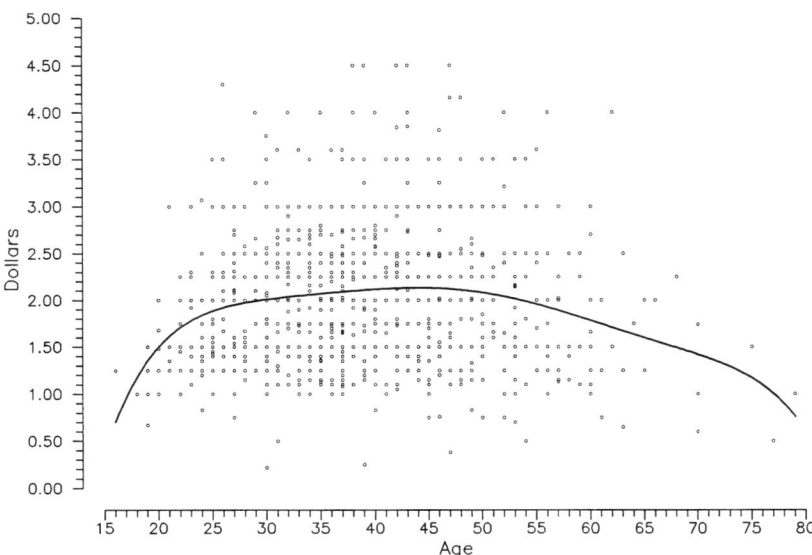

Fig. 11.A2. Age profile of daily wage rates, Kansas, 1884–1887: Raw data and smoothed polynomial.

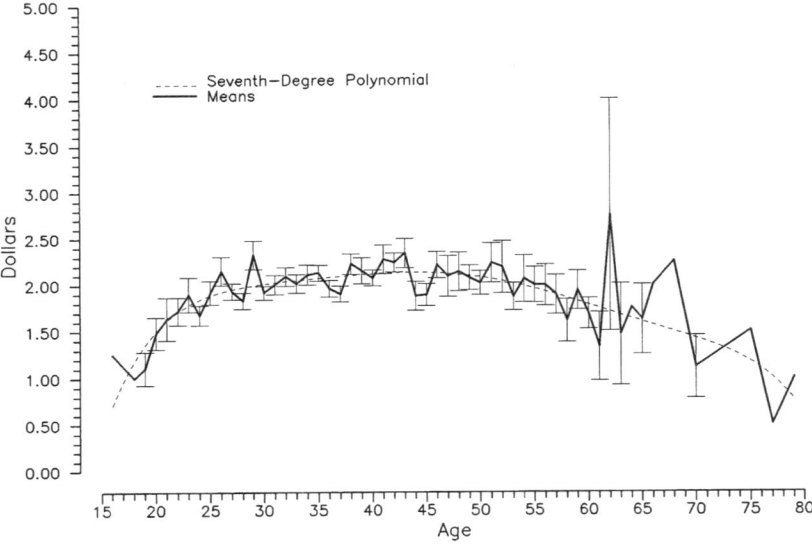

Fig. 11.A3. Age profile of daily wage rates, Kansas, 1884–1887: Standard error of the means.

the vertical lines. Similar procedures were followed in the estimation of age profiles for earnings and days lost.

NOTES

Susan B. Carter has collaborated with us in collecting some of the data sets employed in this chapter. We are grateful for her help and advice. She also offered several suggestions on the first draft that we have taken advantage of in preparing this version. We thank the National Institute on Aging, the National Science Foundation, the Institute of Business and Economic Research, the Laboratory for Historical Research, and the Academic Senate of the University of California for financial support. The data referred to here will be archived at the Laboratory for Historical Research at the University of California, Riverside.

1. Estimates by Spurgeon Bell (1940: 11) and Alvin Hansen (1922: 504) put the industrial workers as a fraction of all gainfully employed workers in 1900 at between 32.4 and 38.4 percent; Stanley Lebergott (1964: 512–513, tables A3 and A4) estimates nonfarm employees (excluding domestic service employees) at 37.4 percent.

2. A sampling of prior views can be found in Bancroft 1958: 38–39; Mushkin and Berman 1947; and Achenbaum 1978. In Ransom and Sutch 1986a, we have traced the historiography of pre-1940 retirement in an attempt to understand the persistent tendency to underestimate the extent of retirement during the sixty years prior to World War II. This issue has more than a purely historical relevance; it has profoundly influenced the thinking of economists on current policy issues. The under-

estimate of retirement is explicit in the work of Michael R. Darby (1979) and implicit in that of Laurence J. Kotlikoff and Lawrence H. Summers (1981). For a corrective, see Ransom and Sutch 1986*b*.

3. The modern concept of labor force participation did not exist prior to 1940. Estimates for the years 1900 to 1930 had previously been based on backward extrapolations of the 1940 data to earlier years (Mushkin and Berman 1947). The new estimates of labor force participation we have made are based on published census data for 1870 and 1880, data from the manuscript censuses for 1900 and 1910, and a special study by the U.S. Bureau of the Census for 1930. For a discussion of these estimates and the methodology employed for our estimates, see Ransom and Sutch 1986*a*, 1988, and 1989*a*, and Ransom, Sutch, and Williamson 1991. Jon Moen (1987) has challenged our approach, but we believe his critique was based on a misunderstanding (see Ransom and Sutch 1989*a*; Ransom, Sutch, and Williamson 1991).

4. The retired are not in the labor force; thus the proportion retired is defined as one minus the labor force participation rate. Census figures report a fall in the rate of labor force participation of men 60 and older from 54.5 percent in 1950 to 32.2 percent in 1980; see figure 11.1. This development is one of the most dramatic changes in labor force behavior to have occurred since World War II. Only the increase in the labor force participation of married women during the same period rivals the change in male retirement in quantitative significance.

5. A private saving plan that protected workers with term life insurance and also provided a lump sum payment after twenty years of contributions was very popular in the late nineteenth century. These instruments were called "tontine insurance policies" and were sold by most insurance companies until they were outlawed in 1906. For a discussion of these plans and circumstances surrounding their abolition, see Ransom and Sutch 1987. Perhaps more than the current era, this period of history seems to fit the assumptions that underlie the life cycle model of saving. That model sees the need to make provisions for retirement as the major motive for private saving (Modigliani 1986).

6. For a more detailed account of Wright's pioneering effort in data collection and its impact on the Massachusetts Bureau of the Statistics of Labor, see Williamson 1967.

7. An index of all of the state reports was published by the U.S. Bureau of Labor (Wright 1902). Wright became the informal leader of the movement to establish the various state bureaus and to further the collection of survey data. In 1885, when Congress established the federal Bureau of Labor Statistics, Wright became its first director. In that capacity he coordinated the efforts to collect data at the state level throughout the 1880s and 1890s. For a more complete summary of the role of Wright in encouraging the collection of this data, see Carter, Ransom, and Sutch 1991.

8. Joan Hannon (1978, 1982*a*, 1982*b*) was one of the first to make extensive use of state labor survey data in computerized format in her analysis of ethnic discrimination in Michigan. More recent research efforts include work by Barry Eichengreen and Henry Gemery relying on a survey of Iowa teachers (Eichengreen 1984, 1987; Eichengreen and Gemery 1986); our own work using data from Michigan, Maine, and Kansas surveys (Ransom and Sutch 1986*a*, 1989*b*); and used by Susan Carter, Peter Philips, and Elizabeth Savoca of a survey from California (Carter 1988; Carter and Philips 1990; Carter and Savoca 1990, 1991, 1992).

9. For a fuller discussion of the objectives and data sets to be collected by the *Historical Labor Statistics Project,* see Ransom 1990 and Carter, Ransom, and Sutch 1991.

10. This point has great significance for evaluating the trends in retirement in the 1870–1940 period evident in figure 11.1, since the fraction of the labor force engaged in agricultural occupations fell steadily from over 50 percent at the outset to less than 25 percent at the end of the period. This shift away from agriculture should have increased the overall proportion of the elderly population that was retired. The fact that such a trend is not evident in the aggregate data implies that retirement among the nonagricultural segment of the population was becoming less common before 1940 (Ransom and Sutch 1988).

11. We also have a survey of 935 farm proprietors from Michigan. Unfortunately, the age of the owner was not asked in this survey, and no use of these data is made in this chapter.

12. There may also have been a bias toward household heads that could have systematically led to the exclusion of older men who were living as dependents in the homes of their grown children.

13. The technique employed in the construction of these curves is explained in the appendix.

14. Data for the census of 1900 was from a public use sample; see Ransom and Sutch 1988. As figure 11.1 indicates, there was a relative stability in the labor force participation of older men during the last quarter of the nineteenth century. This is also true of adult mortality experience (Ransom and Sutch 1989*a*: 5). Thus we believe it is reasonable to extrapolate backward the age distribution of male labor force participation observed in 1900 to the time of these worker surveys.

15. Teaching may not be as different as usually supposed. Susan Carter and Elizabeth Savoca (1992) have analyzed the information in the Iowa survey in more detail. They argue that a teacher's lifetime job tenure was surprisingly long.

16. It is interesting to note that the earnings profile for farm laborers exhibits the least pronounced decline of earnings with age.

17. It is worth noting that this survey was completed prior to the impact of the depression of 1893–1894.

18. We have argued elsewhere that a variety of such "strategies" might be employed, ranging from a dependence on the more traditional family based systems of economic support for older family members to what we characterize as a "life cycle" strategy of saving for old age retirement (Ransom and Sutch 1989*b*).

19. The methods for smoothing the data on days lost is similar to that for the age and earnings distributions presented earlier. See the appendix for details.

REFERENCES

Achenbaum, W. Andrew. 1978. *Old age in the new land: The American experience since 1790.* Baltimore: Johns Hopkins University Press.

Bancroft, Gertrude. 1958. *The American labor force: Its growth and changing composition.* New York: Social Science Research Council.

Bell, Spurgeon. 1940. *Productivity, wages, and national income.* Washington, D.C.: Brookings Institution.

California Bureau of Labor Statistics. 1892. *Fifth biennial report, 1892.* Sacramento.

Carter, Susan B. 1988. "The changing importance of lifetime jobs, 1892–1978." *Industrial Relations* 27(Fall): 287–300.

Carter, Susan B., and Peter Philips. 1990. "Technology, work organization and the gender gap in manufacturing wages, 1830–1980." In *New developments in the labor market: Toward a new institutional paradigm,* ed. Katherine G. Abraham and Robert B. McKersie, 213–238. Cambridge: MIT Press.

Carter, Susan B., Roger L. Ransom, and Richard Sutch. 1991. "The Historical Labor Statistics Project at the University of California." *Historical Methods* 24(Spring): 52–65.

Carter, Susan B., and Elizabeth Savoca. 1990. "Labor mobility and lengthy jobs in nineteenth-century America." *Journal of Economic History* 50(March): 1–16.

———. 1991. "Gender differences in learning and earning in nineteenth-century America: The role of expected job and career attachment." *Explorations in Economic History* 28(July): 323–343.

———. 1992. "The teaching procession? Another look at teacher tenure, 1845–1925." *Explorations in Economic History* 29(October): 401–416.

Darby, Michael R. 1979. *The effects of social security on income and the capital stock.* Washington, D.C.: American Enterprise Institute.

Duggan, James E. 1984. "The labor force participation of older workers." *Industrial and Labor Relations Review* 37(April): 415–430.

Eichengreen, Barry. 1984. "Experience and the male-female earnings gap in the 1890s." *Journal of Economic History* 44(September): 822–834.

———. 1987. "The impact of late nineteenth-century unions on labor earnings and hours: Iowa in 1894." *Industrial and Labor Relations Review* 40(July): 501–515.

Eichengreen, Barry, and Henry Gemery. 1986. "The earnings of skilled and unskilled immigrants at the end of the 19th century." *Journal of Economic History* 44(June): 441–454.

Goldin, Claudia. 1990. *Understanding the gender gap: An economic history of American women.* Oxford: Oxford University Press.

Hajnal, John. 1953. "Age at marriage and proportions marrying." *Population Studies* 7(November): 111–136.

Hannon, Joan Underhill. 1978. "The immigrant worker in the promised land: Human capital and ethnic discrimination in the Michigan labor market, 1889–1890." Ph.D. dissertation, Department of Economics, University of Wisconsin.

———. 1982*a.* "Ethnic discrimination in a 19th-century mining district: Michigan copper mines, 1888." *Explorations in Economic History* 19(January): 28–50.

———. 1982*b.* "City size and ethnic discrimination: Michigan agricultural implements and iron working industries, 1890." *Journal of Economic History* 42(December): 825–846.

Hansen, Alvin H. 1922. "Industrial classes in the United States in 1920." *Journal of the American Statistical Association* 18(December): 501–508.

Iowa Bureau of Labor Statistics. 1885. *First biennial report, 1884–5.* Des Moines: Geo. E. Roberts.

Kansas Bureau of Labor and Industrial Statistics. 1886. *First annual report, January 1, 1886.* Topeka: T. D. Thatcher, State Printer.

———. 1887. *Second annual report, January 1, 1887.* Topeka: T. D. Thatcher, State Printer.

————. 1888. *Third annual report, January 1, 1888.* Topeka: Clifford C. Baker, State Printer.

Kotlikoff, Laurence J., and Lawrence H. Summers. 1981. "The role of intergenerational transfers in aggregate capital accumulation." *Journal of Political Economy* 89(August): 706–732.

Lebergott, Stanley. 1964. *Manpower in economic growth: The American record since 1800.* New York: McGraw-Hill.

Maine Bureau of Industrial and Labor Statistics. 1888. *First annual report, 1887.* Augusta: Burleigh and Flynt, Printers to the State.

————. 1892. *Fifth annual report, 1891.* Augusta: Burleigh and Flynt, Printers to the State.

Michigan Bureau of Labor and Industrial Statistics. 1895. *Twelfth annual report of the Bureau of Labor, year ending February 1, 1895.* Lansing: Robert Smith and Co., State Printers and Binders.

————. 1889. *Seventh annual report.* Lansing: State Printer.

Modigliani, Franco. 1986. "Life cycle, individual thrift, and the wealth of nations." *American Economic Review* 76(June): 297–313.

Moen, Jon. 1987. "The labor of older men: A comment." *Journal of Economic History* 47(September): 761–767.

Mushkin, S. J., and Alan Berman. 1947. "Factors influencing trends in employment of the aged." *Social Security Bulletin* 10(August): 18–23.

New Jersey Bureau of Statistics of Labor and Industries. 1889. *Twelfth annual report of the Bureau of Statistics of Labor and Industries of New Jersey for the year ending October 31, 1889.* Trenton: F. F. Patterson.

————. 1890. *Thirteenth annual report of the Bureau of Statistics of Labor and Industries of New Jersey, for the year ending October 31, 1890.* Trenton: Electric Printing Company.

————. 1891. *Fourteenth annual report of the Bureau of Statistics of Labor and Industries of New Jersey for the year ending October 31st, 1891.* Trenton: John L. Murphy.

Ransom, Roger L. 1990. "A proposal for a historical statistics archive." *Cliometrics Newsletter* (April): n.p.

Ransom, Roger L., and Richard Sutch. 1986a. "The labor of older Americans: Retirement of men on and off the job, 1870–1937." *Journal of Economic History* 46(March): 1–30.

————. 1986b. "Unequalled thrift: An inquiry into the saving behavior of Americans at the turn of the century." Paper presented to the American Economic Association, New Orleans, December.

————. 1987. "Tontine insurance and the Armstrong investigation: A case of stifled innovation, 1868–1905." *Journal of Economic History* 47(June): 379–390.

————. 1988. "The decline of retirement in the years before social security: U.S. retirement patterns, 1870–1940." In *Issues in contemporary retirement,* ed. Edward Lazear and Rita Ricardo-Campbell, 3–37. Stanford: Hoover Institution Press.

————. 1989a. "The trend in the rate of labor force participation of older men, 1870–1930: A reply to Moen." *Journal of Economic History* 49(March): 170–183.

————. 1989b. "Two strategies for a more secure old age: Life cycle saving by late nineteenth-century American workers." Working Papers on the History of Saving, no. 6, Institute of Business and Research, University of California, Berkeley.

Ransom, Roger L., Richard Sutch, and Samuel Williamson. 1991. "Retirement: Past and present." In *Retirement and public policy: Proceedings of the second conference of the National Academy of Social Insurance,* ed. Alicia H. Munnell, 23–57. Dubuque: Kendall Hunt.

U.S. Census Office. 1890. *Eleventh census.* Vol. 7. *Mineral industries.* Washington, D.C.: Government Printing Office.

Williamson, Jeffrey G. 1967. "Consumer behavior in the nineteenth century: Carroll D. Wright's Massachusetts workers in 1875." *Explorations in Entrepreneurial History,* 2d series, 4(Winter): 98–135.

Wright, Carroll D. 1902. *Index of all reports issued by Bureaus of Labor Statistics in the United States prior to March 1, 1902.* U.S. Bureau of Labor. Washington, D.C.: Government Printing Office.

TWELVE

Trends in Old Age Mortality in the United States, 1900–1935: Evidence from Railroad Pensions

George Alter

In his agenda for the historical demography of aging, Peter Laslett calls attention to the need for historical studies of survival at the oldest ages. Although our understanding of trends in mortality is informed by two centuries of European and almost one century of American vital registration, these data provide little guidance on trends in mortality at the oldest ages. Even in a large population, few people survive to the oldest ages, so the mortality rates at these ages are subject to large random errors. In addition, demographers and actuaries have always been mistrustful of the reporting of ages among the elderly. There is a well-documented tendency toward the overstatement of ages above 65 in both censuses and vital registration. Reliable evidence on old age mortality in the United States has only become available since 1940 with the advent of the Social Security system. This chapter will examine new evidence on old age mortality at the beginning of the twentieth century.

Although empirical data on mortality at the oldest ages are sparse, the length of the human life span and the shape of mortality at the oldest ages have been debated for a long time. Medical researchers have been intrigued by experimental evidence suggesting a biological limit to longevity (Sacher 1978; Strehler and Mildvan 1960). Actuaries and demographers have been searching for a mathematical representation of old age mortality (Benjamin 1982; Gompertz 1825; Le Bras 1976; Perks 1932). The Gompertz function, which has been used to approximate mortality at the oldest ages for more than a century, is widely considered less than satisfactory (Bayo 1972; Pakin and Hrisanov 1984). In the last decade interest in old age mortality was renewed by two new theoretical perspectives.

James Fries proposed that the twentieth century has witnessed a tendency toward the "rectangularization of the survival curve" (Fries 1983; Fries and

Crapo 1981). Fries uses official U.S. life tables from 1900 onward to argue that additions to the length of life have not resulted from any increase in the maximum human life span but rather from an increase in the number of people who approach the limits of human longevity. This evidence, he argues, is consistent with biological models of a limited life span. Fries is mainly interested in the implications of this pattern for health policy, and he advocates public health efforts directed toward "compressing" morbidity into the last years of life. Thus, although human life span would not increase, the period between the onset of chronic diseases and the end of life would be shortened. Unfortunately, as we shall see below, U.S. mortality data are not a reliable basis for this kind of analysis.[1]

An alternative perspective with dramatically different implications was introduced by Kenneth G. Manton, James W. Vaupel, and others who have called attention to the implications of heterogeneous "frailty" for the future course of mortality and morbidity. An influential 1979 article by Vaupel, Manton, and Eric Stallard showed that differences among individuals in susceptibility to disease and death can result in misleading trends in aggregate mortality. The term "frailty" has been used to describe differences in the likelihood of death among individuals in the face of a given set of environmental factors. When mortality is high, persons who are relatively more "frail" tend to die at younger ages, and the distribution of frailty among survivors at older ages is quite different from the distribution of frailty at birth. As the level of mortality declines, some individuals who would have died in earlier cohorts reach older ages. These "new survivors" tend to be more frail than those who would have survived when mortality was higher, and the average frailty of the elderly population increases.

Although the magnitude of this effect is still heatedly debated, it has important implications (Coale and Kisker 1986). Vaupel, Manton, and Stallard (1979) showed that changes in the average frailty of the surviving population tend to hide long-run changes in mortality rates at older ages. When mortality is declining, the increasing frailty of the older population offsets some of the reduction in the risk of death. Thus, if the underlying hazard of death was changing at the same rate at every age, old age mortality would appear to be declining more slowly. Indeed, the rising average frailty due to new survivors can lead to increasing mortality rates at some older ages, even though mortality for a hypothetical "standard" individual with a given genetic endowment would have been decreasing at every age.

George Alter and James C. Riley (1989) have explored the implications of frailty models for morbidity. Simulations in this study show that falling mortality can result in rising morbidity as relatively frail individuals have longer lives but are still more likely to become ill. The tendency of some medical interventions to lengthen life without restoring health has been called the "failures of success" (Gruenberg 1977). This is a perspective quite contrary to the implications derived by Fries (see also Riley 1989).

The available evidence on trends in old age mortality in the United States shows them to have been much less consistent than those at younger ages. While mortality has declined more or less continuously at younger ages, progress at older ages has been slow and halting. There have been periods in which mortality decline at the oldest ages stopped and a natural limit on the human life span appeared to have been reached (Fingerhut 1982; Olshansky, Carnes, and Cassel 1990).

The divergent trends in young and old age mortality were very dramatic in the early part of this century. Table 12.1 compares probabilities of death by age in 1901 and 1930 from U.S. life tables for the ten states with reliable death registration in 1901. The table shows rapid progress in reducing mortality at all of the younger ages. The probability of death in five years fell by 40 percent or more at every age under 40. There was almost no change in old age mortality, however.

TABLE 12.1   Age-Specific Probabilities of Death ($_5q_x$) in 1901 and 1930 and Percent Change from 1901 to 1930 for U.S. White Males in the Original Registration States

Age	$_5q_x$ 1901	$_5q_x$ 1930	Percent Change
0	0.1914	0.0838	−56.2
5	0.0217	0.0107	−50.5
10	0.0136	0.0082	−39.7
15	0.0213	0.0124	−41.7
20	0.0323	0.0160	−50.5
25	0.0364	0.0174	−52.1
30	0.0418	0.0211	−49.6
35	0.0482	0.0281	−41.7
40	0.0552	0.0396	−28.3
45	0.0667	0.0552	−17.2
50	0.0835	0.0785	−6.0
55	0.1150	0.1117	−2.9
60	0.1551	0.1580	1.9
65	0.2193	0.2207	0.6
70	0.3020	0.3098	2.6
75	0.4265	0.4290	0.6
80	0.5718	0.5702	−0.3
85	0.7100	0.7008	−1.3

SOURCES: Glover 1921; Hill 1936.

This chapter investigates old age mortality in this period of rapid progress at the younger ages. Annual series of mortality rates at older ages seem to show increasing mortality, with a peak around 1926. This pattern attracted the attention of influential researchers, such as the public health reformer Edgar Sydenstricker (1933) and the actuary Louis Dublin (Metropolitan Life Insurance Company 1929*b*). However, it was by no means certain that the trend had really changed. These apparent increases may have been an echo of the 1918–1919 influenza epidemic or a result of temporary conditions in the 1920s.[2] Furthermore, as noted above, mortality at the oldest ages is always difficult to measure.

The evidence presented here supports the conclusion that an increase in old age mortality did occur in the early twentieth century. Data from three sources will be described: vital registration from the death registration area of 1900, the Pennsylvania Railroad Pension Fund, and an investigation of all railroad pensions by the Federal Coordinator of Transportation. The railroad pension fund data are important, because they are not subject to the age misreporting that seriously impairs the usefulness of censuses and vital registration. These data sets differ in methodology and geographic coverage, but they provide a consistent picture of old age mortality. All these data suggest that mortality above age 80 was either stable or rising in the first third of this century.

TRENDS IN U.S. VITAL RATES

The United States was one of the last industrial countries to develop comprehensive vital registration. Vital registration was the responsibility of the individual states. Massachusetts was the first state to establish a reliable death registration system, and its records are considered complete from about 1870 (Gutman 1956). The U.S. Bureau of the Census began publishing mortality statistics beginning with 1900 for the states and cities in which adequate registration was available. This "original" registration area covered ten states (the six New England states, Indiana, Michigan, New Jersey, and New York) and the District of Columbia. States were added to the registration area as their records were found to be complete. The registration area had expanded to 20 states in 1910, 34 states in 1920, and 47 states in 1930. The death registration system was completed in 1933 when Texas was added.

The gradual expansion of the registration area often confuses the picture of mortality trends in this period. Registration was established first in northeastern states. On balance, these were more industrial and more urban than the southern and western states added later. The early registration states also had fewer nonwhites and more recent immigrants. The net effect of these differences was higher mortality in states with earlier registration. Consequently, mortality tables constructed from the expanding registration area tend to show a decline in mortality, which is an artifact of changing geographic coverage.

Figures 12.1 and 12.2 show age-specific death rates for ages 65–74, 75–84, and 85 and older from 1900 to 1940 for white males and white females in the original registration states. Each of these curves tells a similar story. There appears to have been constant or slightly rising mortality from about 1900 to 1920, a peak in mortality in the mid-1920s, and declining mortality in the late 1920s and 1930s. These visible patterns are confirmed in table 12.2, which shows regression lines fitted by ordinary least squares. The coefficients for the year in these equations estimate the annual decrease in the age-specific death rates. For the entire period from 1900 to 1940, downward trends are found in five of the six series. When only the period from 1900 to 1929 is considered, however, all six series produce upward trends. Furthermore, the rates of increase are correlated with age. The annual increase in the death rate for white males rises from 0.054 per thousand at ages 65–74 to 0.361 per thousand at ages 85 and over. The corresponding estimates for white females are 0.001 and 0.892, respectively. Mortality at ages below 65 was decreasing. Thus there was an overall shift from falling mortality at younger ages to rising mortality at the oldest ages from 1900 to 1929.

The age-specific death rates from vital registration are suspect, however, because of the tendency toward age overstatement at the highest ages. The death rates shown in figures 12.1 and 12.2 are ratios of deaths reported in vital registration and population estimates derived from censuses. Errors in both sources are suggested by the Matching Record Study, which compared ages reported in the 1960 census to a sample of deaths registered in the following year (Hambright 1968). Discrepancies between the census and death certificates were greatest at the oldest ages, and the results of the study

TABLE 12.2   Regression Coefficients for Age-Specific Death Rates, U.S. Death Registration States of 1900

	White Male			*White Female*		
	65–74	75–84	85+	65–74	75–84	85+
1900–1940						
Year	−0.045	0.025	−0.505	−0.170	−0.099	−0.466
Constant	146.5	81.3	1228.4	379.1	306.9	1142.2
R²	0.047	0.004	0.146	0.423	0.053	0.076
1900–1929						
Year	0.054	0.256	0.361	0.001	0.232	0.892
Constant	−43.4	−360.1	−425.9	51.8	−325.5	−1452.1
R²	0.032	0.185	0.051	0.000	0.185	0.183

SOURCE: Linder and Grove 1963.
NOTE: Dependent variables: Age-specific death rates. Independent variable: Year.

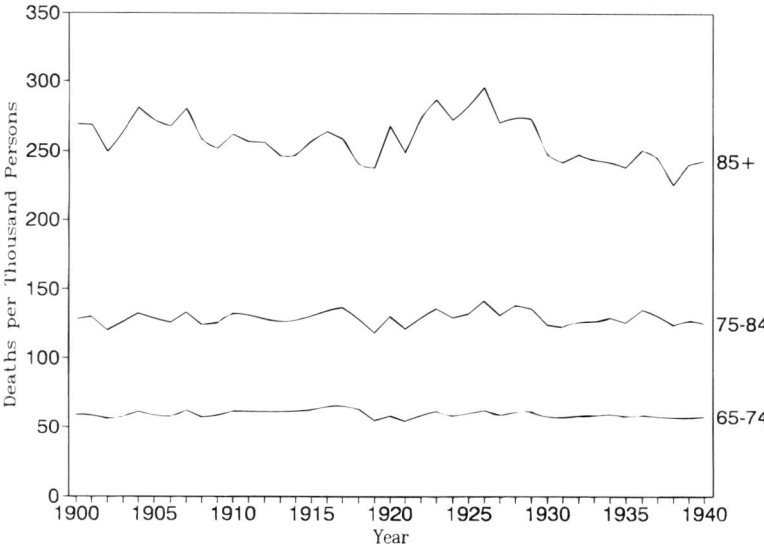

Fig. 12.1. Age-specific death rates, 1900–1940: White males, U.S. death registration states of 1900.

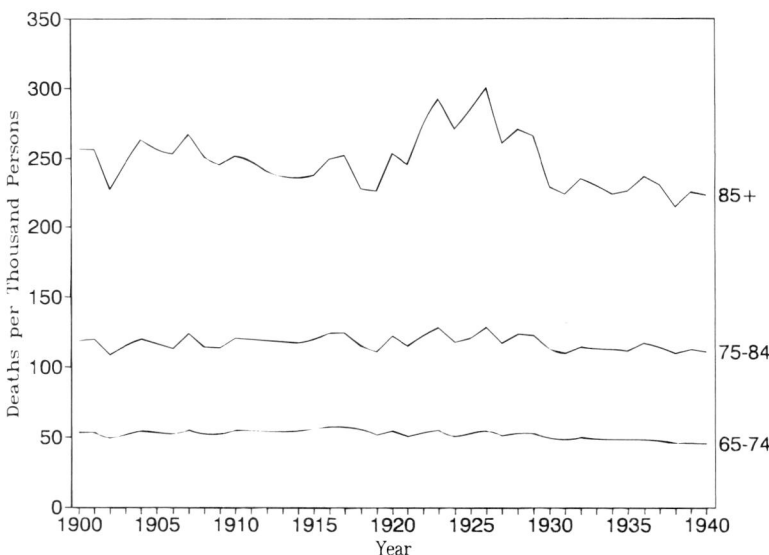

Fig. 12.2. Age-specific death rates, 1900–1940: White females, U.S. death registration states of 1900.

are consistent with a hypothesis of roughly equal age misreporting in both sources. It is likely that age misreporting at the beginning of this century was even more common than it was in 1960.

Since age overstatement tends to be dominant at the oldest ages, the reported age-specific death rates at these ages include some experience of younger people. We can consider the problem in the following way. When age misreporting is present, the observed mortality rate at a given age is a weighted average of the mortality rates of three groups: (1) those who are younger than the reported age, (2) those who are reported at their true age, and (3) those who are older than the reported age. Persons whose ages are overstated (group 1) tend to lower observed mortality, because younger persons have lower mortality rates. Age understatement (group 3) tends to increase mortality by erroneously including older persons in younger age groups. The amount of bias in the observed mortality rate depends on both the numbers of younger and older persons whose ages are misreported and on the differences in mortality at true and observed ages.[3]

Age misreporting will have little effect on the observed death rate when the proportions misreported from younger and older ages are approximately equal. This tends to be the case at the younger adult ages, but it is not likely to occur at the oldest ages. First, there is a tendency for more age overstatement than understatement at these ages. Second, at the upper ages there are many fewer people at older than at younger ages. The high mortality rates at these ages impart a steep slope to the population distribution, which puts more people at risk of age overstatement than age understatement. All of the errors in the final, open-ended age category are errors of age overstatement. Thus age misreporting results in an influx from younger to older age groups. These younger individuals experience mortality rates lower than those of the age groups in which they are reported. This results in an underestimate of the death rates at the oldest ages (Coale and Kisker 1986).

Trends in observed mortality rates will be affected by changes in both age misreporting and in the underlying true mortality rates. On one hand, improvements in age reporting will result in an upward trend in the observed mortality rates at older ages. As the proportions incorrectly reported in higher age groups decline, the mortality rates at these higher ages will tend to increase. On the other hand, a downward trend in mortality at younger ages will tend to produce a decline in mortality at older ages as well. Individuals impart the trends in their true mortality rates to the categories in which they are reported.

The death rates in the U.S. registration area would have been subject to both of these effects. It is possible that age reporting was improving at this time. Ansley J. Coale and Melvin Zelnik (1963) estimated decreasing enumeration errors at most adult ages for the censuses of 1900 to 1930. However, the population aged 85 and over was still significantly overcounted in the 1930 census. Preliminary estimates using stable population methods suggest that at least 10 and possibly more than 25 percent of those reported as 85 and over were really younger than 85 (Alter 1990). This factor would lead to an understatement of the upward trend at these older ages. Thus the effects of improved age reporting were probably offset by declining or less rapidly increasing mortality at younger ages.

On balance, the upward trend in old age mortality observed in the U.S. death registration states appears to be real. It is unlikely that the peak in mortality in the mid-1920s was caused by changes in age reporting.

THE PENNSYLVANIA RAILROAD PENSION FUND

Tabulations of the mortality experience of the Pennsylvania Railroad Pension Fund are available from its inception in 1900. The Pennsylvania Railroad was one of the first corporations to provide modern employee benefits. Sickness insurance and death benefits had been introduced in 1886, and in 1889 the company decided to give pensions to all workers above the age of 70. The new program included mandatory retirement at age 70, and the amount of the pension was based on earnings before retirement. Pensions were also provided for disabled workers aged 65–69 with thirty years of service. To limit future eligibility to long-term employees, the railroad also restricted the hiring of new workers to applicants under age 35.

Annual reports included in the minutes of the Board of Officers of the Pennsylvania Railroad Pension Fund have been used to calculate age-specific death rates. These records fall into two periods. Before 1920, the company was divided into eastern and western operating divisions, and a separate pension fund was maintained for workers in the railroad lines west of Pittsburgh. In 1920, the two pension funds were united, as part of a general reorganization of the company. The board of the smaller western fund did not tabulate its pensioners by age, so mortality rates presented here for 1900 to 1919 refer only to the eastern division of the company. Mortality rates for 1921 to 1936 refer to both divisions combined. In 1937, all railroad pensions were taken over by the Railroad Retirement Board, and the Pennsylvania Railroad Pension Fund limited its activities to providing for workers who did not meet the requirements of the new national system. Annual age-specific mortality rates are not available after the formation of the Railroad Retirement Board.

The Pennsylvania Railroad was the largest corporation in the United States during the nineteenth century, and its pension obligations at the beginning of this century were correspondingly large. By the end of its first year in operation, the fund supported 1,190 pensioners, including 1,054 who were age 70 or older, and 735 more workers retired in 1901. In 1920 when the western lines were added, there were 5,776 pensioners who were almost equally divided between ages 65–69 and 70 and older. At the end of 1936, when the fund was turned over to the U.S. Railroad Retirement Board, there were 11,682 pensioners, 3,428 of whom were aged 70 or more.[4]

Tabulations of mortality by attained age for the lines west of Pittsburgh are not available before the two operating divisions were merged in 1920. However, evidence on mortality in each region by age at retirement suggests that the difference between regions was negligible. Table 12.3 compares mortality in the eastern and western operating divisions for the years 1910 to 1919. Among those who retired at age 70 or older, mortality was nearly the same in each region, 103.4 deaths per thousand in the east compared to 103.9 in the western lines. The difference was somewhat higher for disability retirements at ages 65–69: 89.4 and 96.8 per thousand, respectively. Although these differences do indicate that mortality may have been slightly higher in the lines west of Pittsburgh, they do not represent significant differences.

Reporting of Ages

The pension fund records do not seem to suffer from the kinds of age misreporting that affect other sources of mortality information. Retirements were based on dates of birth already recorded in company personnel files. Since these dates of birth were reported at young adult ages, they would not have been subject to the systematic overstatement common at the older ages. Reporting is also likely to be more accurate when respondents are asked for their date of birth rather than their age, because there is less tendency to round years of birth.[5]

If workers were tempted to misstate their ages, they probably would have reported themselves as younger rather than older. Even before the com-

TABLE 12.3   Death Rates in the Pennsylvania Railroad Pension Fund, by Operation Division and Age at Retirement, 1910–1919

| | Age at Retirement | | |
	70+	65–69	Total
Number of deaths			
East	1,800	1,462	3,262
West	803	320	1,123
Number of lives at risk[a]			
East	17,407.5	16,354.5	33,762.0
West	7,731.0	3,305.5	11,036.5
Death rate			
East	0.1034	0.0894	0.0966
West	0.1039	0.0968	0.1018

[a]Number on December 31 of preceding year plus one-half the number who retired during the year.

pany banned the hiring of workers above the age of 35, younger workers were probably preferred. As retirement age approached, workers whose ages were understated could choose between continued employment or having their records corrected so that they could retire on time.

The minutes of the Board of Officers of the pension fund suggest that the company did attempt to keep its records accurate. Ages could often be checked by comparing different company files, because most workers would have reported their dates of birth more than once. The board considered a number of resolutions that would correct the dates of birth recorded in company files. For example, in 1919, the Board of Officers received a letter requesting the cancellation of mandatory retirement proceedings for a certain worker. The superintendent who wrote the letter claimed to have in his possession a family Bible proving that the correct date of birth was 1854, not 1848 (Pennsylvania Railroad Pension Fund, January 1, 1919).

An important indication of the accuracy of the ages reported in the pension records is the rarity of centenarians in these data. Only two pensioners reached the age of 102, and none exceeded that age. Individuals over the age of 100 are much more common when ages are poorly reported, and deaths are often found at ages 110 and over when age reporting is unreliable.

Selectivity and Representativeness

The mortality experience found in insurance, pensions, and annuities is usually not a representative sample of the entire population. These records differ in two important ways. First, the criteria for admission to these programs are often related to health. For example, insurance companies try to eliminate high-risk cases by requiring medical examinations. In general, the individuals included in insurance and pension records are healthier than the average population. Second, financial aspects of insurance and pensions often limit them to social and economic groups with special characteristics. Both of these problems affect the comparison between the Pennsylvania Railroad pensioners and the general population. For purposes of discussion, the first of these problems will be called "selectivity" and the second, "representativeness."

Actuaries have long been aware that mortality tables derived from insurance records often differ substantially from those based on the general population. The mortality of insurees tends to be particularly low in the first few years after the contracts begin, because persons with detectable disabilities are either refused insurance or placed in special high-risk categories. Pension records usually suffer from a similar selection bias known as the "healthy worker effect" (Fox and Collier 1976). Workers who retire at the mandatory age limit tend to be healthier than those who stop working at earlier ages. Mortality tables based on the experiences of disabled workers show much lower life expectancies than those based on active workers.

These selection effects lead us to expect lower mortality in the railroad pension records than we would see in the general population.

The difference between select and general populations is not constant, however. As the duration of the contract increases, the advantage due to selection diminishes for two reasons. On one hand, most health risks cannot be forecast very far into the future, so the select experience begins to approach the general experience. On the other hand, the high-risk individuals in the general population die more rapidly than others, which brings the average experience closer to the select experience. Most of the effects of selection are gone after five years, and only minor differences exist after ten years.

The rules of the Pennsylvania Railroad Pension Fund removed some of the impact of the selection in the data used here. Although the age of mandatory retirement was 70, workers became eligible for a disability pension at age 65. As we would expect, the mortality of disability retirees between ages 65 and 70 was very high. The disability provision of the pension meant that workers were selected into the pension system at age 65, even though most workers only began receiving benefits at age 70. Thus the healthy worker effect is reduced in these data, because pensioners have already been in the system for five years by age 70. There is some evidence of select mortality at ages 71 and 72, but this effect is gone by age 75.

An additional kind of selection bias can occur when a new program is introduced. The healthy worker effect is probably stronger for employees who retired in the first year of the new pension program than for those who retired later. The first cohort of pensioners did not benefit from the possibility of earlier disability pensions, and many of those who retired in 1900 and 1901 were above age 70 at retirement. Abraham M. Niessen (1948) notes that mortality rates in the first two years of the U.S. Railroad Retirement Board were lower than subsequent experience. A similar effect in the Pennsylvania Railroad pension data is described below.

There is no way to manipulate the pension fund data to make it approximate a random sample of the entire population, but railroad employees seem to be as close to a representative sample of white males as we are likely to find. A breakdown of the Pennsylvania Railroad pensioners by race and sex is not available. However, 93 percent of the early beneficiaries of the U.S. Railroad Retirement Board were white males (Niessen 1948).[6] We also know that the Pennsylvania Railroad Pension Fund applied to all employees of the railroad, company officers as well as manual workers. Since the railroad employed an extensive workforce with a large segment of clerks and other non-manual employees, its distribution of workers by social status is probably closer to the national pattern than a manufacturing firm would be.

Douglas Ewbank has provided me with estimates of infant and child mortality comparing railroad employees to the rest of the population. The estimates are based on reports of surviving children and children ever born in vital registration for the year 1928, and they refer to mortality conditions in approximately 1923. Ewbank has estimated child mortality rates of 0.1323 for railroad employees aged 20–39 and 0.1329 for the total population, a difference of less than 1 percent.[7] Since infant mortality and child mortality are very sensitive to living conditions, we can conclude that railroad workers were not subject to any unusual nonoccupational sources of mortality. Thus railroad workers, if not a representative sample, are at least a close approximation to the national average.

Calculating Mortality Rates

Information in the minutes of the Board of Officers has been used to calculate probabilities of dying for single years of age beginning at age 71. From 1900 to 1936, we have reports giving the number of pensioners by age at last birthday on December 31 of each year. From 1900 to 1919, the reports also give the number of new pensioners and deaths at each age, but after 1919, only the total numbers of new pensioners and deaths are given. Two years are missing from the series. The table for 1902 could not be located. In 1920, the merger of pensioners from lines west of Pittsburgh and changes in reporting procedures made it impossible to compute death rates.[8]

Death rates were computed by dividing the number of deaths by lives at risk. Lives at risk were computed as the sum of the number of pensioners on December 31 of the preceding year and one-half the number who retired during the year. After 1920, the totals of deaths and retirements must be distributed to single years of age. The age distribution of retirees in the years 1917–1919 was used to assign ages to retirees, and deaths were computed by subtracting the number of survivors at the end of the year. Since the overwhelming majority of nondisability retirements occurred at ages 70 or 71, any errors in assigning ages at retirement are minor and have almost no effect after age 75. Annual variations in the distribution of retirements by age are further mitigated by the procedure used to convert mortality estimates to exact ages.

The tables included in the minutes of the pension fund show ages tabulated by age at last birthday. Simple procedures have been used to compute age-specific mortality rates for exact ages in standard life table form. We assume that the population whose age at last birthday was x can be treated as a population aged exactly $x + \frac{1}{2}$. This is a reasonable approximation for data given by single year of age. Probabilities of death for exact ages ($_1q_x$) are derived by computing two-year moving averages.[9]

Trends in Mortality by Age

Figure 12.3 shows annual movements in probabilities of death at ages 71, 75, 80, and 85 ($_4q_{71}$, $_5q_{75}$, $_5q_{80}$, and $_5q_{85}$) for 1900 to 1936 derived from the Penn-

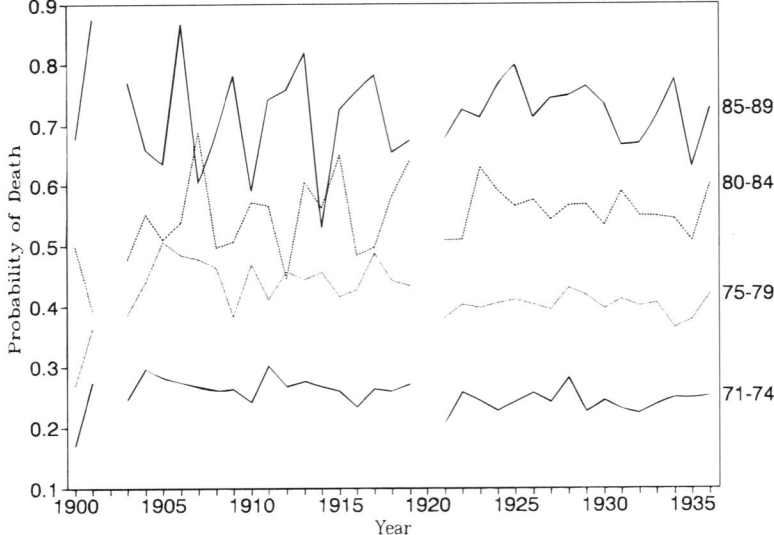

Fig. 12.3. Probability of death, by age: Pennsylvania Railroad Pension
Fund, 1900–1935.

sylvania Railroad Pension Fund data. In table 12.4 and figures 12.4 through
12.7, these mortality rates are aggregated into five-year periods centered on
years ending in 5 and 0. The mortality rates for ages 71–74 have been ex-
trapolated to ages 70–74 to facilitate comparison with U.S. life tables (also
presented in table 12.4 and figs. 12.4–12.7). Trends are easier to detect in
these figures without the confusing influence of annual fluctuations.

The influence of the selection effects described above are apparent in the
first two years of the pension fund. The mortality rates for ages 71–74 were
noticeably lower in the first two years of the pension fund, because currently
employed workers tend to be healthier than those who retire early. This effect disappeared relatively quickly as disability pensions at age 65 became
available, however.

The most remarkable aspect of these data is the difference between the
trends in mortality above and below age 80. The mortality rates at ages
71–74 and 75–79 show clear and steady declines between 1905 and 1935. It
is much more difficult to detect trends at the two older age groups. The age
group 80–84 has a generally rising pattern with the suggestion of a peak
around 1925. Ages 85–89 also peak near 1925, but the overall trend is even
more difficult to identify.

Table 12.4 and figures 12.4 through 12.7 show life table mortality estimates for the U.S. death registration area. Joseph A. Hill (1936) provides

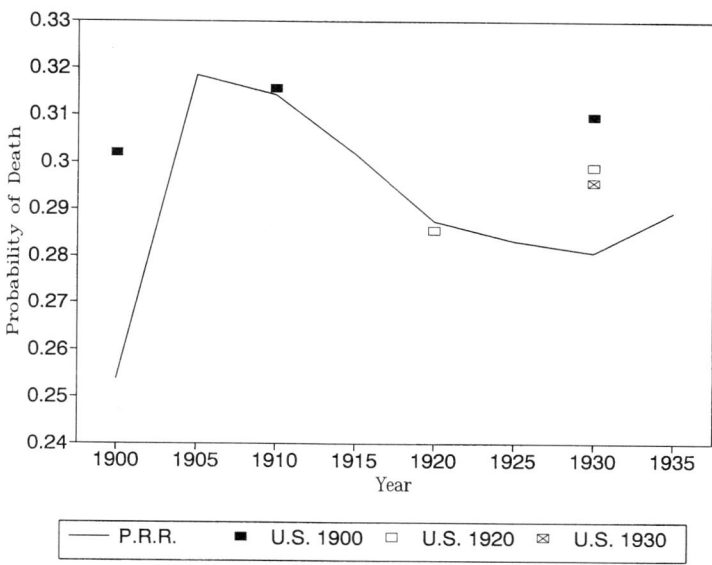

Fig. 12.4. Probability of death at age 70: Pennsylvania Railroad Pension Fund, 1900–1935, and U.S. Life Tables, 1900, 1920, and 1930.

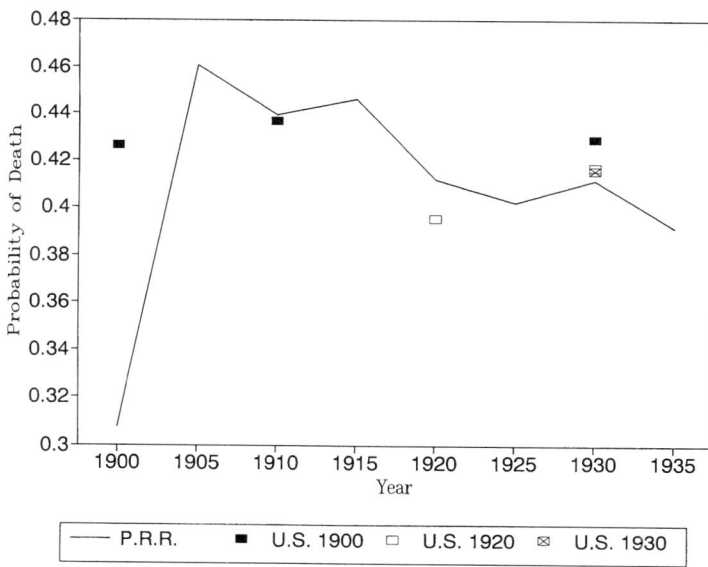

Fig. 12.5. Probability of death at age 75: Pennsylvania Railroad Pension Fund, 1900–1935, and U.S. Life Tables, 1900, 1920, and 1930.

TABLE 12.4　Comparison of Mortality Rates in Pennsylvania Railroad Pension Fund and U.S. White Male Life Tables, 1900–1935 (Probabilities of Death in the Next Five Years)

	Pennsylvania Railroad Pension Fund							
Age[a]	1900–1901	1903–1907	1908–1912	1913–1917	1918–1922	1923–1927	1928–1932	1933–1936
70	0.2537	0.3186	0.3143	0.3018	0.2876	0.2833	0.2808	0.2893
75	0.3077	0.4608	0.4394	0.4461	0.4119	0.4021	0.4114	0.3917
80	0.4765	0.5616	0.5176	0.5581	0.5546	0.5803	0.5610	0.5520
85	0.7584	0.7097	0.7311	0.7297	0.6860	0.7504	0.7099	0.7152
90			0.8284	0.8683	0.8670	0.8189	0.8176	0.8516
95						0.8808	0.6915	0.9613

	U.S. White Male Life Tables			
	1901	1910	1920	1930
70	0.3019	0.3156	0.2854	0.2958
75	0.4265	0.4366	0.3955	0.4157
80	0.5718	0.5769	0.5382	0.5603
85	0.7101	0.7040	0.6850	0.6889
90	0.8274	0.8103	0.7835	0.8041
95	0.9179	0.8940	0.8907	0.9125

Contemporary U.S. death registration area

Registration states of 1900			
70	0.3019	0.3156	0.3098
75	0.4265	0.4366	0.4290
80	0.5718	0.5769	0.5702
85	0.7101	0.7040	0.7008
90	0.8274	0.8103	0.8122
95	0.9179	0.8940	0.9055
Registration states of 1920			
70		0.2854	0.2989
75		0.3955	0.4170
80		0.5382	0.5602
85		0.6850	0.6908
90		0.7835	0.8039
95		0.8907	0.9170
Registration states of 1930			
70			0.2958
75			0.4157
80			0.5603
85			0.6889
90			0.8041
95			0.9125

[a]The probabilities of death for ages 71–74 have been converted to 70–75 using the formula $_5q_{70} = 1.169\ _4q_{71}$.

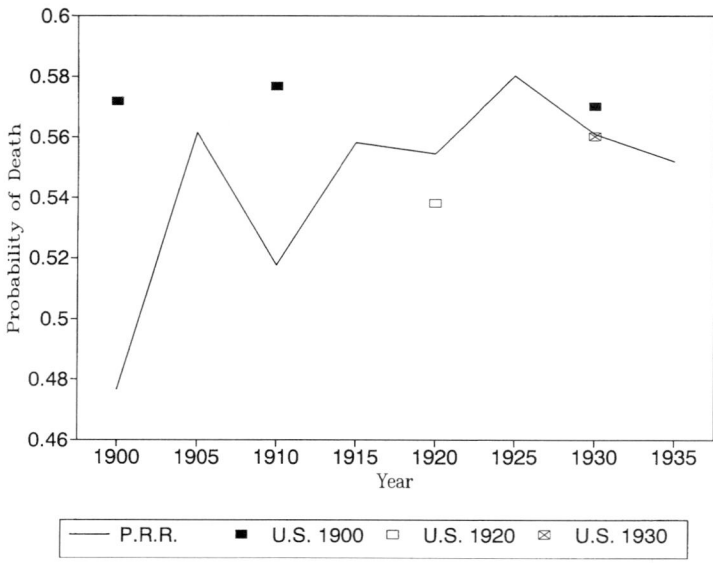

Fig. 12.6. Probability of death at age 80: Pennsylvania Railroad Pension Fund, 1900–1935, and U.S. Life Tables, 1900, 1920, and 1930.

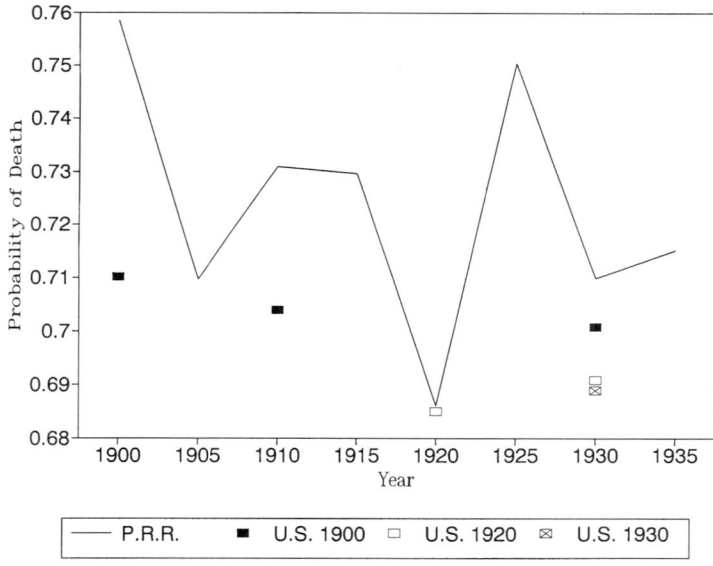

Fig. 12.7. Probability of death at age 85: Pennsylvania Railroad Pension Fund, 1900–1935, and U.S. Life Tables, 1900, 1920, and 1930.

U.S. life tables for 1930 based on the death registration areas of 1900 and 1920. At most younger ages the differences between the earlier and later registration areas would not change our interpretation of the trend in mortality. At these ages, however, the expanding death registration area suggests a larger decline in mortality than the original registration states of 1900. In 1930, the estimates based on the 1900 death registration area are higher than the other two estimates, and the 1930 death registration area yields the lowest mortality rates of all.

It is also reassuring to see that the Pennsylvania Railroad pension mortality was very close to the more general experience captured by the U.S. Bureau of the Census life tables. There is no evidence here that the railroad annuitants were select lives with lower than normal mortality. At age 85 the railroad mortality rates are higher than the U.S. life table estimates. This is probably due to age misreporting errors in the U.S. data, which were discussed above.

A statistical analysis of mortality trends at different ages is presented in table 12.5. Logit regression models have been used to estimate the relationships among age, time period, and the age-specific mortality rates of the Pennsylvania Railroad Pension Fund. The dependent variable in this analysis is the set of death rates for single years of age ($_1q_x$) in each of the years from 1903 to 1935. Death rates based on fewer than 10 lives at risk were excluded, which left 649 observations for the full period. Logit regression was used because the range of the dependent variable is restricted to the interval from 0 to 1. This restriction results in heteroskedasticity, which biases standard errors derived from ordinary least squares regressions. Observations were weighted by the number of lives at risk in all computations.[10] Estimates are provided for three periods. The first period, 1903–1935, uses all of the available data except for the three initial years of the pension fund, which show strong selectivity effects. The second period, 1903–1929, excludes the last six years of the pension fund, in which mortality appears to have been falling at all ages. The third period, 1903–1919, refers to data for only the eastern operating division of the railroad and excludes the possible confounding effects of the western lines added when the two pension funds merged in 1920.

Model I provides a simple estimate of the relationship between age and mortality without distinctions by time period. The logit model of mortality is similar to the Gompertz model, which is more commonly used to approximate adult mortality.[11] In both models the logarithm of the probability of death is almost linear at younger ages, but it increases more slowly at the highest ages as it converges toward 1.0. The estimated coefficient for age in this model represents the rate of increase in the probability of death as age increases. The desirability of additional parameters in modeling the Pennsylvania Railroad Pension Fund data was tested by adding an age-

TABLE 12.5   Logit Regression Models of Probability of Death in
Pennsylvania Railroad Life Tables, 1903–1935

	Years		
	1903–1935	1903–1929	1903–1919
Model I			
Constant	−9.238*	−9.210*	−8.542*
Age	.0927*	.0927*	.0845*
Model II			
Constant	−9.274*	−9.256*	−8.545*
Age	.0932*	.0930*	.0845*
Year	−.0044*	−.0040*	−.0002
Model III			
Constant	−9.252*	−9.502*	−8.966*
Age	.0929*	.0962*	.0901*
Year	−.0057*	−.0062*	−.0014
Year for age 80+	.0057*	.0096*	.0061
Model IV			
Constant	−9.252*	−9.502*	−8.966*
Age	.0929*	.0962*	.0901*
Year for ages 71–79	−.0057*	−.0062*	−.0014
Year for age 80+	.0000	.0034	.0046

NOTE: Dependent variable is life table $_1q_x$.
*The probability of obtaining this result if the true coefficient equals zero is p ≤ .05.

squared term to the logit regression. This additional term did not improve
the fit of the model significantly.

The estimates in table 12.5 support the impression that the shape of the
mortality curve was changing. If mortality at ages 70–79 was decreasing and
mortality above age 80 was constant or increasing, the rate of increase of the
probability of death with advancing age should have become more pronounced. This is exactly the kind of change that we find in Model I by comparing the estimates for 1903 to 1919 to the estimates for 1903 to 1929 or
1903 to 1936. The estimated coefficient for age increases from 0.0845 in the
earlier period to 0.0927 when the 1920s and 1930s are included.

In Model II, the year is added as an independent variable in the logit regression equation. This allows the level of the mortality curve to shift upward
or downward over time. The estimates for all three periods indicate that
mortality was falling, but the change from 1903 to 1919 is not statistically distinguishable from zero.

Models III and IV allow us to distinguish between the trends in mortality
at ages 71–79 and trends over the age of 80. These models are actually
mathematically identical, but they yield tests of somewhat different statisti-

cal inferences. In Model III, a variable is added to distinguish trends in mortality at ages 80 and over from the trend at ages 71–79. This variable is set equal to the year at ages 80 and over but is set to zero under age 80. In Model III, the coefficient for the independent variable "Year" measures the rate of change of mortality at ages 71–79, and the coefficient for "Year for age 80+" measures the difference between the rate of change at ages 80 and over and ages 71–79. The estimated coefficients for this "interaction" variable indicate that mortality decreased less above age 80 in each of the three periods. The difference in trends is greatest for the period 1903 to 1929, and the differences in the periods 1903 to 1929 and 1903 to 1936 are both statistically significant.

In Model IV, the variable for the year is replaced with a variable that is equal to the year at ages 71–79 and zero at ages 80 and over. Since this change does not add any new information, the estimated coefficients for this independent variable are the same as those for the variable that is replaced in Model III. However, the interpretation of the variable "Year for age 80+" is different in Model IV. This variable now provides a direct measure of the trend in mortality at ages 80 and older, instead of measuring the difference between trends above and below age 80. In Model IV, the statistical test associated with this variable considers the null hypothesis that there was no trend in mortality at ages 80 and over. In the previous model the null hypothesis was that there was no difference between the trend at ages 71–79 and the trend at 80 and older.

Model IV indicates that mortality was increasing above age 80 until 1929. When the seven years from 1930 to 1936 are included, however, there is no measurable trend above age 80. This pattern is consistent with other indications in both the Pennsylvania Railroad Pension Fund and the death registration states that old age mortality peaked in the 1920s and declined in the 1930s. It is also noteworthy that the period 1903 to 1919 shows a stronger upward trend at ages 80 and older and a weaker downward trend at ages below 80. This suggests that the mortality peak in the mid-1920s is not due to changes in composition of the pension fund after the western lines were added in 1920. We cannot attach much certainty to the inference that mortality above age 80 was rising, because the statistical tests on Model IV indicate that the estimated coefficients for the "Year for age 80+" variable could differ from zero because of random variations in the data.

The logit regression models in table 12.5 provide statistical confirmation of the impressions derived from figures 12.4 through 12.7. Mortality below age 80 was declining, and there was a significant difference between the trends in mortality above and below age 80. The estimated coefficients indicate that mortality above age 80 was rising in the period from 1903 to 1929, but the statistical tests do not reject the null hypothesis that mortality at these ages was constant.

Thus these data from the Pennsylvania Railroad Pension Fund support the evidence from U.S. vital registration. Both data sets show divergent trends in mortality at the older and younger ages. Furthermore, both data sets point to a turning point around 1926, when mortality at the oldest ages peaked and began to decline.

FEDERAL COORDINATOR OF TRANSPORTATION

In 1934, the Federal Coordinator of Transportation, a short-lived branch of the U.S. government, conducted a major study of employment and pension histories of railroad workers. This was undoubtedly one of the largest studies of its kind ever conducted. The study was motivated by concern for employment during the economic depression and the emerging crisis among railroad pension funds. More than 300,000 employment histories from thirteen railroads and pension histories of 109,096 former male workers from fifty-nine railroads were collected.[12] The pension histories record 644,417 years of experience and 59,165 deaths. In 1940, the U.S. Railroad Retirement Board compiled the results of this survey for use in its actuarial valuation of the railroad pension system.

Since the pension programs examined by the Federal Coordinator of Transportation differed substantially in their provisions, it was necessary to organize them into the six classes shown in table 12.6. Classes 1 and 2 include pension records for workers forced to retire at a compulsory retirement age. In the programs included in class 1, most workers retired at the compulsory age, but in class 2, a substantial percentage of retirements occurred before or after the compulsory retirement age. Classes 3, 4, and 5 identify three kinds of disability retirements. Workers in class 3 were deemed permanently and totally disabled from "any occupation." The disabilities in class 4 were subjected to the less stringent requirement of disability from engaging in the "usual" occupation. The pension programs in class 5 did not distinguish between "any occupation" and "usual occupation." Railroads that allowed both disability and age retirements, such as the Pennsylvania Railroad, contributed histories to class 5 as well as to class 1 or 2. The railroads in class 6 had only disability retirement or did not distinguish between age and disability retirements.

Table 12.6 shows the number of person years of experience in each class of retirement program for workers who retired in three periods: in 1910 or earlier, 1911 to 1920, and 1921 to 1930. The retirement systems with the largest numbers of workers combined compulsory age retirements with disability retirement at older ages. More than half of the experience in these two categories was contributed by the two largest pension systems, the Pennsylvania Railroad (27,431 retirements) and the New York Central Railroad (13,396 retirements). The second panel of the table, presenting the per-

	Year of Retirement		
Class of Retirement[a]	Before 1910	1911–1920	1921–1930
Number of retirements			
1	3,963	7,936	19,371
2	275	1,359	7,962
3	276	383	892
4	46	227	557
5	3,056	9,702	30,414
6	718	3,433	13,483
Total	8,334	23,040	72,679
Percent of retirements			
1	47.6	34.4	26.7
2	3.3	5.9	11.0
3	3.3	1.7	1.2
4	0.6	1.0	0.8
5	36.7	42.1	41.8
6	8.6	14.9	18.6
Total	100.0	100.0	100.0
Actual as percent of expected mortality[b]			
1	122.3	115.2	101.7
2	114.4	124.3	118.3
3	79.6	95.1	90.4
4	91.9	90.5	92.0
5	79.7	83.0	72.1
6	63.3	78.6	73.7
Index of actual/expected mortality			
1	100.0	94.2	83.2
2	100.0	108.7	103.4
3	100.0	119.5	113.6
4	100.0	98.5	100.1
5	100.0	104.1	90.5
6	100.0	124.2	116.4
Total[c]	100.0	104.2	95.1
1, 5[d]	100.0	99.7	87.6
2, 3, 4, 6[e]	100.0	112.1	107.6

SOURCE: Federal Coordinator of Transportation 1940.

[a]Definition of classes: class 1, age retirements with 85 percent retired at compulsory retirement age; class 2, age retirements with significant early and late retirements; class 3, retirement for permanent and total disability to engage in any occupation; class 4, retirement for permanent and total disability to engage in usual occupation; class 5, disability retirement where "any occupation" and "usual occupation" distinction were not applied; class 6, retirement where only disability retirements were made or where separation between age and disability retirement was not possible.

[b]Mortality tables used in standardization: classes 1 and 2, combined annuity table; classes 3–6, disabled life table.

[c]Weighted average of the six classes.

[d]Weighted average of classes 1 and 5.

[e]Weighted average of classes 2, 3, 4, and 6.

centage of retirements by class in each period, shows that there was a change in the composition of retirements over time. Retirements at a compulsory age (class 1) fell from 47.6 percent of all retirements in the period before 1910 to 26.7 percent between 1921 and 1930. Disability retirements (class 5) increased from 36.7 to 41.8 percent, and the retirement systems with less easily classified rules (classes 2 and 6) also grew.

The detailed tabulations done in 1940 do not lend themselves to the computation of age-specific rates, but summary statistics can be used for a standardized comparison. Since the 1940 tables were created for the valuation of pensions, disability retirements were tabulated by years since retirement rather than attained age. This makes is impossible to compute mortality by attained age for the entire population of pensioners. However, comparisons between the railroad pensioners and standard actuarial tables are available. For each class of retirements, we have the ratio of actual deaths to the number of deaths expected under the mortality of the Combined Annuity Mortality Table (classes 1 and 2) or the Disabled Life Mortality Table (classes 3, 4, 5, and 6). These ratios are presented in the third panel of table 12.6, which shows the actual experience as a percentage of the mortality expected under the standard table. Since the standards differ across classes, each class has been indexed to the value for retirements in 1910 or earlier in the fourth panel of table 12.6. Weighted averages of these indexes have been computed using the numbers of retirements as weights. The weighted averages show the standardized experience for all types of retirements and for programs that had both age and disability retirements (classes 1 and 5).

It is important to note that the data in table 12.6 are organized by year of retirement. The data were collected in 1934 and reflect experience up to the end of 1933. Much of the experience of workers who retired in 1910 or earlier occurred after 1910, and some workers who retired between 1911 and 1920 were still alive in 1933. Furthermore, workers who retired in 1910 or earlier were under observation longer and at older ages than those who retired after 1921. Most pensions began between ages 65 and 70, so few of those retired between 1921 and 1930 had passed the age of 80 in 1933. Thus the reader should remember that the time periods in table 12.6 actually overlap, and standardization may not remove all the effects of different age distributions.

Among the six classes of pensions shown in table 12.6, only the compulsory age retirements in class 1 experienced a steady mortality decline over this period. Tabulations of the class 1 retirements by attained age also show steady declines in mortality at each age. As usual, the rate of decline was slower at older ages. The mortality in each of the other classes tended to be highest in the cohort retired between 1911 and 1920, and mortality appears to have been about the same for those retired in 1910 or earlier and between 1921 and 1930.

The trends in the separate retirement classes are not necessarily meaningful, however, because retirement patterns were shifting. As noted above, there was a marked increase in disability retirements at the expense of age retirements. This trend was also apparent in the Pennsylvania Railroad Pension Fund, which relaxed its requirements for disability retirement in 1920 (Pennsylvania Railroad Pension Fund, 19 July 1920). The weighted averages at the bottom of table 12.6 were computed to capture these shifts in disability retirement. When all retirement classes are considered, mortality appears to have increased and then declined. Compared to those who retired in 1910 or earlier, the mortality index for all classes combined is 4 percent higher among the 1911 to 1920 retirements and 5 percent lower for retirements between 1921 and 1930. The weighted average for classes 1 and 5 combined shows the trend among railroads with provisions for both age and disability retirements. Among these pensioners, the mortality decline in class 1 is offset by an increase in class 5 in the middle cohort of retirements. This results in no change from the earliest cohort to the 1911 to 1920 retirements, followed by 12 percent lower mortality among the 1921 to 1930 retirements.

The trends in mortality shown by the weighted averages in table 12.6 are consistent with the mortality experience of the Pennsylvania Railroad Pension Fund described above. We recall that in the Pennsylvania Railroad data, mortality declined at ages below 80, while it increased above age 80. This would create offsetting trends in an overall index, such as the one shown in table 12.6. This fits the pattern of railroads divided between classes 1 and 5. Mortality among these pensioners was constant from the earliest cohort to the 1911 to 1920 cohort of retirements. If we assume that mortality was falling at ages 70–79, then mortality must have been rising above age 80 in that period. The mortality decline noted in the 1921 to 1930 retirements reflects only the downward trend under age 80, because few of these pensioners had passed age 80 when the data were collected in 1934.

One reason that classes 1 and 5 follow the experience of the Pennsylvania Railroad Pension Fund is that the Pennsylvania Railroad experience is included in these results. The Pennsylvania Railroad Pension Fund was by far the largest railroad retirement fund included in the study, contributing 25 percent of the retirement histories. It may well be responsible for the trends in classes 1 and 5. However, even larger increases in mortality are observed in classes 2, 3, 4, and 6, which do not include Pennsylvania Railroad retirees.

A notable aspect of table 12.6 is the contrast between the falling mortality among the age retirements in class 1 and the other classes. The authors of the report suggest that rising mortality among disability retirements may have been a result of stricter criteria for defining disability, but this explanation seems unlikely. Disability retirements were increasing at a much faster rate than age retirements, and we have direct evidence from the Pennsylvania Railroad that their criteria were being relaxed. An alternative explanation is that pension funds were becoming better at identifying disabilities. The diagnostic skills of physicians were improving in this period, and they may have become more able to detect conditions that would result in early death. If those granted disability pensions were not only more numerous but also sicker, we would expect to see improved health among those retired at the mandatory age.

CONCLUSION

It would not have been surprising to find that mortality declined more rapidly below age 80 than above age 80. We know that in the United States and other developed countries, mortality declined more rapidly at younger than at older ages (Dublin and Lotka 1937; Stolnitz 1956). Samuel H. Preston's (1976) analysis of causes of deaths at different ages offers a convincing explanation for these different rates of decline. Mortality at the highest ages is primarily due to degenerative diseases, in particular, cardiovascular diseases and cancer, which are much less likely to respond to public health and medical interventions. Thus the decline in infectious diseases at the beginning of this century had a greater proportional effect on mortality at younger ages.

However, the shift from infectious to degenerative diseases associated with aging does not explain why mortality at the oldest ages was constant or even rising. Since mortality from infectious diseases was declining even at the older ages, mortality from degenerative diseases must have risen for the overall death rate to remain constant.[13] Increases in cardiovascular diseases and cancer were observed at the time, but there was a controversy about the validity of these trends. Medical diagnoses were improving, and there was a decrease in the proportion of deaths attributed to unknown causes and nonspecific conditions, such as senility. The apparent increases in deaths from heart and circulatory diseases and malignant neoplasms were sometimes attributed to better reporting of causes of death (Dublin and Lotka 1937). Edgar Sydenstricker (1933) mentions a controversy about whether cancer rates were actually rising which had been resolved in favor of increasing rates.

Any explanation of the rise in old age mortality at the beginning of the twentieth century must also be consistent with the declining mortality at younger ages. This draws our attention to factors that accumulate slowly with age, which can be grouped into three broad categories: changes in behavior, changes in environment, and the selective demographic effects of earlier declines in mortality.

Two behavioral changes stand out as potential explanations: smoking and diet. Cigarette smoking was clearly rising in this period, but it is unlikely that its effects would have appeared in the cohorts analyzed here. The consequences of smoking are most apparent in individuals who have smoked for a long time, and these men would have been too old to adopt this new habit. Furthermore, smoking was almost strictly a male prerogative at this time, and the rise in female mortality in the U.S. death registration area was as great as the rise in the male mortality.[14]

Dietary changes in the late nineteenth century were quite likely, however, to have increased the risk of cardiovascular disease and possibly cancer as well. Rising incomes, urban life styles, and technological changes, such as refrigeration, may have changed the American diet in unhealthy ways.[15] Richard Doll and Bruce Armstrong (1981) describe a set of "Western diseases" that have been increasing in certain African populations. The cancers identified by them as "Western diseases" were almost all increasing among Metropolitan Life Insurance policyholders between 1911 and 1935 (Dublin and Lotka 1937) and throughout the United States from 1935 to 1974 (Devesa and Silverman 1978). Louis I. Dublin and Mortimer Spiegelman (1952: 428) identified diet as one of the factors accounting for the relatively poor mortality of the United States at older ages when compared to other industrialized countries: "At least one-fifth of our adults are more or less seriously overweight; the proportion is higher for males than for females. Because of our prosperity and abundance, a large number of our people are literally eating themselves to death."

Second, there may have been deleterious changes in the environment, such as pollution or increased housing density. The direction of change in environmental quality is not entirely clear, however. Declining infant mortality rates suggest that public health measures were having a positive effect on water quality in this period, and air pollution was still more dependent on coal-fired furnaces than automobiles. But it is possible that rising cancer rates reflected the accumulation of industrial pollutants from the expansion of manufacturing at the end of the nineteenth century.

Finally, a process of demographic selection might have been responsible. If a population is composed of subgroups with differing susceptibilities to disease, the composition of the population at each age depends on past experiences of mortality (Alter and Riley 1989; Vaupel, Manton, and Stallard 1979). Individuals with high relative risks tend to die at younger ages, so a population becomes less "frail" as it ages. If mortality declines, however, more of the high-risk individuals will survive to old age. When the distribution of relative risks is wide, mortality declines at younger ages can appear to produce mortality increases at older ages. The rising proportion of high-risk, new survivors makes the average mortality at older ages appear higher, even though mortality for individuals of the same relative risk in different cohorts would be declining. Again, Dublin and Spiegelman (1952: 429) anticipated this explanation in their international comparison of adult mortality:

> In other words, the suggestion is that our generally better level of medical care has been prolonging the lives of persons whose health has been impaired by earlier infection. As a result, it is possible that we have among the middle-aged and older persons now in our midst a larger proportion of persons with organic impairments than may be found in other nations.

If this process was at work earlier in this century, it would explain the paradox of worsening old age mortality.

NOTES

I am grateful for the advice and suggestions of Gretchen A. Condran, Douglas Ewbank, Samuel H. Preston, Herbert Smith, James C. Riley, and Ian Timmaeus. I would also like to thank Kay Collins at the U.S. Railroad Retirement Board, Donna Richardson at the Society of Actuaries, and David Weinberg at the Temple University Urban Archives for their assistance in locating unpublished material. This research was supported by NRSA Fellowship 1 F32 AG05471 from the National Institute on Aging.

1. The evidence presented here shows that early-twentieth-century old age mortality rates in the United States were biased downward by age misreporting in censuses and vital registration. This was well known at the time, and actuaries regularly used approximations to close their life tables. Old age mortality in official U.S. life tables was derived by a combination of smoothing, extrapolation, and graduation techniques. For example, the life tables for 1890, 1901, and 1910 arbitrarily assume that $q_{115} = 1$ (Glover 1921: 348–350). Thus the rectangularization of survival curves discussed by Fries is primarily an artifact of the computational methods used to construct life tables and may not reflect any trend in old age mortality.

2. The 1918–1919 influenza epidemic may explain increases in mortality at ages 40 to 60 (Metropolitan Life Insurance Company 1929a). The epidemic removed from the population a group of high-risk individuals who would otherwise have died in later years. This selective mortality reduced death rates immediately after the epidemic, and the rising rates in the 1920s could be seen as a return to the earlier trend. This hypothesis fails to explain rising mortality rates at older ages, however. The impact of the epidemic was concentrated in the early adult ages, and death rates above age 55 did not increase during these years.

3. Assume that the same pattern of age misreporting was present in the census as in the vital registration, namely, that the probability that a person age x would be reported as age y was the same. Then the reported age-specific death rates are really weighted averages of the form

$$O_j = \Sigma \, p_{ij} \, M_i$$
$$= \sum_{i<j} p_{ij} \, M_i + p_{jj} \, M_j + \sum_{i>j} p_{ij} \, M_i,$$

where O_j is the reported death rate at age j, M_i is the true death rate at age i, P_{ij} is the proportion of those reported at age j who are really age i.

The first term represents persons who are younger than age j but are erroneously reported to be age j. The second term, $p_{jj} M_j$, represents those whose age is correctly reported at age j. The last term in the equation captures those who are incorrectly reported at age j from ages older than j. The reported death rate at age j can change either because the proportions who are misreported from other ages have changed (p_{ij}) or because the levels of mortality at different ages have changed (M_i).

4. The numbers of retirements, deaths, and pensioners in the Pennsylvania Railroad retirement fund on December 31 in selected years, 1900 to 1936, are as follows:

	Retirements		*Deaths*		*Pensioners on December 31*		
Year	70+	65–69	70+	65–69	70+	65–69	Total
1900	1,149	143	95	7	1,054	136	1,190
1901	565	170	133	23	1,486	283	1,769
1905	256	147	192	54	1,810	656	2,466
1910	299	244	231	108	2,192	1,177	3,369
1915	314	364	264	166	2,432	2,077	4,509
1920	457	425	266	251	2,891	2,885	5,776
1925	312	835	329	419	3,044	5,289	8,333
1930	348	890	286	594	3,223	6,698	9,921
1935	375	961	303	715	3,324	8,166	11,490
1936	449	926	345	838	3,428	8,254	11,682

5. Since we do not have the records in which dates of birth were originally reported, it is not possible to test these data for age heaping. However, it was possible to test for heaping on certain calendar years, such as those ending in 0 or 5. Ratios were computed comparing the number of pensioners at age 71 in each year to a five-year moving average. These ratios were small and did not show identifiable five- or ten-year cycles.

6. Railroad occupations were highly segregated by race. Railroad porters, the major occupation filled by blacks, were mostly employed by the Pullman Company rather than the various railroads themselves.

7. The methods used to produce these estimates are described in Douglas C. Ewbank 1989. I am grateful to Dr. Ewbank for providing me with these special tabulations.

8. An additional adjustment was made to data for 1933 to compensate for the withdrawal of 125 pensioners of the West Jersey and Seashore Railroad, who were withdrawn from the pension fund when the railroad was leased to the Pennsylvania-Reading Seashore Lines. It was assumed that West Jersey and Seashore pensioners had the same age distribution as others in the pension fund at that time and that they suffered the same mortality during the six months that they were included in the fund in 1933. Since the numbers involved are very small, this adjustment has almost no effect on estimated mortality rates.

9. More formally, the number of person years by age at last birthday is a quantity analogous to the stationary population in the life table, L_x. If we assume that deaths are distributed evenly in each year of life, then

$$L_x = l_{x+.5}$$

and

$$l_x = \tfrac{1}{2}(l_{x-.5} + l_{x+.5}).$$

10. As explained above, the age-specific mortality rates were adjusted to exact ages by averaging adjacent estimates for ages at last birthday. Similarly, the weights used in the logit regression models were derived by averaging the lives at risk for the ages from which the mortality rates were derived.

11. The Gompertz model approximates mortality by the formula

$$\log[\log(1 - {}_1q_x)] = A + Bx,$$

in which x is age and A and B are estimated coefficients. In contrast, the logit model assumes

$$\log[{}_1q_x/(1 - {}_1q_x)] = A + Bx.$$

Many years of actuarial practice have shown that the Gompertz model fits most life tables well over limited ranges of adult ages. There is a controversy, however, about the shape of the mortality curve at the highest ages (Bayo 1972; Bayo and Faber 1983; Kestenbaum 1989; Pakin and Hrisanov 1984). Some estimates suggest that death rates above age 90 increase at a slower rate than the Gompertz curve. The logit model is mathematically similar to the Gompertz model, but it increases less rapidly at higher ages. W. Perks (1932) argues that the simple logit model is superior to the Gompertz model, but he prefers a more complicated four parameter model derived by taking the logit of the logit.

12. The survey obtained records on only 621 female pensioners (Federal Coordinator of Transportation 1940: 20).

13. Preston (1976) shows that the rate of decline of infectious diseases is similar at all ages in an international collection of mortality tables by cause. Comparable statistics are not available for the United States because of changes in the death registration area. However, a similar conclusion can be drawn from the experience of industrial insurance policyholders described by Dublin and Lotka (1937).

14. Wiehl (1930), however, found greater increases in male mortality than in female mortality when she compared 1926 to 1921.

15. This subject needs more investigation before a firm conclusion can be drawn, because the American diet in the nineteenth century was not clearly healthy by present standards. Atack and Bateman (1987: 209) write, "Much of the meat was consumed as fat salt pork; yet despite its unpalatability by modern standards, meat consumption in the 1850s was close to record high levels. . . . The diet was heavy on fats and salt but light on fluid milk, fresh fruit, and green vegetables. Indeed, vegetables were often referred to as 'sauce,' suggesting a role limited to providing flavor or as a garnish, rather than as foodstuffs in their own right."

REFERENCES

Alter, George. 1990. "Trends in old age mortality in the U.S., 1900–1940." Paper presented at the annual meeting of the Population Association of America, Toronto, Canada, May 3–5.

Alter, George, and James C. Riley. 1989. "Frailty, sickness, and death: Models of morbidity and mortality in historical populations." *Population Studies* 43: 25–45.

Atack, Jeremy, and Fred Bateman. 1987. *To their own soil: Agriculture in the antebellum North.* Ames: Iowa State University Press.

Bayo, Francisco R. 1972. "Mortality of the aged." *Transactions of the Society of Actuaries* 30: 1–24.

Bayo, Francisco R., and Joseph F. Faber. 1983. "Mortality experience around age 100." *Transactions of the Society of Actuaries* 35: 21–43.

Benjamin, Bernard. 1982. "The span of life." *Journal of the Institute of Actuaries* 109, pt. 3: 319–341.

Coale, Ansley J., and Ellen Eliason Kisker. 1986. "Mortality crossovers: Reality or bad data?" *Population Studies* 40: 389–401.

Coale, Ansley J., and Melvin Zelnik. 1963. *New estimates of fertility and population in the United States.* Princeton: Princeton University Press.

Condran, Gretchen A., Christine Himes, and Samuel H. Preston. 1989. "Old age mortality patterns in low-mortality countries: An evaluation of population and death data at advanced ages, 1950 to the present." Paper presented at the annual meeting of the Population Association of America, Baltimore, March 30–April 1.

Devesa, Susan S., and Debra T. Silverman. 1978. "Cancer incidence and mortality trends in the United States: 1935–74." *Journal of the National Cancer Institute* 60: 545–571.

Doll, Richard. 1979. "The pattern of disease in the postinfection era: National trends." *Proceedings of the Royal Society of London*, series B, 205: 47–61.

Doll, Richard, and Bruce Armstrong. 1981. "Cancer." In *Western diseases: Their emergence and prevention*, ed. H. C. Trowell and D. P. Burkitt, 93–110. Cambridge: Harvard University Press.

Dublin, Louis I., and Alfred J. Lotka. 1937. *Twenty-five years of health progress.* New York: Metropolitan Life Insurance Company.

Dublin, Louis I., and Mortimer Spiegelman. 1952. "Factors in the higher mortality of our older age groups." *American Journal of Public Health* 42: 422–429.

Ewbank, Douglas C. 1989. "Child mortality differentials by father's occupation, U.S. 1895–1925." Paper presented at the annual meeting of the Population Association of America, Baltimore, March 30–April 1.

Federal Coordinator of Transportation. 1940, November. "Actuarial data and basic tables for valuation of retirement benefits to railroad employees." Washington, D.C.

Fingerhut, Lois M. 1982. "Changes in mortality among the elderly: United States, 1940–78." *Vital and Health Statistics*, U.S. National Center for Health Statistics, series 3, no. 22.

Fox, A. J., and P. F. Collier. 1976. "Low mortality rates in industrial cohort studies due to selection for work and survival in industry." *British Journal of Preventive Social Medicine* 30: 225–230.

Fries, James F. 1983. "The compression of morbidity." *Milbank Memorial Fund Quarterly* 61: 397–419.

Fries, James F., and L. M. Crapo. 1981. *Vitality and aging: Implications of the rectangular curve.* San Francisco: W. H. Freeman.

Glover, James W. 1921. *United States life tables, 1890, 1901, 1910, and 1901–1910.* Washington, D.C.: Government Printing Office.

Gompertz, B. 1825. "On the nature of the function expressive of the law of human mortality and a new mode of determining the value of life contingencies." *Philosophical Transactions of the Royal Society of London* 115, pt. 2: 513–585.

Gruenberg, Ernest M. 1977. "The failures of success." *Milbank Memorial Fund Quarterly* 55: 3–24.

Gutman, Robert. 1956. "The accuracy of vital statistics in Massachusetts, 1842–1901." Ph.D. dissertation, Columbia University.

Hambright, Thea Zelman. 1968. "Comparability of age on the death certificate and matching census record." *Vital and Health Statistics*, U.S. National Center for Health Statistics, series 2, no. 29.

Hill, Joseph A. 1936. *United States life tables, 1929 to 1931, 1920 to 1929, 1919 to 1921, 1909 to 1911, 1901 to 1910, 1900 to 1902*. Washington, D.C.: Government Printing Office.

Kestenbaum, Bert. 1989. "Centenarians: An administrative records perspective." Paper presented at the annual meeting of the Population Association of America, Baltimore, March 30–April 1.

Le Bras, Hervé. 1976. "Lois de mortalité et âge limite" [Laws of mortality and the life span]. *Population* 31: 655–691.

Linder, Forrest E., and Robert D. Grove. 1963. *Vital statistics rates in the United States, 1900–1940*. Washington, D.C.: National Office of Vital Statistics.

Metropolitan Life Insurance Company. 1929a. "A setback in mid-life mortality." *Statistical Bulletin of the Metropolitan Life Insurance Company* 10(February): 1–4.

———. 1929b. "The human life span unchanged." *Statistical Bulletin of the Metropolitan Life Insurance Company* 10(October): 1–3.

Niessen, Abraham M. 1948. "Recent mortality of railroad annuitants." *Transactions of the Actuarial Society of America* 49: 296–302.

Olshansky, S. Jay, Bruce A. Carnes, and Christine Cassel. 1990. "In search of Methuselah: Estimating the upper limits of human longevity." *Science* 250: 634–640.

Pakin, Yu B., and S. M. Hrisanov. 1984. "Critical analysis of the applicability of the Gompertz-Makeham law in human populations." *Gerontology* 30: 8–12.

Pennsylvania Commissioner of Health. 1916–1918. *Annual report, 1914–1916*. Harrisburg: Wm. Stanley Ray, State Printer.

Pennsylvania Railroad Pension Fund. 1899–1937. "Minutes of the Board of Officers." Urban Archives, Temple University.

Perks, W. 1932. "On some experiments in the graduation of mortality statistics." *Journal of the Institute of Actuaries* 63: 12–40.

Preston, Samuel H. 1976. *Mortality patterns in national populations*. New York: Academic Press.

———. 1983. "An integrated system for demographic estimation from two age distributions." *Demography* 20: 213–226.

Preston, Samuel H., and Ansley J. Coale. 1982. "Age structure, growth, attrition, and accession: A new synthesis." *Population Index* 48: 217–259.

Preston, Samuel H., Nathan Keyfitz, and Robert Schoen. 1972. *Causes of death: Life tables for national populations*. New York: Seminar Press.

Riley, James C. 1989. *Sickness, recovery and death*. London: Macmillan.

Sacher, George A. 1978. "Longevity, aging, and death: An evolutionary perspective." *The Gerontologist* 18: 112–119.

Stolnitz, George J. 1956. "A century of international mortality trends: II." *Population Studies* 10: 17–42.

Strehler, Bernard L., and Albert S. Mildvan. 1960. "General theory of aging." *Science* 132: 14–21.

Sydenstricker, Edgar. 1933. *Health and environment.* New York: McGraw-Hill.

U.S. Bureau of the Census. 1900–1940. *Census of population.* Washington, D.C.: Government Printing Office.

―――. 1914–1916, 1924–1926, 1934–1936. *Mortality statistics.* Washington, D.C.: Government PrintingOffice.

Vaupel, J. W., K. G. Manton, and E. Stallard. 1979. "The impact of heterogeneity in individual frailty on the dynamics of mortality." *Demography* 16: 439–454.

Wiehl, Dorothy G. 1930. "Changes in mortality among adults." *Journal of Preventive Medicine* 4: 215–237.

PART FIVE

Conclusion

THIRTEEN

Toward a Historical Demography
of Aging

David I. Kertzer

Over the past decade or so, historical studies of aging and especially of old age have become increasingly popular topics in social history. As recently as 1982, the historian Peter Stearns could write that "as a field of history," old age "remains shockingly untended," a fact he partly attributed to "the shaky esteem the elderly command in contemporary society" (1982: 1). Yet, writing with David Van Tassel just a few years later, Stearns heralded the sudden rise of the history of old age "from virtual nonexistence to its current status as a promising and provocative subfield of social history" (Stearns and Van Tassel 1986: ix).

As Peter Laslett notes in his introduction to this volume, the history of old age follows other pioneering fields in social history in confronting a mass of popular and even scholarly stereotypes that get in the way. It would be naive to claim that these stereotypes act only as a hindrance to scholarly study, since few historians can resist the allure of identifying a broadly accepted stereotype that they can, through historical study, show to be false. The recent history of old age has, indeed, largely been written as just such a series of attempts at myth slaying, much as the early work on household history—identified with Laslett himself—seized on the historical inaccuracy of common notions of the universality of extended family living in the past.

Yet the burden borne by those who study the history of old age is in some ways greater than that borne by students of household history and many other historical subjects, for there are few historical topics with as much contemporary relevance as that of how old people lived and were treated in the past. Concern for the responsibilities of the state and the family toward the elderly—a concern that is in no small part itself a product of the demographic changes examined in this book and particularly what Laslett here refers to as the Secular Shift in aging—has focused a tremendous amount of public and political attention on the costs of various systems of old age assistance. The debates that have ensued involve not simply economic issues but moral ones as well, and these are commonly couched in terms of historical understandings. Is our society moving away from a past in which old people were treated with respect? In which they lived with and were supported by their children? In which they continued to participate in the labor force as long as they saw fit?

The history of old age has tended to swing wildly between two extremes in this history-as-policy debate. A romantic view of the past has produced images of a time when the old were treated with respect, when they occupied positions of power by virtue of their control over family holdings, and when they were surrounded and supported by married children and grandchildren. In this view, the history of industrialization and "modernization" has been a tragic one for the lives of the old: they have become the victims of "progress." In making this argument, scholars have seized not only on temporal distance but on spatial and cultural distance as well, pointing to the non-Western, less industrialized societies as still today maintaining much of the "traditional" concern for the welfare of the elderly that presumably marked Western societies in the past.

On the other side, especially notable among European historians, we find a revisionist view, one that sees a far grimmer story of old age, in which old people crowded meager public charitable facilities in search of a miserable lodging, or a piece of bread, to allow them to survive in a society that gave no quarter to those lacking the brawn or the health to earn their daily living. In this view, old people have never been as well off as they are today, when government programs and social legislation protect them and transfer payments force the young to support them.

The chapters in this book demonstrate that neither of these two scenarios provides an adequate understanding of aging in the past. Part of the problem, of course, is that the terms of the debate have been unrealistically broad. While the demographic changes in Western societies have followed a fairly uniform pattern, from low proportions of elderly to much higher proportions and from low life expectancy to high life expectancy, the social and political arrangements for dealing with the older population have varied considerably from society to society and, indeed, in many cases within societies, by such factors as class and gender. This mirrors anthropologists' findings that in non-Western societies there has been and is today a great diversity of situations in which the old find themselves: from valued and comfortably cared for to devalued and impoverished. This should not be taken as a cry of despair, a despair at our ability to make any generalizations, for certain patterns do indeed emerge, and the fact that they are more complex than earlier generalizations make them no less interesting, either theoretically or in their policy implications.

One of the major issues in the history of old age—and one that ties historical study quite closely to contemporary policy debates—is that of the residence of the elderly: did they co-reside with their children, especially with their *married* children, or were they (residentially at least) on their own once their children had gotten married? This is a question that is taken up in most of the chapters of this book and one that we will want to consider in some detail. Just what obligations an adult child has toward an elderly parent is a matter of considerable policy discussion in the United States today, combining moral concerns about old folks being packed off to institutions with economic concerns about the high cost of such care.

A clear pattern emerges from many non-Western nations, where governments explicitly rely on kin co-residence and kin support of the elderly. The Indian government, for example, relies on the co-residence of old people with their married sons, a norm of care that is in fact commonly followed (Vatuk 1982: 100). Similarly, families are given full responsibility for their elderly members in the Philippines, while in the wealthier Singapore, government support for the elderly is only available for those without children (Treas and Logue 1986: 657). Nor are such patterns foreign to European society, for, as Rudolf Andorka tells us in his chapter, the Hungarian state continues today to rely on the co-residence of older people with their married children to solve problems of old age care. These problems include both the decline in income that comes with retirement—a feature Laslett would associate with the "Third Age"—and the frailty and poor health associated with Laslett's "Fourth Age."

According to traditional Western social theory, societal evolution has entailed movement from a society in which rights and responsibilities were vested in kin groupings to a society in which each individual is an independent actor before the law. This view has been given new expression in work on increased state intervention into the life course and the increased tendency to establish explicit age norms (e.g., Mayer and Müller 1986). In this context, the history of old age, far from being a peripheral subject to be identified exclusively with gerontology and social service, must be seen as a central topic in the history of Western societies. How older people were treated and cared for—and the involvement of state and family in the process—bears centrally on major issues of historical development and social theory, including the extent to which Western societies have followed a distinctive historical path. In addressing these issues, we clearly need not only employ demographic and quantifiable evidence but also a wide variety of more qualitative archival and literary sources. These sources become especially important as we seek to identify the nature of relationships that tied kin and neighbors together beyond households.

In this concluding chapter I would like to take on some of these broad issues, building on the chapters in this book. I begin by reviewing the demographic changes that have radically altered the population dynamics in Western society, contrasting these with those found in the rest of the world, where the situation today is very different. I then turn directly to the guiding model of change in the lives of the elderly—the modernization model—to evaluate it in light of the historical evidence. Following this, I examine the living situation of the elderly in the past in Western societies, arguing that co-residence with children was much more common than many historians and sociologists have led us to believe and that the contrast between the situation of Westerners and non-Westerners in this regard is less than many have supposed. The centrality of gender to the study of the history of aging is then argued by bringing together the results of various chapters of this book, along with other studies, to highlight certain factors that distinguish the situation of men and women in late life. All this leads me to propose a new view of household systems, arguing that to date the commonly employed household typologies fail to take into account the central role that should be accorded the treatment of the elderly.

DEMOGRAPHIC CHANGES

In his introductory chapter, Peter Laslett has provided a clear overview of the dramatic changes in both age structure and life expectancy that have occurred in the West over the past century. As he points out, changes in life expectancy—the most commonly employed measure of individual aging—can be highly misleading in tracing the demographic history of aging.[1]

While the dramatic increase in life expectancy over the past centuries is most striking, we note that the declines in mortality rates for older people were much more modest. Taking the very long view, the anthropologist Kenneth Weiss (1981: 50) asserts that the "number of years added since primitive times to an infant's life has been about 50, to a 15-year-old's life . . . about 30, and to a 50-year-old's . . . only about 12 years." This said, there is no doubt that a 50-year-old today is unlikely to view those additional dozen years as trivial.[2]

Looking at more recent centuries, we find that while the life expectancy of a newborn baby girl in Sweden doubled from 1780 to 1965 (from 38 to 76), the increase in life expectancy of a 50-year-old Swedish woman increased only 8.6 years over the same period; a woman who made it to age 50 in 1785 would live, on average, to age 70 (Weiss 1981: 50). Similarly, to take another example, whereas at birth an Austrian boy born in the late 1960s would live more than twice as long as a boy born there in the 1870s (67 vs.

30 years), an Austrian man aged 60 in the 1960s only stood to live three more years than a 60-year-old of the 1870s (15 vs. 12 more years) (Mitterauer and Sieder 1982: 145). Indeed, as George Alter shows us in his chapter, the historical trend of longevity for those who survived to old age could be quite different than for children at birth. The fact that the mortality rate in old age may have actually risen in the United States in the first decades of the twentieth century is a sobering reminder of this fact.[3]

One of the little-studied areas of the historical demography of aging is, in fact, the course of changes in mortality beyond childhood. While Laslett properly focuses attention on the dramatic changes in demographic rates and age group proportions over the past century in the West, there is reason to believe that changes of significance took place earlier as well. The nature of these changes and their causes are not at all well known. One of the few studies examining changes in age at death over these earlier centuries, conducted in Rouen, France, reveals that whereas only 23 percent of deaths in the period 1660–1709 occurred to those aged 50 and above, 37 percent of all deaths in 1760–1800 took place in these older ages (Gutton 1988: 137). What happened during the eighteenth century to account for these differences remains a matter of speculation, though they likely involve a diminished mortality rate for the very young and rather little change in mortality for the old.[4] Alfred Perrenoud's (1982: 47) study of Geneva, for example, shows a large increase in life expectancy at birth from the early seventeenth to the early nineteenth century (from 24 to 40 years) but a minimal increase for those age 60 (from 12 to 13 years).

As Laslett shows, the dramatic aging of Western populations over the past century is primarily due not to increased longevity among the middle-aged but rather to a sharp decline in fertility. The American population pyramid is in fact becoming less and less pyramidal in shape: in 1900, there were over ten children (under age 18) for every old person (age 65+); today there are only two children per old person (Uhlenberg 1987: 185).

The demographic contrast between the Western and other technologically advanced countries, on the one hand, and the rest of the world, on the other, is breathtaking. While throughout the West older people (age 65+) represent over 10 percent of the population, in countries such as the Ivory Coast and Afghanistan the elderly compose a mere 2 percent.[5] Moreover, while the proportion of elderly in the population has been steadily increasing throughout the West (and in highly industrialized countries like Japan), in much of Africa and parts of Asia the proportion who are elderly has actually been decreasing in recent decades (Cowgill 1986: 22, 25).[6]

Again, though, we need to be careful about using these figures to draw conclusions about the experience of individuals, or to contrast longevous people of the West with short-lived peoples elsewhere. In 1980, for example, though an American baby could expect to live a quarter century longer than a Nigerian baby, American men aged 60 would on average live only three years longer than Nigerian men of that age (Sokolovsky 1982: 3).[7]

MODERNIZATION THEORY

In the influential modernization model of aging, the social and economic changes associated with modernization produce a relative decline in the status and welfare of older people. Demographic forces are thought to play a role here as well, not only in the putative link between small proportions of old people in the population and their high status in the past but also in a somewhat more complicated fashion. The fact that women bore children until they were about 40, combined with the fact that people presumably did not live as long in the past, meant that there was no old age distinct from middle age (Haber 1983: 10).[8] In this view, with the prolongation of life, the limitation of childbearing to the younger fecund years, and the increased movement of adult children away from the parental home, a distinct period of old age became established, one in which the elderly were increasingly isolated and powerless.[9]

The tendency of old people to become more isolated from work and family with modernization has, however, been denied by many scholars. Criticisms come primarily from two sources. First of all, historians have identified past Western societies in which old people were not provided support by kin and suffered from economic privation. Second, anthropologists and others have demonstrated that not all small-scale societies accorded high status to the old. They have shown that in many non-Western societies today, urbanization has not undercut heavy reliance on extended kin relations. On the contrary, such ties continue to provide older people in these societies with security and status.

Part of the confusion in all this stems from the imprecise—perhaps muddled is a better term—nature of the modernization concept. Modernization has been identified variously with urbanization, industrialization, the demographic transition, the spread of public, secular schooling, the spread of state-run welfare institutions, the advent of modern medicine, and many other developments. There is no clear reason why all of these forces should be thought to have the same impact on the status or welfare of older people.[10]

One of the most common claims of the modernization and aging literature is that in the past old people were provided a secure existence through co-residence with their children. Such co-residence was often associated with households that were economic units, providing older people both with continued work roles and with control over property that placed them in a position of authority over their adult children. Critics of the modernization model have jumped at the evidence coming in from the work of the

Cambridge Group and others (Laslett 1972) seeming to suggest that extended families were not in fact common in the Western past. As Brian Gratton (1986: 5) explained, "The most striking criticism [of the modernization model] sprang from the startling discovery that the nuclear household was the predominant form in preindustrial Western societies. This discovery led to the conclusion that the aged could not have exercised power through an extended family."

As various chapters in this book make clear, while we may want to abandon modernization theory for all sorts of reasons, the absence of extended kin co-residence in the European past is not one of them. It is not at all certain that older people in general lived apart from their children in the European past, nor even that they do in all places today. Michael Mitterauer and Reinhard Sieder's (1982) characterization of living arrangements in Austria is of interest here. In harmony with the traditional modernization model, they argue that "historically speaking, the isolation of the aged . . . is a relatively recent phenomenon. It is mainly a result of industrialization and urbanization" (153). They bolster their case by pointing to contemporary Lower Austria, contrasting the high proportion (44 percent) of people over age 60 in the rural population who live with one of their married children to the low proportion (14 percent) among the nonrural population.

Let us, then, review the evidence that is provided both in this volume and in other recent studies regarding this central question: to what extent and in what circumstances did older people in the Western past live with their children?

LIVING WITH ADULT CHILDREN

The "startling discovery" that old people in the European past lived in nuclear family settings and not in multigenerational households leads to another conclusion: the family lives of the elderly in the West were radically different from what was found in the rest of the world. In this view, while outside the West older people have always been cared for by their children, in part through co-residence, in the West the old were left to fend for themselves or to rely on nonkin sources of support, such as those provided by the community, church, or state.

The chapters in this book should lead to the rejection of any such simple revisionist view. Before turning directly to the Western societies, though, let us take a brief look at the situation outside Europe today, for the historical debate over Western exceptionalism is linked to the question of whether today's non-Western family pattern of elderly care represents a kind of system away from which Westerners have moved or whether the Western–non-Western contrast is itself of many centuries duration, predating any of the forces associated with "modernization." For the sake of simplicity, I focus here on South and East Asian societies, avoiding the complexities associated with the high rates of polygyny in Africa or the question of whether Latin American societies can properly be contrasted with the "West."[11]

The predominance of the extended family in the lives of the elderly in South and East Asia today is unmistakable. In India, continued high fertility is often attributed to the felt need to ensure old age support by bearing sons.[12] As Sylvia Vatuk (1982: 72) writes, "In India it is universally expected—or, at least, hoped—that the elderly person will be provided shelter and care by his or her adult offspring, in the setting of home and family." This is seen as the responsibility of the married sons and their wives, and study after study shows a majority of the elderly in fact living with their married sons. In a Delhi study of two thousand old people, for example, 62 percent lived with a married son and only 6 percent with a married daughter (Vatuk 1982: 88).[13] A recent community study of a rural Rajasthan community 700 kilometers southwest of Delhi found two-thirds of all elderly residents living with at least one married son, including one-fourth of all elderly residents co-residing with two or more married sons, all in the same household (Hashimoto 1991: 376).[14] A recent review of the subcontinent concludes that "the majority of South Asian elderly coreside with their offspring" (Martin 1990: 98).

In East Asia we find a comparable pattern, even in urban areas. Eighty percent of Korean parents over 60 lived with one or more of their children in the 1980s, reflecting a deeply felt cultural norm. A study conducted in the mid-1980s of Seoul residents over age 55 found 81 percent of them living with at least one child, including 58 percent living with a married son. The patrilocal bias is strong here as well: only 6 percent lived with a married daughter (Sung 1991: 436, 443). And in Japan, though the trend is very slowly moving away from co-residence of the old with their children, just about two-thirds of all Japanese over age 65 in 1984 lived with a child (Kumagai 1987: 237).[15] A comparable situation is found today in the parts of China for which we have information. A study conducted in the rural suburbs of Shanghai in 1986 found roughly one-third of all those over age 60 living with a married son and about 8 percent living with a married daughter. Among the widowed, a majority lived with their married children, although unlike the other Asian cases mentioned thus far, a significant proportion of widows lived alone (Gui 1988: 160).[16]

The polemics that have followed Laslett's (1965) "world we have lost" thesis, catalyzing the study of household systems in European history, have also had an effect on our understanding of the lives of the elderly in the West and on how these have changed over the past centuries. In the traditional view of the European peasant past as one dominated by multigenerational living arrangements, older people's welfare was guaranteed by their co-

residence with married children, in much the same way as we have seen occurs today in South and East Asia. A corollary of this traditional view is the
progressive residential isolation of the elderly prompted by those changes
loosely identified with "modernization." In the revisionist view, in contrast,
Europe and the West were always different from the East, with European
emphasis on individualism contrasting for centuries with an emphasis on
corporate family units in both Asia and Africa.

Over the past two decades, some of the enthusiasts of the revisionist view
have come under criticism for overgeneralizing from limited English evidence to speak of western Europe or even Europe as a whole (Kertzer
1991).[17] It is now clear—as is evident in both Andorka's chapter on Hungary
and the Kertzer and Karweit chapter on Italy as well as from research on the
Balkans (e.g., Halpern and Anderson 1970) and eastern Europe (e.g., Czap
1982)—that complex family systems were typical of various parts of Europe
in the past. What implications does this have for the lives of the elderly, and
for our understanding of the changes in the position of the elderly over the
past century or two?

The Italian and Hungarian cases point out one kind of exception to the
view of the residential isolation of the elderly in the European past, an exception based on the existence of nonnuclear household systems in large
parts of preindustrial Europe. In central and much of northern Italy, joint
family households rather similar in some ways to those found in South Asia
(i.e., based on the residence of all married sons in the parental home) were
common, and those who lived in such households faced no empty nest
stage, nor did they face the prospect of being left alone on widowhood.[18] In
substantial portions of Hungary, as in much of central and eastern Europe,
complex family household arrangements were as common as nuclear families, and this naturally supported the co-residence of older people with their
married children. This was not simply a matter of patrilocal postmarital residence but, as Andorka tells us, also involved a strongly held norm that ob-
ligated married children to reside with a widowed parent even if the two
generations had not been co-residing prior to widowhood.

One conclusion that might be made in light of such evidence from southern, central, and eastern Europe is that the supposed residential isolation
of the elderly in the Western past pertains only to northwestern Europe and
its descendant societies in North America and elsewhere. This, after all, is
the area said to be the epicenter of individualism, neolocality, and nuclear
family residence. Laslett's claims about the residential isolation of the elderly in the past, though generalized with undue haste by others to Europe
as a whole, after all principally concerned England. It was in this context
that he wrote—in words that he now believes overstate the case—of "the rule
of continued independent residence by the old."

> We have described the old in preindustrial England as having in general been
> left as they were, and where they were, watching their children grow up and
> leave home never to return, and not receiving into their households their own
> elderly relatives for company, nor joining those relatives for the same reason.
> (1985: 227)

In this context, Richard Wall's chapter raises some fundamental questions, for he concludes that in preindustrial times elderly English couples
often lived with children. Here his findings mirror Jean Robin's (1984)
study of the English village of Colyton in 1851–1871. Of the aged parents
(age 70+) of the cohort she was able to follow during these years, more
than half were residing with a child (515). In Wall's figures for his sample
of English communities in the preindustrial period (1599–1796), 49 percent of the men over age 65 and 37 percent of the women of that age lived
with at least one child, with comparable proportions found in the first
decades of the twentieth century.[19]

The implications of nuclear family systems for the residential isolation of
the elderly differ markedly between preindustrial times and recent times
due to demographic changes. The major change of importance here is the
constriction of childbearing to the younger years that has marked recent
decades, combined with the more modest decline in mortality at older ages.
In the past, the relatively late age at marriage combined with higher rates of
adult mortality meant that even in a strict nuclear family system, people
would have spent relatively little of their adult lives living apart from their
children. Of course, those who had never married or had no surviving children would still—in such a system—live alone.

To understand whether a true nuclear family system actually operated
with respect to the elderly, it is not enough to have data on those over age
60 or 65 in general. Instead, we need to see what happened to older people as they lost their ability to run their own independent households. This
typically happened in one of two ways—as a result of illness or frailty, or as
a result of loss of a spouse. The first is difficult to investigate historically
in any systematic, quantitative way (although Ransom and Sutch's chapter shows some of the important research that can be done on this topic).
By contrast, the second offers more direct and widespread possibilities
for analysis.

The pattern here is evident from both Myron Gutmann's chapter
on nineteenth-century Texas and Tamara Hareven and Peter Uhlenberg's
discussion of census results from the northeastern United States in the early
twentieth century. Gutmann's chapter in many ways supports the nuclearity
view, although the frontier characteristics of the Texan population make it
especially inhospitable to multigenerational living arrangements. However,
he notes that where we find older people living with a married child, it is
primarily following the death of the older person's spouse. Whether the de-

gree of frailty of the surviving spouse was a factor in the decision to move in with a married child remains unknown.

The U.S. census data provided by Hareven and Uhlenberg show that more than three-fourths of all older widows were living with children in 1910, and Daniel Scott Smith's studies of the 1900 U.S. census point to a similar pattern. Of those women aged 65 to 74 without a spouse, 36 percent lived with a married child and another 29 percent lived with an unmarried child. Of the unmarried men of the same age, 30 percent lived with a married child and another 21 percent lived with an unmarried child. Among the eldest group (age 75+), 42 percent of the unmarried (primarily widowed) women lived with a married child and another 32 percent with an unmarried child. Similarly, 48 percent of the eldest unmarried men lived with a married child and another 21 percent with an unmarried child. Smith concludes that in the pre-World War II period, "older couples typically lived with unmarried children, the widowed old with married children, and the never married, especially spinsters, with their siblings" (1982: 91, 107). The elderly who lived with married children, then, did so as a result of joining existing households of their children following their own widowhood. The result is that for all Americans over age 65 in 1900, a sizable proportion (roughly 30 percent) did indeed live in households containing three generations (Smith 1979: 290).[20]

This is a rather striking figure for a society practicing neolocal residence. Indeed, what I would like to suggest is that such evidence must force us to revise our notions of Western nuclear family systems. But before I draw out such conclusions, it is well to focus our attention on a key element whose implications must themselves be considered very carefully: gender.

GENDER AND OLD AGE

The historical demography of aging does not take us very far unless we recognize the fundamental significance of gender. Among the most important topics for historical research here is the differential impact of demographic changes on the lives of older men and women, as well as the societal implications of these changes. As Laslett's introduction points out, old age itself has become increasingly feminized in the West. In Canada, for example, at the beginning of this century there were 105 men over age 65 for every 100 women, a proportion that may be partially attributable to gender disparities in immigration to Canada. By contrast, in 1976, there were only 78 older men for every 100 older women (Denton and Spencer 1980: 12). The United States shows a similar pattern, with a sex ratio of 102 for those over age 65 in 1900, sinking to 67 in 1985, or, in other words, three older women for every two older men. For those in the oldest age groups the imbalance had become even more dramatic, with only two men over age 85 for every five women (Uhlenberg 1987: 189).

The history of the sex ratio disparities at older ages is still not well known, though the overwhelming predominance of women at older ages in the West today is certainly a recent phenomenon. Andorka, for example, notes that in Hungarian villages of the eighteenth and nineteenth centuries, there were more older men than women, and Wall points out that gains in female life expectancy have far outpaced those in male life expectancy in Europe over the past decades.

But the fact that the predominance of women at the upper age range is largely a twentieth-century phenomenon should not blind us to the fact that older men and women in the past were also greatly affected by sex differences in demographic rates. In the Western past, the two principal gender differences involved remarriage propensities and age at marriage (i.e., the marital age gap). Indeed, these two are linked, as Andorka points out for Hungary, where, following widowhood, men were not only more likely to remarry than were women but in such second marriages were likely to marry women substantially younger than themselves (for Europe more generally, see Dupâquier et al. 1981). This relationship is probably also responsible for the large marital age gap (over seven years) found by Gutmann for Texan men over age 50 in the late-nineteenth-century censuses. The higher the rate of male remarriage compared to female remarriage, the more likely it is that old men will have a spouse present in their household and the more likely old women will be widows, even in the absence of any difference in male and female life expectancy.

Cultural norms encouraging male remarriage and discouraging female remarriage are found widely around the world (though they are not universal). Similar patterns appear in both South and East Asia (Palmore 1987: 98–99). As is shown in my chapter with Nancy Karweit, men were two or three times more likely to remarry following widowhood in nineteenth-century Casalecchio, Italy, a pattern not dissimilar to that found throughout most of Europe at that time. One of the intriguing findings not only of that research but of work in Germany and elsewhere in Europe is that through the nineteenth and into the twentieth century there seems to have been a continuous decline in the rate of remarriage for both men and women (Mitterauer and Sieder 1982:15). Even today, though, the gap between male and female remarriage rates remains and, indeed, may well have increased. In the mid-1980s, elderly widowed American men had remarriage rates more than eight times greater than women's (U.S. Senate Special Committee on Aging 1988: 137). In this respect, American society has been evolving in a direction more closely approximating traditional Hindu society.[21]

The implications of these demographic differences are starkly apparent in figures on the marital status of the older population in different societies.

A comparison of widows and widowers in the "less developed" and "more developed" countries of the world around 1980 shows a curious pattern. While the proportion of the population that is over age 65 is vastly different between the two—only 4 percent of both men and women in the former countries compared with 10 percent of the men and 15 percent of the women in the latter—the sex differences in marital status are remarkably similar. In the less developed countries, just 16 percent of the old men are widowers compared to 54 percent of the old women, while in the more developed countries, 18 percent of the old men and 52 percent of the old women are widowed (Palmore 1987: 95–96). Different demographic forces lead to an uncannily similar result: while life expectancy differences between men and women are much less in the developing countries—a fact that would lead to more similarity in widowhood rates between men and women—the marital age gap tends to be larger and rates of male remarriage often higher.[22]

In some parts of Asia, at least, these rates have remained stable over the past century. In India in 1881, for example, 28 percent of the men over age 60 were widowed compared to 84 percent of the women. Ninety years later, the proportions widowed were 22 percent for men and 69 percent for women (Vatuk 1982: 73). Something oddly similar has been happening in the United States, for with all the other changes taking place, the proportion of those over age 65 who were married changed only modestly between 1900 and 1985. The proportion of married men rose from 71 percent to 79 percent, while the proportion of married women declined from 24 percent to 16 percent (Uhlenberg 1987: 189). Historical changes in sex differential remarriage and mortality rates combined with changes in divorce rates to bring about this result.

These demographic differences have a powerful impact on living arrangements of the old, leading to stark differences between men and women. It appears that these differences are even greater today than they were in the past. Wall points out that a smaller proportion of elderly women lived with a spouse in England and Wales in 1981 than had been the case in preindustrial times. Loss of a spouse, though, had very different implications for men and women. This was true not only because of men's greater ability to remarry but also because loss of spouse more often meant social demotion—away from household headship—for women than for men, as discussed in my chapter with Nancy Karweit.

RETHINKING HOUSEHOLD SYSTEMS

Our understanding of living arrangements in the European past has been conditioned by a series of household models highlighting the contrast between nuclear and complex family systems, the latter encompassing "stem," "joint," and "multiple family" households. These two main types are thought to have radically different implications for the lives of the old. In the nuclear family model, the individual lives in an ever-shrinking household as her or his children grow up and establish their own independent households at marriage. In old age, in this model, the individual lives either with a spouse or, more commonly as one grows older, alone. By contrast, in the complex family household, one or more of the parents' children remain in the parental household after marriage, bringing in their spouse and repopulating the household with their own children. In such a system, older individuals live in a supportive household environment, surrounded by kin of the second and third generation, until the end of life.

What these models share is a virtually exclusive focus on norms of postmarital residence as the diagnostic element of household systems: a nuclear family system is one in which newlyweds establish their own independent household at marriage; a stem family system is one in which one—but only one—child brings his (it is usually a son, not a daughter) spouse into the parental home, while a joint family system is one in which multiple children may (and generally should) remain in the parental home after marriage, bringing in their spouses.

Of these three classic types, only one—the joint family—is characterized by a household formation point other than marriage. The second transition arises from demographic vagaries: in a joint family system any family having more than one child per generation bringing a spouse into the household would become unduly large within a couple of generations. The result is a provision for the splitting of households into constituent groups of kin, a splitting that comes not with marriage but at some later time (Hajnal 1983: 69).

What I would like to propose here is that complexity comparable to that used in dealing with complex family households be added to our model of the nuclear family. The cultural norm of neolocality does not by itself produce a pure nuclear family system. The fact that people establish their own households at marriage need not exclude a phase of complex family coresidence as a part of the normal life course. For a pure nuclear family system to be found, we must have an additional element: the lack of any norm leading married couples either to take in frail or widowed elderly parents or to move in with them. By contrast, where such norms operate, we are not in the presence of the classic nuclear family system at all. Rather, we find a variant, one that might in fact have had as broad a historical distribution as the pure nuclear family system. We may call this a nuclear reincorporation household system. If we were as attuned to look at the latter end of the life course as we are to look at youth and young adulthood, the significance of reincorporation to household systems would have been established long ago.[23] Instead, while we now have a fairly good map of the historical distribution of various postmarital residence systems throughout Europe, our understanding of the residential lives at the older end of the life course is distorted by the error of linking neolocality to pure nuclear family systems.

England and its descendant societies have been viewed as the type cases of the nuclear family system. So influential has the historical work on these societies been, in fact, that sociological and historical texts today are full of wild overgeneralizations about the nuclear family household as having been the norm throughout "Western" or "European" history. But even as we look at the data in this book from Richard Wall on England or Tamara Hareven and Peter Uhlenberg from the northeastern United States, we must ask whether a pure nuclear family system actually operated in these societies in the past.[24]

I propose, in short, that we shift the terms of the debate over household complexity in the past in northwestern Europe (and other areas marked by neolocality).[25] To date the historical debate has largely been framed in terms pitting those arguing for a nuclear family system against those arguing for a stem family system. Low cross-sectional proportions of complex family households have thus been alternatively explained as either demonstrating a nuclear family system at work or showing the results of developmental cycle factors in a stem family system. For example, Steven Ruggles (1987) argues that the proportions of three-generation households in nineteenth-century England and America show a preference for stem family principles, kept in check by various demographic constraints.[26]

What I am proposing here has implications for both sides of this debate, for where nuclear reincorporation principles are at work, both sides of the nuclear versus stem family household debate may be wrong, or at least misleading. The champions of the nuclear family may be wrong through oversimplifying the developmental cycle of family life, while the champions of the stem family may be wrong in interpreting the co-residence of two adult generations as indicating a nonneolocal system of postmarital residence.

We are, unfortunately, very far from knowing the distributions of a nuclear reincorporation system versus a pure nuclear household system. The difficulty of even being able to tell the difference between a population following the rules of stem family formation as opposed to nuclear reincorporation, using common cross-sectional methods, is cogently demonstrated in Gene Hammel's chapter in this volume.

These difficulties are compounded by the fact that in actual practice, behavior reflects norms only as filtered through a complex prism of other forces. In any given community, the frequency of reincorporation is the product not only of abstract cultural norms but also of such demographic factors as the availability of adult married children of the right sex, as well as various economic factors. Wealthier individuals may have had less need for reincorporation, being able to arrange their own support system through hiring servants and able to generate income without needing a spouse (in the case of the widow especially) and in the face of declining physical strength for manual labor.

To what extent such support was provided by the collectivity (as Laslett 1988, 1989 and Richard Smith 1984 argue for preindustrial England) as opposed to the family remains an open question, a question of no small historical significance. Nor is this a question lacking in contemporary policy relevance, as debates over the propriety of state versus family responsibility for the elderly rage in the public arena. Such debates resound with references to the great historical changes that have taken place in family life and care of the elderly, references that more often than not reflect a poor understanding of the history of aging, demography, and family life.

The research agenda for the emerging historical demography of aging, as these examples make clear, is a rich one. The work to be done not only promises to provide us with a much better idea of how older people lived in the past but precious insight as well into the lives of all members of society, young and old. Moving away from an exclusive youth-centered viewpoint to take a perspective from the later years of life will continue to challenge some of our most deeply held paradigms of society in the past and enrich our theoretical models of society.

NOTES

I would like to thank George Alter, Gene Hammel, Daniel Scott Smith, and especially my coeditor, Peter Laslett, for their helpful and provocative comments on an earlier draft of this chapter. As their comments showed, the historical demography of aging, though new, is a contentious field, and my comments in this concluding chapter do not necessarily reflect those of either my coeditor or the authors of the chapters herein.

1. An example of this can be found in Kumagai's (1987: 225) characterization of the rapid increase in life expectancy (from the mid-40s to around 80) in Japan over the past half century as a "longevity revolution." Since the bulk of the increase simply involves the increasing proportion of babies and small children who survive, it may be misleading to portray this as a revolution in "longevity."

2. These estimates are not universally accepted, and prehistorical demography remains a poorly developed field.

3. See also Preston 1970.

4. Although changes in the age structure produced by other forces could also have played a role.

5. These figures are for 1980.

6. According to figures from the United Nations, the proportion of elderly in Third World countries dropped from 7.1 percent to 6 percent over the period 1950–1975 (Okojie 1988: 3). African census figures regarding older ages must be read with some caution, due to problems of age misreporting.

7. Further comparative data of this sort may be found in Hoover and Siegel 1986: 22.

8. The way in which some proponents of this view present their data may be misleading, however. Carole Haber (1983: 11), for example, quoting Fischer's classic study of aging in American history, provides a table entitled "Demographic Life Cycle in America, 1650–1950," which at half-century intervals shows for men and women a series of average ages for marriage, last birth, and so on. For example, the table shows an average age at death for women in 1700 of 52, when the woman's last child is born at age 42. This gives the impression that the average mother would die when her youngest child was only age 10. Of course, the life expectancy of a woman still alive at age 42 would be well beyond age 52, leading to significantly different conclusions about the life course in the American past.

9. For a statement and defense of modernization theory and its implications for aging, see Cowgill 1986: 181–200.

10. For a critical view of the usage of the modernization concept in historical family research, see Laslett 1987.

11. South and East Asian societies also have the virtue for my purposes of being the locus classicus of Hajnal's joint household systems, which he contrasts with the simple household systems of northwest Europe (Hajnal 1983).

12. The continued importance that expectations of reliance on children for support in old age have on continued high fertility in much of the Third World is documented in Bulatao 1979.

13. This was based on a random sample of residents of metropolitan Delhi, aged over 60, conducted in the mid-1970s. The heavy patrilocal bias is evident in a study of a Bangladeshi village, conducted at the same time, that found 62 percent of those over age 60 living with a married son, another 16 percent with an unmarried son over age 15, and only 2 percent with a married daughter (Cain 1981: 378).

14. The joint family household, in which all sons live together with their parents, remains the cultural ideal in this community.

15. The proportion dipped from 82 percent in 1960 to 65 percent in 1984.

16. The proportion of those living alone rose steadily from 12 percent among those aged 60–64 to 39 percent for those over age 80.

17. From the publication of the now classic volume, *Household and family in past time,* Laslett and his colleagues at the Cambridge Group have noted the diversity of household systems found in Europe, especially through attention paid to Serbia and, later, Russia. However, this aspect of their message tended to get lost in the enthusiasm of many scholars for the finding that European peasantry and nuclear family co-residence were not incompatible.

18. This pattern extended far beyond Italy, into southern and central France and Iberia as well. Bourdelais (1986), for example, shows in his study of the village of Prayssas in Agen in the nineteenth century that the multiple and extended family system ensured that older people would live in households with their children until their death.

19. Richard Smith (1984: 419) has commented on the remarkable stability of the proportion of English elderly living with married children from preindustrial times into the twentieth century.

20. See also Smith 1984.

21. Of course, among the reasons for this increasing sex difference in remarriage rates at older ages is the sex ratio in the American population at these ages, for there are many more available women than men.

22. Life expectancy of males at birth is actually higher in a number of South Asian countries today than is female life expectancy, and even at age 65 men in Bangladesh and Pakistan can expect to live longer than women (Martin 1990: 96).

23. But see Laslett's (1988) discussion of "nuclear hardship," an important stimulus to the proposal I make in these paragraphs.

24. A similar northwestern European example has recently been provided for the Belgian city of Vervier in the nineteenth century, showing that older widows and widowers tended to live with a married child, especially when no unmarried children were available (Alter, Cliggett, and Urbiel 1992).

25. A good example of a neolocal system in southern Europe is provided by Da Molin's (1990*a*, 1990*b*) study of a series of communities in southern Italy from the seventeenth through the nineteenth century. It also provides a good example of my thesis, for while she describes these communities as demonstrating the "nuclear structure of the southern Italian family" (1990*a*: 524), she also tells us that "a widow who was needy was never abandoned by her family . . . but rather taken into their homes and assisted" (ibid.: 52).

26. The demographic constraint debate, first raised in this context by the influential work of Levy (1965), has led to a series of attempts to disentangle the impact of demographic forces on household composition patterns through the use of microsimulation, the latest of which is found by Hammel in this book. On the role of demographic constraint in limiting the frequency of complex family households, see Kertzer 1989.

REFERENCES

Alter, George, Lisa Cliggett, and Alex Urbiel. 1992. "Household patterns of the elderly and the proximity of children in a nineteenth-century city, Verviers, Belgium, 1831–1846." Paper presented to the RAND Conference on Economic and Demographic Aspects of Intergenerational Relations, March, Santa Monica, California.

Bourdelais, Patrice. 1986. "Vieillir en famille dans la France des ménages complexes (L'exemple de Prayssas, 1836–1911)" [Growing old amid family in the part of France marked by complex households (The example of Prayssas, 1836–1911)]. *Annales de Démographie Historique 1985*, 21–38.

Bulatao, Rodolfo A. 1979. *On the nature of the transition in the value of children.* Honolulu: Papers of the East-West Population Institute.

Cain, Mead. 1981. "The consequences of reproductive failure: Dependence, mobility, and mortality among the elderly of rural South Asia." *Population Studies* 40: 375–388.

Cowgill, Donald O. 1986. *Aging around the world.* Belmont, Calif.: Wadsworth.

Czap, Peter. 1982. "The perennial multiple family household, Mishino, Russia, 1782–1858." *Journal of Family History* 7: 5–26.

Da Molin, Giovanna. 1990*a*. "Family forms and domestic service in southern Italy from the seventeenth to the nineteenth centuries." *Journal of Family History* 15: 503–528.

————. 1990*b*. *La famiglia nel passato: Strutture familiari nel Regno di Napoli in età mo-derna* [The family in the past: Family structures in the kingdom of Naples in the modern era]. Bari: Cacucci.

Denton, Frank, and Bryon Spencer. 1980. "Canada's population and labour force: Past, present and future." In *Aging in Canada,* ed. Victor W. Marshall, 10–26. Don Mills: Fitzhenry and Whiteside.

Dupâquier, J., E. Hélin, P. Laslett, M. Livi Bacci, and S. Sogner, eds. 1981. *Marriage and remarriage in populations of the past.* New York: Academic Press.

Gratton, Brian. 1986. "The new history of the aged: A critique." In *Old age in a bu-reaucratic society,* ed. David Van Tassel and Peter N. Stearns, 3–29. New York: Greenwood Press.

Gui, Shi-Xun. 1988. "A report from mainland China: Status and needs of rural el-derly in the suburbs of Shanghai." *Journal of Cross-Cultural Gerontology* 3: 149–167.

Gutton, Jean-Pierre. 1988. *Naissance du vieillard* [The birth of the aged]. Paris: Aubier.

Haber, Carole. 1983. *Beyond sixty-five.* Cambridge: Cambridge University Press.

Hajnal, John. 1983. "Two kinds of pre-industrial household formation system." In *Family forms in historic Europe,* ed. Richard Wall, Jean Robin, and Peter Laslett, 65–104. Cambridge: Cambridge University Press.

Halpern, Joel M., and David Anderson. 1970. "The zadruga: A century of change." *Anthropologica* 12: 83–97.

Hashimoto, Akiko. 1991. "Living arrangements of the aged in seven developing countries." *Journal of Cross-Cultural Gerontology* 6: 359–381.

Hoover, Sally L., and Jacob S. Siegel. 1986. "International demographic trends and perspectives on aging." *Journal of Cross-Cultural Gerontology* 1: 5–30.

Kertzer, David I. 1989. "The joint family revisited: Demographic constraints and complex family households in the European past." *Journal of Family History* 14: 1–15.

————. 1991. "Household history and sociological theory." *Annual Review of Sociol-ogy* 17: 155–179.

Kumagai, Fumie. 1987. "Satisfaction among rural and urban Japanese elderly in three-generation families." *Journal of Cross-Cultural Gerontology* 2: 225–239.

Laslett, Peter. 1965. *The world we have lost.* London: Methuen.

————. 1972. "Introduction: The history of the family." In *Household and family in past time,* ed. Peter Laslett and Richard Wall, 1–89. Cambridge: Cambridge Uni-versity Press.

————. 1985. "Societal development and aging." In *Handbook of aging and the social sciences* (2d ed.), ed. Robert H. Binstock and Ethel Shanas, 199–230. New York: Van Nostrand Reinhold.

————. 1987. "The character of familial history, its limitations and the conditions for its proper pursuit." *Journal of Family History* 12: 263–284.

————. 1988. "Family, kinship and collectivity as systems of support in pre-industrial Europe: A consideration of the 'nuclear-hardship' hypothesis." *Continuity and Change* 3: 153–175.

————. 1989. *A fresh map of life.* London: Weidenfeld and Nicolson.

Levy, Marion J., ed. 1965. *Aspects of the analysis of family structure.* Princeton: Prince-ton University Press.

Martin, Linda G. 1990. "The status of South Asia's growing elderly population." *Journal of Cross-Cultural Gerontology* 5: 93–117.

Mayer, Karl U., and Walter Müller. 1986. "The state and the structure of the life course." In *Human development and the life course,* ed. Aage B. Sørensen, Franz E. Weinert, and Lonnie R. Sherrod, 217–246. Hillsdale, N.J.: Lawrence Erlbaum.

Mitterauer, Michael, and Reinhard Sieder. 1982. *The European family.* Trans. Karla Oosterveen and Manfred Horzinger. Chicago: University of Chicago Press.

Okojie, Felix A. 1988. "Aging in sub-Saharan Africa." *Journal of Cross-Cultural Gerontology* 3: 3–19.

Palmore, Erdman. 1987. "Cross-cultural perspectives on widowhood." *Journal of Cross-Cultural Gerontology* 2: 93–105.

Perrenoud, Alfred. 1982. "Le recul de la mort: Structure par âges et facteurs sociaux" [The decline of death: Structure by age and social characteristics]. In *Le vieillissement,* ed. Arthur Imhof, 43–76. Lyon: Presses Universitaires de Lyon.

Preston, Samuel H. 1970. *Older male mortality and cigarette smoking.* Population Monograph Series, no. 7. Berkeley: Institute of International Studies, University of California.

Robin, Jean. 1984. "Family care of the elderly in a nineteenth-century Devonshire parish." *Ageing and Society* 4: 505–516.

Ruggles, Steven. 1987. *Prolonged connections: The rise of the extended family in nineteenth-century England and America.* Madison: University of Wisconsin Press.

Smith, Daniel Scott. 1979. "Life course, norms, and the family system of older Americans in 1900." *Journal of Family History* 4: 285–298.

———. 1982. "Historical change in the household structure of the elderly in economically developed societies." In *Old age in bureaucratic society,* ed. Peter Stearns, 248–273. New York: Holmes and Meier.

———. 1984. "Modernization and the family structure of the elderly in the United States." *Zeitschrift für Gerontologie* 17: 13–17.

Smith, Richard M. 1984. "The structured dependence of the elderly as a recent development: Some skeptical historical thoughts." *Ageing and Society* 4: 409–428.

Sokolovsky, Jay. 1982. "Introduction: Perspectives on aging in the Third World." *Studies in Third World Societies* 22: 1–22.

Stearns, Peter N. 1982. "Introduction." In *Old age in preindustrial society,* ed. Peter N. Stearns, 1–18. New York: Holmes and Meier.

Stearns, Peter N., and David Van Tassel. 1986. "Introduction: Themes and prospects in old age history." In *Old age in a bureaucratic society,* ed. David Van Tassel and Peter N. Stearns, ix–xx. New York: Greenwood Press.

Sung, Kyu-Taik. 1991. "Family-centered informal support networks of Korean elderly." *Journal of Cross-Cultural Gerontology* 6: 431–447.

Treas, Judith, and Barbara Logue. 1986. "Economic development and the older population." *Population and Development Review* 12: 645–673.

Uhlenberg, Peter. 1987. "A demographic perspective on aging." In *The elderly as modern pioneers,* ed. Philip Silverman, 183–204. Bloomington: Indiana University Press.

U.S. Senate Special Committee on Aging. 1988. *Aging in America: Trends and projections.* Washington, D.C.: Government Printing Office.

Vatuk, Sylvia. 1982. "Old age in India." In *Old age in preindustrial society,* ed. Peter N. Stearns, 70–103. New York: Holmes and Meier.

Weiss, Kenneth M. 1981. "Evolutionary perspectives on human aging." In *Other ways of growing old,* ed. Pamela T. Amoss and Stevan Harrell, 25–58. Stanford: Stanford University Press.

INDEX

Designer:	U.C. Press Staff
Compositor:	BookMasters, Inc.
Text:	10/12 Baskerville
Display:	Baskerville
Printer:	Haddon Craftsmen, Inc.
Binder:	Haddon Craftsmen, Inc.